Samuel Pepys A Life

Also by Stephen Coote

Byron – The Making of a Myth
William Morris
A Short History of English Literature
A Play of Passion – The Life of Sir Walter Ralegh,
John Keats – A Life,
W. B. Yeats – A Life
Royal Survivor A Life of Charles II

Samuel Pepys
A Life

STEPHEN COOTE

Hodder & Stoughton

First published in Great Britain in 2000
by Hodder and Stoughton
A division of Hodder Headline

10 9 8 7 6 5 4 3 2 1

A CIP catalogue record for this title is available
from the British Library.

ISBN 0 340 751231

Typeset by Palimpsest Book Production Limited,
Polmont, Stirlingshire

Printed and bound in Great Britain by
Mackays of Chatham PLC, Chatham, Kent

Hodder and Stoughton
A division of Hodder Headline
338 Euston Road
London NW1 3BH

For
Toni

Du kennest mich wieder,
du lockest mich zart
Hermann Hesse

CONTENTS

LIST OF ILLUSTRATIONS		ix
ACKNOWLEDGEMENTS		x
INTRODUCTION		xi
CHAPTER ONE:	*Educating Samuel*	1
CHAPTER TWO:	*Waiting on Events*	25
CHAPTER THREE:	*Restoration*	43
CHAPTER FOUR:	*Getting Started*	67
CHAPTER FIVE:	*The Life of this Office*	95
CHAPTER SIX:	*The Right Hand of the Navy*	127
CHAPTER SEVEN:	*The Years of Agony*	157
CHAPTER EIGHT:	*Perpetual Trouble and Vexation*	193
CHAPTER NINE:	*Darkness*	213
CHAPTER TEN:	*An Encirclement of Enemies*	237
CHAPTER ELEVEN:	*At the Admiralty*	261
CHAPTER TWELVE:	*Pepys and the Popish Plot*	283
CHAPTER THIRTEEN:	*The Uses of Adversity*	305
CHAPTER FOURTEEN:	*Return to the Admiralty*	323
CHAPTER FIFTEEN:	*Retirement*	351
REFERENCES		361
BIBLIOGRAPHY		371
INDEX		375

LIST OF ILLUSTRATIONS

The execution of Charles I, artist unknown.
Magdalene College from Loggan's *Cantabrigia Illustrata.*
Samuel Pepys by John Hales.
Elizabeth Pepys attributed to John Bushnell.
Charles II by John Michael Wright.
George Monck, 1st Duke of Albemarle, artist unknown.
Edward Montagu, 1st Earl of Sandwich, artist unknown.
Sir William Penn by Lely.
Sir Anthony Deane by John Grennhill.
The Great Fire of London, Dutch School.
Royal visit to the Fleet by Williem van de Velde.
The Dutch attack on the Medway by Ludolf Bakhuizen.
The last page of the Diary.
Pepys in the middle age by Kneller.
James II, artist unknown.
Anthony Ashley Cooper, 1st Earl of Shaftsbury, artist unknown.
William III, artist unknown.
John Evelyn by Robert Nanteuil.
Sir Christopher Wren by Kneller.
Boat action during the Third Dutch War by Ludolf Bakhuizen.
Samuel Pepys by J. Cavallier.
A bookcase from Pepys Library.
The destruction of the Mole at Tangier by Dirk Stoop.
The Royal Naval Hospital at Greenwich by Canaletto.
Pepys in 1700 by John Closterman.

ACKNOWLEDGEMENTS

I wish to thank the Master and Fellows of Magdalene College, Cambridge, and the Curators of the Bodleian Library for permission to quote from manuscripts in their possession.

Illustrations 1, 3, 4, 5, 6, 7, 15, 16, 17, 18, 19, 25 are reproduced by permission of the *National Portrait Gallery*; 2, 13, 21, 22 reproduced by permission of *Pepys Library*, Magdalene College, Cambridge; 8, 9, 11, 12, 14, 20, 23, 24 reproduced by permission of the *National Maritime Museum*; 10 reproduced by permission of the *Museum of London*.

INTRODUCTION

When I was writing *Royal Survivor*, my biography of Charles II, the handsome volumes of Pepys's *Diary*, magnificently edited by Robert Latham and William Matthews, were constantly open before me. Like anyone familiar with that monument of modern scholarship, Pepys's personality exercised its magnetic pull over me. As I became more engaged with the man and began to gather information about his life both before and after the writing of the *Diary* itself, so I was intrigued by the fact that here was a figure who was not only of intense interest in his own right but was present at virtually every great historical event of his age.

As a schoolboy Pepys saw the execution of Charles I. As a young man he was an eye-witness of the events that led to the fall of the Cromwellian regime. He sailed with the fleet that brought Charles II back in 1660. He rapidly established himself as the most able administrator in the country's leading industry: the navy. As a result, he was not only closely involved in the Second and Third Dutch Wars but in the profound shifts that those wars helped to engender – the rise of party politics especially. Because of this, it seemed possible to trace the development of a man in a period of profound social change, to follow Pepys's metamorphosis from revolutionary teenager to a man accepting and, indeed, welcoming the return of the monarchy.

Like the nation itself, Pepys felt the deep pull of traditional securities and identified with a regime which, was soon subject to ever more searching criticism. During the national madness of the Popish Plot, Pepys was a victim of those who sought to limit the powers of the monarchy to which he had wholeheartedly given his support. During the brief reign of James II it is possible to see Pepys deeply devoted to a form of government that the majority of influential people no longer required. The revolutionary schoolboy had become the increasingly redundant conservative. That Pepys's principles ran deep – that he was not simply a man constantly changing with changing times – is suggested in that after the Glorious Revolution he chose to incur the penalties paid by the so-called Non-Jurors (those who refused to take the oath of allegiance to William and Mary) rather than compromise his beliefs.

The period of Pepys's retirement shows him pursuing his wide variety of cultural interests. These, too, add to the fascination of the man, for Pepys throughout his life maintained an intense interest in the theatre, in book and print collecting and, above all, in music. He was, in the phrase of the day, a 'virtuoso'. Nothing suggests this more perfectly than his interest in the Royal Society. His was not the concern of the professional scientist, although he kept himself abreast (sometimes with difficulty) of the great scientific publications of the era and, indeed, gave his imprimatur to the greatest of all these works: Newton's *Principia*. Pepys was, by this time, president of the Society, a post given to him in recognition of his outstanding administrative ability.

It is this last that points to perhaps the most abidingly fascinating aspect of Pepys's life when seen as a whole: his professionalism, his engagement with the world of work. A constant theme throughout the extraordinary wealth of the *Diary* – running parallel with his marriage and his love affairs, his cultural interests, his political observations, his friendships, pleasures and sorrows – is Pepys's growing sense that his identity as a man was firmly rooted in the means by which he earned his money. I have tried to show the strands that made this up, to do justice to his Puritan background and his ambition, his delight in power and status, his sense of fulfilment in creating, as far as he could, a well-oiled and efficient bureaucratic machine. I have also tried to suggest how these talents related to his being a bourgeois in a time of increasingly autocratic monarchy and to show how, in a period of personal desolation with his wife dead and his eyesight failing, work was at least his worldly salvation. I have hinted, too, at the price I think he paid for this.

CHAPTER ONE

Educating Samuel

He elbowed his way through the crowd and looked on the scene with the alert, life-hungry eyes of a boy of fifteen. It was difficult to see very much, but in the far distance, beyond the immense press of bodies, he could just glimpse the mounted soldiers ranged around the scaffold by the Palace of Whitehall. Behind them, the officials and the instruments of execution were all in place. So much was proper, for this was a moment of the highest solemnity, the 'saddest sight that ever England saw'.[1] After seven years of civil war the people had finally brought their king to trial and ordered his death. Clerks, their hands numb in the bitter January air, prepared to make notes for the benefit of posterity. Others prayed. The executioner and his assistants, hideously disguised in thick frieze coats, false hair and false beards, looked on as King Charles I prepared himself to speak.

A great silence fell on the crowd as Charles claimed that, far from being guilty of bringing bloodshed and ruin to his country, he was dying as 'a Martyr to the People'. The boy, like practically everybody else, was unable to hear what he said. Nor did he greatly care. What were the excuses of a tyrant to him? Instead, he contented himself with watching as the axe fell and the King's severed head was lifted up by its hair to be displayed to the groaning crowd. Justice of a sort had been done, and now, as the multitude dispersed, the bright-eyed boy scampered back to school with a phrase from the Bible echoing in his head: 'the memory of the wicked shall rot'.[2] He, at least, was exultant. He had watched history in the making. Monarchy was at an end. His own people had won the fight for freedom, and Cromwell and his men were casting the world anew.

Such piety and political tumult had surrounded the boy for as long as he could remember. His parents were God-fearing Puritan people of modest means, to whom he had been born on 23 February 1633, in a room above their tailoring business in Salisbury Court, a thoroughfare that ran down from Fleet Street to the north bank of the Thames. He was the fifth of eleven children brought into the world by John and Margaret Pepys, and eight days after his birth he had been carried to St Bride's church across the way and there baptised Samuel according to the Anglican rite. As custom dictated, he was then put out to a wet-nurse, one Goody Lawrence, in the little Middlesex village of Kingsland, an area where his mother had relatives. The infant Samuel survived the manifold risks of illness that attended the early days of every seventeenth-century child and soon returned from Kingsland to his parents' house in London, the city that was to be the focus of his entire life.

For families like the Pepyses, London was a dark, crowded, dirty city, the cheek-by-jowl houses being 'the scurviest things in the world . . . nothing but wood and plaster and nasty little windows, with but one casement to open, the storeys were low and widened one over another, all awry and in appearance ready to fall'.[3] A thick cloud of pollution hung constantly above this dark and ramshackle capital.

The smoke from innumerable manufacturers' furnaces and family hearths, warmed by sulphurous sea coal, created so lethal a cloud that almost half who 'perished in London die of phthisical and pulmonary distempers'. The inhabitants were 'never free from coughs and importunate rheumatisms, spitting of impostumated and corrupt matter'. Summer often brought the plague, and always the terrible, gut-wrenching smells of unswept stables and the noxious vats of soap-makers, tanners and the alum manufacturers whose product was so essential to finishing the cloth Samuel's father made into suits.

Some of the more important London streets were paved, a number more were cobbled, but many were 'so miry and foul as is not only very noisome, dangerous and inconvenient to the inhabitants thereof but to all the King's liege people'. All sorts of rubbish clotted the central drains of these streets and was left saturated and stinking with the rain that sheered off the gutterless roofs. Hackney carriages, drovers and a myriad other people jostled acrimoniously through these noisy thoroughfares as they went about their business: merchants to the Exchange, lawyers to the Inns of Court, servants to the public conduits. The noise was oppressive too. Horseshoes and iron-clad wheels rattled on the stones. Notoriously foul-mouthed arguments broke out between the drivers of goods vehicles jammed at the crossroads. Street vendors called their wares in raucous voices. Pig gelders blew their horns and, if they were lucky, practised their trade on their screaming victims at the street corners. And, above this din, preachers and fanatics were forever shouting about salvation.

As Samuel grew into boyhood, he came to see that his father's business was a respectable enough trade and that John Pepys himself was a respectable if unexciting man, labouring timorously in his cutting-room, 'his journeymen sitting about him, each man with his pint of ale and halfpenny loaf before him'.[4] John Pepys was one of those for whom making anything more than a meagre living was a mystery and who looked with dependent eyes on the initiatives of others as he sought solace in the music he loved, as his son was also to do. Although originally from the Fens, John Pepys had laboured for years in London without any conspicuous success, burying eight of his children in the nearby churchyard and receiving little comfort from his wife, a difficult and improvident woman of poorer status than himself. She had once been a laundress and now involved herself in the more extreme forms of Puritanism. Samuel and his surviving siblings – Thomas, Paulina and John – grew up in the atmosphere she helped to create, of moral certainties, strict prohibitions, and a conviction of being the elect of God.

As his boyhood years passed, the influences that played over Samuel at home became increasingly important in the world outside. A little while before his ninth birthday, events reached their first crisis. After eleven years of personal and increasingly autocratic rule, King Charles had been obliged to call a session of Parliament. Long-nurtured resentments came to a head and the dark and dirty streets around Samuel's home were filled with sudden tumult, a noise that was to resound through his whole life. 'Some hundreds of the citizens came down with swords and staves,' wrote one observer. The crowd was insisting on adding its voice to those Members in the chamber at Westminster who were demanding an end to arbitrary taxation and what they saw as the detestable popery of the King's religious policies. So fierce was the attack that men like Samuel's father were obliged to board up their premises. 'The citizens for the most part shut up their shops,' wrote one observer, 'and all gentlemen provide themselves with arms as in a time of open hostility.'[5] The tension continued to mount when the King failed to arrest the five Members who were leading the opposition against him, and eventually, having won the enmity of the greater part of its citizens, the bewildered monarch fled his capital.

The months that followed saw turmoil and resolution in London. Whoever held the capital – 'that proud unthankful city' as Royalist propagandists called it – held real power. Samuel was growing up in a capital preparing itself for war. Radical ideas were circulating in the streets and, as conflict became inevitable, a newly constituted Committee of Safety took control of the London militia. Over the following months Samuel became used to the sight of armed and leather-jacketed soldiers swaggering with pikes and muskets through the London streets and training on St George's Fields beside the great defensive wall the citizens had thrown up to protect themselves. Behind that wall, or the 'lines of communication' as they were called, the citizens themselves went about the task of spiritual reformation, setting up righteous government and preparing for the millennium. Zealous Puritans frequently interrupted services that smacked of the popery apparently beloved by the King. They altered the liturgy to suit their prejudices, smashed the faces of the carved stone saints, pulled down altar rails and organs, and instituted a rigid observance of the Sabbath. Sunday, they decreed, was a day to be spent in thoughts of the New Jerusalem. Travel and sports were banned, inns and taverns were closed, and only the milkmaids were allowed to break the silence of the streets as they cried their wares in the early mornings or the late afternoon.

All of this was agreeable enough to the little family in Salisbury Court, but the growing Samuel and his parents soon had worrying medical problems to bear. In particular, they became increasingly aware that he was suffering from a stone in his urinary system, which was perhaps caused by a high intake of protein and the fact that the flour in the bread the family ate was adulterated with chalk dust to whiten it. Certainly, the stone caused the boy great discomfort for there was a constant and growing pain in his kidneys. In the heat of summer his skin became hot and prickly, while he found it difficult to make water in the cold of winter. On some occasions, when he succeeded, his urine was flecked with blood. As he would write decades later: 'I remember not my life without the pain of the stone in the kidneys (even to the making of bloody water upon any extraordinary motion) till I was about twenty years of age.'[6] It was all most distressing to a bright and intelligent little boy and, in an effort to relieve his anxieties, he was sent for a while with his brother Tom to board with his old wet-nurse in Kingsland. There, in the open fields, Samuel could temporarily forget his problems as he practised shooting with his bow and arrows.

The stone in Samuel's kidneys was to be the cause of one of the first great crises of his early adult life, but other experiences were also directing the future course of his career. His father's relatives played an important role here, for if John Pepys himself was an ineffectual man it is clear that other members of his family had powers of mind and character that his winning and clever son had inherited. Across the court from Samuel and his parents, for example, lived another John Pepys, an ageing lawyer whose considerable professional success (he had appeared at the trial of the Gunpowder Plot conspirators) enabled him to keep a coach and a grand establishment at Ashtead in Surrey to which Samuel was occasionally invited, much to his delight. In later life he would recall Ashtead as 'my old place of pleasure'. After all, it was there that the acutely sensuous little boy, full of curiosity, had his first experience of calf-love while walking with a Mrs Hely, talking earnestly to her 'and taking her by the hand, she being a pretty woman'. John Pepys had, besides, a kindly daughter called Jane, who would one day do Samuel a great service.

Other distinguished members of the Pepys family retained their ties with the Fens. For many generations the Pepyses had been administrators at the abbey of Crowland in Cambridgeshire and had settled in the nearby villages of Cottenham and Impington. Samuel's father had been born in the last, and the boy's great-uncle Talbot Pepys still lived there. This family patriarch had distinguished himself in the law and served as treasurer of the Middle Temple, as well as briefly becoming MP for the borough of Cambridge, whose Recorder he now was. Other Pepyses also resided in the area, and at some time around 1644 young Samuel was sent to live with them, probably at his uncle Robert's house in Brampton.

There were a number of possible reasons for this move. A Parliamentarian victory in the civil war was very far from certain at this stage, while conditions in London itself were growing increasingly harsh. There were food and fuel shortages, punitive rates of taxation and a worrying sense of economic decline. It was said that 12,000 houses and shops in the city were standing empty, and the Commons were told that 'our rich men are gone because the city is the place of taxes and burdens'. The supplies of the cloth essential to John Pepys's business had been interrupted by the fighting, and unpaid tailors would soon be complaining that 'our trade is so spoiled that no man now will give any credit'.[7] It is hardly surprising that John and Margaret Pepys should want their oldest child at least to be free of these privations, but what is certain is that by moving Samuel out of London and into the area inhabited by his father's relatives the boy was being placed among people deeply committed to Puritanism.

Nothing could have made this clearer to Samuel than the proximity of his most distinguished relations, the Montagus. Sir Sydney Montagu (who died in 1644) was the youngest brother of the Earl of Manchester and Lord Montagu of Broughton. He was thus a member of one of the richest and most distinguished families in the kingdom, and his house at Hinchinbrooke was an ample tribute to his status. He had entertained Charles I there on a number of occasions, for if Sir

Sydney was a Puritan of the most severe type and much given to theological speculation, he was also an ardent Royalist. His legal training had prepared him for distinguished positions at court, but a deep vein of romanticism flowed through this otherwise crusty man. In what was clearly a love match he had married Paulina Pepys, Samuel's great-aunt, and a local woman with no more to recommend her than her merits. The couple had two sons. The first was lost in a tragic accident, but when Paulina herself died young she left behind her a second boy, Edward Montagu, who was to have the most profound influence over Samuel's life.

Even now Samuel knew that the civil war had thrust Edward into the public arena at a mere eighteen years of age. The conflict that split the nation also divided families, and young Montagu was as wholly given over to the Parliamentarian cause as his father was to the King's. He had married into a distinguished Parliamentarian family and was soon afterwards given a colonel's commission in the Parliamentarian forces of the eastern counties, which were commanded by his cousin, the Earl of Manchester. By July 1644, Edward Montagu had fought in his first set-piece battle at Marston Moor where he so distinguished himself that he was invited to represent his commander-in-chief when the city of York surrendered soon afterwards. It is impossible that young Samuel, grinding away at the Latin exercises set by his master at Huntingdon Grammar School, should not have heard of the exploits of his glamorous cousin, of how he had become a supporter of Cromwell the rising star and of how, newly rewarded with a command, he and Cromwell's New Model Army had played an important part in the defeat of the Royalist forces at the battle of Naseby.

It was perhaps the confidence inspired by this victory that was responsible for the boy's return to London. Certainly, the city that he came back to on the verge of his adolescence was vibrant, exciting and often wild with religious extremism.

'God is making here a new world,' declared a Scottish divine.[8] This was not an atmosphere that made for consensus, and the London of Pepys's early teenage years was riven with dissent, even the house in Salisbury Close echoing to such debate, one of Samuel's aunts being 'a poor, religious, well meaning, good, humble soul, talking of nothing but God Almighty'.[9] Such talk could be dangerous when taken to extremes and, while the moderate majority in the city sought mild reforms, many others were worried by the growth of sectarianism. There were large numbers of people in London who wanted to turn the world upside-down, and the city was loud with anarchic discussion. Pepys was growing up in a world were the old securities, the old certainties, were under serious threat.

There were those who asserted that only 'visible saints' should rule the earth and, looking enviously about them, swore that 'there ought to be a community of goods, and the saints should share in the lands and estates of gentlemen and rich men'. The influential Levellers developed such notions especially and urged the abolition of the House of Lords and the monarchy. They had visions of England becoming a republic – a democracy, even – and could write ecstatically that 'the old world is running up like a parchment in the fire'. Although there were still those (and they were perhaps a majority) who knew that fire burns, in this desperately excited and unstable time they were unable to make themselves heard. When they tried to stage a counter-revolution in London they failed miserably, and in the summer of 1647, when Pepys was just fourteen, he watched as the New Model Army marched into the city while the people cheered them to the echo.

By this time Pepys himself had been a pupil at one of the most eminent institutions in the capital for something over a year. St Paul's School fronted the road on the east side of the old Gothic cathedral, close to where the booksellers offered their wares. It was the largest of London's fee-paying schools (Pepys himself had an exhibition or scholarship) and it was also the most Puritan. The Latin motto placed above the entrance by the great Dean Colet gave an idea of the education offered there. St Paul's School was 'an academy for the instruction of boys in the faith of Christ, the best and greatest, and in good literature'. Its 153 pupils corresponded to the number of fishes caught in the miraculous draught, and their education was designed to equip them with sufficient literary skills to study the Bible and the early Church fathers. By so doing they would begin to know God, to love him, and so prepare themselves for the heavenly gift of faith. Throughout his adult life Pepys was to show himself a man well versed in religious texts and a great connoisseur of sermons, but if St Paul's School helped nourish his faith it also kindled his intense intellectual curiosity.

A good grounding in classical literature was designed to make the Paul's boys able to perform 'justly, skilfully and magnanimously all the affairs, both public and private, of peace and war'.[10] This was an ideal Pepys's career was to fulfil magnificently. He would mature to become the one man able to run the navy as his country set about expanding its maritime trade, while he would fill his leisure hours with the widest range of intellectual pursuits from the writing of history to an interest in the new science. His teachers were a seminal influence in this. Samuel Cromleholme, the then Sur Master of St Paul's, was a bibliophile and clearly an inspiring man whom Pepys was to honour for his 'abundance of learning and worth', for all that he would later see that he was in part at least a 'conceited pedagogue'. John Langley, the High Master, was on first acquaintance a more awe-inspiring figure who 'struck a mighty respect and fear into his scholars, which however wore off after they were a little used to him'.[11] From such men as these Pepys acquired a deep love of learning and a knowledge of the classics sufficiently lasting for him to be able later to choose a phrase of Cicero's for his personal motto: *mens cujusque is est quisque* – 'as is the mind, so is the man'.

None the less the man himself was far from formed, and the early weeks of 1650 were a trying time for the family in Salisbury Court. Samuel's future hung in the balance. Trading conditions in London were now so bad that the Merchant Tailors were attempting to suppress unfortunate rivals such as his father, and John Pepys was obliged to petition the Company for membership and to offer a reasonable sum to 'avoid trouble and molestation'. Money was clearly tight in the Pepys household, and if the talented Samuel was to have a more promising career than his father's, help would have to be sought elsewhere. In February 1650, young Pepys stood before the master and wardens of the Mercers' Company in the hope of winning one of the scholarships to Cambridge that were reserved for promising Paulines. He was on the threshold of a new world and his talent, as it always would, gained him entry to it. Samuel won an exhibition and, in the summer of 1650, he was entered as a sizar at Trinity Hall where he had distant family connections.

It is probable that he and those around him were thinking of a career in the law, but events did not take such a predictable course. With the death of the King, the country at large was in the grip of the Commonwealth men, and Puritan zealots nurtured ever fiercer dreams of a New Jerusalem and rule by the saints. A purged Parliament passed bills abolishing the monarchy as 'unnecessary, burdensome and dangerous' while also sweeping away the House of Lords as 'useless'. Such wild-eyed enthusiasm was not to everybody's taste and, in the quiet prettiness of Magdalene College, Cambridge, the master, Dr Edward Rainbowe, felt unable to compromise his Royalist conscience. He was quickly replaced by one John Sadler, a rising Commonwealth man who, by chance, lived in Salisbury Court. Clearly he had noted his talented young neighbour and, in October 1650, Pepys was entered at Magdalene.

The curriculum taught to the two thousand undergraduates gathered in the university was already eight hundred years old and was rooted firmly in the methods and outlook favoured by the scholars of the early Middle Ages. It was rigidly concerned with logic and disputation, drew its forms of enquiry from Aristotle and was systematic to a quite extraordinary degree. An undergraduate like Pepys, conscientiously following the course, aspired to an encyclopedic range of knowledge that could be seen as a coherent and interrelated whole. It was not easily acquired. Lectures lasted for an hour and were given between seven and eight in the morning, an uncomfortable and chilly experience which, in the winter months especially, was accompanied by a great deal of coughing and the shuffling of chilblained feet.

What was learned at lectures was then put to use in disputations: elaborate and highly technical debates between students, which placed considerable demands on verbal dexterity, memory and the handling of complex logical procedures. It was a harsh training. Syllogisms flashed like rapiers as the young men tried to create arguments that would confound their opponents and lead them into admitting that the truth of a proposition was quite the reverse of what they had initially asserted. If such disputations sharpened the wits they also encouraged a rather tiresome contentiousness, but it was the declamation – the formal set speech richly garnished with quotations from the great authors of antiquity – which was designed to train a man to think and write in a style that was smooth, plain, full and masculine. Throughout his life Pepys would be keenly aware of the value of order, system and style. His university studies encouraged this, and that he worked hard is suggested by the fact that he was awarded two college scholarships.

It is probable that Pepys also acquired another skill at

this time. Undergraduates were expected to take certain of their lectures down whole, a practice known as 'diting'. It is hardly surprising that methods of shorthand were much in favour among hard-pressed students, and Pepys's familiarity with Thomas Shelton's popular *Tachygraphy* probably dates from this period of his life. The alphabet of lines and curves on which Shelton based his system was comparatively simple to use, and by 1635 the university press at Cambridge was issuing the book for a large local market. A competent exponent of Shelton's shorthand, who might well use it for taking down sermons and speeches as well as lectures, would be able to record what he heard at something like a hundred words per minute. Fluency with Shelton's system was to prove enormously useful to Pepys, not only in his later professional work but also in that most secret of projects which ultimately secured his fame – his *Diary*.

Life at Cambridge was not just a matter of attending freezing lecture halls and transcribing reams of Aristotelian argument. The influence of a great university is subtly pervasive, providing those receptive to it with attitudes and values altogether more intangible than the ideas specifically taught there. This was clearly so for Pepys. He had come from a London riven with sectarian strife to a seat of learning that placed little value in the severer forms of dogmatism. 'Nothing spoils human nature more than false zeal. The good nature of an heathen is more God-like than the furious zeal of a Christian.'[12] The words of the provost of King's College may have seemed remote to an unknown undergraduate but they represented none the less a poise of mind that many would hanker after as events in England took their increasingly tumultuous course.

Similarly, the science taught in the university's scholastic curriculum may have seemed pedantic and dry, but contact with his tutor, Samuel Morland, surely gave Pepys some inkling of the new spirit of enquiry that was abroad and in which he too would soon become deeply interested. Morland was a scholar who could as readily invent a calculating machine as research into the history of the Waldensians. Hydrostatics fascinated him, and at various times he was to turn his agile mind to ear trumpets, portable cooking stoves and techniques of espionage, all in the hope of filling his increasingly empty purse. Morland was to return penuriously into Pepys's life but now, on their first acquaintance, he helped introduce the clever if rather narrow youth to the wider vistas of Cambridge thought.

And, as always, there was music. Pepys came from a musical home, and throughout his life music was the art that, above all, could move him to the fibre of his being. None the less, the Interregnum was not a propitious time. The court, the Church of England and the theatre – all once great centres of musical activity – had been proscribed, and only domestic music-making still flourished. A great deal of music was played at Cambridge, and Pepys certainly had musical friends at the university, for all that he appears to have had no formal instruction in the subject. Like his father, he could play the viol, to which he added such instruments as the violin, the lute, the theorbo and the flageolet. He was a competent sight-reader and was blessed with an acceptable bass-baritone voice. Above all, he adored music for its own sake. 'Music is the thing of the world I love most,' he wrote later.[13] It appealed to his intellectual curiosity and to a spirit that, for all its Puritan self-discipline, was easily, deliciously tempted into pleasure. Beneath the severe surface encouraged by Pepys's homelife ran the deep, sensuous currents of a man whose feelings and sensations were easily stirred.

Cambridge helped liberate these too. The unofficial curriculum of the university – the contact with young men of his own age – was as fruitful to the growing Pepys as his other university experiences. He was introduced to the city's public houses where he learned to sing 'Full forty times over', which he later described as 'a very lewd song', and on one occasion at least indulged himself so copiously that he staggered back to Magdalene where, in the agony of a hangover, he was admonished in front of the fellows for being scandalously overseen in drink. No doubt his friends encouraged him: Bob Sawyer, the future attorney-general with whom he shared his rooms, Fossan, Hoole, Castle and Nicholson with whom he studied, scholarly Richard Cumberland, and Christopher Anderson, relaxing from his medical studies with a girl when he could win the interest of 'an exceeding pretty lass, right for the sport'. Pepys's own sexual interests surely stirred and dominated his days, but if nothing is known of any encounters he might have had at this time, his fantasy was certainly active and he threw his more sentimental energies into composing a romance. He rediscovered the manuscript of this a decade after abandoning it and 'liked it very well, and wondered a little . . . at my vein at that time when I wrote it'.[14]

Such were Pepys's pleasures as an undergraduate, but Cambridge was not an unclouded horizon, and the most delightful afternoon could bring him up short with his old pain. Sometime during the summer of 1653 Pepys and a group of friends walked over to Aristotle's Well. It was a hot day, they were thirsty, and the cool running water was deliciously inviting. Pepys drank copiously before returning to college where he was suddenly doubled up in agony. It was, as he recognised, the old problem of his stone taking a turn for the worse. Many years later he coolly analysed what had happened. The weight of the water he had drunk that afternoon 'carried after some day's pain the stone out of the kidneys more sensibly through the urethra into the bladder'.[15] Now the discomfort would be frequent and sometimes unbearable.

Pepys had not only his health to worry about. He graduated in March 1654 and returned to London with no very clear or brilliant prospects before him. Nor did the time seem opportune, for London and the nation at large were once again in the grip of tumultuous events. A year earlier an exasperated Cromwell had marched into the House of Commons and told the members of the Rump Parliament gathered there that 'the Lord has done with you and has chosen other instruments for the carrying on his work'. For seemingly endless months the men who had agreed to the execution of Charles I had prevaricated over reform. Meanwhile, those outside the House who had not lapsed into a sullen acceptance of events – the army especially – agitated ever more furiously for the establishment of a kingdom fit for God's people. Pepys was once again witnessing a capital torn with dissent.

London showed him what anarchy could mean. The Levellers were demanding that the ordinary soldiers mutiny against their senior officers and seize power in the name of the people. The Diggers argued for a wholesale redistribution of wealth, declaring that the earth was 'a common treasury'. There were fears too of Royalist uprisings in support of the murdered King's son Charles, and terrible disturbances in Ireland. This was a time of bloody conflict. Armed rebellion against the Commonwealth was repressed with the utmost ferocity, while naval victories against the rival Dutch showed England to be 'a new Rome in the west'. Now Cromwell had acted in his own right, acted as some said with 'the spirit . . . so upon him, that he was overruled by it; and he consulted not with flesh and blood at all'. He wanted an assembly of the godly but, when the Nominated Parliament was elected, it rapidly disintegrated and resigned its power. The army was again the dominant force in the land and it was they who persuaded Cromwell to accept the Protectorship of the country and embody executive power in his own person.

If this was a period of the gravest uncertainty in the public sphere it was also an unsettling time for a young unemployed graduate like Pepys. To add to his troubles, he had fallen deeply in love and, in the imperious force of his passion, was determined to marry. The girl's name was Elizabeth St Michel. She was just fifteen, she was half French, and she came from an improvident family which, for all its aristocratic pretensions, had lost its fortune when it renounced the Catholic Church. Few alliances could have been more reckless, more downright foolhardly even, but Elizabeth was achingly desirable. She was naïve and unformed, fascinating in her sometimes un-English ways, a child who stirred Pepys's sexual nature to its core and brought suddenly to the forefront of his mind all his need to assert his masculinity, his dominance, that combination of the overbearing and the deeply affectionate which ran through his short frame and glowed in his large, enquiring eyes.

Like music, Elizabeth 'did wrap up my soul' so that there were moments when the lovelorn Pepys felt dizzy and even 'sick'. He would have Elizabeth at whatever cost, and whether she was ripe for him or not. Certainly, she was very young for marriage since girls in the second half of the seventeenth century did not usually begin menstruation until their fifteenth year. This disparity in Pepys and Elizabeth's maturity would later cause grave problems but, for the moment, Pepys himself was ablaze with passion and it is possible that he arranged a strictly illegal Anglican marriage service in October 1655 since, in his curiosity and uncertainty, he had acquired the habit of attending illicit Anglican ceremonies. What is certain is that the marriage was solemnised in the required form of a civil ceremony conducted at St Margaret's, Westminster, on 1 December 1655. It was followed by a wedding feast – modest enough, no doubt – that was held in a tavern on the steep slope of Old Fish Street.

Pepys had got his way and now he would have to try to make a life to support his desire. A job was the first essential and, with a job, a home. Both came in their most modest form through the agency of Edward Montagu and, as so often in Pepys's career, his fortunes were directed by actions on the wider political stage. When Cromwell assumed the Protectorate, Montagu's career flourished mightily. He was appointed to the Protector's Council of State and the following year was made a Treasury commissioner. The country had already won a series of magnificent victories against their great trading rivals the Dutch and now, with an enthusiasm for naval combat that rivalled the heroic days of the Armada, Cromwell was resolved to go to war with Spain. Montagu was required to superintend the vast quantity of paperwork needed to equip the fleet and, in the month of Pepys's marriage, he was appointed to the Admiralty Committee. He brought considerable if not always successful powers of application to his work, and by the start of January 1656, had been promoted to Joint General at Sea with the great but ailing Admiral Blake. The quantity of business Montagu had to transact, along with the likelihood of his frequent absences at sea, meant that he needed an able young man to look after his affairs at home, and early in March 1656 he despatched his first surviving note to 'Samuel Pepys at my lodgings in Westminster'. Pepys was now his illustrious kinsman's man-of-business with everything to learn about minor responsibility and the correct handling of superiors and rivals.

It was Pepys's task to pay sums of money to various of Montagu's colleagues, to order swords for him, caps for his children, and rich hangings for his home at Hinchinbrooke. It was also his duty to keep Montagu informed about events in the country at large when his 'honoured master' was at sea. The fact that Pepys and Elizabeth were now living in a tiny apartment in the Palace of Whitehall provided for them by Montagu gave Pepys an excellent vantage-point from which to observe all that was going on. He told Montagu about the activities of the lunatic religious fringe and of how a fanatical preacher from one of the sects had yet again set up the tiresome cry that the spirit within him was more powerful than the government who censored him. With the fascination for all aspects of human life that ran so deep within him, Pepys also told Montagu how he had observed Cromwell holding his sides with laughter as the gentlemen of his court paraded grotesquely before him dressed up in some captured popish vestments.

Above all, Pepys noted the changing tone of Whitehall. With the assumption of the Protectorate, Cromwell had taken on monarchical powers and these were now suggested by the increasing pomp with which he was surrounded. The palace was no longer a chaotic scrimmage, unregulated and swarming with people. 'He that sees the strictness used for stopping that free passage of strangers through Whitehall, and the ceremony used in passing the presence chamber, will say Sir Gilbert Pickering is a perfect Lord Chamberlain, and who meets Colonel Jones with a white staff in his hand will acknowledge him as perfect a Controller,' Pepys wrote. There is a light vein of irony in this, but what Pepys was describing was an outward, visible sign of that monarchical stability so many were hankering after, the worth of which Pepys himself was now coming to appreciate.

Pepys also had other duties to attend to. Montagu's first expedition as Joint General at Sea proved something of an anticlimax. He and Blake had hoped to capture the Spanish treasure fleet but, arriving too late, missed it and had to content themselves with bringing home two prizes won by a fellow officer and variously estimated as being worth between £600,000 and £1 million. Montagu was obliged to claim his share through the Prize Office and Pepys was put in charge of this task, itemising the silver furniture, the bullion and the spices that were now his master's. Such a responsibility was surely congenial to Pepys, giving him a sense of self-worth and answering to a deep and previously unexperienced delight in organising people, dealing with bureaucrats and pleasing those in high places. The task also brought out his humanity and curiosity for, along with the treasure, Montagu brought home the sons of the governor of Peru who had himself died in the struggle to capture his ship. It was Pepys's responsibility to see that these boys were lodged as their station required, and it was probably while attending to this that he took the opportunity to learn those elements of Spanish that would later be so useful to him.

However, Pepys was nothing more than a humble factotum doing a job considerably smaller than his abilities warranted, and he did not always do it to the required standards. Like many able young men, there was a side to Pepys that was easily distracted from duty, slothful even, and self-indulgent. For example, it was his task to keep Montagu's lesser servants in order, a job to which his youth and nature did not always suit him. With their master often away, the servants grew bored and the maids especially began to go to disreputable local cook-houses where one of them met a man with whom she eloped, taking some of Montagu's household goods along with her. There was the inevitable inquisition into the matter and Pepys was found to have behaved indiscreetly. He protested (perhaps too much) that this was not so, vowed that he himself kept regular hours, and swore that in the future he would do all he could to prevent 'the disrepute of a maid's going to a victualling house in neglect of your Honour's own doors'. Pepys was clearly perturbed that he had let things slide, for he knew how dependent on Montagu he was. 'It troubles me,' he wrote, 'to hear what your Lordship's apprehensions are concerning me. The loss of your Honour's good word I am too sure will prove as much my undoing as hitherto it hath been my best friend.'[16]

Pepys was learning fast, but the lessons of his public life were altogether more easily mastered than those he had to face in the little turret room he and Elizabeth occupied in the vast, sprawling Palace of Whitehall. Pepys had married for love and now he had to face everyday realities. The mere presence of Elizabeth roused him intensely, but his ardour was coupled with exasperation. Elizabeth was hopelessly untidy and careless in little domestic details. She totally lacked other women's seemingly effortless ability to make a home, for all that she tried so hard. When Elizabeth washed Pepys's dirty clothes it was like watching a child at play. She was at once serious and incompetent, and her inability was made worse by the fact that she was frightened of her husband, frightened of a man who was clever, demanding, sexually more mature than she was, and who was racked with guilt at his own outbursts of anger and frustration. They were, besides, very poor. Once Pepys had to pawn his lute for forty shillings. Such petty hardships hammered at his self-respect and made him even more difficult to live with. Nor could Elizabeth provide him with the intellectual companionship he craved. Pepys's mind roved easily over the fields of European civilisation but Elizabeth was happiest when lost in a French romance whose tedious, irritating plots she would recite at length.

And Elizabeth had a will of her own – desires of her own too. She was a teenager and naturally flirtatious. When Pepys caught her looking at another man, and making those little gestures with which she had captured his heart, jealousy tightened round him like a crown of thorns. It was what he would later call his 'old disease' and there was nothing he could do about it. There were furious rows and passionate reconciliations, but sometimes, even in the intimacy of their bed when desire consumed all other feelings, there were difficulties. Elizabeth suffered from a recurring abscess on her labia, which made intercourse extremely painful and left both partners with a passion for each other that they could not easily satisfy. At one time things were so bad between them that Elizabeth left her husband and went to live with friends in Charing Cross. How long she was gone is not known, but she was back by the close of 1657, and the shamefaced couple started all over again because they loved each other.

Pepys needed Elizabeth more at this time than perhaps he dared admit. There were moments as he was going about Montagu's business in the savagely cold winter of 1657–8 – seeing a merchant, perhaps, dealing with the Prize Office, or shopping for the family – when the stone in his bladder doubled him up in a pain that was, in his own word, 'insupportable'. It was obvious that something had to be done, but the prospect of an operation was alarming. Pepys had to weigh up the possibilities carefully, and his thoughts ran with a seriousness he had never known before. The operation might prove fatal, and would certainly be excruciatingly painful. The details were unthinkable, but as the cold that held London in its grip brought the usual distressing symptoms to the all but unknown young manservant, he realised he would have to take his chance and, by March, he had made his decision.

Pepys was only twenty-five, still young enough for the securities of his childhood to be a tangible support to him, something real and immediate. In Salisbury Court, amid that warren of people who had always been so good to him, there lived an eminent surgeon called Thomas Hollier. Hollier specialised in lithotomies, or operations for the stone, and was, by the standards of his time – when anaesthetics were unknown and septicaemia unrecognised – a successful practitioner. Quantities of his patients survived his ministrations. To Hollier Pepys would go, and the operation itself would be performed in the nearby house of John Pepys of Ashtead's daughter. Jane Turner, as she now was, had married well and her house was probably larger and more suitable than Pepys's parents' home. Besides, the house of a relative was a place where his mother and father would feel obliged to guard their emotions. Pepys had worries enough not to have to deal with those. The crisis had touched his deepest nature. He had prepared his mind for death and resolved that if by Providence he survived then he would hold a 'solemn feast' of celebration every year to thank the God who had preserved him.

Pepys was as ready as he could be, and on 26 March 1658, he made his way to the Turners' house. There Hollier and his knife were waiting for him. No doubt prayers were said before Pepys was tied with a rope to what served as the operating table and Hollier began his work: making an incision about three inches long between his patient's anus and scrotum prior to opening his bladder, removing the stone in about fifty agonising seconds and, in the process, so damaging the ducts from Pepys's testicles that for the rest of his life he would be sterile but not impotent. Pepys himself would never know the truth of this, but now, when the operation was over, Hollier gave the offending stone to his patient. It weighed some two ounces and was about the size of a tennis ball. Pepys would eventually have a box made for it and show the specimen to his friends. He had survived a great crisis, and now his love of life flooded through him with renewed energy as he readied himself for a future that would take him on an extraordinary course and eventually involve him in the affairs of his country at the highest level.

CHAPTER TWO

Waiting on Events

With his recovery a new era opened in Pepys's life and with it came a new job. He was now a clerk in the Exchequer on a salary of £50 a year which, in the manner of the time, he supplemented with fees and gratuities. To celebrate this rise in status Pepys and Elizabeth moved into a 'poor little house' in Axe Yard, a cul-de-sac close to the modern Downing Street. There, in addition to a bedroom and a dining room, Pepys had his own study and dressing room. The pride in possession that ran so deeply in him was stirred, as was his concern with money. He had been poor and even now he was far from being a rich man. None the less, with the carefulness that was characteristic of him, he began saving hard and, in two years, had £40 to invest with Uncle Robert in Brampton. Pepy's income from the Exchequer also allowed him and Elizabeth to hire a maid, and in late August 1658 Jane Birch joined the little ménage. She was a mild-mannered, rather untidy girl who, much to Elizabeth's relief, did the laundry and other chores for them. There were occasions on which Pepys lost his temper with the girl – Jane's ways offended his insistence on order and good appearance – and once he beat her with a broom, later regretting it. He grew fond of her, though, and Jane was the first of many such girls who were to join the Pepys household, sometimes with disastrous results.

Quite how Pepys came by his new job at the Exchequer is unclear, for the Exchequer itself was hidebound with hereditary life appointees. Family influence may have had its part to play and it is possible that Montagu, for whom Pepys still ran errands, had a hand in his kinsman's fortunes since he belonged to the same political circle as Pepys's new employer, George Downing. What is certain is that Pepys's new boss was an ogre who commanded his clerk's hatred and admiration in equal measure, for George Downing showed Pepys how hard, how vain and how ruthless a successful man of affairs could be. Downing himself was then in his early thirties and had his eye constantly on the main chance. He was rising high in a country where he had not been born for he was of New England stock and an early graduate of Harvard. Once he had crossed the Atlantic, Downing sided with the Parliamentarians and, having served first as a chaplain and then, as Scout-Master General to Cromwell's army in Scotland, he entered politics. In 1657 he was appointed English Resident at The Hague where he conducted himself with all the quarrelsomeness that he thought became an ambassador living among his country's bitterest trading rivals.

Downing was, none the less, a man of vision, and in his company Pepys became familiar with the profoundly influential idea that Britain should destroy the naval power of the Dutch and so break their monopoly on the carrying trade. This was an old and long-treasured ambition that had found its most forthright expression in the writings of the most glamorous of the Elizabethan sea-dogs. 'He that commands the sea,' wrote Sir Walter Ralegh, 'commands the trade, and he that is lord of the trade of the world is lord of the wealth of the world.'[1] England was particularly well placed to assume this position since the country was close to the main trade routes, was abundantly supplied with deep-water harbours and, being an island, had no land borders to defend or expand. All its energies could thus be devoted to naval power and, with this, England could develop an ever-increasing prosperity. From now on wars would be fought principally for commercial advantage, a notion that was eventually to move to the centre of Pepys's concerns.

For the moment, the work Pepys was required to do was not particularly arduous. He would rise at daybreak and get himself ready while Elizabeth read to him, then he might take his breakfast at a tavern on the way to the Exchequer office in the Palace of Westminster. A bewildering range of business was conducted there since the Exchequer was at one and the same time a law court, the depository of the national finances, and an auditing department where money was both received and disbursed. This last was the particular responsibility of the tellers of the Exchequer and their deputies, like Pepys, who were supposed to 'attend constantly every morning throughout the year (except on Sundays and the great festivals) and in the afternoons when need requires for the receiving and paying of . . . treasure.'[2] It was a teller's job to count the money when it came in. The cash itself was then receipted by an auditor and recorded in duplicate by the clerk of the pells. The means used for this last were antiquated in the extreme: long hazelwood tally sticks were cut with a series of graded notches representing the amounts received. These tally sticks were then split down the middle and one of the halves was given to the person who had paid the money while the other remained with the Exchequer. Both parties were thus provided with a cumbersome if foolproof record of their transaction.

So much for business. The Exchequer buzzed with people and Pepys, exercising his vigorous gift for friendship, soon had a numerous acquaintance there. John Hawley introduced him to the ways of the Exchequer, to its work and its manner of being convivial. Many hours were whiled away with Hawley and his companions in the local taverns. Wood's in Pall Mall was the venue for a weekly get-together with such friends as the musical Vines brothers, William Bowyer, whose rubicund father was the *pater familias* of the clerks, Will Symons and joke-cracking Peter Luellin. Samuel Hartlib, the son of the philosopher, was another colleague, while Pepys also had many friends from other walks of life. There was Wootton the City shoemaker with whom he drank occasionally, the great scholar William Fuller, who was now eking out an existence at the school attended by Montagu's sons, and Henry Moore the lawyer, who spoke so well and so judiciously that Pepys always found it difficult to part from him.

Nor were Pepys's friendships confined to men. He had a quick eye for the attractions of the opposite sex. He noted, for example, the wife of one of Montagu's followers who, he declared, had 'the best complexion that ever I saw on any woman'. There were other beauties to be found amid the crowded stalls of Westminster Hall where Pepys went shopping. He liked to buy newsbooks and pamphlets from Miles and Ann Mitchell, for example, and he was friendly with their daughter-in-law Betty whom he called his 'wife' because she looked so much like Elizabeth. The linen-sellers of Westminster Hall were often pretty too. Pepys noted particularly the attractions of Betty Martin and her sister Doll, women with whom he would eventually become entangled, for it was already apparent to him that his wife could not wholly satisfy his sexual curiosity and appetite. Pepys's eyes flickered across any company in which he found himself, searching out food for his fantasies and, eventually, for the relief of his pressing needs.

For the moment all this was innocent enough, and sometimes Pepys's acquaintances would visit him at work. If there was nothing much to do, he would take them back to Axe Yard for a dish of steaks and rabbit, and a game or two of cards. He was on call none the less, and these convivial episodes were likely to be interrupted by one of Downing's messengers summoning Pepys to attend to some errand. When it was despatched Pepys might go on to visit other friends such as Dr Whore in Cannon Row, Westminster, where the physician, accompanied by two professional musicians, would be singing 'songs of his own making'. Pepys might also drop in on Montagu, now a Cromwellian baron, who also had a musical house and offered excellent conversation.* Sundays were necessarily different. Pepys usually spent his Sunday mornings going to church and listening with critical interest to the preacher. His taste for sermons was maturing and now began to reflect the ideas and aspirations of his generation. He was becoming increasingly disgusted by those who claimed divine inspiration then delivered it 'with a great deal of noise and a kind of religious tone'. Such sermons he found frankly 'dull', although they still appealed to his parents and to those rather trying relatives he might find in Salisbury Court on a Sunday evening, 'sometimes all honey with one another, and then all turd, and a strange rude life there is among them'.[3]

There is a feeling here of Pepys having grown away from his modest roots, and along with this went a growing distaste for the extremism that had surrounded him as he grew up. It was boring, uncouth and, as he increasingly realised, unproductive. Now a great national crisis was to show that a growing number of people felt as he did. On 3 September 1658 Oliver Cromwell died. The man who had ruled as king in all but name was mourned with the pomp that became a monarch. His black-draped effigy was exhibited in Somerset House for two months so that a long, winding procession

* Pepys often referred to Montagu in his *Diary* as 'my Lord'.

of the curious could pay their last respects. When the public appetite had been satisfied, the wax image was clothed in crimson and adorned with the crown and sceptre that the living Cromwell had always declined. The image was then placed upright on the catafalque and illumined by the light of five hundred flickering candles. Finally, the hearse was drawn in procession to Westminster Abbey accompanied by hooded mourners marching to the funeral beat of muffled drums.

Such pomp could not disguise the fact that Cromwell had held the nation together through a unique combination of character and circumstances, and now Pepys was to witness the divisions and insecurities with which the country was truly riven. His intense and natural interest in political events is suggested by his membership of the Rota Club where some of the best minds in the country met to discuss the current state of affairs in debates that were 'the most ingenious, and smart' that a man could wish to hear, so sharp indeed that 'the arguments in the Parliament house were but flat to it'.[4] Such debates suggested that the passing of the Protectorate to Cromwell's son Richard was smooth in appearance only, and certainly belied the government's boast that the nation was so calm 'there is not a dog that wags his tongue'. There were too many unsettled questions, too many rifts below the surface of national life, too many intractable problems for this to be so.

Here was an intensely uncertain world, for men of Pepys's generation were not only disillusioned by the religious extremism they saw about them but by the succession of constitutional experiments that had followed the execution of King Charles. While religious zealots still proclaimed their savage visions, self-seeking politicians bickered in an apparently endless round of inefficiency. Financial problems made matters worse. Cromwell's naval victories had been ruinously expensive, the national debt mounted frighteningly and the depleted ranks of the New Model Army were restless and unpaid. Richard Cromwell was not the man to sort such problems out. He had neither the experience to control Parliament nor the stature to appear on the European stage. For all that he might send Pepys's patron Montagu to the Baltic in an attempt to mediate between Sweden and Denmark, international politics were as far beyond his grasp as the problems he faced at home.

In this time of mounting uncertainty the ever-loyal Pepys took personal charge of My Lord's plate and made sure that it was placed safely in the great chest at the Exchequer. He was wise to do so, for a dizzying series of events was now propelling the nation into ever deeper crisis. Senior army officers were demanding that the Parliament that could not pay them should be dissolved. When this was refused they rallied their men round London, and Richard Cromwell, with a mere two hundred men to protect him, fast became 'Tumble-Down-Dick' and retired into private life. The army then recalled the old Rump Parliament, which had ordered the execution of the King, but the returned Members were adamant that they would assert their authority over the armed forces, both the army that had brought them back to power and the navy now sailing off the Baltic with Montagu in command.

The Members in Westminster viewed Montagu himself with particular suspicion for they believed that he was not wholly sympathetic to their aims. Their doubts were perfectly justified since Montagu was by this time a firm supporter of the sort of monarchical authority Oliver Cromwell had exercised during the Protectorate. Even the Rump Parliament was not so foolish as to make an enemy of their naval commander while he was at sea, however, and they contented themselves with sending out a commission empowered to take over the peace negotiations in the Baltic. These were uncertain times and a Royalist double agent of singular incompetence was also sent over to sound out Montagu concerning a proposed uprising. During these tense days Montagu listened to everyone but revealed his deepest feelings to none of those about him. Certainly, he did not betray his concerns to Pepys, who had sailed out with letters for him. Instead, Montagu persuaded his men that their best course was to return home. On his way back he learned that the planned Royalist insurrection had been put down, and now, as he landed, he was stripped of his appointments and was obliged to wait silently at Hinchinbrooke as the Rump Parliament was replaced by a military Committee of Safety.

Pepys kept Montagu in touch by letter with events in a London seething with discontent. The apprentices were out on the streets protesting at the actions of the army and demanding the election of a free Parliament. They collected some 20,000 signatures on a petition that outlined their grievances in detail, and by 5 December they were ready to present this to the Common Council of the City. Every effort was made to prevent them, and a tense atmosphere grew up between the serried ranks of soldiers marshalled in the streets and the great mass of ordinary people, who were determined that their voice should be heard. Violence broke out, and Pepys described it for My Lord with all the vividness and delight in the reality of concrete detail of which he was becoming a master:

> The soldiers as they marched were hooted at all along the streets, and where any straggled from the whole body, the boys flung stones, tiles, turnips, etc., and, with all the affronts they could give them; some they disarmed, and kicked, others abused the horse with stones and rubbish they flung at them; and when Col. Hewson came the head of his regiment they shouted all along: 'A cobbler! A cobbler'; in some places the apprentices would get a football (it being a hard frost) and drive it among the soldiers on purpose, and they either darest not (or prudently would not) interrupt them; in fine, many soldiers were hurt with stones, and one I see was very near

having his brains knocked out with a brickbat flung from the top of a house at him.[5]

Pepys had been used to protest in the London streets from the time of his boyhood, but now matters had turned sour indeed. The crowd exasperated the soldiers beyond endurance and, perhaps on Hewson's orders, they fired. Some half-dozen youths were killed and several others were wounded. Events were running out of control. Widespread violence was threatened, a further huge petition was prepared, seconded by yet another from the seamen and watermen of London. The demand was yet again for 'a free and legal Parliament' to redress grievances, and by now it was perfectly clear that the Committee of Safety had no control over the capital. At the end of the month the Rump had once again resumed power.

It was in this winter of veering fortunes that Pepys himself made a decision of the utmost importance. As the old year turned into 1660 he sat down to review the state of affairs both in his personal life and in the broader, public world that was so noisily venting its confusion in the streets outside. He himself was withdrawn, silent, meditative. This was a solemn moment as his mind, neat but capacious, began to survey each of the many elements of his existence. 'Blessed be God,' he wrote, 'at the end of the last year I was in very good health, without any sense of my old pain.'[6] The problem of the stone that had tortured him for years had been cured and, with the sense of physical relief, came a feeling of spiritual gratitude: simple, modest and, in the end, all the more touching for that.

Pepys's personal circumstances were modest too. 'I lived in Axe Yard,' he wrote, 'having my wife and servant Jane, and no more in the family than us three.' Pepys wanted more, and children especially: the convivial clerk of the Exchequer, working, entertaining and enjoying himself, knew disappointment and was hurt by the barrenness of his difficult marriage. 'My wife, after the absence of her terms for seven weeks, gave me hopes of being with child, but on the last day of the year she hath them again.' Characteristically, Pepys said nothing about Elizabeth's feelings on the matter, but certainly there was little in his outward circumstances to support his usual natural ebullience. Instead, from the perspective of the year's end, everything was rather meagre. For all his saving from his salary and the perquisites of his office, Pepys felt himself 'very poor' and he recognised how, in the difficult times through which he was living, even his continuing in his job was 'somewhat uncertain'.

It is likely that Pepys drafted these sentences in rough before transcribing them (in Shelton's system of shorthand) into the stout octavo stationer's notebook he had bought from John Cade of Cornhill. He proceeded with great care, for what he was writing had been conceived as no casual whim. Pepys would bring to his task all his longing for order, decency and method. When he had turned back the first bare page of the notebook – so exciting, so tempting in its virgin purity – he took a ruler and, dipping his pen in red ink, drew a line about half an inch from the top of the page and a second margin down the left-hand side. Then, taking up another pen and a different coloured ink, Pepys began writing. He shaped the symbols precisely, legibly. Although the pages of the notebook were not lined and were too opaque for him to use a ruled backing-sheet, his sentences would run in a straight and orderly manner while the spaces between the lines would also be exact and regular. Pepys was making a balance-sheet of his world. The accountant of the Exchequer office was doing his annual audit. The young man brought up in a Puritan household was examining his worldly state. The historian was writing the history of himself. Above all, the artist was at work. Pepys had resolved that he would write an account not just of the previous year but of every day that followed in the next. He would keep a diary – a journal, as he preferred to call it – and he would bring to it all the care, the attention to detail, and the rich and vivid self-awareness he had lavished on his first page. Like many great writers, he knew that he was his own best subject, and the scores of blank pages that remained to be filled would contain his self-portrait and his history of his times.

Those entries would require a different style from the one he had used so far. On his first page Pepys had tried to view his life in general terms but now, as day succeeded day, he would have to show with microscopic particularity the impulses that made up the man he actually was and his world as he experienced it. He would have to capture the blankness of New Year's Day 1660, for example, when he 'dined at home in the garret, where my wife dressed the remains of a turkey, and in the doing of it she burnt her hand'. He would have to show domestic crises such as the one that loomed soon afterwards when his landlord's agent called for the half-yearly rent and, since there was no money in the house, Pepys had to take the man round to his office where, with seventeenth-century insouciance about such matters, he paid him with funds borrowed from the Exchequer.

Pepys would have to suggest as well the reality of a great city as it lived its infinitely various life about him. He would have to evoke the very substance of London, as when, on the night of 16 January, he 'sat up till the bell-man came by with his bell, just under my window as I was writing of this very line, and cried, "Past one of the clock, and a cold, frosty, windy morning."' Such life was too delicious not to record and, having done so, Pepys 'went to bed and left my wife and the maid a-washing still'. And always there was more. Pepys would show his own days as they followed one after the other, idle days when there was 'nothing to do at our office', or busy days when, dressed in 'my suit with great skirts', he hurried round the London streets attending to Downing's business or My Lord's. He would describe himself being lured into Harper's tavern by a couple of friends who, amid the tobacco smoke and chatter, introduced him to Muddiman the hack journalist whose conversation, well-informed and outrageous, gave Pepys a very clear idea of a man who claimed to write for the greater glory of the Parliamentarians but in reality 'did it only to get money and did talk very basely of many of them'.

Not that Pepys himself was without his money worries. He was poor and he had to be careful. After he had parted from Muddiman, he called on My Lord's daughter who it was feared had smallpox, then met with a couple of acquaintances whom he took home and 'gave a bottle of wine and the remainder of my collar of brawn'. As the convivial evening came to an end, there was a knock on the door. It was John Hawley with bad news. Pepys had been 'missed' at the office. Worse, his bosses were now demanding that he pay back the money he had borrowed for the rent 'at which I was put to a great loss how I should get money to make up my cash, and so went to bed in great trouble'. This was hardly surprising. After all, Pepys's job was on the line, but the following morning he had recovered his nerve. He had a clear idea of what he would do and felt as confident as a man in his position could. He trudged his way through streets dirty with slush from the recent thaw and went to borrow the £10 he owed from John Crew, a distinguished Presbyterian friend of My Lord. Then he returned 'to my office and was able to pay my money'. A crisis had been averted and, to celebrate, Pepys and a friend 'drank a pint of wine at the Star in Cheapside'.

Beneath this engaging surface of daily life profound forces were at work and Pepys observed these too. He knew that the most powerful army in the country was that in Scotland under the command of General Monck. Monck himself had strongly disapproved of the southern army's actions in dismissing the Rump Parliament, and on the first day of 1660, as Pepys himself was beginning work on his *Diary*, Monck began to move his troops south towards London. It was clear that the military forces quartered in Northumberland were too weak to oppose him, and every mind in England was focused on what Monck would do. Monck himself was a rough, enigmatic man and he held the balance of power. In his hands lay the future of the country: the decision as to whether the Rump would be maintained by his soldiers or whether he would call for a 'free Parliament'.

There was no doubt as to where the majority opinion in London lay. Protests had made clear the people's disgust with the Rump, while the elections to the Common Council had given this view legitimate form. Pepys knew at the start of the year that the councillors had 'sent to Monck their sword-bearer, to acquaint him with their desires for a free and full Parliament' and, being of their opinion and knowing in his heart of hearts that such elections would mean the return of the monarchy, Pepys watched and listened intently to everything that happened. He learned that the Prince's Lodgings in Whitehall were to be prepared for Monck. On 9 January he 'heard for certain that Monck was coming to London'. Four days later he was told that Monck's letter to the Common Council was a 'cunning piece', which carefully veiled his intentions, but by the beginning of February, the city was full of his soldiers and soon the great man would be there in person.

As Pepys watched these events they were also attended to with intense interest by members of the little exiled court of Charles Stuart, now living in poverty in the Low Countries. For years Charles had exerted might and main to win back the throne that was rightfully his and, in the process, had learned the hard political lessons of guile and deceit. After his father's death he had led a Scots army into England only to be defeated at Worcester and then have to flee for his life.

There had followed aimless, shiftless years on the Continent, years fuelled by hopes of Royalist insurrections in England and made bitter by continuous disappointment. Charles had eventually negotiated an allowance of sorts from the King of Spain, but this was rarely paid and there were times when, having sold his plate, he was obliged to eat his meagre daily meal off a plain trencher. Disillusion, cynicism and an intense belief in his hereditary rights characterised the tall and saturnine exile, who was now edging towards his thirtieth birthday and who was too schooled in the uses of the world to give easy credit to hope or to trust the motives of those about him.

What the exiled court could only learn from messengers, Pepys saw with his own eyes and heard with his own ears. His personal enthusiasm for monarchy warmed with the nation's. On 30 January he woke and, before he was even out of bed, 'fell a-singing of my song "Great, good and just"', a cavalier lyric by Montrose that put Pepys 'in mind that this was the fatal day, now ten years since, His Majesty died'. Pepys's excitement had confused him since Charles I had actually been executed eleven years before, but it is a measure of how far Pepys had come in this time that the boy who had eagerly joined the crowds outside Whitehall in 1649 and prophesied that monarchy would be forgotten now wanted nothing more than the restoration of Charles II.

He watched the uncertain course of events with intense interest and wrote it all down. He noted that as Monck marched ever closer to London so he ordered the troops stationed there to be withdrawn, but the soldiers, unpaid and surly, were not easily to be commanded. The restoration of the King was far from certain and on 2 February, as Pepys was carrying £60 from the city for My Lord, he heard gunfire and found the Strand full of soldiers ready to mutiny and 'bawling and calling in the street for a free Parliament and money'. But now even the weather seemed to welcome the changes about to sweep across the nation. The following day was brilliantly sunny. An exultant Pepys played on his flageolet in St James's Park and then, having conducted his business, went walking with friends 'all over Whitehall whither General Monck was newly come and we saw all his forces march by in very good plight and stout officers'. Here, surely, was the army of liberation, and the mass of people greeted it with enthusiasm. 'Boys do now cry "Kiss my Parliament" instead of "Kiss my arse",' Pepys noted, 'so great and general a contempt is the Rump come to among all men, good and bad.' The way had been paved for the restoration of the King and euphoria was universal and tumultuous:

> In Cheapside there was a great many bonfires, and Bow Bells and all the bells in all the churches as we went home were a-ringing. Hence we went homewards, it being about 10 a-clock. But the common joy that was everywhere to be seen! The number of bonfires, there being fourteen between St Dunstan's and Temple Bar. And at Strand Bridge I could see at one view . . . 31 fires. In King's Street, seven or eight; and all along burning and roasting and drinking for rumps – there being rumps tied upon sticks and carried up and down. The butchers at the Maypole in the Strand rang a peal with their knives when they were going to sacrifice their rump. On Ludgate Hill there was one turning of the spit, that had a rump tied upon it, and another basting of it. Indeed, it was past imagination, both the greatness and the suddenness of it. At one end of the street, you would think there was a whole lane of fire, and so hot that we were fain to keep still on the further side merely for heat.[7]

A few weeks later it became apparent that My Lord wished to have a confidential word with Pepys. He invited him to walk in the Whitehall garden where, with the circumspection that had become second nature to him, Montagu asked his young cousin 'how things were with me' and suggested that, with the great changes about to sweep the country, Pepys look for 'some good place'. Montagu would help him. The path to promotion was being cleared for Pepys, and Montagu himself 'asked me whether I could without too much inconvenience go to sea as his secretary, and bade me think of it'. My Lord's patrician manner is exactly caught as he handed a great opportunity to Pepys, wrapping it in self-effacing courtesy and a studied diffidence of manner. It would not do to be over-enthusiastic about such things at such a time and, rather than let an excited Pepys talk, My Lord gently deflected the conversation to 'things of state' before reminding Pepys with firm politeness that 'he would have me to go' with him to sea.[8]

The opportunity with which Pepys had been provided seemed golden but he needed some persuading to take it. He was a Londoner born and bred. The narrow streets of the city – winding, dark and dirty – were his natural home. The cries of the numerous hawkers were altogether more familiar to him than the strange language of sailors. Besides, as his father had recently told him, Uncle Robert of Brampton had declared his intention of leaving his small estate to Pepys and was even now so sickly a man that 'he doth believe he cannot continue in that condition long'. Modest security had its temptations and Pepys could not make up his mind. Slowly others persuaded him and pointed out the advantages that would accrue. Pepys met an acquaintance in a tavern, for example, who told him it would be perfectly possible for Montagu's man to enter the names of five or six extra servants on the muster role, pay them what he pleased and pocket the difference. The perquisites of office had their attractions, however dubiously come by, but altogether more alluring for an intelligent young man of twenty-seven was the challenge of a future that might lead anywhere. Slowly Pepys's resolve hardened and, on 9 March, in the Painted Chamber at Whitehall, he told My Lord 'that I was willing and ready to go with him to sea'. A delighted Montagu welcomed Pepys into his entourage and suggested that he write to Downing telling him of his decision, 'which I did'.

The one person Pepys had not fully consulted in this great matter was his wife. The problem of what to do with Elizabeth nagged him. She was young, attractive and flirtatious. Pepys was a man easily made jealous. To try to relieve his anxieties, he went to Harper's tavern and did not leave until about ten o'clock, by which time he was fairly drunk – sufficiently drunk to swear the next day that he would 'drink no strong drink this week, for I find that it makes me sweat in bed and puts me quite out of order'. Then he went to see his father. He found him in his cutting room and broached his difficulty. The old man thought it best that Elizabeth be sent to board at the Bowyers' country house in Buckinghamshire. The *pater familias* of the Exchequer clerks and his wife would keep an eye on her. When Elizabeth was told what had been decided for her, she was angry and upset. Not only was she to be left alone while her husband faced heaven only knew what dangers, but Pepys had broken the news to her with that overbearing insensitivity he seemed to reserve almost exclusively for her and which comes out even in his *Diary* entry. 'I took occasion to tell my wife of my going to sea.' Elizabeth's feelings did not greatly matter. Her submission was all that was required, and when Pepys returned to the house that evening he found Elizabeth 'making caps for me', like the docile child he wanted her to be.

Meanwhile, the new secretary shone in his master's light. His sudden rise in status meant that he was invited to dine by luminaries of the Navy Office. He needed his own little entourage too, and he hired a serving-boy and a clerk. Such trappings of office delighted Pepys's self-esteem, but more deeply satisfying was the great amount of work he suddenly had to do for Montagu. He was no longer idle and unfocused, but a young man of intelligence and ability who was fully stretched: sorting papers, writing reports, and dealing with the crowds of petitioners who appealed to him for work – men like the parson who wished to be a preacher on one of My Lord's ships and offered him a gratuity for his efforts. There were personal matters to attend to as well. The rent on Axe Yard had to be settled. Debts had to be paid. Essential belongings had to be packed in a borrowed sea-chest. And, of course, there was Elizabeth.

For all his thrusting, overbearing ways, Pepys loved his wife and, in these days before his parting, he was determined to show it. Prudence dictated that he make a will and in it he left everything to Elizabeth: money and all those possessions he prized so greatly, save for his more scholarly books which he bequeathed to his brother John. Elizabeth herself, half French as she was, should have his books in that language. Pepys had done all he could and at last the time came for him and Elizabeth to part. On the morning of 17 March the couple 'bade Adieu in bed'. When Pepys had sealed his will he took Elizabeth by coach to the Chequers in Holborn from where she would go to the Bowyers. Then he readied himself for whatever the future might bring.

CHAPTER THREE

Restoration

What the future brought in the short term was torrential rain. The continuous downpour over London was so intense that it was possible to row boats along Whitehall. This did not prevent Pepys from setting his hand to the 'infinity of business' he was now required to attend to. The logistical details of putting the fleet to sea were manifold, but for all that the work was onerous Pepys rejoiced in it, finding that the pressure, the responsibility and the sheer complexity of the problems involved absorbed his intellect and used his energies to the utmost. His vigour was extraordinary and the exercise of it was a delight. To work in this way was to find great satisfaction and a newly alert view of life. It was to discover himself.

The secretaryship was also an easy way of making money. Captain Williamson, newly commissioned as commander of the *Harp*, offered Pepys a gold coin and twenty shillings in silver for his help. The scrimmage of tradesmen and junior officers who took Pepys to dine at the Pope's Head in Chancery Lane were likewise keen to oil the ducts of bounty.

As Pepys's purse grew heavier his wry amusement grew proportionately, but the warning voice of the Puritanism in which he had been raised also made itself heard. 'Strange,' he wrote, of those who were so assiduously courting him, 'how these people do now promise me anything; one a rapier, the other a vessel of wine or a gun, and one offered me his silver hat-band to do him a courtesy. I pray God keep me from being proud or too much lifted up hereby.'[1] There was little danger of that, for among the many jostling to put their snouts in the trough there appeared a figure who was regularly to embarrass Pepys and for whom he was bound to feel responsibility.

Balthasar St Michel was Elizabeth's brother, a wheedling, comic liability of a young man whose belief in his own gentility was as assured as the narrowness of his means. Brother Balty was after a job – not one in which he would have to work, Pepys would understand, but one that would provide him with status and cash. Balty wanted to be, in the phrase of the day, a Reformado, an officer without fixed responsibilities. The prospect made Pepys cringe, but he could not shirk his family duties. He knew Balty of old and could etch his portrait in the acid of his contempt. 'I perceive he stands upon a place for a gentleman that may not stain his family; when God help him, he wants bread,' he wrote.[2] Pepys would have to do something for him, and when Balty, with all the dexterity of the parasitical, contrived to get himself invited to dine with Pepys and My Lord, Montagu disencumbered Pepys of his embarrassment by personally seeing to it that Balthasar was made a Reformado under a captain he himself disliked.

The honour of the St Michels had been saved and Pepys could give his attention to matters altogether more important. There was still a mass of paperwork to attend to: letters to write, letters to read, commissions to draft and, for reasons he could not yet ascertain, passes to make out for numerous friends of My Lord's who, it seemed, had all decided to make their way to Holland. To be sure, it was delightful to receive letters aboard ship from highly placed officials in the Admiralty addressed to Samuel Pepys, Esq., 'of which God knows I was not a little proud'. To crack open the wax seals of other letters and find gold and silver coins secreted in them was also a pleasure of which it was difficult to tire. The work was demanding. There were times when Pepys was at his desk until midnight and then, after only three hours' sleep, worked on until nine the following morning. Such strenuous labour was not always made easier by the two assistants he had hired to lighten his load. His landlubber clerk Burr took a boat to shore at the least opportunity, and when his boy Eliezer spilt beer over a mound of documents an exasperated Pepys boxed his ear.

There were compensations all the same. It was deeply agreeable to see the respect with which My Lord was treated, even by those who had earlier been his rivals. Vice-Admiral Lawson, for example, was known as an ardent Republican and as the man who had sailed the fleet up the Thames in support of the Rump. He was yesterday's man. Lawson was a seaman of the greatest skill and experience, brave and loved by his men. It would be worrying indeed if such a figure were to show himself aggrieved but, as the guns thundered to welcome Montagu aboard the *Swiftsure*, Lawson showed himself 'very respectful to my Lord, and so did the rest of the commanders of the frigates that were thereabouts'.

The respect shown to Montagu was shown to Pepys in his turn. My Lord's secretary was not a man to be on the wrong side of, but the many who now chose to ingratiate themselves with Pepys warmed to him and were pleased to find that an official could also be a friend. Pepys, for his part, not only enjoyed their companionship but the sense of authority he had now acquired. 'I was infinitely pleased,' he wrote, 'to see what a command I have to have everyone ready to come and go.'[3] His world was changing fast and, in the rare minutes of free time that Pepys could find, his *Diary* became his means of coming to an understanding of a new way of life. His happy-go-lucky days of rubbing shoulders with clerks were gone and now there came men with a courtesy of behaviour that was altogether more satisfying. This was how the successful made the world work, and the tailor's son with his Cambridge education was resolved to be of their company and to confide his wonderment strictly to his *Diary*.

Here, aboard ship, was a world of carefully guarded hierarchies. Only the captain took precedence over Pepys at the lavish formal meals held in the great cabin, but the captain, Pepys noted, was scrupulously civil.[4] The two men got to know each other sufficiently well for Pepys to tell him of his operation for the stone, and on the anniversary of his lithotomy – a personal and profound occasion – the captain knocked on the door of Pepys's cabin and stayed drinking wine with him until eleven o'clock that night, 'which is a kindness he doth not usually do to the greatest officer in the ship'. A few days later, when Montagu had installed himself on his flagship, the *Naseby*, 'the Captain would by all means have me up to his cabin; and there treated me huge nobly, giving me a barrel of pickled oysters, and opened another for me, and a bottle of wine, which was a very great favour'. Such conviviality was delightful, 'everyday bringing me a fresh sense of the great pleasure of my present life'.

His content made Pepys marvellous company and he was adroit enough to exploit the rewards it brought. After all, he had a future to make. His relationship with Montagu became particularly close, especially when the fleet headed out to sea and Pepys, the inveterate landsman, 'began to be dizzy and squeamish'. My Lord was sympathetic, offered his bilious and overworked secretary yet another plate of oysters, then allowed him to take the rest of the afternoon off and pace the deck. The following day Pepys had begun to find his sea-legs, and when the *Naseby* dropped anchor in the middle of the English battle fleet Pepys enjoyed the spectacle hugely. 'Great was the shout of guns from the castles and ships and our answers, that I never heard yet so great rattling of guns.' The smoke was so thick that the company could not see one another on board. Pepys had moments of melancholy none the less (he was probably missing Elizabeth), and if at times he played music with Montagu and the officers to delight them, at others he played it to cheer himself. On one of these last occasions, realising that his secretary was feeling a little down, Montagu summoned him to dine with him and gradually, over the next few days, opened his heart to him. Montagu was sounding out how loyal Pepys could be and how discreet, for the voyage on which they were embarked was of the greatest national importance.

It was becoming obvious to Pepys that Monck and the Council of State were resolved 'to make way for the King's coming', but Montagu knew for certain what his secretary only guessed at. As always, Montagu was guarded, but gradually the need for circumspection fell away and on May Day 1660 – 'the happiest May Day that hath been many a year to England' – he made the position clear. The House of Commons had for some time been in secret negotiations with Charles Stuart in order to prepare for his return to his throne. Now the King's reply had been received, and it was Pepys himself who read it out to the assembled captains of the navy. The message was reassuring, conservative, tactful. There were deep wounds to heal and deep uncertainties to resolve. In response to the Commons' invitation the King offered not only a promise of religious toleration but 'a free and general pardon' to all enemies of the House of Stuart save only those whom Parliament chose to except. It was essential to show an apparently sincere regard for the

Members at Westminster, and Charles wrote to the Speaker saying, 'We do assure you upon our royal word that none of our predecessors have had a greater esteem for Parliaments than we have.' For the moment this struck the right note, even as it pointed to the political and religious difficulties in which Pepys himself would later be embroiled as the King, with breathtaking guile, would seek to assert his ancient prerogative rights of waging war and calling and dismissing Parliament without that body's consent.

Pepys and Montagu had already drawn up the letter in which the navy would express its loyal thanks to the King for what he had promised (for form's sake, Pepys pretended to draft it as the officers were debating the issue) and in the end 'not one man seemed to say no to it, though I am confident many in their hearts were against it'. Then, when he had heard the seamen cry, '"God bless King Charles!"', Pepys visited every ship in the fleet to read the King's Declaration aloud. He was in his element. He was suddenly the loyal servant of the Crown conspicuously busy at the forefront of affairs, received everywhere with 'respect and honour', and privy to great secrets. When he returned to the *Naseby* in the evening, a delighted Montagu showed him letters written by Charles and his brother the Duke of York 'in such familiar style as to their common friend'. Pepys was delighted and amazed. My Lord was at the very centre of power, and a few days later, after Pepys had carefully added his own name to the copies of the navy's reply to the King, Montagu told him the real purpose of their voyage. They were even now sailing to fetch Charles Stuart home from Holland and exile.

By Monday morning, 14 May, 'The Hague was clearly to be seen by us', and Pepys, 'with child to see any strange thing' as he wrote, was desperate to go ashore and feast his curiosity. Eventually he was given permission to do so and got into a little boat. The weather was so bad that, as the party neared the low and barren shore, a wave washed over them. Nothing daunted, Pepys managed to find a place on a coach making its way to the city. On board were 'two very pretty ladies, very fashionable and with black patches, who very merrily sang all the way' and flirted openly with 'the two blades that were with them'. Pepys took out his flageolet and played as they sang but, in so doing, dropped his sword and had to send his boy back for it. He gave him sixpence when he returned 'but some horse had gone over it and broke the scabbard'. There were compensations all the same. The Hague was 'a most neat place in all respects' and brimming over with English people, one of whom showed Pepys the sights. After a day of exploring, Pepys returned to the Dutch court where he caught his first glimpse of a figure who was eventually to have the most profound effect on his career: William of Orange, the orphaned son of Charles Ist's eldest daughter and the heir to the Dutch royal house who was, Pepys declared, 'a very pretty boy'.

It was probably the sudden arrival of so many strangers in The Hague which meant that Pepys had to make do that evening with a salad and two or three mutton bones shared between ten for his supper. Despite the poor food, the following morning he was all for sightseeing again and, accompanied by a schoolmaster who 'spoke good English and French', he went souvenir shopping, buying a little basket for Elizabeth and altogether more extravagantly for himself three books 'for the love of the binding'. After that, Pepys returned to the fleet and to the work that awaited him. He entertained a Dutch admiral in Latin (the sure grounding of his schooldays was standing him in good stead) and then he was rowed ashore once again, 'intending to find one that might show us the King incognito'. He took Montagu's son Edward along with him, and eventually they both squeezed their way through an immense press of people into the royal presence. There they were rewarded when Charles 'kissed the child very affectionately'. Pepys himself then kissed the hands both of the King and his brother before taking the boy to see Edward Hyde, the future Lord Chancellor 'who did lie bed-rid of the gout' but none the less 'spoke very merrily to the child and me'. Such was Pepys's first glimpse of the grandees who, remote in their terrifying authority, would soon be the puppet-masters of his days. Even now he was careful to record his impression of the King especially, writing that he 'seems to be a very sober man' – a remark which was to prove that first impressions can be deceptive indeed.

But now the hurly-burly of euphoria swept Pepys up in its thrilling, irresponsible wake. Over the last few weeks he had worked as he had never worked before, and now he was determined to play. There were worries all the same. He had left young Montagu in the charge of a colleague called Mr Pierce 'with direction to keep him indoors all day till he heard from me'. The boy was not having this, and soon Pepys heard that he and Pierce had gone off sightseeing to Delft. He made his own way there, met Edward on the road, but soon lost the lad again and only after an anxious interval met up with him in a picture shop in The Hague, 'at which I was very angry with Mr Pierce and shall not be friends, I believe, a good while'. A relieved Pepys gave the tiresome boy into his uncle's care, having met the man by chance in the street, and went off to enjoy himself with an old friend from his Cambridge days, his room-mate Charles Anderson who was in The Hague with a fellow physician. All three were determined to see the sights and went 'to a Dutch house where there was an exceeding pretty lass and right for the sport'. It being a Saturday night the girl, who was a barmaid, was too busy to pay much attention to them and they sat drinking till midnight by which time Anderson was sufficiently tight to stagger home with Pepys vowing that he would have the girl, 'which he told me he had done in the morning'.

With his friend's luck in mind Pepys, accompanied once again by young Montagu, took a wagon to Scheveling where they were to stay the night. There were several people sleeping in the room where Pepys put up, including a pretty Dutch woman on her own whom Pepys, spurred on partly by drink, had 'a month's-mind to'. To his chagrin he lacked the courage of his convictions. He watched her get up, 'then I rise and walked up and down the chamber and saw her dress herself after the Dutch dress, and talked to her as much as I could; and took occasion, from her ring which she wore on her first finger, to kiss her hand; but had not the face to offer anything more'. Still hung over, Pepys did some sightseeing blearily before making a rough passage back to the *Naseby*. By this time he was feeling distinctly bilious. He needed a rest and, 'having spoke a word or two with my Lord, being not very well settled, partly through last night's drinking and want of sleep, I lay down in my gown upon my bed and sleep till the 4 a-clock gun the next morning waked me'. He was still very confused. He thought it was eight the previous night, 'and rising to piss, mistook the sun rising for the sun setting'.

The *Diary* gives the happy impression of a bright and somewhat self-important young man drawn into great events and fascinated by all he saw, but for once it is of as much interest for what it does not record as for what it does. A great part of Pepys's future career was to be given over to the titanic struggle between the English and the Dutch for commercial and, above all, maritime supremacy – to the rivalry from which Downing insisted the nation must emerge victorious. Pepys himself gives only the slightest hints of his moving through a society very different from his own. Above all, he gives no impression of Dutch wealth and Dutch power, or of a social and political system wholly at odds with the monarchical form of government to which he had given his heart.

This was the golden age of the Dutch republic, the period of 'True Enlightenment'. The long war against the tyranny of imperial Spain had been won, the House of Orange had been temporarily subdued, and now the Seven Provinces, led by their regent patriciates, argued out policy through consultation and compromise at meetings of the States General convened at The Hague. There, the wealth of the States of Holland inevitably made the merchants' of Amsterdam's interests the dominant voice for trade was the foundation of the republic, its glory and its strength. The Dutch themselves were well aware of this. 'What constitutes the wealth of the republic?' asked one. 'The opulence of its trade. And what is the source of that trade? Good government. For nothing is more attractive for the whole world than freedom of conscience and security of possession.'[5] Here was an orderly and open society that surprised foreigners (Englishmen especially) by 'the strange freedom that all men took in boats and inns and all other common places, of talking openly whatever they thought upon all public affairs, both of their own state and their neighbours'. Although its moral prohibitions could be severe, the Dutch had created for themselves a literate society disinclined to revere a hereditary aristocracy, tolerant of religious dissent, relatively free as to the restrictions placed on women (as Pepys had fumblingly discovered), possessed of enormous energy and, above all, ambitious for self-enrichment.

The Dutch merchants of the United East India Company had pushed the nation's trading empire as far as India and Sri Lanka. The West India Company traded in African gold, ivory and slaves. From its bases in the West Indies they had established an entrepot trade for Spanish goods from the New World and the commodities that came from Nieuw Amsterdam on the island of Manhattan. Transported in Dutch ships, these goods were held in Dutch warehouses along the bustling river Ij until the time was ripe to sell them to a hungry market. Thus enriched, groups of Dutch merchants, sure that their credit was guaranteed by the mighty Exchange Bank of Amsterdam, could proceed to buy forests, vineyards, grain, tobacco and tar cheaply, sell them when the price was high, then speculate on the Amsterdam stock exchange which, between noon and two, became a frenzy of 'shouting, insults, impudence, pushing and shoving' as deals were made and confirmed with a traditional double handshake. There was little to compare with this in England. Here was capitalism at its most thrusting, enterprising and sophisticated, a system that was the envy of Europe and whose success had built the elaborately plastered and balustraded houses through which a drunken Pepys had picked his uncertain way back to his ship.

A couple of days later he was 'beginning to be settled in my wits again'. This was just as well, for what now followed was one of the great pageants of English history and Pepys was determined to be both its observer and its recorder. News now came that the Duke of York and his younger brother Gloucester were coming aboard. Montagu was rowed out to meet them while Pepys and the rest stood 'at the entering port'. Guns were fired as the dukes neared, after which 'they went to view the ship all over and were most exceedingly pleased with it'. Both of these near godlike figures seemed to be 'very fine gentlemen', while York's secretary, Mr Coventry, was likewise a man Pepys would hold in the highest regard. Now four of the people who would help run the Royal Navy were brought together for the first time 'upon the quarter-deck . . . under the awning, the Duke of York and my Lord, Mr Coventry and I'.[6]

They spent an hour allotting each ship its place and function in the forthcoming voyage home then, when their work was done and the grandees had dined and departed, 'news is sent us that the King is on shore'. This called for great rejoicing salvoes to be fired. Pepys, in the heady rush of loyalty that was surging through him, determined to fire the gun by his own cabin. This was not a wise idea for 'holding my head too much over the gun, I have almost spoiled my right eye'. He had a lucky escape, but his eye was still inflamed the following morning when the King and a large crowd of royalty and aristocrats came aboard the *Naseby*, which the King rapidly rechristened the *Royal Charles*. Then, when the dining was done and the farewells had been said, the sailors 'weighed anchor, and with a fresh gale and most happy weather we set sail for England'.

Once the convoy was under sail, Charles beguiled all those about him with his charm of manner and his stories. Pepys watched him and listened with the most intense curiosity, almost certainly making there and then the shorthand notes that he would later transcribe into his *Diary*, creating his memorable portrait of a 'very active and stirring' Charles II 'walking here and there, up and down' on the quarter-deck as 'he fell in discourse of his escape from Worcester'. Pepys was enthralled. Incident followed incident as Charles felt free at last to tell the world of those brave and loyal people who had helped him in the days of his adversity. Pepys, the first to hear the story, noted it down assiduously as his new master told of his 'travelling four days and three nights on foot, every step up to the knees in dirt, with nothing but a green coat and a pair of country breeches on and a pair of country shoes, that made him so sore all over his feet that he could scarce stir'. Such pathos recalled in a moment of triumph was, to Pepys, almost unbearable and 'made me ready to weep'.

This was an age of the easy public demonstration of emotion but there was nothing insincere about Pepys's feelings. He had spent the earliest and most formative years of his life amid bewildering political change and now, it seemed, stability was at last returning to his confused country. King Charles, telling his pathetic story to a group of rapt listeners, was far more than a vulnerable man. He was the living witness of the fact that in England at least experiments in republicanism were at an end. Older, vaguer and more potent beliefs were taking their place. As the country's true and legitimate monarch, Charles was enveloped in a quasi-mystical cloud patched up from religion and law, tradition and superstition, mythology and political theorising. There was still a divinity that hedged this king and events had proved it. It was Providence – the will of God – people said, that had returned him to his throne. The needs and machinations of men had had little to do with it. He was a sacred figure. It was treason even to think of Charles's death, let alone to speak or write about it. It was forbidden to curse him in public or private, forbidden to question that his power extended everywhere. Life, honour, law and peace all stemmed from him. He alone had the right to summon Parliament and create the peers, judges and bishops who helped both to shape and administer his legislation and to govern the Anglican Church – his Church, that purest flower of Protestantism and the institution of which he alone was the supreme and unquestioned head.

Pepys, like so many of his fellow countrymen, saw his new king through this confusing veil of relief and awe, and it helped confirm his commitment to the Stuart cause. In this he would fundamentally never waver, even if experience was to hone his criticism and temper his admiration. Even now a saving humour made sure he kept things in proportion for, as the great flotilla arrived on the English coast and the King himself hurried to make for land, so Pepys and some others followed the royal party in a second barge that contained one of the royal spaniels, 'which shit in the boat, which made us laugh and me to think that a King and all that belong to him are but just as others are'.

When Charles himself finally landed at Dover after his years of exile 'the shouting and joy expressed by all was past imagination', but for Pepys himself the following day was something of an anticlimax. He had watched history in the making. He had mixed with the greatest of the land. Now the pageant had moved on and he felt himself 'very uncouth all this day for want thereof'. There were compensations all the same. Royal benevolence was scattered with a liberal hand, and Charles had given no less that £500 for his flagship's officers and crew and £50 for Montagu's servants. The currencies in which this was paid were confusing, Pepys getting sixty ducats from the first gift and seventy guilders from the second but, by the start of June when he had worked it all out, the results were deeply satisfying. The nine weeks of intense work he had passed in helping to restore Charles II had seen him double his capital and he was now worth nearly £100.

It was all most pleasing and it seemed that there was more to come, for My Lord was now appointed Earl of Sandwich and a Knight of the Garter. These were far more than decorative honours in the old, hierarchical world that was returning. A peer of the realm had legal privileges and moral responsibilities, which supposedly made him a being altogether superior to his fellow men. A contemporary commentator made this clear when he wrote that, as distinguished from ordinary people; 'peers of noble birth and education are more generous, heroic spirits, and not so apt to be overawed by regal threats, nor seduced by inward and private ends from the public good'.[7] Lord Sandwich, as Pepys's patron must now be called, had entered that heroic and exalted circle whose valour and patriotism were reckoned an essential bulwark to the monarchy and whose prestige was such that ordinary people could not criticise them without fear of the pillory and losing their ears. Pepys accepted this with appropriate deference and was later rather puzzled to find that although he adored such people 'with all the duty possible, yet the more a man considers and observes them, the less he finds difference between them and other men'. Such a realisation was later to lead to a crisis in his relations with Sandwich but, for the moment, he basked in the fact that My Lord was a friend and highly pleased with his secretary. Pepys had proved his worth beyond all expectation and Sandwich would keep him by his side. '"We must have a little patience,"' he told Pepys, '"and we will rise together. In the meantime I will do you all the good jobs I can."'[8]

On Thursday, 7 June, a royal summons arrived commanding Sandwich and his entourage to London. They travelled by way of Canterbury where Pepys, ever curious, inspected the cathedral and Thomas à Becket's tomb. Two days later the party arrived in the capital. They disembarked at Temple Stairs and Pepys spent the afternoon in Sandwich's company as My Lord attended on the King. Many of Pepys's days were now to be spent in this manner, and although he found court attendance 'infinite tedious', he knew it was essential if he were to further his career. Sandwich himself was continuing to ride high and the favours showered on his master meant that Pepys, too, was a man to whom many looked, stretching out their hands and offering gratuities in turn for favours.

It was all very pleasant, but how long could it last? Euphoria would eventually have to settle into the habits of every day, and if Pepys's prosperity were to continue it was essential that he secure himself a good, permanent post. Sandwich was well aware of this. He recognised his responsibilities towards his industrious secretary and the fact that the wide range of his own duties meant that an able assistant was absolutely necessary to him. For days now Pepys had been living with 'much business and some hopes of getting some money thereby', and on 18 June, when he had accompanied Sandwich home, My Lord 'told me that he did look after the place of the Clerk of the Acts for me'. For a man who had only his education and abilities to recommend him, this was a dazzling prospect indeed. The clerk of the acts was secretary to the Navy Board which, in its turn, was responsible for the entire civil administration of the fleet. The post was a prize worth hoping for and the thought of it dominated Pepys's dreams.

Initially it was for My Lord to show that his bounty had muscle, and on 23 June Sandwich told Pepys that 'he had obtained a promise' that the clerkship would indeed be his, 'at which I was glad'. The whole of that Sunday Pepys's mind was 'full of thoughts for my place of Clerk of the Acts'. This was partly because, as Sandwich had told him, 'it was not the salary of any place that did make a man rich but the opportunity of getting money while he is in the place'. This was to prove goldenly true, but for all Sandwich's assurances, there followed a hair-raising scramble for office. Competitors were everywhere. First Pepys had to go to the Admiralty and talk with Mr Turner, who he knew was a rival for the clerkship. Fortunately, the man was 'very civil to me and I to him, and shall be so'. After all, in a small world especially, there was no point in making an enemy of one's competitor. Allies were also a necessity and Pepys, using the network of contacts he had built up over the recent weeks, took the opportunity to have a word 'about my business' with the Duke of York's secretary, William Coventry, 'who promised me all the assistance I could expect'. Pepys and Sandwich then went to see the Duke who, as Lord High Admiral, ordered Coventry 'to dispatch my business of the Acts in which place everybody gives my joy as if I were already in it, which God send'.

The Duke's warrant for the place duly arrived at the end of the month, but even patronage from the highest in the land was no absolute security. Competition now reared itself in the form of the previous holder of the office, Thomas Barlow. The insecurity was worrying in the extreme, and Pepys spilled out his concerns to My Lord, who promised him his whole-hearted support in blocking Barlow's application. Pepys was sufficiently calmed by this to sit up writing business letters until two in the morning but he still felt it necessary to beg the help of Sir George Carteret, the treasurer of the navy. Pepys had learned that his rival Barlow was in London and was thrown into near despair. There seemed so much to lose: status, high-quality work, the chance of making himself wealthy. Pepys had already heard that there was a project afoot 'for all us secretaries to join together and get money by bringing all business into our hands', and few men can resist a quango.

What followed was the sort of nightmare that only bureaucrats can devise. Securing his patent was the necessary final preliminary to validating the Duke of York's warrant, and it would require all Pepys's pushiness and vitality to obtain it. He sought the advice of the solicitor-general. He persuaded Sandwich to hasten the secretary of state in the essential business of obtaining the royal signature. The signed document was then taken to the Privy Seal Office, which authorised the issue of letters patent, and Pepys went over to the House of Lords to ask advice of an old Cavalier friend as to who best could engross the patent for him. He was recommended to a Mr Beale who grandly informed Pepys that he had no time to write out the patent in the required Chancery hand, and it became necessary to scour Chancery Lane for someone who could do the job. It seemed that no one could for every scrivener in London was busy with such work. Pepys was desperate, and it was only late that night that he procured the services of a musical friend, Mr Spong, who agreed to come round to Sandwich's lodgings and write out Pepys's bill that night in the required way.

When Spong had finally finished, Pepys was able to hurry to Worcester House and secure the chancellor's '*Recepi*' before rushing back to the opprobrious Beale's for a docket. The latter was not pleased. Pepys's haste was unseemly and the patent had been ill drawn-up by another hand. Mr Beale, it appeared, was going to be obstructive and Pepys realised that he would have to dip his hand in his purse. He brought out two gold pieces 'after which it was strange how civil and tractable' Mr Beale was. With the docket, Pepys hurried back to Worcester House where, elbowing his way through the great crowd and saying that he was running an errand for My Lord, he managed to get into the chancellor's office and get his seal passed at the last moment. The clerkship of the acts was finally his and, with Elizabeth in a hackney coach beside him, Pepys went to pay a £9 fee to Beale and bore his illuminated patent out to show his wife. The entire nerve-wracking process had cost him upwards of £40, but at last he was firmly on the ladder to success.

The clerkship of the acts brought with it a suitable symbol of Pepys's new status, and this, too, he was keen to show Elizabeth. They were to move into the house that went with the job, a stately apartment on the east side of Seething Lane, close to Tower Hill. Although the rooms here were probably rather small, the Pepyses were to enjoy (in addition to a kitchen and the larders, store-cupboards and cellars that went with it) a range of amenities, which included a study for Pepys, a dining room, a dressing room, a parlour, a 'matted chamber', 'red', 'blue' and 'green' chambers, along with another for dancing and music. Such a home deliciously magnified the couple's dignity, and Pepys had already persuaded his fellow officers on the Navy Board to agree to his having a door inserted that opened on to the leaded roof so that he, his guests and his wife might enjoy a fine view of London on summer evenings. They lost no time in moving in. Elizabeth, for all her lack of practical skills, saw to the packing up of their household goods and her own clothes. By 17 July all was ready and Pepys, his wife and a neighbour took a coach to Seething Lane, overtaking the carts piled high with their belongings as the drivers watered their horses in the Strand.

It had been a busy day. Not only had the Pepyses moved house, Pepys himself had finally come to an agreement with Barlow about the clerkship. He discovered that his erstwhile rival was 'an old consumptive man and fair-conditioned' with whom it was possible to do business amicably. Each side proceeded carefully but, 'after much talk, I did grant him what he asked – *viz.*, £50 per annum if my salary be not increased and £100 per annum in case it be to £350; at which he was very well pleased'. Pepys was in high good spirits. His job was secure, he had a fine new house and servants to attend him as well. So delighted was he in these that even when he returned home that night from seeing Sandwich and found his footboy asleep when he should have been guarding the house Pepys refused to berate him but had 'a great deal of sport' trying to wake him up. The boy later proved thoroughly unsatisfactory and was dismissed, but altogether more important was another new arrival, a boy of just eighteen called William Hewer. For the moment Hewer's duties were generally to attend Pepys both at his office and in the house. It seemed, however, that he too had his shortcomings – young Hewer was prone to late nights and bad company – but he was loyal, tender-hearted and 'so obedient that I am greatly glad of him'. Gradually there would grow up a friendship between them that would last a lifetime.

The Navy Board itself had a long history dating back to the reign of Henry VIII. It was run by four principal officers: the treasurer, Sir George Carteret; the comptroller, Sir Robert Slingsby; the surveyor, Sir William Batten; and Pepys, the clerk of the acts. Three commissioners assisted them and were attended by staff clerks. All were responsible to the Duke of York as Lord High Admiral and ultimately to the King. The board was required to meet twice a week and its responsibilities ensured that it was the largest of the spending departments, accounting for nearly a quarter of government expenditure. The size of the navy the board had inherited from the Cromwellian regime partly ensured that this was so for, to the battle fleet of Charles I with its mighty three-decker *Sovereign of the Seas* and sixteen other warships, Parliament had added a large number of cruisers to protect the nation's commerce.

It was the duty of the Navy Board to keep these ships in good repair and, when possible, to augment their number. In particular, they had to supply the materials required for these purposes. Nearly all of this – timber, masts, iron, canvas, hemp and tar – was imported by merchants whom the board had contracted, and corruption, as Pepys soon discovered, was rife. The board also supervised rates of pay and the victualling of the fleet. This last was entirely in the hands of a single contractor named Denis Gauden, a thoroughly unsatisfactory position that Pepys was eventually to spend a great deal of his energy trying to rectify. Finally, the Navy Board was responsible for the control and safety of the royal dockyards. These were situated in Deptford, Woolwich, Chatham and Portsmouth, and together they made up the most considerable of all the nation's industries.

For the moment, the overriding need was to save money, a problem that was to bedevil Pepys's career. He was already worried by it. 'The want of money puts all things, and above all things the Navy, out of order,' he wrote, 'and yet I do not see that the King takes care to bring in any money, but thinks of new designs to lay out money.' Indeed, matters were so bad that Pepys and his colleagues were finding it impossible to pay off the seamen in full and eventually they presented the Duke of York with 'our project of stopping the growing charge of the fleet, by paying them in hand one moiety [half] and the other four months hence'. The Duke approved, 'and we returned by his order to Sir G. Carteret's chamber, and there we did draw up this design in order to be presented to the Parliament'. These were to be Pepys's first brushes with the Members at Westminster and they were not encouraging for the committee men especially were recalcitrant, their opposition providing a hint of Pepys's lifelong struggle to fund his master's policies from a reluctant Commons. The ordinary sailors were angry about their arrears of pay, while it was necessary to keep the workers in the dockyards pacified too.

On one occasion it was necessary to do rather more than this. In January 1661, the defeated forces of religious sectarianism made one last, pathetic attempt to show their power. A London cooper named Thomas Venner led three dozen of his congregation to seize London and impose the rule of the saints. There was a hysterical overreaction. It was obvious that the rebels would want to seize the naval dockyards and arsenals, and the Navy Office was ordered to station guards in them. Pepys himself was woken by the great tumult of people in the streets 'and got my sword and pistol, which however I have no powder to charge'.

He went out to find London full of soldiers and the wretched insurrectionists 'expecting Jesus to come and reign here in the world presently'. Pepys and the comptroller then made their way to Deptford where they chose four captains to command the guards at the dockyard. There was no real danger, but the whole experience was interesting to Pepys in unexpected ways: not only did he see the great wealth gathered by Mr Davis the storekeeper (who put him up overnight in a most 'princelike' manner) but he was profoundly impressed by the deference shown to him. 'Never till now did I see the great authority of my place, all the Captains of the Fleet coming cap in hand to us.'[9] Here was an outward and visible acknowledgement of his status and the sort of moment that fixes for ever in a man's mind a notion of his own importance.

Meanwhile, Sandwich's benevolence continued to flow unabated, whether it came in the form of a half a deer shot on his estates and 'smelling a little strong' or the altogether more rewarding gift of a clerkship of the Privy Seal. This was to Sandwich a minor office that had first been granted him personally and which he was happy enough to pass on to Pepys. Pepys himself had already had experience of the Privy Seal Office when trying to secure his patent, and now he managed to secure temporary leave from the Navy Board so that he could deputise for Sandwich during one month in every quarter. The work was undemanding and, at first, highly lucrative. Pepys soon learned how to reduce his hours at the Privy Seal Office to an essential minimum, but he eagerly gathered the fees paid to him for witnessing the seal granted to every applicant seeking letters patent from the Crown. When he added up his takings at the end of the first month, Pepys found that he had earned the princely sum of £132 for little effort. Sandwich's words were coming true. Public office was indeed a way to private riches.

There were nagging dissatisfactions too. Elizabeth's medical problems in particular aroused Pepys's concern and irritation in equal measure. The first Sunday in August saw her 'much in pain', and Pepys went to see Dr Williams 'who had cured her once of this business' and obtained an ointment from him. Its effects were not immediate, and the following day, having come home from his morning's work, he was obliged to dine alone, 'my wife being ill in pain a-bed – which I was troubled at, and not a little impatient'. The often overbearing husband could be selfish and petulant, and his mood was not helped by Elizabeth's domestic shortcomings. It was all very well and charming to play with the 'very pretty' puppies to which their dog had given birth, but when Pepys afterwards went upstairs to sort out his papers he found Elizabeth's clothes strewn all over the place and lost his temper with her. He was 'troubled' at this and the quarrel was made up, but such incidents were annoying. Pepys was an efficient and ever more busy man who felt threatened by unnecessary mess and the lowering effect it had on his self-esteem. That he then felt petty when he lost his temper did not help matters either.

He needed, besides, continuous sexual stimulation. Pepys

was far from being the sort of man who could work hard all day then spend the evening in monastic quietude. Sex fed his energy and his curiosity, and when Elizabeth failed to satisfy him he began to look elsewhere. There were those attractive linen-sellers in Westminster Hall, for example. On 4 August Pepys 'bespoke some linen of Betty Lane' then plucked up the courage to take her for a drink in the Trumpet where he sat talking with her '&c'. The abbreviation covers a wealth of thoughts and fantasies: Pepys's memories of two people in young adulthood intrigued by each other's presence.

Eight days later he pursued Betty again. It was a Sunday and he had been to a service at Whitehall where the ultra-Royalist chaplain had preached on the text '"To whom much is given, of him much is required."' The morality of the sermon appeared to make little impression on the comfortable, fee-rich civil servant – Pepys was more impressed by the 'brave anthem' that was sung – and when he left the chapel he dined at My Lord's (who was away visiting a relation) then took a post-prandial walk. During this he happened to run into Mrs Lane once more. Here was too good an opportunity to miss. A pretty linen-seller, however worldly-wise, was sure to be impressed by a man with friends in high places, and Betty was inveigled into My Lord's garden where Pepys shared a bottle of wine with her before suggesting that they go to Axe Yard (still happily vacant), where he was 'exceeding free in dallying with her, and she not unfree to take it'.

Axe Yard was expensive, but a second house had its uses and Pepys was ready to exploit them. Besides, his erstwhile neighbour there, Mrs Crisp, had a pretty daughter. Early in September Mrs Crisp invited Pepys to a party, a bibulous and delightful occasion blessed by the presence of the fair Diana Crisp. Pepys was intrigued and sat drinking and talking to the girl until 'she began to be very loving to me and kind, and I fear is not so good as she should be'. Two days later Pepys was to discover that this hypocritical little flurry of censoriousness was entirely justified. He had been making sure that everything was all right in Axe Yard and was standing idly at the door when Diana happened to pass by. Pepys beckoned to her and took her 'into my house upstairs and there did dally with her a great while, and find that in Latin "*nulla puella negat*".'* After that he took a boat home, sorted his papers and, with a mind unclouded by guilt, gave his wife a music lesson 'in which I take great pleasure'.[10]

Elizabeth was still something of a child to Pepys, someone to indulge and who could be made to reflect his growing status. The following day, when she was a little pettish, Pepys decided to pamper her and 'went along with her to buy a necklace of pearl which will cost £4. 10s – which I am willing to comply with her in, for her encouragement and because I have lately got money, having now above £200 in cash beforehand in the world'. Pepys could afford to be complacent and he rather enjoyed it. Indeed, there was much now to reflect his social position and, in a world where hierarchy was open, explicit and all-important, he was quick to note the honours paid to him. Few things said more about a man than where he sat in church, and Pepys was now conspicuous even there. When, dressed in his new silk suit, he walked into St Olave's in Seething Lane on a Sunday morning, the churchwardens were careful to usher him into the highest pew. Soon a special gallery would be built for him and his colleagues at the Navy Office. Mr Pepys, it seemed, had arrived.

* 'the girl denied nothing'.

CHAPTER FOUR

Getting Started

On 24 January 1661, Mr and Mrs Samuel Pepys threw a dinner party for several members of the Navy Board at their house in Seething Lane. It was a rather grand affair costing all of £5 and was a great success, even though the chimney smoked a little, a common problem at the time for the flue had probably been built for wood fires rather than the newer sea coal. This was irksome, since one of Pepys's purposes in inviting his guests was to show them the great improvements he had made to his home. Much of his time and a great deal of his money had been lavished on these, since Pepys was determined to live in style. As soon as he and Elizabeth moved into Seething Lane he persuaded carpenters from the Navy Office to refloor his dining room, and by late September the plasterers had moved in and were putting the house into such a 'sad pickle' that 'my wife was fain to make a bed upon the ground for her and I; and so there we lay all night'.

Mrs Crisp, the beautiful Diana's mother, came to advise about the furnishings, while at the start of October Pepys's father was also giving his opinion 'about the hangings for my rooms, which are now almost fit to be hung, the painters beginning to do their work today'. The covering of bare, limewashed plaster with material hung from eyelets in the walls was *de rigueur* for an upwardly mobile couple in Restoration London, and Pepys eventually chose green serge hangings and elected to have gilded leather for the upholstery of his dining-room chairs. The whole process was pleasing to his delight in possession, even if it was inconvenient and expensive. 'My layings out upon my house in furniture are so great,' he wrote in his *Diary* 'that I fear I shall not be able to go through them without breaking one of my bags of £100, I having but £200 yet in the world.'[1]

Nor was it only money that Pepys was worried about. He had problems with his neighbours too, problems of a disgusting kind that a man such as he would not tolerate for a moment. Pepys described these difficulties frankly. 'This morning one came to advise me where to make a window into my cellar in lieu of one Sir W. Batten had stopped up', he wrote, 'and going down into my cellar to look, I put my foot into a great heap of turds, by which I find that Mr Turner's house of office [lavatory] is full and comes into my cellar, which doth trouble me.' This was hardly surprising, for the regular emptying of cess-pits by night-soil men was more often an ideal than a reality in Restoration London. 'I will have it helped,' Pepys wrote in his *Diary*. He would too, and on 25 October – five nauseating days later – 'the vault at the end of my cellar was emptied'.

But sanitary problems were still not at an end. Elizabeth's untrained dog habitually fouled the house, and Pepys was so irate that he was determined to keep the animal in the now cleansed cellar. This resulted in a quarrel followed by a nightmare in which Pepys dreamed 'that my wife was dead, which made me that I slept ill all night'. Now, however, at the start of 1661, it seemed that everything was more or less under control and Pepys could throw his first dinner party in Seething Lane. Among those invited were 'the two Sir Williams', Navy Office colleagues of great importance to him: Sir William Batten and Sir William Penn. Both were men of wide naval experience, and it suggests the enormous delight that people took in Pepys's company that officials so apparently distinguished should dine with the young clerk of the acts who, as yet, knew next to nothing about the ways of the navy in which they had spent their careers.

Penn was a handsome, round-faced man, 'a merry fellow' who 'sings very bawdy songs' and who was, as Pepys was well aware, extremely cunning. Penn was also familiar with the techniques of modern naval warfare. He had fought as vice-admiral under Blake in Cromwell's Dutch Wars and was thoroughly experienced both with the modern 'great ships', massive in size and bristling with ninety to a hundred guns, as well as with the tactics by which they were ranged to windward of the enemy and in line ahead so that they could release their fire-power without being troubled by smoke. Penn had played a leading role in the Cromwellian capture of Jamaica, and he added considerable administrative insight to tactical expertise. Much of this last he had summarised in a memorandum presented to the King in 1660, which set out the advantages of attaching commissioners to the Navy Board – men who would act together without being hidebound by too many rules – and a number of these proposals had been accepted. Indeed, Penn himself was now a commissioner. He was also the recipient of Pepys's as yet secret contempt. Pepys could rarely find a good word to say for Penn. The very qualities that had recommended him to the King blinded the clerk of the acts to his merits, for here was a rival who might at any time prove dangerous. Meanwhile, Pepys would entertain him generously and cover his feelings with smiles of welcome.

Batten, too, was not a popular figure with Pepys. His merits had caused him to be appointed surveyor of the navy, but

Pepys was largely blind to these. The two men were rivals for the perquisites of office (Batten was magnificently skilled in feathering his own nest) while Pepys thought Batten was a poor speaker, a bad bookkeeper, slow and little able to choose the right men to work with him. Batten himself was by now nearly sixty years old, and while he was clearly an officer it was Pepys's view that he was certainly not a gentlemen. Batten was, in the phrase of the day, a tarpaulin: a man schooled in handling ships, and born to the horny-handed skills this needed rather than to the rank and education that supposedly made a man a leader of men. Elizabeth made matters yet more difficult by strongly disliking Lady Batten, whom she regarded as high-handed, for all that before her marriage the woman had been, as Pepys one day pointed out, another man's whore.

For the moment such feelings had to be concealed, and Pepys was adept at using his charm. 'I perceive none of our officers care much for one another,' he confided to his *Diary* early in 1661, 'but I do keep in with them all as much as I can.' Besides, there was much real pleasure to be had in their company. As Pepys wrote on 5 April 1661, 'at night to Sir W. Batten's and there very merry with a good barrel of oysters, and this is the present life I lead'. It was agreeable to be in the society of men of the world, for all they were competitors. They were hospitable and always ready to drink deep as Pepys himself often was. After work on 5 June 1661, for example, Pepys went out on to the leads of his house to play music and escape the summer stuffiness of being indoors. After a while 'Sir W. Penn came out in his shirt into his leads and there we stayed talking and singing and drinking of great draughts of claret and eating botargo [dried fish roe] and bread and butter till 12 at night, it being moonshine'. Pepys went to bed 'very near fuddled', and the following day had to confess to his *Diary* that his head 'ached all night and all this morning with my last night's debauch'. Here, as he knew, was his 'great folly', and he often paid for it not just in money but in such violent hangovers and worse. There was even an evening when 'I was forced to call the maid, who pleased my wife and I in her running up and down so innocently in her smock, and vomited in the basin, and so to sleep.' On another occasion Pepys brought up his breakfast of pickled herrings in Sandwich's 'house of office'.

Nor did events in the public world pass Pepys by. For all the euphoria that had greeted the return of Charles II, an example had to be made of his enemies and, in particular, of those who had executed his father. On 13 October 1660, Pepys was present at the judicial murder of one of the regicides:

> I went out to Charring Cross to see Major General Harrison hanged, drawn and quartered – which was done here – he looking as cheerfully as any man could do in that condition. He was presently cut down and his head and his heart shown to the people, at which there was great shouts of joy. It was said that he was sure to come shortly at the right hand of Christ to judge them that have now judged him. And that his wife doth expect his coming again. Thus it was my chance to see the King beheaded at Whitehall and to see the first blood shed in revenge for the blood of the King at Charring Cross.

Despite the irony and reflection in this passage, Pepys was not a vindictive or cruel man and the revenge heaped on the regicides soon began to sicken him. A little less than a week later he was writing how 'I saw the limbs of some of our new traitors set upon Aldersgate, which was a sad sight to see; and a bloody week this and the last have been, there being ten hanged, drawn and quartered.' Enough was enough, and by the start of December Pepys was finding his countrymen's desire for revenge excessive. On 4 December he heard how 'the Parliament voted that the bodies of Oliver, Ireton, Bradshaw, and [Pride] should be taken out of their graves in the Abbey and drawn to the gallows and there hanged and buried under it. Which (methinks) doth trouble me, that a man of so great courage as he [i.e. Cromwell] was should have that dishonour, though otherwise he might deserve it enough.'

Besides, there was a new world to make. April 1661 saw the King's coronation. The nation and London in particular threw itself wholeheartedly into a lavish display of euphoria at monarchy revived. Great triumphal arches in the most accomplished classical style spanned the route that Charles's procession was to take. As Pepys walked home from a visit to his father he noted how 'all the way is so thronged with people to see the triumphal arches that I could hardly pass for them'. Poets and painters, architects and historians had set themselves to fashioning the most elaborate imagery to celebrate Charles's accession to the throne. Entering into his kingdom in the thirtieth year of his life, Charles was a figure to be compared to Christ entering on his ministry. He was a new David, a new Solomon. His benevolent rule would see Eden returned and the Age of Gold come again. The decoration on the arches celebrated such fond imaginings, and one in particular spoke directly to Pepys. It celebrated the Pax Britannica, which would be achieved as the nation sought world-wide domination through trade and commerce, its merchant ships protected by an invincible navy. Science, and navigation in particular, would bring the country mastery of the seas, trade would bring plenty, and plenty would bring peace. The clerk of the acts was one of the men to ensure this would be so, for here was the political programme that would dominate much of Pepys's professional life.

At the centre of everything was the King himself. On 22 April, Pepys rose early, put on his fine velvet coat for the first time and, with the Battens and Sir William Penn, made his way to a flag-maker's in Cornhill where, in a private room amply supplied 'with wine and good cake', he watched the passing pageant. Charles was making the traditional progress from the Tower to Whitehall preliminary to his coronation. The streets were 'all gravelled; and the houses hung with carpets before them, made brave show'. Lavishly caparisoned horses and a fine company of soldiers, 'all young comely men, in white doublets', passed exultantly before Pepys and then came the King himself 'in a most rich embroidered suit and cloak' looking 'most nobly'. Behind him rode My Lord in a costume so sumptuous that he had been obliged to ask Pepys to act as his agent in raising £1,000 to pay for it. Pepys succeeded by dint of persuading a wealthy Puritan cousin to advance the money for which he and Uncle Robert were required to stand security. This was a debt of honour and had to be accepted, but it remained a burden for many years, part of the price Pepys had to pay for his own standing in the world. None the less, it would be mean to think of such things at a moment like this, 'so glorious was the show with gold and silver'. It dazzled the eyes and Pepys had to look away, but not before he noticed how the King and the Duke of York acknowledged the presence of the Navy Board as they went by. One of the young women leaning out of the windows also caught Pepys's gaze and intrigued him sufficiently for him to chat with her 'which made good sport among us'.

Pepys rose at four the following morning. The boy who had elbowed his way through the crowd to see the execution of Charles I now pushed his way through the dense congregation packed into Westminster Abbey to witness the coronation of his son. Pepys managed to scramble up on to the great scaffold that had been built across the north end of the Abbey 'where with a great deal of patience I sat from past 4 till 11 before the King came in'.[2] The pageantry delighted him, and Pepys eagerly noted the bishops in their copes of cloth-of-gold, the 'magnificent sight' of the nobility in their state dress, and finally the King himself with his sceptre carried by My Lord. It was a 'very great grief' to Pepys that he could not see the ceremony of the anointing, but he heard the great shout that went up when the crown was placed on Charles's head and listened as a general pardon was read out by Sir Edward Hyde, now Lord Chancellor. After that, silver medals were 'flung up and down', but Pepys could not come by one. So great was the excited noise that it drowned the music, but by this time Pepys had more urgent things to worry about. 'I had so great a list to piss, that I went out a little while before the King had done all his ceremonies and went round the Abbey to Westminster Hall.'

So fervent was Pepys's monarchism that in his description of the coronation Charles the man is wholly subsumed in Charles the king, the gilded symbol of the nation. There is no hint of the political problems that underlay the scene and which were eventually to catch Pepys in their wake. There is no suggestion either of the forces that had returned the Stuart monarchy: the deep Anglican commitment of the conservative gentry especially, the resolve of those men who had seen their ancient powers fall into the hands of fanatics and who were now determined to wrest them back. They were determined to have a king who was neither too poor nor too dependent to stand at the head of a nation where they would have their rightful Parliamentary sway. Nor does Pepys's exultation of Anglican ceremonial allow for the religious divides in the country and the gentry's determination to secure their State Church against all opposition, whether Catholic or Nonconformist. Slowly and with growing skill, partly by design and partly in response to events, these men would make a world for themselves where all might yet be conformable to their vision – a vision of an England where the manor house and the vicarage stood firm for established order, a kingdom where no monarch could be an autocrat and no religious dissident a man of power.

Pepys, the devoted servant of the Stuarts, would shape his

career in such a world and see it ended by it. Now, however, having relieved himself, he went into Westminster Hall where there was more pageantry to be glimpsed, more gestures of the nation's loyalty to witness. 'The King,' he wrote, 'came in with his crown on and his sceptre in his hand – under a canopy born up by six silver staves, carried by Barons of the Cinq Ports – and little bells at every end.' The great of the land then sat down to eat as their first course was carried in by the Knights of the Bath. Bowing heralds led loyal subjects into the King's presence, and the Lords Northumberland, Suffolk and Ormonde rode into the hall on horseback before each change of course. At last the King's champion entered, armoured and with his spear and shield carried before him. A herald loudly proclaimed that 'if any dare deny Charles Stuart to be lawful King of England, here was a Champion that would fight with him; and with those words the Champion flings down his gauntlet; and all this he doth three times in his going up towards the King's table'. It is Pepys's sheer delight in all this that is so characteristic: the eye for detail, colour and human incident, his ear for 'the music of all sorts', and his pleasure in walking up and down and looking 'upon the ladies'.

London was the focus of the nation's rejoicing, and it was Pepys who noted that as darkness fell 'the city had a light like a glory round about it, with bonfires'. Out in the streets 'gallants' laid hold of Pepys and his friends 'and would have us drink the King's health upon our knee, kneeling upon a faggot; which we all did, they drinking to us one after another – which we thought a strange frolic'. It was Pepys's good luck then to meet up with Mr Thornbury (Yeoman of the Wine Cellar to the King) who took Pepys along to his house where they all continued to toast King Charles until one of the gentlemen 'fell down stark drunk and lay there spewing'. But by now Pepys himself had had too much to drink. He had no sooner gone to bed 'but my head began to turn and I to vomit, and if ever I was foxed it was now – which I cannot say yet, because I fell asleep and sleep till morning – only, when I waked I found myself wet with my spewing'. Pepys had another agonising hangover, and the only remedy, it seemed, was to go out for a 'morning draught' of hot chocolate.

Such unbuttoned ease after so many years of Puritanical deprivation appealed deeply to the pleasure-loving Pepys, and if his *Diary* is a chronicle of great public events it is also a journal of his own exhausting conviviality and his constant curiosity about all aspects of the life he encountered. He had a well-considered philosophy of pleasure. 'The truth is,' he wrote in March 1666, 'I do indulge myself a little the more pleasure, knowing that this is the proper age of my life to do it, and out of my observation that most men that do thrive in the world do forget to take pleasure during the time that they are getting their estate but reserve that till they have got one, and then it is too late for them to enjoy it with any pleasure.' Here is the very essence of the man, his thoughts vivid with observation, positive and outgoing, and yet at the same time checked by a prudential and even calculating awareness of his own advantage. The hedonist and the Puritan are balanced. Here is the man who could drink himself stupid at the coronation yet also at the start of every year prepare those sombre balance sheets of his worldly state. The equilibrium was precarious all the same, and what is so engaging about Pepys at this time – and often so painful to observe – is not any smooth integrity of personality he might momentarily have achieved but the constant war he fought with his conflicting selves. 'As is the mind, so is the man.'

The fleshly Pepys delighted in food especially. Eating and drinking play a great part in his record of his days. 1661, for example, began with Pepys and his family dining on 'a barrel of oysters, a dish of neat's tongues, and a dish of anchovies – wine of all sorts, and Northdown ale'.

As the month wore on he recorded his delight in a leg of pork given to him as a present and 'a good dinner and very handsome' given by Mr Ackworth, the storekeeper at Woolwich. But woe betide those who did not live up to the mark. Mrs Pierce, the purser's wife, earned herself a minute place in immortality when she served Pepys 'a calf's head carbonardoed, but it was [so] raw we could not eat it'. Mrs Pierce, Pepys decided, 'is such a slut that I do not love her victuals'. But occasionally his own entertaining fell seriously below accepted standards as when, on 26 June 1662, he ordered his kitchen to serve a pickled sturgeon he had foolishly kept for some seven weeks. The result was predictable. 'My stomach was turned,' he wrote, 'when my sturgeon came to table, upon which I saw very many little worms creeping, which I suppose was through the staleness of the pickle.'

Even so, while Pepys could take a genuine pleasure in eating sheep's trotters and 'umble pie' (which was made from the umbles, or entrails, of venison) his celebrations for the anniversary of his operation for the stone were grand affairs consisting of plates of carp, salmon, chicken, ox tongues and cheese. In 1663, he would treat a dozen guests to 'a fricassee of rabbits and chicken, a leg of mutton boiled, three carps in a dish, a great dish of a side of lamb, a dish of roasted pigeons, a dish of four lobsters, three tarts, a most rare lamprey pie, and a dish of anchovies'. Such gargantuan generosity necessitated suitable place settings and, as his income rose, Pepys was able to entertain at a lavishly prepared table. He carefully recorded buying six spoons in 1661, further 'spoons, forks and a sugar box' in 1664, 'a case of very pretty knives with agate hafts' in the same year, and yet more knives in 1666 and 1667. Presents such as the £500 worth of solid silver plate that he was given in 1666 augmented this, and eventually Pepys was able to boast of having no less than thirty silver plates on which to serve his bounty.

Clothes, too, delighted Pepys, for a smart appearance was proper to a rising man. In 1661 he was wearing a white coat made out of one of his wife's old petticoats, but soon he was having his bands trimmed with deep ribbons of the Flemish or Venetian lace that was coming to be fashionable. That year also saw him wearing a sword 'as the manner now among gentlemen is'. Not that Pepys regarded his sword as a weapon: it was a fashion accessory, and during the only violent incident in which he was involved during this period – the day in May 1663 when he was attacked by a great dog – he was so confused that he completely forgot to draw it. A hat likewise was essential, for elaborate rules about where and before whom one should stand bareheaded were a means of emphasising social status. On 28 January 1661, Pepys 'bought a hat, cost me 35s'. This was a considerable sum, but Pepys believed that money spent on his appearance was wisely invested, and his delight in his 'Jackanapes coat with silver buttons' is as evident as was his pride when he wrote 'this morning came home my fine Camlott cloak with gold buttons – and a silk suit; which cost me much money and I pray God to make [me] be able to pay for it'.

As for his hair, Pepys was still wearing his own in 1661 but it was long and curled and difficult to keep clean so, in 1663, he started wearing a periwig. It was not until the start of January 1664, however, that he decided to shave off his moustache. Shaving, indeed, was one of those areas in which he was particularly fussy. In the early 1660s Pepys smoothed his face each weekday with a pumice-stone and on Sundays indulged in the luxury of having a barber come to the house before church. By 1664 he had bought himself a cut-throat razor and could enjoy the perfectly smooth cheeks that appear in all his portraits, such as that painted by John Hales in 1666, which shows Pepys holding a copy of his song 'Beauty Retire'.

Next to a beautiful woman, music remained Pepys's principal pleasure. He knew this all too well. 'Music and women I cannot but give way to,' he guiltily declared, 'whatever my business is.'[3] Music surrounded him and he relished it with an all-embracing gusto whether it was 'the music of a booth at Southwark Fair' or Henry Lawes' *Third Book of Airs*, which he took with him when he sailed to bring back the King. Lawes, indeed, was the leading composer in this period before the supremacy of Purcell, whether he was writing catches – 'fooleries', Pepys called them – such as were commonly sung in taverns, or the more sophisticated declamatory air with its attempt to honour the importance of the words through an apt balance of melody and recitative elements. Music brought Pepys company and solace in solitude. It also brought him a measure of exasperation, for he had no formal training in the art he so deeply loved and was determined both to remedy this and to compose.

Such ambitions were to cause him much trouble and expense. At the start of 1662 Pepys resolved to take lessons from one John Birchensha.[4] All through January and February of that year he was taught at a cost of £5 a month, 'which is a great deal of money and troubled me to part with it'. He practised hard, and so enthusiastic did he become that even Sundays found him 'composing some airs (God forgive me)'. Many *Diary* entries from this period suggest how keen he remained, and 'so to music and then to bed' being a typical and often repeated sentence. The task he had set himself was difficult all the same, and Pepys was at first unwilling to confess how large a part Birchensha had played in 'finishing my song of "Gaze not on swans" in two parts, which pleases me well'. It was only after three weeks that he could be more honest with himself and write of this song and another that they were works 'which Mr Birchensha set for me a little while ago, I find them most incomparable songs as he has set them – of which I am not a little proud, because I am sure none in the world hath them but myself'.

By this time, however, Birchensha himself had disappeared angrily from the scene. He had invented a mathematical machine – his 'great card of the body of music' – to aid composition. Pepys, although impressed, presumed to criticise the system and there was a row which Pepys skilfully, if rather meanly, exploited to his own advantage. 'We fell to angry words,' he wrote, 'so that in a pet he flung out of my chamber and I never stopped him, being intended to have put him off today whether this had happened or no, because I think I have all the rules that he hath to give, and so there remains nothing but practice now to do me good – and it is not for me to continue with him at £5 per mensem.'

One of the most fruitful places to hear music in public was the theatre, and Pepys the amateur musician was also an avid play-goer. On 3 January 1661, he went to see the King's Company in their Vere Street Theatre 'where was acted *Beggars' Bush* – it being very well done; and here for the first time that ever I saw women come upon the stage'. It was a historic moment in the history of English drama. Pepys had earlier seen the play performed by an all-male cast, but it was the King himself who had decreed that female roles should now be played by actresses, giving as his reason that this would allow plays to 'be esteemed not only harmless delights but useful and instructive representations of human life'. Here were the seeds that led to the great flowering of Restoration drama. The Puritans had closed down the theatres in 1642 (it is possible that Pepys had enjoyed performances as a little boy prior to this), and although there had been intermittent productions before the return of Charles II it was the royal warrant granted on 9 July 1660 to Thomas Killigrew and Sir William Davenant to raise companies of actors in London that was responsible for the refounding of the theatrical life that Pepys so often, and sometimes so guiltily, enjoyed.

Beggars' Bush was performed by the King's Company, and Pepys himself reckoned that their theatre was 'the finest play-house, I believe, that ever was in England'. This was a pardonable exaggeration from an enthusiast, for the little building, seating about five hundred people, was plain and had no provision for scenery. Killigrew the impresario, 'a merry droll, but a gentleman of great esteem', as Pepys called him, claimed the rights over the great heritage of Elizabethan and Jacobean drama. When, in May 1663, he moved to the Theatre Royal he was able to stage these and other modern works with a lavishness that pleased Pepys greatly. By 1666 Killigrew's leading actors, Charles Hart and Nell Gwyn, were developing that quintessential form of Restoration drama: the witty encounter of a contemporary rake with a high-spirited and independent heroine. Meanwhile Davenant, the impresario of the Duke's company, specialised in somewhat bombastic heroic drama and farcical comedy, the latter particularly appealing to Pepys who called *Sir Martin Mar-all* 'the most entire piece of mirth, a complete farce from one end to the other, that certainly was ever writ'. Pepys was not a man to sit po-faced in the theatre. Raucous laughter was essential to his enjoyment of life.

All aspects of stagecraft fascinated Pepys and the friendship of actors delighted him. In 1660, when he went to his first play as an adult he invited the young star, Edward Kynaston, to drinks afterwards. The company of actresses, meanwhile, offered more prurient thrills. Pepys adored going backstage, and later the conversation of Nell Gwyn, that 'merry bold slut', and one of her female companions provided a delicious frisson.[5] 'But Lord their confidence,' he wrote, 'and how many men to hover about them as soon as they come off the stage, and how confident they are in their talk.' Such raciness was thrilling and naughty, but the delights of backstage life could be equalled by those front of house. The close press of a crowded audience stirred Pepys's appetites, and the theatre was as good a place as a church to ogle women. On 28 January 1661 he was again at the Vere Street theatre 'and here, I sitting behind in a dark place, a lady spat backward on me by a mistake, not seeing me'. He 'was not troubled at it at all', however, for she was, as he noted, 'a very pretty lady'.

Pepys was no very subtle critic of the stage. He liked what was smart and modern, even what was meretricious. Notoriously he dismissed *Romeo and Juliet* as the worst play 'that ever I heard in my life'. It is true that the actors in this performance were under-prepared and fluffed their lines, but Restoration audiences demanded a refinement they believed Shakespeare lacked, and Pepys was a Restoration man. He was even disappointed by *A Midsummer Night's Dream*, dismissing it as summarily as Hippolyta ridiculed the mechanicals. Here was a play 'which I have never seen before, nor shall ever again,' Pepys wrote, 'for it is the most insipid ridiculous play that ever I saw in my life'. Only the spectacle saved it. 'I saw, I confess, some good dancing and some handsome women, which was all my pleasure.' When Shakespearean dialogue palled, Pepys could always look at the actresses' breasts. He had, none the less, a sure sense that all this pleasure was just an insubstantial pageant. When he went backstage at the King's Theatre while it was being enlarged, for example, Pepys cast his eyes over the unused props and costumes. 'But to see their clothes,' he reflected, 'and the various sorts, and what a mixture of things there was; here a wooden leg, there a ruff, here a hobby-horse, there a crown, would make a man split himself to see with laughing.' The theatre, he knew, was a snare and delusion. 'How fine they show on the stage by candle-light,' he wrote, of the sad items littered around him, 'and how poor things they are to look at too near hand.'[6] The Puritan was never far from the pleasure-seeker, and Pepys fought long, hard and unsuccessfully to master the temptations of the stage.

An improving book might help, and Pepys read with the

gusto he brought to all his activities, propping up a book while he ate, nursing it to him as a lighterman rowed him along the Thames, or even reading by the light of a linkboy's torch as he made his way through the narrow London streets. In such ways he managed to read at least a book a month and he bought volumes for his library extensively. These were often purchased as loose quires, but Pepys had already acquired a taste for fine bindings (a craft in which the period excelled) and 5 January 1661 saw him going home by coach having visited 'Paul's churchyard to bespeak Ogilby's *Aesop's Fables* and Tully's *Offices** to be bound for me'. Both works suggest a taste for moral improvement, and Pepys's library at this period contained a number of such works. Bacon's *Faber Fortunae* was a particular favourite, the notion of every man as the architect of his own destiny being an idea with particular appeal.

His library contained a respectable quantity of theological works, but Pepys's principal interest in this area was Church history and his historical reading was wide indeed. Continental history had its appeal for him, but the immediate past was of altogether greater interest. Biographies of earlier Stuart worthies were eagerly read, but even now he had the true historian's taste for primary sources and eagerly purchased Rushworth's *Historical Collections* for the reprints of documents they contained. Travel books also appealed to Pepys – he enjoyed a Spanish guide to Rome – and we have seen that he had sufficient books in French to leave his collection of them to his wife in his first will. Pepys read Latin enthusiastically (sometimes he would rise early in the morning to read Cicero) while he also had a taste for the mannered intricacy of Renaissance Latin and enjoyed the works of Erasmus particularly. Shakespeare on the page sometimes disappointed him as he did in the theatre.

* i.e. Cicero's *Offices*.

Pepys bought *Henry IV* on the way to a production 'but my expectation being too great, it did not please me as otherwise I believe it would'. There is no mention in the *Diary* of *Paradise Lost*, the supreme work of Restoration English literature, nor, rather surprisingly, could Pepys at first acquire the contemporary taste for Butler's satiric epic *Hudibras*.

Ephemera was also increasingly to fascinate him (he later put together a remarkable collection of printed ballads) and, like many of his contemporaries, he was not above enjoying 'mighty ingenious' books of prophecy, ghost stories, accounts of marvels and even the occasional work of pornography. Indeed, Pepys's encounters with a well-known dirty book of the time provide an amusing but telling insight into his character. On 13 January 1668, after a fairly uneventful day at the office, Pepys made his way 'homeward by coach and stopped at Martins my bookseller, where I saw the French book which I did think to have for my wife to translate, called *L'École des filles*'. No doubt Pepys, judging by the title of the work, had imagined it to be an improving-conduct book, which would broaden Elizabeth's mind even while subduing her to the drudgery of translation. He was shocked to find the truth quite otherwise. 'When I came to look into it,' he wrote, with somewhat strained prudery, 'it is the most bawdy, lewd book that ever I saw, rather worse than *Putanta Errante* – so that I was ashamed of reading in it; and so away home.'

The pull of *schadenfreude* was to prove stronger than Pepys had imagined. Some three weeks later he was back in Mr Martin's shop and was now one of those shuffling, slightly shamefaced figures who browse at length along the more disreputable shelves. Eventually, after an hour of furtive reading, Pepys bought the book 'in plain binding (avoiding the buying of it better bound) because I resolve, as soon as I have read it, to burn it, that it may not stand in the list of books, nor among them, to disgrace them if it should be found'. Such glorious self-deceit was taken yet further the next day. It was a Sunday and the dutiful Pepys was 'doing business' while also reading a little of *L'École des filles*. Perhaps, amid the comparatively mild and even rather charming descriptions of the delights of physical love and sexual slang in the book, Pepys came across such useless pieces of information as the author's assertions that a woman can avoid becoming pregnant if she moves constantly during intercourse and avoids simultaneous orgasm. Certainly – perhaps because it was Sunday – the book's didactic purpose was apparently uppermost in Pepys's mind. *L'École des filles*, he wrote 'is a mighty lewd book, but yet not amiss for a sober man once to read over to inform himself in the villainy of the world'.

Pepys also made sure he was versed in contemporary science. The writings of the great Boyle he found very difficult indeed, but he was fascinated by the new work being done in statistics, and once he had bought a microscope in 1664 (paying no less than £5. 10s. 0d. for it) he eagerly perused Henry Power's *Experimental Philosophy* and, above all, Hooke's *Micrographia*. The marvellous illustrations in this last book – particularly memorable is the flea drawn on a gigantic scale – make it one of the great works of the age, and Pepys voiced the opinion of many when he wrote that *Micrographia* was 'the most ingenious book that ever I read in my life'. It is wholly typical of Pepys, however, that this enthusiasm for science was not confined to his library. People and institutions kindled his interest far more keenly than solitude, and it was in the company of his friend the scientific instrument-maker Ralph Greatorex that, on 23 January 1661, Pepys went 'to Gresham College (where I never was before) and saw the manner of the house, and find great company of persons of honour there'.

Pepys was viewing what would become the Royal Society after Charles had granted its charter in July 1662. He was also getting an early glimpse of the fashionable new taste for scientific enquiry. 'The truth is,' a contemporary would write 'a spirit of learning came in with the Restoration, and the laity as well as the clergy were possessed with a generous emulation of surpassing one another in all kinds of knowledge.' At the highest level – that of Newton and Boyle – what these men were attempting to do was to get beyond a passive fatalism in the face of nature and the received wisdom of the ancients, replacing these with a quest for those laws that would show the world acting at all times and in all places according to consistent and verifiable rules. This was the heroic labour of professional men of genius, but around them clustered lesser lights interested to varying degrees in what they were doing and happy enough with the amateur status of 'virtuosi'. Among these men was Pepys who, on 3 May 1665, recorded that he was present at one of the Society's meetings at which he saw 'a cat killed with the Duke of Florence's poison. And saw it proved that the oil of tobacco, doth the same effect, and is judged to be the same thing with the poison, both in colour and smell and effect.' Ever fascinated by the curious, he added that he 'saw also an abortive child, preserved fresh in spirit of salt'.

Pepys's association with the Royal Society would really begin to flourish after 1664. None the less, he was already part of that generation who were not content to see the world through Aristotle's eyes alone, who knew about telescopes and microscopes and had even handled them, men who had no problem with the fact that the earth moves round the sun and who believed that knowledge advances and that its progress may be followed by those with the wit to do so. Intelligence of itself was not enough, however, and Pepys had no adequate formal training in science. In particular, he lacked a knowledge of mathematics and, knowing that numeracy was of use to his work, he set about learning his multiplication tables with characteristic enthusiasm. He arranged for Cooper, the mate of the *Royal Charles*, to come and give him his first lesson at his office on 4 July 1662. The lessons continued for a month and many *Diary* entries from this time begin in a similar way: 'up by 4 o'clock, and hard at my multiplication table'.

High theory did not greatly interest Pepys but he enjoyed experiments and he had a relish for the beautifully crafted gadgets and gismos that came with the new science, and which were either useful in his profession or curious in their own right. He began to assemble a fine if small collection of these. In addition to his microscope he had, among other things, a 'weather-glass', or thermometer, a double-horizontal dial by which (with some difficulty) he could tell the time, and a 'rule', which not only served as a ruler but, with the aid of dividers placed on the scales engraved on it, could be used to solve elementary mathematical problems, somewhat in the manner of a modern pocket calculator. Thus prepared, Pepys was able to undertake not just the daily routine of his work for the Navy Office but such expeditions to the dockyards as the one he made to Portsmouth in April 1662 – a trip in which the whole man stands self-revealed.

It was only with difficulty that Pepys had persuaded Elizabeth not to come with him to Portsmouth but to go instead to the rural seclusion of Brampton. This was to be an all-male expedition, and after a breakfast of buttered eggs in Lambeth, Pepys, Hewer and Penn were joined by Sir George Carteret and his friend Dr Clarke, physician to the King's Household and a fellow of the Royal Society. The good doctor broke the ice by telling a tale bawdy even by Restoration standards 'of the monkey that got hold of the young lady's cunt as she went to stool to shit, and run from under her coats and got upon the table, which was ready laid for supper after dancing was done'. Laughter made the men as equal as they could be, and by the time the party arrived in Guildford, Dr Clarke and the clerk of the acts were such firm friends that they could punningly refer to each other as cousins. Jokes soon gave way to more serious talk, and by the time they had settled in Portsmouth Clarke, beguiled by Pepys's charm and sensing the gusto of his curiosity, began an 'exceeding pleasant' conversation about the new science during which 'he offers to bring me to the college of the virtuosos . . . and to show me some anatomy, which makes me very glad'.

But Pepys was now having trouble with his eyes. For the moment he put this down to the number of healths he had been obliged to drink in a town excited by the prospect of the imminent arrival of Charles II's new queen, the Portuguese Princess Catherine of Braganza. A flattering encounter with the Duke of Ormonde 'who owned and spoke to me' resulted in Pepys being able to see the lavish apartments prepared for Catherine while, in an interval from the long hours of work he was putting in for the Navy Board, he caught a glimpse of the radiantly beautiful Mrs Pearse, the wife of a distinguished naval surgeon and friend. Pepys 'being in haste, could not learn of her where her lodgings are, which vexes me'. He spied Mrs Pearse again a few days later accompanied by 'another lady', and seized the opportunity to entertain them both to wine and sweetmeats before Dr Clarke arrived. All four spent the evening 'playing and laughing' until the men were forced to leave as the town gates were about to be locked.

Clarke and Pepys had enjoyed themselves so much that, on the way home, they worked out a ruse whereby work would keep them in Portsmouth for a day longer than planned. As a result, a second evening with the amiable Mrs Pearse and her companion was spent playing cards, but as the two men made their midnight way home they were intrigued to try to work out who their friend's companion was. Although Mrs Pearse herself denied it, the fact that she was 'old and handsome and painted and fine, and hath a very handsome maid with her' led both men to think she was a bawd. They were not to find out the truth of this for, after a couple of evenings that might have come from a Restoration comedy, Pepys had the altogether more serious duty of accepting the 'Burgesship' of Portsmouth and then taking all those present for a drink. His work already brought its dignities and responsibilities.

The following day, May Day, the officers of the Navy Board left Portsmouth very early, but the journey back was not pleasant. By the time Pepys was ready to overnight in Guildford he was angry and uneasy. There were strains under the surface of his professional life and these were making him sore. There had already been a disagreement between himself and the two Sir Williams about choosing masters for the fleet. The knights had disdained to take Pepys's advice and, behind his back, had ignored his recommendations. Carteret was furious both at the irregular procedure and the omission of Pepys's man, while Pepys himself at once saw where his advantage lay. Carteret, the treasurer of the navy, was a very grand figure indeed. He had supported Pepys, and if Pepys now drew back from too familiar an acquaintance with Batten and Penn, the two Sir Williams would surely realise that he was not a figure to be trifled with.

Tactlessness had already deepened the acrimony. At the close of 1662, as Pepys, Penn and Batten were returning from a business meeting, Batten had suggested that they stop off for a drink at the Three Tuns in Charing Cross. A pretty barmaid worked there, and Pepys made a remark about her and Batten, which made Penn laugh and Batten furious. So angry was he indeed that he persuaded Penn to join with him and pull rank on Pepys. A fortnight later they rebuked him for his absence from a meeting, 'saying that without their Register they were not a committee'. This was a calculated insult and Pepys was in 'some dudgeon' at being treated merely as a taker of minutes. The terms of his employment made it clear that he was far more than this and, besides, his ambitions were at stake. As he sat thinking the matter over it became clear to him that he could not brook such an insult and he realised that 'I must keep myself at a little distance with them and not crouch, or else I shall never keep myself up even with them.' From now on relations between the three men would often be strained.

Nor was this squabbling simply a matter of bruised egos and sly manipulation. Pepys's intense curiosity had joined with the Puritan streak in him to alter his attitude to his work. The fundamental conflict in his personality was driving him to explore those characteristics that would soon begin to make him a great civil servant: his love of order and efficiency, his need to control and reduce to method, and, above all, that necessary combination of ambition and the desire to dominate, which exulted him personally even as his efforts were given to the service of the State. Pepys was changing, deepening, becoming more himself. Easy, boozy, high-spirited junketing underwritten by bouts of intense labour was no longer enough. At the sombre moment of his reckoning at the end of 1661 Pepys chastised himself for having been 'a very great spendthrift in all manner of respects'. He promised to reform.

Pepys knew his weaknesses well enough and swore 'a solemn oath about abstaining from plays and wine'. He wrote this resolve down, possibly in a little notebook, and from time to time, and on Sundays especially, read it over. Every day renewed the campaign, and by the close of January Pepys believed he was winning. On the last Sunday of the month he went to church twice and, at the close of the day, noted down his improved state: 'But thanks be to God, since my leaving drinking of wine, I do find myself much better.' Soon he was forming 'a resolution of keeping within doors and minding my business and the business of the office'. His determination paid off. 'All day either at the office or at home, busy about business till late at night – I having lately followed my business much,' he wrote on 13 March 1662. 'And I find great pleasure in it, and a growing content.' When his boy failed to wake him early, he gave him a sound thrashing.

Pepys's new-found righteousness sharpened his eye for the shortcomings of others and he was all for probity now. He would follow the Instructions issued by the Lord High Admiral to the letter. There it was laid down that among the duties of the clerk of the acts was that of keeping a record of the market price of all goods to be purchased – timber, masts, hemp, tar and so on – 'so His Majesty be not forced for want of true and timely information of the market to give exorbitant prices'.[7] Many of these items had to be brought from abroad, and it was again the duty of the Navy Board to obtain weekly statements from the Customs House so that an eye could be kept on which merchants had imported what, in order that the Navy Board might thereby avoid being tied to one supplier when 'divers might afford more choice at easier rates'. Pepys's new zeal unmasked numerous abuses as he conducted his market research, stomping over London Bridge and into Thames Street to discover the going rates for goods. These were, as he expected, much lower than the Navy Board had been told and it brought him 'great content' to find this out and 'save the King money'.

The same monarchist enthusiasm drove him in 'the business of the flag-makers'. The scam was flagrant, the flag-makers 'having 8d per yard allowed them by pretence of a contract, when no such thing appears; and is 3d more than was formerly paid and than I now offer the Board to have them done'. Other abuses also attracted his eye. William Hughes, the Woolwich rope-maker, had written to Batten complaining about the quality of the rope supplied by the great Sir Richard Ford. Pepys hurried down to Woolwich and, ever empirical, ordered tests to be carried out on the rope. He found it to be 'very bad' and saw that it broke easily, which was not surprising since 'some of it hath old stuff that hath been tarred, covered over with new hemp, which is such a cheat as hath not been heard of'. The following day. Pepys had Ford's contract 'stopped' but his honesty had its price. Ford himself became an avowed enemy and an irate Batten ensured the dismissal of the hapless Mr Hughes.

As Pepys well knew, Batten was not averse to lining his own pockets. The Lord High Admiral's Instructions had made it perfectly clear to all that trading by members of the Navy Board in commodities required by the fleet was illegal. The Instructions had gone on to stipulate that because of 'the ill consequence of it' principal officers were 'to take care that neither themselves nor any inferior officers in the Navy trade in any such commodity, or any way go shares with any merchant in any way for commodities sold to the Navy'. The penalty for being caught out in such illicit trading was dire for 'if any shall be detected to do so, they are to inform the Lord High Admiral of it, that such officers shall be dismissed the service'. In fact, it was usual for members of the Navy Board to turn (or pretend to turn) a more or less blind eye to such deals and to enjoy the profits as did Batten who, as a result of his activities, lived 'like a prince' in his country house in Walthamstow.

Indeed, Batten would stoop very low to support his way of life. He already had his hands in the Chatham Chest, the fund set up for disabled seamen and, as early as 3 July 1662, Pepys had resolved that it would be a 'meritorious act' to sort the matter out. After all, the Instructions made it clear that members of the Board 'are to be liable to trace one another in their distinct and several duties'. Partly as a result of this there was constant friction between the two men, but it was the other Sir William who was the more serious problem, and there is rare venom in Pepy's *Diary* entries about him. Pepys found Penn both underhand and hypocritical, ever ready to try to turn office rules and precedents against him (without success, for the rising bureaucrat was well versed in such procedures) and then covering his spite with an ingratiating pleasantness. Pepys was revolted. 'Whatever the matter is, he doth much fawn upon me, and I perceive would not fall out with me, and his daughter mighty officious to my wife; but I shall never be deceived again by him, but do hate him and his traitorous tricks with all my heart.' There were further unpleasant incidents, but Pepys himself felt increasingly safe. He was a rising man with friends in high places, and he had already prepared his approach to the greatest in the land.

At the close of 1661 the Duke of York, the Lord High Admiral of England, asked the officers of the Navy Board about the ancient practice of foreign ships saluting the English at sea. Pepy's colleagues gave their opinions on this tendentious issue but, since Pepys himself knew nothing about the subject, he was obliged 'to study a lie' in order not to lose face. After the Duke had left he told the great man's secretary, William Coventry, that as a schoolboy he had heard the historian Selden 'often say that he could prove that in Henry the 7ths time he did give commission to his captains to make the King of Denmark's ships to strike to him from the Baltic'. Now he had to make good that claim. On his way home from the office, Pepys bought Selden's tome on maritime law, 'having it in my mind to write a little matter, what I can gather about the business of striking sail and present it to the Duke, which I now think will be a good way to make myself known'. Pepys was becoming fully the professional, a man skilled in handling his colleagues, skilled in the affairs of the navy, bright, energetic and committed. This was just as well, for now, deep in the Palace of Whitehall, the Lord High Admiral was meditating war.

CHAPTER FIVE

The Life of this Office

The Lord High Admiral was a man whose face was frozen in a sneer of unquestioning superiority. Even his portraitists, torn between flattery and the desire to capture his personality, could never entirely soften this away, for if the expression had been acquired by birth it was confirmed by experience. That experience had been, in its way, quite as remarkable as his elder brother the King's. Both had been present as boys at the battle of Edgehill, and it was the Civil War that had set the Duke's opinions for life and confirmed his belief that a successful leader, for all he might be duplicitous, should never yield to opposition or harbour a liberal idea. He hankered after authoritarian certainties in both religion and politics, and he added to this an ambition for martial glory. He had spent many of the long years of the Interregnum as an officer in the French army fighting under Turenne, and he had achieved considerable renown. Now, after his return to influence in the wake of his brother's restoration, he looked eagerly about him for a cause in which to shine.

That cause was not far to seek. The Duke held his position

as Lord High Admiral by right of birth, and he brought to his office considerable energy and a crowd of followers eager to support his ambitions. He had a genuine love of the sea, and if in 1660 he knew little about ships, the taste for yachting he shared with his brother soon taught him much about sailing, navigation and other technical matters. Above all, the sea gave him the opportunity of appearing a national figure, an aristocratic hero. Such *hauteur* was important, for it helped condition his policies. In particular, he and the crowd of enthusiastic naval officers about him looked at the rich and bourgeois Dutch traders across the North Sea with a mixture of envy and contempt. The Duke himself had recently founded a Company of Royal Adventurers into Africa and, with a combination of courtiers and London merchants, had resolved to break the profitable Dutch monopoly on black slaves run from the Gulf of Guinea. The success of an initial raid was encouraging and Pepys wrote of how 'we go now on with great vigour in preparing against the Dutch, who they say will now fall on us without doubt, upon this high news come of our beating them so wholly in Guinea'. Excitement rose yet again when an expedition to North America overcame Dutch merchants who were trading with British colonists along the Hudson. In 1664 the Dutch port of Nieuw Amsterdam was seized and renamed New York in the Duke's honour.

Here, it seemed, was proof that mere republicans could indeed be subdued by the natural superiority of aristocratic warmongers, that there were 'certain sparks and secret seeds of virtue' in noble persons 'from which grows fruit more early and more vigorous than that which the industry of the vulgar can produce'.[1] Contempt for the Dutch deepened and, with it, jealousy. In the prosaic analysis of Pepys's colleague Captain Cocke: 'the trade of the world is too little for us two, therefore one must down'.[2] Such bluntness suggests the relatively unsophisticated state of economic thinking at this time. It was a widely held belief that the world's wealth consisted of bullion, that this was of a more or less fixed quantity, and that it was every ruler's duty to seize as much of it for himself and his subjects as he could. Ideas of competitive pricing and the expansion of markets were still in their infancy, and war (or the threat of war) seemed the obvious solution. It certainly seemed so to Pepys's erstwhile boss Sir George Downing.

Downing believed that the great Cromwellian victories at sea had so cowed the Dutch that they would make concessions whenever pressed. Labouring night and day at his office in The Hague, he did everything he could to deprive his hated rivals of their share of world trade. He bullied, he cajoled, he threatened. He put his own slant on the direction of English foreign policy when explaining it to the Dutch. He argued that even though the two nations had signed a treaty, many grievances were still to be reconciled, and he roundly declared that the English would have no hesitation in using force if they did not get satisfaction. After all, had not the English passed a Navigation Act aiming at 'the increase of shipping and encouragement of the navigation of this nation'?

War was becoming inevitable and other issues spurred it on. While the republican Dutch hardened their resolve not to be browbeaten, the Duke of York turned his ear to Downing's efforts to foment hostilities and believed he heard in them whisperings of his own political advantage. If the Dutch were defeated and their wealth fell into English hands then not only would the nation itself be enriched but the Crown would so hugely profit from the increase in tax revenues that it might yet free itself from an opprobrious Parliament, which, the Duke believed, exercised a power altogether unbecoming to the glory of monarchy. An ever greater exaltation of royal power was a European-wide phenomenon and was, besides, a Stuart family tradition. The Duke's grandfather, James I, had memorably declared to his Parliament that 'the state of monarchy is the supremest thing on earth: for kings are not only God's lieutenants, and sit upon God's throne, but even by God himself are called Gods'. Charles I had given his life for this cause and soon Charles II, with all the guile and cynicism of a hard-bitten survivor, would be seeking to extend his prerogative powers to their limits and even beyond.

Such ideas held a deep appeal for York's altogether cruder and more dogmatic mind, while the example of states across Europe nourished his ambitions. At the start of the century many European countries had representative assemblies that enjoyed varying degrees of power and influence. Parliaments in England and Scotland, *diets* in Germany and Poland, *risdags* in Sweden and Denmark, the *cortes* in Spain, the States General in France and even the *zemsky sobor* in distant Russia provided some check on royal absolutism. Gradually, as the century progressed, this restraining power was diminished by monarchs seeking ever greater personal influence. The *cortes* became a cipher. No assemblies of the *zemsky sobor* were called between 1654 and 1682. By 1672 Karl XI of Sweden had established himself as an autocrat and his heirs were deemed 'responsible to none on earth for their actions'. Frederik III of Denmark would follow a similar route, but it was the France of Louis XIV that provided the most alluring image of royal absolutism. The States General had not been called since 1614, and were not to be summoned again till the eve of the Revolution. In his own mind at least, the Sun King illumined virtually every corner of Europe and, where his light shone, the influence of the Catholic Church flourished too.

Such an exaltation of royal magnificence had its appeal not only for those who gloried in it by right of birth. To many of their subjects it appeared to be the pledge of order, security, the safe continuance of daily life. Men of Pepys's generation were all too painfully aware of the bloodshed and anarchy that ravaged a country when monarchies and parliaments were at odds. During the English civil war tens of thousands had died on the battlefields or of the famine and destitution that followed war. The confusing alternations of political experiment that came afterwards had solved nothing and, for the greater number of people, an eager-eyed longing for the New Jerusalem and the rule of the saints had been replaced by a deep homesickness for the old securities. Monarchy was the natural, the divinely sanctioned form of government. The authority of a king was sacred. He was the image of God's majesty, the fount of justice, the defender of true religion, the embodiment of the power before which every knee should bow. In such a world as this, order in the State was for many an altogether more pressing concern than questions of individual liberty, and a man's best efforts might be given, like Pepys's, to serving his king. The hawk-eyed young naval officers about York, thinking greedily of the prizes and promotion war would bring, urged him on. War would bring opportunities for action, and action would bring wealth. Besides, what had they to fear? Surely it was an easy matter for people such as themselves to repeat and even surpass the great victories won by Cromwell?

Fired by such arguments, York turned his attention to the state of the Royal Navy and, in particular, to Pepys and his colleagues in the Navy Office. He had a certain instinct that his plans could be brought to fruition only by an efficient civil service and like other autocrats (or would-be autocrats) across Europe he looked increasingly to intelligent, ambitious men of middling rank to serve his end. The clerk of the acts was one such man. Just as Louis XIV would surround himself with able advisors from often modest backgrounds – Le Tellier, Pomponne, Colbert and the bullying Louvois – so the Stuarts would come increasingly to rely on Pepys. He was, for the moment, a humble enough figure, but as time passed and Pepys came increasingly to find his identity in his work he would emerge as an important type of figure: a bourgeois and a bureaucrat willingly committed to monarchical supremacy.

Even now Pepys laboured hard to detect and right the abuses in the shipyards and was occasionally discouraged by the apathy around him, writing of how he went 'home to supper and to bed, being weary and vexed that I do not find other people so willing to do business as myself when I have taken pains to find out what in the yards is wanting and fitting to be done'. Such grim feelings were none the less a spur to his own desire for excellence, for quality, the strengths in his personality that he was determined to force on those around him. Like the true civil servant he was, Pepys wanted accurate records of all work done and he chafed at the slipshod attitudes of the dockyard managers and 'their ignorance and unwillingness to do anything of pains and what is out of their old dull road'. He would persist, however, and his persistence gave him pleasure. 'I like it well and will proceed in it,' he wrote, eventually detecting in such efforts the mainspring of his bureaucratic energies. 'My delight is in the neatness of everything and so cannot be pleased with anything unless it be very neat.' This was, he confessed, 'a strange folly'. It was, none the less, the basis on which he would eventually make the navy into one of the greatest fighting forces in western Europe.

His self-satisfaction was not unclouded, for the Lord High Admiral's interest in the Navy Board soon resulted in the appointment of another commissioner in the form of his secretary, William Coventry. Fearing a rival, Pepys was immediately suspicious, and his discomfort was increased by an angry outburst from Sir George Carteret against the new arrival. Would Pepys have to join forces with the treasurer against the man? On 15 May 1662, Pepys was present at the Privy Seal Office when Coventry received his letters patent, 'at which I know not yet whether to be glad or otherwise'. Coventry's reforming zeal was acknowledged, and while this appealed to one side of Pepys it ruffled others. It was difficult to get a purchase on the man, for if Sir George had told him that Coventry 'hath already feathered his nest in selling of places', Pepys himself was well aware that Coventry had an eagle's eye for the dishonesties of others and he resolved to cancel a trip to Hampton Court, writing that he was 'afeared now to bring in any accounts for journeys; and so will others I suppose be, because of Mr Coventry's prying into them'. Pepys, the model of probity, was not above fiddling his expenses from time to time, but a row between Coventry and Sir George as to whether the Exchequer or the treasurer should pay a victualler's account (if Sir George paid he was entitled to a rake-off of threepence in the pound) soon showed how fierce Coventry could be.

This was precisely the sort of rigour that the professional Pepys admired, and by the middle of July the two men were becoming friends. On 11 July they dined with each other, 'fell to talk of business and regulation', and began to appreciate each other's qualities. 'Upon the whole, my heart rejoices to see Mr Coventry so ingenious and able and studious to do good,' Pepys wrote. He was pleased, too, that his colleague showed him so much 'frankness and respect'. This acknowledgement was quite unforced on Coventry's part. He was a man able enough to admire quality in others, and by August he was telling Sandwich that Pepys was 'the life of this office'. By the close of September, Pepys was determined to have Coventry as his ally. It had taken him six months to move from suspicion to friendship, but now a relationship was blossoming between the two men which was to be one of the most formative of Pepys's life. In the company of William Coventry – aristocratic, witty, clear-minded, stylish and energetic – Pepys began to discover something more about his own deepest professional impulses and his previously barely recognised needs. Coventry offered him an aristocrat's view of public service as something to be followed for the public good, and by the close of October, as they were walking in the Navy Office garden together, Coventry made his ideals plain:

> . . . he said, in these words, that he was resolved, whatever it cost him, to make an experiment and see whether it was possible for a man to keep himself up in Court by dealing plainly and walking uprightly without any private gain a-playing. In the doing whereof, if his ground doth slip from under him, he will be contented; but he is resolved to try and never to baulk taking notice of anything that is to the King's prejudice, let it fall where it will – which is a most brave resolution. He was very free with me; and by my troth, I do see more real worth in him than in most men that I do know.[3]

Here is one of those moments when somebody embodying half-acknowledged aspirations is encountered, a moment whose influence is both permanent and profound. From now on Coventry appears repeatedly in the *Diary* as an ideal of public service: the enemy of waste, dishonesty and inefficiency, a man suave, courageous and committed to his cause.

Not that the patrician and the parvenu were always in complete accord. Pepys's work was bringing him into contact with a number of leading London merchants and he had a keen appreciation of their abilities. This was not shared by Coventry, who looked on such people with disdain, believing that trade would besmirch his honour. He felt he could 'never expect reputation' by acting in concert with such men, but it helps to place Pepys both socially and culturally to see how he was unaffected by such attitudes. To him, a self-made millionaire was a figure to respect. He could learn from such people and also do business with them. Both activities were keenly interesting and it was, besides, flattering to be courted by such men as the great timber merchant Sir William Warren as he set about using Pepys in his campaign to prise the navy timber contract away from his rival William Wood.

On a June evening in 1662 Warren took Pepys down to Wapping to explain the timber industry to him. Timber was by far the largest and most important of the Navy Board's requirements, for even a single ship of the Third Rate would require anything up to three thousand cartloads. English oak was deemed to be by far the most satisfactory material for building hulls but it was increasingly difficult to obtain in sufficient quantities and was, besides, very expensive. Imported timber consequently became ever more important and was the chief of the 'East Country' goods bought from Poland, Prussia, Bohemia and Norway. Warren now showed Pepys the differences between the three principal types of Norwegian deal 'and told me many pleasant notions concerning their manner of cutting and sawing them, the watermills, and the reason how deals become dearer and cheaper'.

Such knowledge was the very stuff of Pepys's profession, and he listened to Warren with all the intelligence and interest he invariably brought to such matters. Warren, knowing his man, responded in kind, and took Pepys to his timber yard 'where vast and many piles of deals, spars, and balks and Euphroes', lay neatly piled. Warren explained to his fascinated companion that 'deals' were used for decking, 'spars' for booms and bowsprits, while 'balks' were rough hewn timber and 'euphroes' giant Norwegian spars some thirty feet long. Pepys was intrighed for he had not known these things before. Such knowledge was both pleasure and power, 'and indeed', he wrote, he was 'very proud of this evening's work'. Warren, too, was pleased, and a couple of years later he could be confident that the 'firm league' made between him and the clerk of the acts would be mutually beneficial.

Warren would have a virtual monopoly over supplying the navy with timber and Pepys would prosper greatly from the commission he received.

For the moment, Pepys and Warren had what seemed a mutually beneficial agreement and one that would, Pepys chose to believe, also bring advantage to the King, for by such arrangements Pepys might to some degree ensure that favourable (or at least not grossly profiteering) deals could be made on behalf of the navy. But Pepys not only learned and profited from the merchant princes of London. Craftsmen, too, had much to teach him, and his friendship with Anthony Deane, the assistant shipwright at Woolwich, was lasting and important to both men. Deane visited Pepys's office on 12 August 1662, when he promised he would 'discover to me the whole abuse that His Majesty suffers in the measuring of timber, of which I shall be glad'. Six days later Pepys rode out to Epping Forest with Deane 'and there we saw many trees of the King's a-hewing and he showed me the whole mystery of the off-square, wherein the King is abused in the timber that he buys, which I shall with much pleasure be able to correct'. This he would do by using the rules Deane had taught him to confute dishonest suppliers, and it is typical of Pepys's practical enthusiasm that, while the two men were waiting for dinner in nearby Ilford, 'he and I practised measuring of the tables and other things till I did understand the measure of timber and board very well'.

It was clear to Pepys that Deane was a master of his trade – indeed, he was the most skilful ship-designer of his day – and a friendship based on mutual respect was once again profitable to both men. Deane was promoted through Pepys's agency, while Pepys himself had as a friend a man whom he could nearly always trust. But woe betide Deane when he slipped up. If Pepys knew how to ingratiate he was also capable of the magisterial rebuke. He would not tolerate shoddy standards even from a close friend, and moments of professional wrath were one inspiration for a literary form Pepys was soon to master: the official letter. When Pepys caught Deane out he made his feelings transparent:

> I will not dissemble with you because I love you. I am wholly dissatisfied in your proceedings about Mr Browne and Mr Wheeler . . . Mr Deane, I do bear you still a good respect, and (though it may be you do not think that worth keeping) I should be glad to have reason to continue it to you. But, upon my word, I have not spared to tell the Board my opinion about this business, as you will shortly see by a letter we have wrote to Commissioner Taylor. Wherein I have been very free concerning you, and shall be more so if ever I meet with the like occasion.[4]

The professional Pepys was not a man to trifle with, and it was this figure – keenly intelligent, shrewd, practical and alert – who now visited the naval dockyards regularly in his management of the King's business.

The dockyards themselves were the sites of England's greatest industrial enterprise and covered many acres. Here were the slips, the wet docks and the dry, the ropewalks, the warehouses and the masthouses, the sawpits and the timber piles, the masts lying in protective mud or in ponds. In such places as these, amid myriad activities, Pepys met the clerical and executive officers, supervised their work, and monitored the discipline they tried to impose on their often turbulent workmen – that army of sawyers and sailmakers, coopers and caulkers, joiners and jacks-of-all-trades – who toiled (or were supposed to toil) through an eleven-hour day for low wages that were often in arrears and who, at harvest time, were apt to abscond in pursuit of extra work. It was the duty of the clerks of the cheque in each yard to maintain order among these raucous, grumbling labourers, and this proved no easy task.

When Pepys visited the dockyard at Chatham in the summer of 1662, for example, he found 'great disorder by multitude of servants and old decrepit men' and realised he would have to do something about it. Chatham was the principal naval dockyard and thus vital to the nation's defences. Situated on the Medway and close to London, its vast storehouses held supplies of Wealden timber and gave work to some three hundred men. It was essential to monitor their performance and record their absences by means of a daily muster, while Pepys's solution to the discipline problem was to introduce call books in which the clerks of the cheque were to itemise all work done. Similarly, the efficiency of the storekeepers had to be regulated, while the clerks of the survey's reports on supplies also had to be gone through. All of this was a preparation for the work of the craftsmen who built and repaired the ships, the master shipwrights, the master attendants and their numerous subordinate officers whose titles were both apt and evocative: the master caulker, and the boatswain of the yard, the master mastmaker, the master carpenter, the master boatmaker and the master ropemaker.

The ships these men built were a glorious sight, for this was a period that knew no reason why an instrument of death should not also be a work of art. What impressed first, apart from the sheer size of the vessels, was the baroque profusion of ornament with which they were covered: the leonine figureheads, the human and animal forms writhing on the bulk heads, the wreaths round the gun ports, the carved domes and spires projecting from every angle, and the wooden giants or 'quarterpieces' flanking the gilded arms of the House of Stuart on sterns as fanciful as reredoses. None the less, the technical requirements of these floating masterpieces made the severest demands. They needed, obviously enough, to be strong, but they had also to be fast, manoeuvrable and little prone to roll in a storm or heel under full sail. They also had to be balanced so perfectly that the huge weight of cannon they carried could be placed high and remain as steady as possible. Hulls had to be narrow or 'fine' to minimise water resistance, and equalling out these conflicting elements was a technical skill of the highest order in which English shipwrights excelled.

Pepys rapidly became familiar with the ways in which such ships were constructed, with the laying of elm keels in overlapping sections, with the brave sight of the eighty pairs of ribs, or 'frames', which gave the hull of a large ship its shape, with the planking that covered these on the outside and the 'ceilings' that covered them within and which were, in their turn, secured by 'riders', 'breasthooks' and 'crutches'. A conscientious naval official who had not been bred to the sea had also to learn the internal arrangements of a ship. The lowest level was the 'floor', where provisions and water were kept. Above this was the 'orlop', where cables were kept and some of the cabins were placed, along with the cockpit which, during combat, was used as a surgery. The powder magazine was also to be found at this level, while immediately above it were the cannon, mounted on one, two or even three battery decks. The great cabin for the senior officer – often a lavish affair 'very curiously wrought and gilded with divers histories, and very much other work in oil colours' – was to be found at the after end of the upper deck.

In addition to building new ships, the dockyards also repaired existing vessels, whether they were tiny Sixth-Raters or the massive First Rates. When Pepys first took up his work at the Navy Board he discovered that the King had inherited fifteen First-and Second-Rate vessels of which the most prestigious was the *Royal Charles* on which the King had sailed back after his long years in exile. Originally, the vessel had been built on Cromwell's orders by Peter Pett, whose family had for several generations held a virtual monopoly of

Thameside shipbuilding and whom Pepys himself regarded as a rogue.

Cromwellian associations were still causing problems at the close of 1663, for the prow of the *Royal Charles* was decorated with a mounted figure of the Protector trampling on his enemies while Fame held a garland over his head. There was widespread rejoicing when this objectionable imagery was removed and the carved head of Cromwell himself was hung from a gibbet. For all his monarchism Pepys did not share in the joy since the accountant had got the better of the patriot. 'God knows,' he wrote, 'it is even the flinging away of £100 out of the King's purse,' for it had been proposed that the offending image should be replaced (as indeed it was) with a great Neptune borne across the waters in a shell drawn by seahorses. The magnificently redecorated vessel was none the less the pride of the navy and the nation's flagship – a symbol of the prestige to which Restoration England aspired.

With Pepys's responsibilities came both honours and more duties, the rewards of a successful man. In the middle of February 1662 he was sworn a Younger Brother of Trinity House, while soon after relinquishing his post at the Privy Seal Office (which had become an unprofitable chore), he was told that he had been nominated as a member of the commission set up to manage England's newest possession: Tangier, the north African port that had come to England as part of the new Queen's dowry. This was a sure recognition of Pepys's outstanding ability for he would be consulting with some of the greatest men in the land: the Duke of York, Prince Rupert, Monck (now the Duke of Albemarle), Sandwich, William Coventry and such lesser lights as Thomas Povey, the exquisitely mannered treasurer of Tangier.

For all that he was thoroughly incompetent, Povey was to have a considerable influence on Pepys since he was a fellow virtuoso, a man of taste and culture, and a fellow of the Royal Society. 'I find him a fine gentlemen,' Pepys wrote, 'and one that loves to live nobly and neatly.' He was soon to discover that this was something of an understatement. On 19 January 1663, Mr Povey threw a dinner party that left Pepys both astonished and impressed. 'He made a most excellent and large dinner,' Pepys wrote, 'even to admiration; he bidding us in a frolic to call for what we had a mind and he would undertake to give it to us – and we did, for prawns – swan – venison after I had thought the dinner was quite done, and he did immediately produce it, which I thought great plenty.' Povey's hospitality was matched by his pride in his house. He had a fine collection of 'delicate pictures', his rooms were floored with woods of several colours, he had magnificent furniture, a 'bath at the top of his house', painted mangers in his stables, and a grotto and a vault in his garden. He also had a prodigious wine cellar equipped with a well to cool 'bottles of all sorts', which were neatly ranged around 'in that order and plenty as I never saw books in a bookseller's shop'.

Pepys himself was not in a position to compete with such a prodigious display but he was still determined that his house in Seething Lane should be as splendid as he could make it. He had hung his pictures by the start of 1662, had arranged for pewter sconces to light the stairs, and seen to it that he was well supplied with such essential comforts as good sea coal. He remained dissatisfied all the same and he gradually formed the ambitious resolve to add another storey to his house. The project soon showed itself dogged with misfortune. When all the tiles had been removed torrential rain fell unremittingly for five days. The house was saturated, and while Pepys moved his belongings into a spare room of Sir William Penn's he thought it best to send Elizabeth to Brampton. This was not a wise move: her absence soon made him sexually restless and unhappy, and his fantasy began to rove into forbidden areas. He had – 'God forgive me' – lustful imaginings about Penn's maid and even about his own Jane Birch, but these he stifled 'for fear she should prove honest and refuse and then tell my wife'.

Family problems also proved irksome and long drawn-out, but if Pepys was an erring husband he was a loyal brother and a dutiful son. He had invited his unprepossessing sister Pall to Seething Lane in January 1661. Determined to make it clear that he was a peacock among the sparrows, he pointedly refused to let her sit at table with Elizabeth and himself. Pall was to have little more status than a servant, and the hurt, resentful girl made herself so awkward that it was clear she would have to go. September saw her 'crying exceedingly' as she left for Brampton. Nor were his other siblings any more congenial. Brother John failed to live up to the promise of a young man who had taken his Cambridge Bachelor of Arts in 1663, and he drifted into holy orders without any obvious signs of a vocation: he would rise only on his brother's back.

However, while John was a disappointment Tom was a liability. He was poorly educated and had followed his father into the tailoring trade. Pepys realised he would have to find him a wife with a dowry if he were ever to have adequate capital. Such a woman was never met with and, by the autumn of 1663, Tom's incompetence meant that his business was foundering. Worse was to follow, for winter and spring found him 'deadly ill'.[5] Pepys was horrified when he heard that Tom was dying of the pox, furious when the housemaid told him that his brother was deeply in debt, and appalled by hints of a homosexual affair, which might not only bring dishonour on the family but worse since, for all that Pepys claimed ignorance of what it really was, 'the detestable and abominable vice of buggery committed with mankind or beast' was a capital offence.

Pepys decided Tom was 'a ruined man', but was principally worried by the thought of the mess that he himself would inevitably have to clear up. None the less, his pity was moved as well as his contempt, and when Pepys stood by his brother's deathbed and saw him unable to string two words together 'it made me weep to see that he should not be able when I asked him, to say who I was'. Pepys's spirits rose to ordering a barrel of oysters when he learned that whatever Tom was dying of it was not a venereal disease, but the sight of a brother's death was unbearable and Pepys's grief was genuine if short-lived. He was not a man to feel false emotions for one feebler than himself and his honesty was tough and realistic. 'I had real grief for a while', he wrote of Tom, 'while he was in my sight, yet presently after and ever since, I have had very little grief indeed for him.'

Nor was it only his siblings whom Pepys had had to deal with. His parents, too, drew on his vigour in order to solve their problems. Uncle Robert had died in July 1661 and was soon followed by his wife. Robert Pepys had gone to his grave in the fond hope that 'all occasions of differences and suits of law [be] avoided amongst my brethren and kindred about my estate', but matters soon made litigation inevitable. Pepys was drawn in, for the greater part of Uncle Robert's real estate had been willed to him and his father, the reversionary interest descending to Pepys himself after his father's death. It fell to Pepys to sort through the accounts, and he discovered that charges against the estate had reduced its value to a quarter of its gross worth. Worse, a number of the deeds had been lost, which meant that the estate would by rights be inherited by Uncle Robert's brother Thomas, his heir-at-law. Thomas and his two sons had been left a paltry annuity and legacies respectively, and all three determined to pursue their rights with vigour.

By a decision of the local manorial court, Uncle Robert's property in Graveley passed to Thomas by default, but when the far more substantial property at Brampton was awarded to Pepys and his father, despite the lack of deeds, Thomas Pepys again swung into action, claiming a breach of manorial custom. An out-of-court settlement was only reached in February 1663 by which, in exchange for a portion of Uncle Robert's personal estate, Thomas Pepys agreed to waive his rights over Brampton and Pepys and his father to surrender their claim to Graveley. The matter had been settled after a fashion, but the details of the arrangement were such that Pepys periodically feared that more litigation might ensue. Meanwhile, he preened in front of his colleagues at the Navy Office, boasting that 'the estate left me is £200 a year in land, besides monies, because I would put an esteem upon myself'.

Pepys was not the only one who sought esteem. Elizabeth, too, was hankering after visible signs of status. In the attempt to make her a more interesting companion Pepys had introduced her to music and mathematics but, if he wanted her to shine, it would be by his light and in ways that he approved. When Elizabeth beautified herself with borrowed hair the Puritan in him rebelled. Beneath the tenderness he undoubtedly felt for her – Pepys was proud of her ability to draw, delighted when they read to each other, and gratified by her readiness to please him – there was a mean undercurrent to his affection that was sufficiently marked for others to notice. Sandwich's wife certainly saw it and resolved to have her say. 'My Lady did mightily urge me to lay out money upon my wife, which I perceived was a little more earnest than ordinary; and so I seemed to be pleased with it and do resolve to bestow a lace upon her.' In order to make it clear to Lady Sandwich that her word, if not law, was at least something to be obeyed, Pepys told Elizabeth to make a selection of laces but to leave the final choice to her superior. A lace costing all of £6 was finally chosen, and Pepys himself was left to writhe in secret at his enforced generosity. 'I think it too much,' he wrote, 'and I pray God keep me so to order myself and my wife's expenses that no inconvenience in purse or honour follow this my prodigality.' Elizabeth's domestic shortcomings continued to rile him too, but it was her insistence that she have a lady companion that provoked the first of a new series of crises.

Pepys knew that his relationship with Elizabeth was going through one of its rough phases and he was distinctly tetchy. Matters came to a head one grey November afternoon when a letter from Elizabeth arrived in his office.[6] Pepys stuffed it angrily into his pocket unread, promising that he would burn it in front of her when he got home. By the time he got back to his house, however, his mood had turned sullen and he went to bed. The following morning Elizabeth reopened the campaign. 'She began to talk,' Pepys wrote, 'and to be friends, believing all this while that I had read her letter, which I perceived by her discourse was full of good counsel, and relating the reason of her desiring a woman, and how little charge she did intend it to be to me.' Poor Elizabeth, her rather pathetic wheedling was soon met with such a torrent of anger that she cried out hysterically to her husband that Pepys could 'put her away, and take one of the Bowyers if I did dislike her'.* After a while matters appeared to improve but actually got worse. Brother Balty was now involved and, in the effort to relieve his sister's distress, had found what he thought was a suitable companion for her. She was a Miss Gosnell, a talented, attractive creature, and Pepys relished the thought of her living under his roof. In December she came. For three days Pepys hurried back from the office at all hours to catch a glimpse of her. Then she left. Brother Balty had told her of the Pepyses' supposed access to the court and to highlife. He had overplayed his hand, and the petulant Miss Gosnell upped and went to seek her fortune on the stage.

Elizabeth was on her own again, feeling lonely and neglected. She watched her busy husband becoming ever wealthier and her mind turned once again to dreaming of a companion. She

* The Bowyers were friends from Pepys's Exchequer days, see pp.25–41.

wondered at first if the unfortunate Pall might fit the bill, and Pepys promised to consider the matter. After all, if he had to spend money in this frivolous way it was preferable to spend it on his sister rather than on a stranger. In the end he did nothing and, on 9 January 1663, a now desperate Elizabeth renewed the attack. She put her case squarely to her husband then called for their serving-maid Jane to bring her a bundle of papers that she kept locked in her trunk. The girl did as she was told, and Elizabeth shuffled through the letters until she found a copy of the missive she had sent to her husband's office the year before. She began to read it out, and the row that ensued is best told in Pepys's own words:

> She now read it, and was so piquant, and wrote in English and most of it true, of the retiredness of her life and how unpleasant it was, that being writ in English and so in danger of being met with and read by others, I was vexed at it and desired her and then commanded her to tear it – which she desired to be excused it; I forced it from her and tore it, and withal took her other bundle of papers from her and leapt out of the bed and in my shirt clapped them into the pockets of my breeches, that she might not get them from me; and having got on my stockings and breeches and gown, I pulled them out one by one and tore them all before her face though it went against my heart to do it, she crying and desiring me not to do it. But such was my passion and trouble to see the letters of my love for her, and my will, wherein I had given her all I have in the world when I went to sea with my Lord Sandwich, to be joined with a paper of so much disgrace to me and dishonour if it should have been found by anybody. Having torn them all, saving a bond of my Uncle Robert's which she hath long had in her hands, and our marriage licence and the first letter that ever I sent her . . . I took up the pieces and carried them into my chamber, and there, after many disputes with myself whether I should burn them or no, and having picked up the pieces of the paper she read today and of my will which I tore,

The execution of Charles I, artist unknown, 1649.

Magdalene College from Loggan's *Cantabrigia Illustrata*.

Samuel Pepys by John Hales, 1666.

Elizabeth Pepys attributed to John Bushnell, 1672.

Charles II by John Michael Wright, c.1660–65.

George Monck, 1st Duke of Albemarle, artist unknown.

Edward Montagu, 1st Earl of Sandwich, artist unknown.

Sir William Penn by Lely.

Sir Anthony Deane by John Grennhill.

The Great Fire of London, Dutch School, 1666.

Royal visit to the Fleet by Willem van de Velde.

The Dutch attack on the Medway by Ludolf Bakhuizen, 1667.

The last page of the Diary, 1669.

> I burned all the rest. And so went to my office – troubled in mind.[7]

The battle was continued during the couple's midday meal, but it was Elizabeth who won this round against her selfish husband. Pepys had arranged for Dr Pierce and Dr Clarke to come to dinner with him, and Elizabeth seized her opportunity. 'I went to my wife and agreed upon matters; and at last, for my honour am forced to make her presently a new moiré gown to be seen by Mrs Clarke.' Pepys winced at the expense but recognised that 'it sets my wife and I to friends again, though I and she never were so heartily angry in our lives as today almost, and I doubt the heart-burning will not soon over'. Pepys knew that he had behaved shamefully, 'and the truth is I am sorry for the tearing of so many poor loving letters of mine from sea and elsewhere to her'. Perhaps he apologised when he returned late that evening from the office, for the day ended on a very different note from that which had begun it. 'So home – mighty friends with my wife again, and so to bed'.

Nor was it only Elizabeth with whom Pepys was having trouble at the start of 1663. He had rewarded his erstwhile mathematics tutor Richard Cooper with a place as master on a ship sailing to Tangier under the buccaneering Captain Robert Holmes. By early March the voyage was over and word came to Pepys that Cooper had conducted himself disgracefully. He wrote to ask the truth about these allegations, informing him that 'you are said to be a mutineer, a man ignorant in your duty that hath several times endangered the ship and very often been drunk'. If this were true it would do Pepys's own reputation no good and he wrote to Commissioner Pett at Chatham for an impartial view of Cooper. Pett replied that he considered the man a weak-brained drunkard but that he would probably be able to continue at his post provided he were supplied with a competent master's mate.

When Holmes came before the Navy Board to witness against Cooper his fury was evident. He demanded that the man be discharged forthwith, but Pepys objected that it was unfair to condemn him unheard. Tempers flared, and for all that his colleagues on the board stood by him, Pepys was sorely troubled and not a little afraid of Captain Holmes's vengeance. He passed a painful weekend and then, on Monday evening, ran into Holmes on My Lord's doorstep. It was a ghastly coincidence, but the seaman and the bureaucrat were too shrewd to make a scene. Instead they exchanged civilities and, in the conversation that followed, Holmes 'did as good as desire excuse for the high words that did pass in his heat the other day, which I was willing enough to close with'. At the next meeting of the Navy Board the matter of Cooper's misbehaviour came up again and by now the evidence was clear. Cooper was 'a fuddling, troublesome fellow, though a good artist [mathematician]; and so am content to have him turned out of his place'.[8]

At home, too, things appeared to have quietened down, for early in March 1663 Elizabeth acquired her heart's desire: a lady's companion. Her name was Mary Ashwell and she was little more than a child, fresh out of a school in Chelsea. Pepys found her pretty and 'ingenious at all sorts of fine works which pleases me very well and I hope will be very good entertainment for my wife without much cost'. He was delighted to find that Mary was also musical and hastened to buy her a virginal book. He was more attracted by her than perhaps he was prepared to admit, for the child proved to be 'a merry jade' and her high spirits for a while drove out the Puritan in Pepys. He began to relax in her company, playing music and cards and going on walks to pick cowslips or hear the nightingales sing. The *Diary* also records that sure symptom of Pepys in a relaxed mood: visits to the theatre. His vows were not forgotten but he persuaded himself that he had not broken them because the Theatre Royal in Drury

Lane to which he had recently gone had not been built when he wrote out his pledge. Such was the charm of the girl that Elizabeth, too, was delighted and seemed to derive courage from the companionship she had now found. Certainly, she answered her husband back more spiritedly than she had before, and even rounded on him during one disagreement and called him 'pricklouse', a hurtful reference to his father's trade. The quarrel was made up and the result was an increase in Elizabeth's wardrobe along with an enhancement of her talents, for now she acquired a master to teach her to dance.

The introduction of Mr Pembleton into the household was a disaster.[9] His mincing manners turned Elizabeth's head and so entranced did she become that she would brook no criticism of her newly acquired skill and even persuaded Pepys himself to take lessons. Soon Mr Pembleton was visiting twice a day. Pepys began to think there was more to his wife's friendship than he had imagined, and when he returned home one day to find the couple deep in conversation his 'old disease' flared again. The jealous Pepys is a pathetic figure, at once cruel, irrational, and crippled with guilt. His feelings tormented him and he hated himself. His mind was gripped with lurid fantasies. He retreated to his office 'pretending business'. He tried to listen in on the dancing lessons, walking up and down in his chamber as he did so to discover 'whether they danced or no or what they did'. He was low and he knew it. 'I am ashamed to think what a course I did take by lying to see whether my wife did wear drawers today as she used to do, and other things to raise my suspicion of her.' Pepys was disgusted by his own hypocrisy and felt that he deserved to be beaten 'since God knows that I do not find honesty enough in my own mind but that upon a small temptation I could be false to her, and therefore ought not to expect more justice from her'.

His suspicions none the less mounted and his fantasies grew

out of all proportion. He watched in torment as his wife and her dancing master held hands as they went down the river for a game of ninepins. He hated 'that man'. Pembleton was, he decided, 'a pretty neat black man, but married'. How could such an inconsiderable figure upset him so much? 'It is a deadly folly and plague that I bring upon myself to be so jealous.' It seemed that Pembleton was forever in Seething Lane, and Elizabeth's spirits so rose in his presence that Pepys feared that 'without great discretion I shall go near to lose . . . my command over her'. Dancing was a sin, the Puritan in him said, a sin 'whereby her mind is taken up from her business and finds other sweets besides pleasing of me'. The wretched Pembleton even followed them to church, and Pepys began to feel that he was losing his sanity. During the week the tormented bureaucrat rushed back from his office to see whether the beds had been tumbled on. They had not.

Elizabeth was aware of what was troubling her husband and promised that she would not see Pembleton alone in the house. Eventually the lessons came to an end, but Elizabeth believed that she had learned more than dancing. She was fighting back. She wanted to hurt her husband, to humiliate him for his jealousy, and she believed that the presence of her companion would stop any outrageous behaviour on Pepys's part. He saw that Elizabeth was a changed woman. 'Her spirit is lately come to be other than it used to be,' he wrote, 'and now depends upon her having Ashwell by her, before whom she thinks I shall not say nor do anything of force to her, which vexes me and makes me wish that I had better considered all that I have of late done concerning my bringing my wife to this condition of heat.' He faced a fury he could not subdue and, in his tortured state, he decided that the only thing to do was to send Elizabeth to stay with his parents in Brampton. Time alone might heal the pain.

It did not. It merely changed its form. For all that he summoned his Puritan feelings to his aid – renewed his vows, forswore strong drink, worked long hours, and took up his battle against corruption in the navy with renewed vigour – Pepys was restless and wretched. And the more severely the Puritan pursed his lips, the more restive the old Adam became. Sexual jealousy was replaced by a sexual desire that was harassing, promiscuous and insistent. He watched the grandees of the court pursuing their notoriously bawdy lives. He was repelled and attracted in equal measure. He felt, as many people did, that such licence was wrong. He laboured all day for the King's cause, and then noted in his *Diary* Charles II's excessive self-indulgence and feared for the nation over which he ruled. It concerned him greatly to think that the King was 'at the command of any woman like a slave'.

Pepys gave the matter a great deal of thought and listened intently to gossip, eventually deciding that Charles was essentially a fondler of women. 'The King,' he wrote, 'doth spend most of his time in feeling and kissing them naked all over their bodies in bed – and contents himself, without doing the other thing, but as he finds himself inclined; but this lechery will never leave him.' Here was the problem. Such self-indulgence clearly weakened the moral fibre of both the King himself and his court. The moral lead supposedly provided by a hereditary aristocracy was under threat. The courtiers' conversation was 'so base and sordid that it makes the ears of the very gentlemen of the backstairs to tingle'. The Puritan in Pepys revolted and he wrote that it was surely necessary to have 'at least a show of religion in government'. After all, 'sobriety . . . is so fixed in the nature of the common Englishman that it will not out of him'.

Lady Castlemaine, Charles's *maîtresse en titre*, gave Pepys special cause for concern since he recognised all too well how alluring this imperious and lascivious woman was. He knew, as everybody else did, that by April 1663 she had been given rooms in Whitehall and that she dipped her avaricious hands into every corner of the public purse. Pepys worried about her influence over the King in political matters especially, and over the coming months he was to believe that policy was driven by lust. 'My Lady Castlemaine rules him,' he wrote of Charles, 'who hath all the tricks of Aretino* that are to be practised to give pleasure – in which he is too able, having a large——; but that which is the unhappiest is that, as the Italian proverb says, *Cazzo dritto non vuolt consiglio*.'†[10] And yet Pepys could understand what drove Charles. For all his moral indignation his responses were in fact altogether more ambivalent, more human. On 21 May 1662, when walking through the gardens at Whitehall, he 'saw the finest smocks and linen petticoats of my Lady Castlemaine's laced with rich lace at the bottoms, that I ever saw; and did me good to look upon them'. He hankered after a print of her and eventually got one. He hankered after gossip about her too and, when a serving-maid brought him an item of tittle-tattle, he made a pass at the girl and became so roused 'that I spent in my breeches'.

Other royal mistresses caught Pepys's eye, the beautiful Frances Stuart in particular. He watched as this alluring, vacuous girl appeared to replace Castlemaine in the royal affections. He could not help his prurient interest. He watched them all out riding and 'I followed them up into Whitehall and into the Queen's presence, where all the ladies walked, talking and fiddling with their hats and feathers, and changing and trying one another's, but on another's heads, and laughing'. The scene was a voyeur's delight. 'It was the finest sight to me, considering the great beauties and dress, that ever I did see in all my life.' *La belle Stuart* in particular captivated him. The others were beautiful 'but above all, Mrs Stuart in this dress, with her hat cocked and a red plume,

* Pietro Aretino, an Italian writer of the renaissance famed for his erotica.
† A man with an erection heeds no advice.

with her sweet eye, little Roman nose, and excellent *Taille*, is now the greatest beauty I ever saw I think in my life'. That night the laughter of the women, the red plume and the little Roman nose tortured him. Pepys went to bed and, in his excitement, played with himself like a schoolboy.

But masturbation fantasies were not enough. Pepys needed the warmth and smell of a real woman to focus his desires. He ransacked his memory for thoughts of old girlfriends. At the end of June he bumped into Betty Lane, the linen-seller from Westminster Hall whom he had seduced in Axe Yard. She had changed, and not for the better. She was now 'monstrous fat'. But what did it matter? She had once been willing – but now it seemed she was not, or not very. She protested long that 'she never went abroad with any man as she used heretofore to do', but 'one word' was sufficient to persuade her 'to go with me and to meet me at the . . . Rhenish Winehouse – where I did give her a lobster and do towse her and feel her all over, making her believe how fair and good a skin she had'. This was true, but there was too much of it, and, besides, he knew it of old. Desire palled. Pepys grew 'weary' and his jaded fantasies were brought to a sharp close by someone flinging a stone at the window and crying out: '"Sir, why do you kiss the gentlewoman so?"'[11]

He pursued other women: a girl met casually in a tavern whom he kissed three or four times, although 'God forgive me, I had a mind to something more.' He trailed another girl he had known across Palace Yard. He fondled Sir William Penn's maid and kissed her. He thought of prostitutes, but when he went looking could not find one. None of these were what he wanted, anyway. And then his mind threw up an image that eventually would not easily let him go. Down in the yards at Deptford was a woman who kindled fantasies altogether more dangerous and exciting – altogether more guilty – than a passing parade of aristocratic whores or the plump familiarity of an old girlfriend. Mrs Bagwell was pretty, honest, socially his inferior and married to a carpenter on the *Dolphin*, a man for whom Pepys had done some manner of professional favour. This combination of obligation and desire, the thought of spoiling someone vulnerable and pure – the challenge of it all – roused Pepys and shamed him in equal measure. The shipyards where he was master now became his hunting-ground for sex.

On the wet Thursday afternoon of 9 July 1663, Pepys had himself rowed down to Deptford 'and there mustered the yard, purposely (God forgive me) to find out Bagwell, a carpenter whose wife is a pretty woman, that I might have some occasion of knowing him and forcing her to come to the office again'. Mrs Bagwell would be mastered by distributing the pettier official favours that were Pepys's to give and the means to victory was her husband. Luck, it seemed, was on his side. He met both Mr and Mrs Bagwell on his way to the yard for, hearing that he was on his way, they had came out on purpose to thank their patron. Pepys was not going to give a hint of his intentions as yet. 'I spoke little to her,' he wrote, 'but planned means of getting her to come to the office.' Meanwhile, he endured the well-meant pleasantries of the cuckold-to-be.

Young Mr Bagwell was keen to show himself agreeable to his powerful boss and wanted to display how familiar he was with the yards. Perhaps Mr Pepys would like to see Sir William Penn's lodgings? He would, and Mr Bagwell 'went along with me to show me Sir W. Penn's lodging, which I knew before, but only to have a time of speaking to him and sounding him'. After all, one had to put up with a little boredom. One had to be circumspect too. The following week found Pepys back in Deptford and Bagwell keen to renew his acquaintance and invite Pepys home. The Bagwells' was a neat little house, and they were proud to entertain an important visitor. 'They had got wine for me and I perceive live very prettily; and I believe the woman a virtuous modest woman.' Pepys was not yet fully ready for the attack (perhaps his conscience was stirred by the couple's simple well-meaningness) and, for the moment, he contented himself with walking back through Rotherhithe with the husband and asking him questions about naval matters. Mrs Bagwell was a triumph for another day.

Decency had won – temporarily – and soon Pepys had other concerns. During the first week of August he learned that his wife and her lady companion had come to blows in Brampton. It was his own fault, he decided. He had given Elizabeth her way far too much over the past year and he would take care to tame her on her return. This soon came to pass, and by the end of the month the now detested Mary Ashwell had left amid a flurry of other domestic crises: the loss of the cookmaid, the re-employment of a drunken one and the hire of a louse-ridden charity girl who promptly ran off in the clothes with which she had been provided. Pepys had her whipped by the parish authorities when she was caught, then turned to his wife.

The tiffs about housekeeping continued. There were even occasional sightings of the obnoxious Pembleton. It appeared that these posed no real threat, and the relationship between Pepys and Elizabeth took up its old course, squabbles alternating with moments of 'great content playing and dallying with my wife'. In the autumn they travelled together up to Brampton on his father's business, and when Elizabeth was made ill by drinking too much cold beer on a warm day Pepys suddenly realised the depth of his passion for her. Elizabeth 'became so pale and I alone with her . . . that I thought she would have died, and so in great horror, and having a great trial of my true love and passion for her, called the maids and the mistress of the house'. All was soon well. Elizabeth tried to settle back into improved domestic ways, and Pepys with her.

But this relative domestic calm was clouded by ominous

rumours. Pepys had been troubled for some time with the knowledge that the libertine life of the court had infected the moral health of My Lord and he was deeply concerned. Sandwich had been seriously ill during the winter of 1663 and had spent the spring recuperating in Chelsea. His landlady there had a daughter, Betty Becke, with whom he had become infatuated. Gossip was rife and Pepys was appalled. His own liaisons had at least been handled with a measure of discretion, but Sandwich was openly flaunting his folly, smearing his reputation and so threatening his own standing that Pepys sensed danger.

With the country edging towards war it was essential that the aristocracy show evidence of that moral excellence which was their *raison d'être*. Pepys's *Diary* became the confidant of his fears, and its pages show him trying to come to terms with the problem and make his attitude clear. 'I perceive,' he wrote, 'my Lord is dabbling with this wench, for which I am sorry, though I do not wonder at it, being a man amorous enough, and now begins to allow himself the liberty that he sees everybody else at court takes.' The moral climate could be blamed for Sandwich's behaviour, but it could not excuse it. Nor would the problem itself go away. Pepys tried to convince himself that it was not his responsibility and that it was not for him to get involved. 'I am very sorry to see that my Lord hath thus much forgot his honour, but am resolved not to meddle with it,' he wrote. Besides, there were other, more potent forces that might make his patron see the folly of his ways. 'Let him go on till God Almighty and his own conscience and thoughts of his own lady and family do it.'

Such voices, it seemed, were silent, while others were quick with gossip. Ned Pickering, a young satellite of Sandwich's for whom Pepys had no very high opinion, cornered him and poured out 'the whole business of my Lord's folly'. Pepys was hurt by this seeming overthrow of a noble mind. 'I am ashamed,' he wrote, 'to see my Lord so grossly play the beast and fool, to the flinging off of all honour, friends, servants and everything and person that is good.' Here was scandalous self-abasement that might ruin Sandwich for ever. Instead of attending to his great responsibilities he wanted to 'have his private lust undisturbed with this common whore'. He was little better than an infatuated adolescent who chose to drool his time away 'playing on his lute under her window and forty other poor sordid things'.

Something had to be done. The gossip at Whitehall was now so intense that Pepys feared for Sandwich's job and, with it, his own. Not only morals but survival itself now appeared to be at stake. Pepys resolved to act. He would speak with Sandwich but, when he went to see him, his courage failed. The difference in rank between them was too great, the matter so personal. A deeply troubled Pepys then took the civil servant's option and drafted a letter of reproof. Sensibly, he put it aside for a few days. Less sensibly, he discussed it with friends. The matter was so difficult. After all, he knew of 'the duty which every bit of bread I eat tells me I owe to your Lordship'. But the wretched business had to be faced and, with elephantine circumlocution, Pepys drew his patron's attention to what the gossips at Whitehall were saying:

> Another sort, and those the most, insist upon the bad report of the house wherein your Lordship, now observed in perfect health again, continues to sojourn, and by name have charged one of the daughters for a common courtesan, alleging both places and persons where and with whom she hath been too well known, and how much her wantonness occasions, though unjustly, scandal to your Lordship, and that as well as to gratifying of some enemies as to the wounding of more friends I am not able to tell.[12]

The girl was apportioned the greater part of the blame, and

no one, Pepys lyingly reassured Sandwich, knew the contents of the letter.

There was no reply. Pepys passed an agonising time and then, on Sunday, he and Sandwich met as My Lord was preparing to go to chapel at Whitehall. Pepys's anxious questioning had by now reassured him that the letter had had something of the desired effect, but the well-bred Sandwich was not prepared to display his shamefaced feelings. Who, he asked Pepys, had given him his information? A stuttering list of names spilled out, but My Lord should know that his servant was tender for his honour and that nobody else had heard about the letter. Sandwich demurred. He believed that Pepys had shown it to others and he watched as the terrified man broke down in tears. Then, with the courtesy that was natural to him, Sandwich began 'to talk very cheerfully of other things, and I walked with him to Whitehall and we discussed of the pictures in the gallery'. But Pepys was still in an agony of doubt. Had he done himself irreparable professional damage? Time would tell, but it suggested that he was safe. Sandwich left Chelsea, he loaned Pepys his coach, he helped him to a lucrative job on the Fishery Commission. This was all to the good for, as the rift in the two men's relationship narrowed, so the country at large was being readied for war.

CHAPTER SIX

The Right Hand of the Navy

Readying the navy for war was a monumental task, which placed huge demands both on Pepys himself and on the public purse. Money was a constant worry. For all that the service had inherited a splendid fleet from the years of the Cromwellian regime, the nation's first duty had been to decommission large parts of its potentially destabilising army rather than build up and maintain its forces at sea. As a result, it had proved impossible to settle all of the navy's liabilities, and when Pepys first arrived at the Navy Office a mountain of debt and interest charges loomed over every initiative. The fact that this money was in large part owed to the merchants, who alone could provide the materials for maintaining the fleet, resulted in a serious deterioration of the ships and yards, and meant that Pepys's early responsibilities had been to retrench and root out corruption.

The disabling financial problems with which he had to wrestle stemmed from a number of causes. Chief among these was that the administration of the national revenue was bedevilled with antiquated practices and ways of thinking that were wholly inadequate to solving contemporary problems. King Charles's early parliaments had been determined that he should have a sufficient revenue to carry out the day-to-day duties of government, but the received belief of many was that monarchs should 'live of their own', that ideally they should fund national expenditure from the great range of their hereditary and traditional resources. Even now these were regarded as being inadequate, and the members of Charles II's first Parliament (like those of the Interregnum before it) believed not only that they could adequately assess the shortfall but that it was their duty to make it good. To this end they resolved 'that the present King's Majesty's revenue shall be made up [to] twelve hundred thousand pounds a year'.

For all its good intentions, Parliament's gesture was riddled with problems. Its accounting procedures were rudimentary in the extreme, the collection of taxes was often inefficient, securing credit on anticipated revenues was difficult and expensive, while the fact that Parliament had effectively become responsible for granting the King a sufficient ordinary revenue (let alone the extra sums required by war) inevitably led to friction. Pepys was to be continuously harassed by such problems. Already, in 1663, Parliament had instructed the Navy Office to reduce the annual running expenses of the service from £374,743 to £200,000, and challenges so forbidding provided an enforced training in financial stringency. Civil servants like Pepys were required to hone their skills. A growing professionalism characterises the forward-looking administrators of the Restoration period, and men like Pepys sought to strengthen royal authority – and thus, they supposed, the political stability of the nation – by insisting on reason, system, a mastery of the facts.

One of Pepys's early initiatives makes this especially clear. By the start of 1664 he had resolved to make himself thoroughly familiar with the details of every contract drawn up by the Navy Office. This required a prodigious amount of work and, as the country moved ever nearer to war, so the *Diary* shows the efforts he felt obliged to make. He was frequently to be found going 'to the office, where very busy till 11 at night'. The pressure was considerable if deeply rewarding. 'Up, and all the morning very busy with multitude of clients, till my head begin to be overloaded'. Later the same day his head was 'ready to burst with business'. August 24, 1664, saw him 'up by 6 a-clock and to my office . . . despatching business in haste', while the end of the month saw him 'up by 5 a-clock and to my office' where, with the invaluable Will Hewer and another, 'we despatch a great deal of business as to the ordering my papers and books which were behind-hand'.

Pepys continued to be busy all that morning, but he also recognised how duties had to be balanced with pleasures. He went home for his lunch with Elizabeth, who had got him 'some pretty good oysters', and when Pepys had eaten these he went 'to hear my boy play upon a lute which I have this day borrowed'. Music could always comfort, 'and indeed, the boy would with little practice play very well'. There were small but irksome private matters to attend to as well, and as the pressured navy official hurried about his work so he had one day to go 'to Westminster to my barber's, to have my periwig be lately made cleansed of its nits'.

Perhaps this was not altogether a chore, for the barber, Mr Jervis, had an extremely pretty maid. Her name was Jane Welsh, and she was far from being the only young woman upon whom Pepys cast his eye at this time. The grinding weight of work sharpened his sexual appetite and he sought out promiscuous encounters with women friends old and new. Betty Lane, for example, reappeared on the scene. She was never far from Pepys's thoughts when his sexual urges mastered him and, on 4 January 1664, he cruised Westminster Hall looking for her. He wanted her and felt guilty about wanting her. Shame made him a hypocrite and he confessed that he was 'glad' they did not meet up. Less than a fortnight later they did. Pepys recorded the fact in his *Diary*, using that polyglot mixture of languages which so ambivalently hid and revealed his delight and disgust. A practised man of the world now, Pepys took Betty 'to the cabaret at the Cloche in the street du roy, and there, after some caresses, je l'ay foutee sous de la chaise deux times, and the last to my great pleasure'.* Deeply satiated, he wondered if, in his ravenous desire, he had gone too far, but Betty Lane was easy-going, complaisant, and when it was all over, 'I did perceive that je n'avais fait rien de danger à elle'.†

Such fears were natural in all extra-marital contracts and seriously inhibiting. A couple might succeed in practising *coitus interruptus*, but other contraceptive methods were primitive in the extreme: rudimentary condoms, made from sheep's intestines or a ribbon tied on with a lace, were primarily intended to protect men from disease. Nor did ignorance of the physiological facts improve matters: if his partner reached orgasm a man might very well worry that he had made her pregnant while if she did not he could assume he had got off scot-free. Pepys was riddled with guilt. He returned to his office and, for a while, the arrival of a new slide rule calmed his thoughts with its cool and beautifully fashioned mathematical indifference. The mood did not last, however, and he went to bed that night 'with my mind un peu trouble pour ce que j'ai fait today'.‡ He was worried that he might have got Betty Lane pregnant and he hoped this encounter with her would be 'la dernière de toute ma vie'.§

It was not, of course. Nor did it seem that she was pregnant. A meeting on 1 February confirmed that. It was better to

* 'to the Bell Tavern in King Street . . . where I had her twice'.
† 'I had done nothing to offend her.'
‡ 'with my mind a little troubled for what I did today'
§ 'the last in all my life'

marry her off, though. Perhaps he should urge on her the match with his old friend John Hawley, which had been in the air for years. Betty would have none of it. Very well, then, 'I am resolved wholly to avoid occasion of farther trouble with her.' Pepys was in a temporarily virtuous mood, as he had shown when the lovely Mrs Bagwell came to the office two days earlier in the hope of getting her husband promotion. 'I liked the woman very well and stroked her under the chin,' Pepys wrote, 'but could not find in my heart to offer anything uncivil to her, she being I believe a very modest woman.'

But the man of virtue could easily turn Puritan bully, and when Pepys met up with Betty Lane in April the occasion showed him at his most unpleasant. He pressed her again to marry Hawley. Once more she would have none of it. Pepys turned on her and 'made her angry in calling her old and making her know what herself is'. And, because of what she was, he wanted her again but could not have her because 'her body was out of temper for any dalliance'. Menstruation was considered particularly dangerous to the male lover since, while there was no doubt whatsoever that his semen was by its very nature good for a woman, menstrual fluid was considered to be full of evil humours. It was better to avoid such contamination and, after three or four hours together, Pepys left Betty, having extracted her promise that she would say, if asked, that they had seen each other for a mere fifteen minutes.

The next thing Pepys heard was that he had got what he wanted. Betty Lane had married. She was Betty Martin now. Irresistible ideas rushed into his mind. A couple of days before, he had had an innocent little meeting with Jane Welsh, his barber's maid, at a tavern in Brewer's Yard where he 'did sport with her, without any knowledge of her though'. Now he wanted more from a woman and the new Mrs Martin seemed the perfect choice. 'I must have a bout with her very shortly, to see how she finds marriage.' Pepys discovered the next day. He went to her lodgings 'to give her joy' and she willingly let him, for Mr Martin was 'a sorry simple fellow . . . a man of no discourse'. As Pepys left, 'she urged me to appoint a time, as soon as he is gone out of town, to give her a meeting next week'.[1]

They met two days later. The July heat was strong and Pepys was walking towards Westminster by way of Fleet Alley when he eyed a particularly attractive prostitute, one of perhaps some 3,500 who openly solicited in the capital. Pepys made it obvious what he wanted but 'honour and conscience' got the better of him. Besides, he was frightened of catching a disease. It seemed better to have sex with a known woman, a safe, married woman and, 'much against my will', Pepys took a coach to Mrs Martin's lodgings where he arranged to take her to 'the old house at Lambeth Marsh'. There he gave her something to eat and drink, then had her twice. Afterwards, he felt he could not understand her and was rather contemptuous of a woman who wittered on about how she loved her husband and how she didn't, and who gave herself to him for five shillings. Perhaps it was better to pay for straight, commercial sex. Pepys took Betty back across the river and went to have another look at the brothels in Fleet Alley. The woman he had seen earlier on was still soliciting. Pepys was intrigued, disgusted and, above all, frightened. He

> went in and there saw what formerly I have been acquainted with, the wickedness of those houses and the forcing of a man to present expense. The woman, indeed, is a most lovely woman; but I had no courage to meddle with her, for fear of her not being wholesome, and so counterfeited that I had not money enough. It was pretty to see how cunning that Jade was; would not suffer me to have to do in any manner with her after she saw I had no money; but told me then I would not come again, but she was now sure I would come again – though I hope in God I shall not, for though she

be one of the prettiest women I ever saw, yet I fear her abusing me.[2]

The appalling verb is the key to a host of unquestioned attitudes and superstitions about women and sex, most of them based on fear: fear of being robbed perhaps, fear of being degraded, certainly fear of a situation where Pepys would not be in control. Above all, Pepys's fear was of catching a disease. The 'great pox' was a true terror, and a promiscuous man might well examine himself after a chance encounter for the chancres and sores that were the harbingers of a terrifying regime of mercury-vapour baths and mercury-based pills, which eventually loosened the hair and teeth, softened the gristle of the nose, and softened the brain too. The nightmare image of a cadaver lay easily beside the naked body of a random conquest and goes a long way to accounting for Pepys's preferences for the supposed chastity of married women, for those he might safely hazard were virgins (or, at any rate, little experienced) and for being masturbated by those whom he could persuade to the act.

It does not, however, account for his marked predilection for women of a lower social class, and now his thoughts returned to Jane Welsh, his wig-maker's maid. On 3 September he strolled into his barber's and 'had good luck to find Jane alone'. He chatted to her and found out that the Jervises intended to try to marry her off and only allowed her out on her own at sermon time on a Sunday. Pepys asked her if she would meet him in Westminster Abbey the following Sunday. Fearful of insulting a customer, Jane agreed, and Pepys left the shop thinking she was 'a good-natured as well as a well-looked girl'. But she was not an easy catch. The following Sunday she stood him up, and Pepys was left to loiter in the Abbey for three hours pondering that it had been an unlucky week for him. He had arranged that the lovely

Mrs Bagwell (another lower-class woman) should visit him in the office, but she too 'came not'.

Then, on his way back from the Abbey, Pepys bumped into Jane, who was standing by a tavern door. He 'took her in and drank with her' and she made another vague promise of a date. Pepys had to press his interest now, and returned to the barber's shop the following day. Jane was there and, when the coast was clear, Pepys went upstairs 'and drank with her, kissing her – but nothing more'. They agreed to meet the following Sunday, but again she stood him up. The following day she was cold to him and a hurt Pepys shrank into a shell of self-righteousness. 'It is no matter,' he wrote, 'I shall be the freer from the inconveniences that might follow thereon – besides offending God Almighty and neglecting my business.' Jane allowed him to stroke her under the chin once more on 3 October, but it was clear that the affair was petering out and, besides, Pepys had other fish to fry.

Mrs Bagwell had finally turned up at the office. He 'kissed her only', but she made clear she did not like it, 'saying, that did I do so much to many bodies else, it would be a stain to me'. Pepys refused to believe the woman was quite so virtuous as she seemed to be and determined to lay siege. The old lure of a job for her husband would be the bait, and she appeared to take it. On 20 October Mrs Bagwell returned to the office where 'I caressed her, and find her every day more and more coming, with good words and promise of getting her husband a place, which I will do.' On 8 November 1664, they were together 'a good while' and promised to meet again shortly. They did so a week later. With 'much ado' Pepys persuaded Mrs Bagwell to follow him to a tavern in Moorfields 'and there I did caress her and eat and drank'. It was clear she was not going to surrender easily. 'Many hard looks and sithes [sighs] the poor wretch did give me, and I think verily was troubled at what I did.' None the less, 'after many protestings, by degrees I did arrive at what I would, with great pleasure'. By this time it had started raining, and Pepys gallantly escorted his conquest back into town until she knew where she was and could find her own way home. After that, they had sex with each other regularly: unsatisfactorily after a dinner-party at the Bagwells' own home, when Pepys had sent the husband out on an errand, in 'a cabaret where elle and I have eat before', and at the Bagwells' home yet again when the poor woman pulled a muscle in the forefinger of Pepys's left hand as she struggled to resist him.

Meanwhile, as he seduced the wife of a ship's carpenter, Pepys was still in pursuit of suppliers trying to cheat the navy itself. A typical day might see him despatching 'much business' before going down the Thames to Woolwich to investigate a man who was believed to be putting inferior-quality hemp in the navy's ropes then tarring them over to hide his dishonesty. Pepys's Letterbook is an impressive and sometimes chilling record of the correspondence he had with such people. Men like the Deptford shipwrights might have thought they could bamboozle Pepys then hide from him behind the mysteries of their trade, but they could not. Pepys could talk technicalities with the best of them and he was determined in true civil service fashion to have the correct procedures properly followed.

The Deptford shipwrights had failed to follow the protocols in the matter of some 'Knees', which joined the deck-beams to the sides of a ship. They received a pointed letter. 'I return you the enclosed bill for Knees (though signed) that you may certify them (as the Duke commands) to be agreed by contract.'[3] It was exasperating to Pepys that these men regularly failed in such all-important paper matters as certifying goods received. He explained that their 'omission' was a serious issue that 'often puts us upon a necessity either of delaying satisfaction to merchants (as now in this case of Mr Castle's) or of passing their bills unjustifiably'. The shipwrights were to return their answer tomorrow and, when they did not and merely tried to laugh at him, they were magisterially rebuked for their impertinence by a man 'not used to ask questions to . . . little purpose'.

Nor was this all that Pepy's work consisted of. In addition to chasing scoundrels, deals had to be brokered. On one occasion, after a dinner of 'a good dish of mackerel', Pepys set about discussing with his dining companions their 'contract for tar', along with another contract 'of canvass'. It is clear that he enforced hard terms 'against their will, to the King's advantage, which I believe they will take notice of to my credit'. But it was not only such administrative and business sides of his work that interested Pepys. He was fascinated also by the technical problems it posed. When he learned that there was a shortage of wadding for the guns he wondered if the leather shavings left over by shoemakers might supply the want, and he wrote to Admiral Myngs's father for the opinion of an experienced tradesman. Myngs did not think the shavings were suitable since they were only 'very small snips', and Pepys wondered if tobacco stalks might be used instead.

Such a pragmatic approach to practical difficulties was wholly in keeping with Pepys's interest in the proceedings of the Royal Society, of which he became a fellow on 8 February 1665. By then he had been interested in the Society for a year or more and he knew many of its members and fellows. Peter Pett the shipwright was one such, as was the mathematical and musical Lord Brouncker, who shared Pepys's interest in shipbuilding and was appointed a naval commissioner in 1664. Brouncker was also the first president of the Royal Society and round him were gathered a large number of Pepys's most distinguished acquaintances: John Wilkins, Lord George Berkeley, and John Dryden 'the poet I knew at Cambridge'. By early 1664, Pepys was attending meetings regularly. On 14 April his appetite had been whetted by hearing about Hooke's experiments on the expansion and contraction of glass, which he declared were 'very pretty, and true'. Musical experiments particularly fascinated him, and on 5 October he went to see a demonstration of a new instrument called 'the Arched Viol'. The experiment itself was unsuccessful (the instrument could not be kept in tune) and altogether more important to Pepys was the fact that earlier that day Mr Crocker, the engraver and calligrapher, had promised to bring him 'a globe of glass and a frame of oiled paper' so that he could read by candlelight without being disrupted by the glare.

Pepys had been worried by his eyesight for some time. Early in 1663 he had recorded how 'my eyes begin to fail me, looking so long by candlelight upon white paper'. At the start of April 1664, reading an old manuscript on shipbuilding, he had had to put it aside for the same reason, but the problem would not go away. On 4 May, Pepys dined at home and then went 'to my office, where very late, till my eyes (which begin to fail me nowadays by candlelight) begin to trouble me'. The following day he was still concerned, writing that his eyes were 'beginning every day to grow less and less able to bear with long reading or writing – though it be by daylight, which I never observed till now'. What he was suffering from was a combination of long sight and astigmatism, minor complaints in the modern world, but in the seventeenth century problems that might suggest to a man that he was going blind.

Nor was it only his eyes that worried Pepys: occasional spasmodic pains had made him worry that he might be falling victim to his old complaint of the stone. His doctor reassured him that all was well, but on 14 May the pain was so great that Pepys was forced to go to bed and take a 'glister' or enema. It did him little good, but 'at last, after two hours lying thus in the most extraordinary anguish, crying and roaring, I know not whether it was my great sweating that [made] me do it, but getting by chance among my other tumblings, upon my knees in bed, my pain began to grow less and so continued less and less, till an hour after I was in very little pain, but could break no wind nor make any water; and so continued and slept well at night'. Two days later the pain returned, as it did periodically over the next few months. It was a trying time. In the office he was 'busy till my brains ready to break with variety of business' and he was exasperated by the incompetence around him, believing 'the service like to suffer by other people's neglect'. Meanwhile, his pain made him 'mighty melancholy, to think of the ill state of my health'.

There was nothing for it but to see a doctor. Mr Hollier's diagnosis was not comforting. Having once assured Pepys 'that I could not possibly have the stone again, he tells me that he doth verily fear that I have it again and hath brought me something to dissolve it – which doth make me very much troubled and pray God to ease me'.[4] Dark memories of the dreadful operation in 1658 clouded Pepys's mind and he shuddered, but still the pain would not go away. By 1 July he had consulted another physician and received yet another diagnosis. Dr Burnett 'assures me that I have an ulcer either in the kidneys or bladder'. Pepys was given some unsatisfactory advice about what to do but left wondering why 'Mr Hollier should never say one word of this ulcer in all his life to me'. By 14 August that good doctor had changed his mind once more. Pepys was now suffering from 'nothing but cold in my legs breeding wind', which he had caught by wearing a dressing-gown. Clearly the problem, which was probably renal colic, was righting itself and, a week later, after Pepys had taken a dose of Epsom water, no more is heard of the complaint.

He pushed on. There were important people to see, important points to master, and a successful civil servant must be seen to be versatile. On 29 February 1664, Pepys had had a two-hour private conversation with Sir Philip Warwick, secretary to the Lord Treasurer. The record of the meeting contained in the *Diary* gives a vivid impression of two men of the highest calibre discussing questions of policy with the quick and serious intelligence of people used to dealing with such matters. Pepys shrewdly analysed Warwick's motives for talking to him in the first place, saying that 'he seemed to take pains to let me either understand the affairs of the Revenue or else to be a witness of his pains and care in stating of it'. Certainly, Warwick was thorough and Pepys's daunting interview gave him a clear and invigorating insight into the enhanced professionalism now being increasingly expected of senior civil servants.

For example, Warwick's conversation impressed on Pepys the importance of adequate record-keeping. 'He showed me,' Pepys wrote, 'many excellent collections of the state of the revenue in former Kings' and late times and the present.' Here was the security of fact, for from his records Warwick was able to prove 'how the very assessments between 1643 and 1659 . . . came to above 15 millions'. From such moments as these came Pepys's own growing realisation of the importance of being well versed in the immediate historical background of a problem and, in time, he would devote much of his formidable energy to establishing such matters for the Navy Office. His naturally enquiring mind had a genuine relish for the accumulation of detail but, for all his fascination with the past, Pepys's efforts in this direction were far more than a pleasing antiquarian diversion. Such knowledge was power and with it he would be able to defend both himself and the Navy Board from the loose, emotive attacks that would one day be launched by critical Members of Parliament determined to prove that Pepys and his fellows squandered the money provided for them.

Warwick also made Pepys aware of the importance of seeing the nation's difficulties in an international perspective. 'He showed me,' Pepys wrote, 'a discourse of his concerning the revenues of this and foreign states.' From his analysis of the incomes of the nation's competitors Warwick was able to show 'how that of Spain was great, but divided with his kingdoms and so came to little'. The wealth achieved by Louis XIV, on the other hand, might be envied but the conditions under which it was accumulated could not be reproduced in England since 'it is at the will of the Prince to tax what he will upon his people; which is not here'. The arbitrary and absolutist nature of French authority was, as always, deeply repugnant to the majority of Restoration Englishmen, while the sophistication of the Dutch remained an abiding source of fascination. Warwick managed to prove both to his and Pepys's satisfaction 'that the Hollanders have the best manner of tax, which is only upon the expense of provisions'. From the monies raised by this it was possible to 'conclude that no other tax is proper for England but a pound rate or excise upon the expense of provisions'.

The practice of writing memoranda was clearly coming of age, and Pepys would in time show himself to be one of its masters. As both Warwick and Pepys himself were all too painfully aware, the vaunted skills of civil servants were no grounds for complacency. Analysis could point to the most dangerous national weaknesses – the precise nature of the shortfall in tax revenues especially. Warwick went on to show Pepys exactly how serious this was by revealing to him 'every particular' of the problem and the fact that 'the £1,200,000 which the Parliament with so much ado did first vote to give the King, and since hath been re-examined by several committees of the present Parliament, is yet above £300,000 short of making up really to the King the £1,200,000'. There was no gainsaying Warwick's deeply disturbing conclusions (for all that the Treasury itself had not yet the structures and resources to solve them) and Pepys was obliged to confess that 'I believe him truly'. After all, his own daily experience at the Navy Board illustrated what Warwick had shown him, and both men knew that the consequences of the King's indebtedness were dire in the extreme. An active Parliament and an impoverished king were real threats to political stability.

Pepys had spent two hours with a mandarin, but if he was fascinated and concerned by what the conversation revealed, the nation's grandees could be distinctly uncomfortable people, and it was Clarendon, the Lord Chancellor himself, who gave Pepys his greatest scare at this time.[5] The zealous clerk of the acts believed he was acting on an official warrant when he had the trees in Clarendon Park, Wiltshire, marked with the navy's broad arrow as a sign that they should be felled. In fact, the Crown had reserved for its own use only such trees as had already been cut down, and the gouty Clarendon – fat, imperious and brilliant – created an angry scene about the problem one night at his sumptuous home in the Strand. Sandwich was present and tried to interpose on Pepys's behalf, but the Lord Chancellor would have none of it. He spoke against Pepys 'in the highest and most passionate manner that ever any man did speak, even to the not hearing of anything to be said to him'. Pepys had behaved 'most ungentlemanlike with him', Clarendon declared, and had sent Anthony Deane, 'the veriest fanatic that is in England', to mark the trees, 'on purpose to nose him'.

Pepys knew that his own intentions were entirely innocent, but how did one persuade the greatest representative of the law of England of this when that man was in a state of apoplectic fury? Pepys was terrified. There was no telling what he might lose: his honour, his job, his freedom. What on earth could he do? Sandwich advised him 'to wait presently upon my Lord and clear myself in the most perfect manner I could, with all submission and assurance that I am his creature both in this and all other things'. Pepys hurried over to Worcester House immediately but found Clarendon involved in business and, taking Sandwich's advice again, resolved to make a second attempt. He arrived just in time to find the Lord Chancellor leaving his dining room, and there 'I accosted him, telling him that I was the unhappy Pepys that had fallen into his high displeasure, and came to desire him to give me leave to make myself better understood to his Lordship – assuring him of my duty and service'. The replete Chancellor was in a good mood and 'he answered me very pleasingly: that he was confident upon the score of my Lord Sandwich's character of me – but that he had reason to think what he did, and desired me to call upon him some evening.' Pepys begged to be allowed to come that night, and Clarendon agreed.

Pepys duly returned to find the Chancellor still at work, but when he was done Clarendon himself called, '"Come, Mr Pepys, you and I will take a turn in the garden."' The Lord Chancellor was helped down the stairs and, going out into the garden, 'there walked with me I think above an hour, talking most friendly yet cunningly'. Pepys pleaded his case. 'I told him clearly how things were. How ignorant I was of his Lordship's concernment in it. How I did not do nor say one word singly; but what was done was the act of the whole Board.' Clarendon understood, and saying that he had thought Pepys must have been responsible for the outrage since he was the only member of the Navy Board not known to him personally, he made it clear that he had no very high opinion of Pepys's colleagues. He none the less thanked Pepys himself 'for my desire and pains to satisfy him'. Things were getting better and, when Pepys asked Clarendon with which of his servants he should consult to conclude the matter, 'he told me nobody, but would be glad to hear from me himself'. In a world of patronage, this was a strong hint and Pepys took it. 'I see what he means, and will make it my work to do him service in it,' he wrote, adding: 'Lord, to see how we poor wretches dare not do the King good service for fear of the greatness of these men.'

If Pepys was justified in being wary of Clarendon he always had the stomach for a fight with his colleagues. His energy, initiative and mastery of detail had roused their jealousy and now, as the country inched its way towards war, the principals of the Navy Office fought each other tooth and nail. The issue, as so often, was timber. For some years now Sir William Batten had done nicely out of his friendship with the great timber merchant William Wood. Wood had his monopoly, Batten had his commission, and both were pleased. Now the upstart clerk of the acts was rocking their comfortable arrangement.

Pepys had done his homework and, in Sir William Warren, had found a man to supply timber more cheaply than before. He had done all this on his own initiative, 'the whole business from beginning to end being done by me out of the office'. His lazy-minded colleagues had let the business go through on the nod, for Pepys had only had to present his case and they agreed to sign a contract for £3,000 worth of masts 'without the least care or consultation either of quality or price, number or need of them, only in general that it was good to have a store'. The plummy-voiced complacency of this last remark is almost audible, while Pepys's delight in outmanoeuvring his colleagues and discreetly lining his own pocket in the King's service is ringingly clear. 'But, good God! to see what a man might do, were I a knave.'[6] He was not a knave. He had merely played the accepted game with an adroitness the others could not match. He knew Warren's timber was the best, he knew it was cheap, and he knew he could prove it.

Soon he would have to. The continuing saga of his family's involvements in Brampton required Pepys's presence there and his colleagues took advantage of his being away. Batten now gave it out as his opinion that the navy already had a sufficient stock of masts. He gathered around him those who agreed with him and began to mutter about the superior quality of the masts supplied by his friend Wood. On his return, Pepys, had to defend himself and he did so with that strategic mastery of office politics that is the hallmark of a great administrator. He knew his facts and he had his allies. He wrote carefully reasoned letters to Coventry and George Carteret, both active and intelligent men, to prove that Warren had offered the better deal. His wood was cheaper, better in quality and was already lying in the river. The last point alone guaranteed a saving of £220 in transport costs, and the mutually profitable arrangement between Pepys and Warren continued.

The result of such dealing, apart from readying the country for war, was Pepys's own growing wealth and comfort. Pretty and valuable things began to appear in the house on Seething Lane: a silver state cup from the clerk of the ropeyard at Woolwich, cutlery, a pair of silver candlesticks, snuffers from Mr Harris the sailmaker, and that most delightful toy, a silver watch. 'Lord!' Pepys wrote in that tone which is so uniquely his, 'to see how much of my old folly and childishness hangs upon me still that I cannot forbear carrying my watch in my hand in the coach all this afternoon, and seeing what o'clock it is one hundred times.'

He had to be careful, though. Preserving moral standards in such a world was a delicate business and fine if not always very straight lines had to be drawn. It was customary for a clerk paying out money to receive a percentage, but bribes were a different matter. In this grey area Pepys set himself a rule (to which he did not always manage to adhere) that he would not accept money in advance as his condition for showing a contractor a favour, but if a contract were awarded on its merits (and such contracts were supposed to be made at full meetings of the board where all the factors involved could be 'maturely scanned') then he saw no harm in accepting either a fee or a percentage of the profits. It was all so agreeable – almost too agreeable sometimes. When Pepys went for a drink with Sir William Warren in the Sun tavern, the good merchant gave him a pair of gloves for Elizabeth. Pepys could feel something hard through the paper in which they were wrapped, said nothing and went on talking. Then, 'when I came home, Lord, in what pain I was to get my wife out of the room without bidding her go, that I might see what these gloves were, and by and by, she being gone, it proves a pair of white gloves for her and 40 pieces in good gold: which did so cheer my heart that I could eat no victuals almost for dinner'.[7]

Not that things always went so easily. At the close of 1667, Warren obtained Pepys's help in getting a contract for shipping hemp from Genoa.[8] Pepys was as usual perfectly clear in his own mind that the terms of the contract ensured that it was 'a service to the King'. The terms may indeed have been favourable to the Crown but the outcome, as far as Warren was concerned, was not. He made a loss on the deal and was therefore only able to pay Pepys £60 out of the £100 he had promised him. This called for tactful handling, and Pepys's account of the matter in his *Diary* shows what a nimble negotiator he had become.

First of all he told Warren that he 'would demand nothing of his promises though they were much greater, nor would have thus much [i.e. the £60], but if he could afford to give me but fifty pieces it should suffice'. Warren knew his man and brought Pepys 'something in a paper'. It was obvious what this 'something' was but haste would be unseemly, and 'I told him that I did not insist on anything, and therefore prayed him to consult his ability before he did part with them and so I refused them one or twice till he did a third time offer them, and then I took them.' With the money handed over, it was Warren's turn to angle for a favour and he said that he would present Pepys with another £50 'if I would undertake to get him £500 paid on his bills'. Pepys played the problem deftly. 'I told him I would by no means have any promise of the kind, but that I should do my utmost for nothing to do him that justice.' The implication, of course, was that if Pepys succeeded Warren would quietly pay him for the favour. The deal had been struck, 'and so we parted, he owning himself mightily engaged to me for my kind usage of him'. This was how a man became rich, and by the start of 1665, Pepys found he was worth £1,349. The Puritan in him rejoiced 'to think how God doth bless us every day more and more'.

It was surely right to spend a little of this wealth on worldly finery, and the man who now chatted confidently with his merchant friends on the Exchange was determined to cut a fine figure. Along with the periwig (so glorious an addition that the Duke of York claimed he did not recognise him in it), Pepys now went about his business in a dark suit trimmed with scarlet ribbon and a velvet cloak. All this was rich (as well as being painfully expensive) but it was not ostentatious and, so dressed, Pepys could make an impression on the world and advance his career. His ability to bring order where there was confusion was widely appreciated, and nowhere more so than among the members of the Tangier Committee, a body that was now to move close to the centre of Pepys's concerns.

At first it had been hoped that the port would be a base for a lucrative trade in corn, hides, oil, copper and such luxuries as gold and feathers. None the less, Tangier soon proved to be a considerable liability. It was remote, poorly defended and surrounded by hostile Arab forces. Above all, it was under-capitalised and expensive to run. It was reckoned that maintaining Tangier cost the government some £70,000 a year but this was insufficient and the outpost became something of a Cinderella among the English plantations. Many of the two thousand men in its crumbling garrison had been lured there under false pretences and were obliged to live off rotting victuals unwanted elsewhere. A large proportion of the six hundred civilians were criminals and minor political offenders, and problems proliferated both on the ground and back in London among the members of the Tangier Committee itself.

The treasurer of the committee, for example – Pepys's friend the elegant Mr Povey – was altogether less competent as an accountant than he was as a host. The books for the Tangier Committee were in a terrible mess. 'Such accounts,' the dismayed Pepys observed, 'I never did see; or hope again to see in my days.'[9] High words were exchanged around the committee table, and a rattled Povey, wholly unable to defend himself, eventually took Pepys to one side and offered him his post on the condition that they could share the profits. This was a golden offer, as Pepys was fully aware, but it would mean strenuous work. He gave the matter deep consideration. The Tangier Committee would take up valuable time and energy that might be better spent on the navy, and Pepys was in a 'doubtful condition what to think of it'. There was much to-ing and fro-ing, much canvassing of opinion, but eventually the matter was decided. At the meeting of the Tangier Committee on 20 March 1665, Povey stood down declaring that in order that 'the work might be better done and with more quiet to him, he desired, by approbation of the Duke, he might resign his place to Mr Pepys'. The Duke of York was more than happy to give his consent and the other grandees concurred.

From now on, Tangier would play a not inconsiderable part in Pepys's career, if for no other reason than that it proved itself 'one of the best flowers' in the carefully tended garden of his perquisites. The short-term profits to be made from it were considerable for a man like Pepys and he gleefully recorded in his *Diary* the rapid enrichment it brought him. For example, the victualling contract, which he was allowed to draw up himself, brought him £300 a year 'which doth overjoy me'. Nor was it only personal gain that brought him pleasure. Pepys brought his customary efficiency and loyalty to the task and claimed he could 'with a safe conscience say that I have therein saved the King £5,000 per annum'. He did not add that he had been complicit in fixing the price (thereby making the nation pay for his profits) or that he prevaricated endlessly in paying Povey his share.

It says much about Pepys's belief in his own abilities (as well as the views of his superiors) that he took on the role of treasurer to the Tangier Committee two weeks after war had been officially declared on the Dutch. In this, too, the Duke of York would place a great deal of his trust in Pepys, the rising bureaucrat of the Navy Board. The Duke had also conducted a deft Parliamentary campaign to raise funds for his war. He employed Sir Thomas Clifford to redirect the interest of a Commons committee from the decay of the cloth trade to the general decline of English business then packed the committee itself with Members known to have anti-Dutch sentiments. So successful was this that, with the help of carefully manipulated accounts provided (with Pepys's help) by the Navy Board, the House of Commons accepted how the 'honour, safety and future wealth' of England demanded that the country go to war. In order to support their enthusiasm the Members made vast grants of supply: £2.5 million in the session of 1664–5 and a further Additional Aid of £1.25 million in October 1665. These sums would prove difficult to collect, however, and desperate shortages of money seriously hampered the immense efforts Pepys was required to make over the coming months.

Yet the Parliamentary grants of supply were of unprecedented amounts. There were those who saw in them an unrivalled opportunity for significantly overhauling the mechanisms of the nation's economy and, in particular, of solving the ever-pressing problem of raising adequate credit to fund the government's borrowing requirement. Up until this time, and in the absence of the state and civic banks that so facilitated trade in such advanced European cities as Venice, Amsterdam and Hamburg, King Charles had been largely dependent for his borrowings on individual wealthy financiers like Thomas Viner and Edward Blackwell, London grandees who operated a range of services that might loosely be described as 'banking'. Clarendon wrote of them as 'men known to be so rich, and of so good reputation, that all the money of the kingdom would be trusted or deposited in their hands'.[10] This money they would lend to the King on the security of his tax revenue.

Clarendon went on to relate how they would be summoned before Charles when there was a need 'for present money'. There then followed elegant and gentlemanly negotiations based, Clarendon averred, on mutual advantage, respect and trust. It was all very satisfactory, both to the grandees and to the Stuarts, 'for there is nothing surer, than that the confidence of the King's justice, and the unquestionable reputation of the Lord Treasurer's honour and integrity, was the true foundation of that credit which supplied all His Majesty's necessities and occasions; and His Majesty always treated those men very graciously, as his very good servants, and all his ministers looked upon them as very honest and valuable men'. There were those who strongly disagreed, and asserted that the financiers, charging what was widely regarded as an extortionate 10 per cent rate of interest, were profiting unreasonably from their stranglehold on the nation's finances. Among these critics was Pepys's old boss Sir George Downing. Downing's experiences both at the Exchequer and in Holland had convinced him of the need for institutional reform. The ease and sophistication with which the Dutch government raised credit particularly impressed him and he saw the need to solicit funds in England from a wider public than the great financiers along with the necessity of creating some form of national bank.

This was not a new cry, but the efficiency of the enemy was

a spur to action and Downing taunted his fellow countrymen by claiming: 'you are not so good husbands of your money nor do you lay it out so carefully and with that advantage as they'.[11] His proposals for reform were neat, simple and apparently commonsensical. Parliament should guarantee war loans made to the King by private individuals and interest should be paid on these regularly. Official, numbered receipts would be issued for monies so deposited, and loans would be repaid in strict sequence by Exchequer officials administering funds specially set aside for the purpose.

Downing was a vigorous and persuasive campaigner for his cause, but for all that he got his way, there were those who harboured severe doubts about his scheme and his boast that 'he would make his Exchequer the best and the greatest bank in Europe'. Clarendon, with the intuition of a deep conservative, believed that the close involvement of Parliament in Downing's scheme tarnished the authority and independence of the King and decried his plan as 'introductive to a commonwealth, and not fit for a monarchy'. More modest men had different objections. Pepys, all too familiar with the bureaucratic torpor of the Exchequer, agreed with a colleague who declared that 'it will be impossible to make the Exchequer ever a true bank', and he had, besides, another objection shared by many of his contemporaries. The King could all too easily renege on his debts and Pepys himself, fearful of 'the unsafe condition of a bank under a monarch', preferred at this time to keep his own savings in an iron chest in the cellars at Seething Lane.

He was perhaps untypically cautious, but all the time that men such as he were unprepared to invest their money on the nation's behalf – to fund what would eventually become the national debt – the immense difficulties caused by inadequate credit would remain. As far as the navy was concerned, Pepys and his colleagues would have to deal with them. Indeed, they would have to deal with an alarming multitude of problems as they readied the biggest fleet the country had ever known for combat on an unprecedented scale. Constantly crippled by financial difficulties, they would have to ensure the efficiency of the dockyards on which the war effort ultimately depended. Pepys especially had already expended great efforts in starting to solve the most basic problems: the deteriorating condition of many of the ships, the depleted stocks of timber, canvas, rope and masts, the endemic graft, corruption and incompetence. Constantly burdened by a mountainous £1.3 million of debt, he and his colleagues had slowly won back the confidence of their suppliers. They had even been able to add two Second Rates to the fleet, the *Royal Oak* and the *Royal Catherine*. Now they would have to strain to complete one more Second Rate, five Third Rates and five lesser ships, and do this against a marked reduction in trade and the consequent fall in government revenue.

The problem of raising credit simply would not go away, and nothing, it seemed, could be done. Even the Lord Treasurer threw up his hands in despair when Pepys pleaded to the Privy Council for money. '"Why, what means all this, Mr Pepys?" he cried. "This is true, you say, but what would you have me do? I have given all I can for my life. Why will not people lend their money? Why will they not trust the King as well as Oliver? Why do our prizes [captured enemy ships] come to nothing that yielded so much heretofore?"'[12] This was the cry of a man who simply did not have the mental qualities to face a new and unprecedented challenge: the capacity to adapt, analyse and innovate – qualities that Pepys himself was learning and which he would soon be required to develop to the full.

Even now, as the country moved towards war, the provision of credit was far from being his only problem. Inevitably, Pepys also became involved in the difficulties of mustering men and ships. All the nation's seamen (with certain jealously guarded exceptions) were liable for service, as were merchant vessels. Not everyone, however, was prepared to accept these obligations and, on 15 January, Pepys appeared with Sir William Penn before members of the Privy Council to argue that ships of the Levant Company should be prevented from sailing to the Mediterranean because 'the King having resolved to have 130 ships out by the spring, he must have above 20 of them merchantmen'. So far only a mere dozen merchant ships had been secured and there was, besides, a crying need to enlist the men who would sail them.

Penn himself had prepared the report on this and consequently delivered it. Pepys listened grudgingly to him, saying that he 'spoke pretty well to the purpose, but with so much leisure and gravity as was tiresome'. The in-fighting and grudges of the Navy Board did not let up even in time of war. Meanwhile, Pepys himself was soon looking into the matter of the Barking and Greenwich fishermen and trying to determine whether some of their number might be recruited without affecting London's supply of fish. 'I am glad of the occasion to make me understand something of it,' he wrote, and midnight of 3 March saw Pepys labouring over a memorandum on the subject and arguing that these men had no justified claim to be free of the pressgangs, those terrible posses who seized men and boys from homebound merchantmen, wherries on the Thames and even the rural fields.

The press-gangs troubled Pepys's conscience and stirred his humanity.[13] He knew that their existence was morally indefensible and administratively essential. Warfare at sea required the recruitment of some 30,000 men and the Privy Council issued orders for a general impress. Whenever this occurred Parliament raised loud criticisms, but throughout his career Pepys had to issue orders to the effect that 'the impresting of men for supply of the King's ships not to be stopped, notwithstanding the enquiries on foot in Parliament, touching the matter'. As a careful civil servant he sent repeated warnings to press officers to avoid the legal problems that would follow an over-enthusiastic pursuit of their task and, when matters got out of hand, intervened personally to check the worst abuses. For example, he took action when Charterhouse schoolboys were 'seduced from Southwark Fair and shipped against their wills'. On another occasion, when a band of men was impressed without being paid, Pepys did the only thing his conscience dictated and 'did there out of my own purse disperse £15 to pay for their pressing and diet last night and this morning'. The whole business grieved him. 'To see poor, patient labouring men and housekeepers leaving poor wives and families, taken up on a sudden by strangers, was very hard . . . a great tyranny.'

Crews recruited in such ways were said to be fit only for rats, but their numbers were supplemented by a surprising number of volunteers (many of them eager for prize-money) and all were under the command of a bewildering array of non-commissioned officers, chief among whom were the 'masters', warrant officers appointed by the Navy Board and responsible for navigation and the proper working of the sails and rigging. When such seasoned veterans were promoted to be commissioned officers they were known (as were the surviving officers of the Cromwellian navy) as 'tarpaulins'. Pepys was fully aware that there was continuous friction between these professionals and the so-called 'Cavalier' or 'gentlemen' officers, who were often the younger sons of the aristocracy and owed their places to patronage rather than experience. These 'gentlemen commanders' had been encouraged by a royal initiative of 1661 – it was part of a much wider campaign to move aristocratic patronage back to the centre of influence after the Interregnum – but it brought with it many problems. There was not only the rivalry with the tarpaulins but factional in-fighting of the most ferocious sort which, like these men's frequent absence at court and demands for privilege, caused severe disciplinary problems. In time Pepys was to develop firm views on this issue and make significant efforts to solve the problem but, for the moment, he was obliged to watch the 'gentlemen' squabbling among each other in the most dangerous way.

Gentlemen and old salts alike had to be fed and watered, and victualling was yet another of the board's responsibilities. Its room for manoeuvre here was severely limited for the supply of victuals had reverted after the Interregnum to being a monopoly. From his huge complex of stores and slaughterhouses on Tower Hill, Denis Gauden was expected to supply the entire fleet with beef, pork, biscuit, peas and beer at the rate of sixpence a day per man in peace-time and eight pence during hostilities. War put an intolerable strain on this system. The sheer quantity of food and drink required was enormous. A navy of 16,000 men required 500 tuns of water every week, but this often went putrid and the effects of the widespread dysentery that resulted were revolting and disabling in the extreme. Beer was often of poor quality, food frequently rotted, and bad provisioning might even result in a fleet's having to return to port. This was yet another problem Pepys would eventually address.

The combined pressures of warfare and running what was effectively a vast business were exposing the most alarming difficulties – difficulties that would soon have very serious political repercussions too. Under these circumstances it is hardly surprising that Pepys's forebodings about the forthcoming war were deep and constantly expressed in both his *Diary* and his correspondence. It was all agonisingly difficult and intensely worrying. He had laboured mightily and was becoming indeed, as the great Albemarle declared, 'the right hand of the Navy here'. He had sat up night after night by guttering candles and, with painful eyes, drafted memoranda. He had consulted with the greatest in the land. He had turned his seemingly inexhaustible intelligence to a host of problems.

But he knew, deep in his heart, that the navy was barely ready for what was now expected of it. None the less, a war against the Dutch had been decided upon and 'we all seem to desire it', Pepys wrote, 'as thinking ourselves to have advantages at present over them; for my part I dread it'.[14]

CHAPTER SEVEN

The Years of Agony

The Dutch and English fleets engaged off Lowestoft in June 1665. The sound of gunfire could be heard as far south as the capital but news of the battle itself came in slowly. For uncertain sweaty summer days the streets of London were loud with rumour. The English had won, people said. The crew of the *Charity* had shamefully surrendered. Others knew for certain that Lord Sandwich had been killed. Pepys bided his time. At the start of June 1665, dressed in a new silk suit, which had cost him a princely £24, he entertained an unknown girlfriend at Tothill Fields where he did 'as much as was safe with my flower' before escorting her home, after which he sat at his desk too full of remembered delight to concentrate on his correspondence. The following day he set about helping a clerk who had been wrongfully arrested, and on Sunday 4 June he cast up his accounts and found he was worth £1,400 – the richest he had ever been. There might have been a lot more money in the future but Pepys believed he had lost a lucrative victualling contract and was annoyed. The accounts of the Tangier Committee were in good order, however, and Pepys was congratulated on what he had achieved. And still the long, hot summer hung over everything. Electric storms lit up the night skies, while in Drury Lane Pepys saw 'two or three houses marked with a red cross upon the doors, and "Lord have mercy upon us" writ there'. The plague had arrived in town.

On 8 June, news of the battle at last came through. Pepys heard it first at the Lord Treasurer's office. The Duke of York, Prince Rupert, Sandwich and Coventry were all well. This was confirmed when Albemarle, 'like a man out of himself with content', repeated the news to Pepys. The Dutch had failed to get advantage of the wind so were unable to use their fireships. The mighty navies, high-pooped and gilded, their coloured ensigns straining at their mastheads, had engaged with terrible ferocity. Pepys the inveterate landsman noted down the details, copying out Coventry's report of the action and then summarising it in his *Diary*. He wrote of how the Earl of Falmouth, Lord Muskerry and Richard Boyle had been killed by a single chain-shot as they stood on the deck of the Duke's ship. Then he added the gory detail that rumour gave. The blood and brains of the dying men had spattered the Duke of York's face, while the flying head of Mr Boyle had knocked the Duke himself to the deck, 'as some say'. There was more to come. 'Admiral Opdam blown up. Trump killed . . . all the rest of their admirals . . . killed. We have taken or sunk as it is believed, about 24 of their best ships. Killed and taken near 8 or 10,000 men; and lost, we think, not above 700'.[1]

To the ecstatic clerk of the acts, whose ceaseless labours had made the encounter possible, the battle of Lowestoft was 'a great victory, never known in the world'. For the moment Pepys did not realise the full implications, did not see that the forty-three fleeing Dutch vessels that he was told had arrived safely in Texell would be the core of a revived Dutch navy, the centrepiece of a renewed struggle. Nor, for the moment, did he think of the cost and the immense financial problems ahead caused by the fall in tax revenues from the decline in trade, losses to Dutch privateers, the plague, the closing of the Baltic and the pressing of seamen. This was a time for celebration. Pepys ordered a great bonfire to be lit at the Navy Office gate. There was a party, dancing in the streets, and Pepys went down to distribute four shillings to the revellers. It was all 'mighty merry', and he went to bed that night 'with my heart at great rest and quiet, saving that the consideration of the victory is too great for me presently [immediately] to comprehend'.

The invisible enemy was less easily routed. Plague deaths rose with the summer heat, and by July over two hundred stinking corpses were being borne through the London streets each week. Preachers promised their sombre congregations that there was an afterlife, but many had little time to prepare for it. On 17 June, as Pepys was travelling through London in a hackney coach, he was suddenly jerked to a halt as his driver stumbled to the ground complaining that he was 'very sick and almost blind'. Helping the victim was too dangerous. Self-preservation must come before compassion, so 'I light and went into another coach, with a sad heart for the poor man and trouble for myself'. A few days later it seemed as if the whole city was trying to flee. Wagons and coaches crowded Cripplegate where Pepys stopped off at the Cross Keys for a drink and had a pleasing chat with the tapster's wife. In the middle of death, he was in life – abundant life, but he took precautions variously sombre and sensible all the same. He chewed tobacco. His mother, in London for a visit, was returned to Brampton. Elizabeth was despatched to Woolwich. Coventry quit the capital with the rest of the court, but Pepys determined to sit matters out, to work hard and to play hard.

The absence of Elizabeth had a predictable effect. As the mortality bills soared to over a thousand a week and the sick were sealed in their houses until their corpses could be carried away for night burial in plague pits, Pepys sought out sex. He went to Hampstead with Mary from the Harp and Ball at Charing Cross and found himself 'much pleased'. She was pretty and compliant, willing like so many in this terrible time to seize the day and offer Pepys 'what pleasure almost I would with her'. Mrs Bagwell, too, was willing. He saw her on 8 August when she went with him to his office 'en lequel jo haze todo which I had a corason a hazer con ella'.* And, in addition to his own affairs, Pepys was asked to arrange a romance.

It had been agreed that Sandwich's daughter, Lady Jeminah Sandwich, should marry Sir George Carteret's oldest boy.[2] Sandwich himself was tied up with the fleet and had asked Pepys to arrange the details of the match. This was an important and responsible task – the King and the Duke of York were both interested in its outcome – and Pepys soon concluded arrangements that were highly satisfactory to both sides. Carteret in particular was delighted, and for a while the haughty grandee became 'so light, so fond, so merry, so boyish' that Pepys was entranced. He was even more delighted by the company of Lady Carteret, generous and charming as she was, and clearly determined to play the perfect mother-in-law. Perhaps she was partly trying to make up for her son, an unprepossessing and shy youth who clearly had no sexual experience and was terrified by the whole business. Pepys met him when he was invited over to the Essex house of Lady Sandwich's sister where the interested parties were staying. Young Carteret was a pathetic specimen. 'But, Lord', wrote Pepys, the seducer of Mrs Bagwell and a dozen others, 'what silly discourse we had by the way as to love-matters, he being the most awkward man ever I met with in my life as to that business.' Pepys

* 'where I had everything I desired to have with her'

would have to help all he could, and what followed were scenes that could have come from a Restoration comedy.

When it was suggested that the two young people be left alone to begin their courting, Pepys, fearing a ridiculous and perhaps an upsetting scene, advised against it and took the young man aside for an avuncular talk. Did young Carteret like the girl? The youth just managed to stammer out that he did 'but Lord! in the dullest, insipid manner that ever lover did'. Clearly he needed some help, and the following day Pepys again took him aside and, walking up and down the gallery, showed him how he should always lead his future wife by the hand then taught him how to turn a compliment. Carteret was grateful. These things did not come naturally to him, he said, and he proved the point when, as they went to church, he failed to pluck up sufficient courage to take his fiancée's hand. That evening the couple were left alone together (one of the children in the house accidentally shutting the door on them) but the following day it was clear that the courtship had not been a success. Young Carteret had failed to impress or even to rouse pity, and the Lady Jeminah merely answered Pepys's enquiry with a blush and a statement to the effect that she would always honour her parents' wishes.

The wedding was held on the last day of July, which saw Pepys up 'very betimes' and dressed in a new silk suit trimmed with gold buttons and gold lace. He and the Carteret parents had the unfortunate experience of being stuck on the Isle of Dogs for nearly three hours and they arrived at the church just in time to see the wedding party leave. The bride looked 'mighty sad' and a concerned Pepys put this down to her natural gravity. He was clearly impressed by the aristocratic solemnity of the whole occasion, however, the ability of these people to enjoy themselves without becoming raucous, and Pepys's own behaviour – so unselfconsciously recorded – suggests something of the vulgarity of the parvenu. He got into the bridegroom's chamber while Carteret undressed and 'there was very merry', presumably cracking the sort of jokes men are wont to make on such occasions. He then saw the couple bedded, kissed the bride and watched as the curtains round the bed were solemnly drawn, 'and so good-night'. Here was a manner of life Pepys was not fully used to and he was impressed. 'The modesty and gravity of this business was so decent, that it was to me, indeed, ten times more delightful than if it had been twenty times more merry and jovial.' He was very satisfied too with the part he had played in arranging it all.

The following morning he went to greet the blushing couple then spent a pleasant day before returning to London, but even amid these festivities the horrors of the plague could not be forgotten. Some 1,800 Londoners had died of it the previous week. When Pepys returned to the wedding party a few days later everybody asked him what the mortality bills had risen to and, as he repeated the dreadful number – 2,010 – so it seemed 'it was a sad question to be so often asked me'. There were, too, appalling stories of the plague to tell. Pepys was told how the maidservant of a local landowner had absconded from the pest-house. Because she did not answer a knocking on her door it was at first believed she was dead and arrangements were made for her burial. No one, however, would make themselves responsible for interring the corpse, and the worried landowner was wandering distractedly over the nearby common when, to his utter horror, he bumped into the poor girl. She was immediately obliged to return to the hospital in one of the close-curtained pest coaches, but her misfortunes were not yet over. Some lively young men passing by believed the coach contained a beauty travelling incognito, and one of them 'thrust his head . . . into her coach to look, and there saw somebody look very ill, and in a sick dress and stunk mightily'.

This stink of death was everywhere in London and, as

August waxed insufferably hot, the mortality bills reached a terrible six thousand a week. The authorities did what they could. They ordered that fires in movable pans should be placed in the streets so that disinfectants could be burned on them. Makeshift pest-houses were built. A small army of men dug mass burial pits and carted the corpses to them. Wednesdays and Fridays were given over to fasting and public prayers, but still the plague raged on. All efforts to halt it seemed hopeless. Unburied bodies piled up in Greenwich and armed watchmen forbade access to them. Pepys's compassion was stirred and, along with it, his curiosity.

He saw the brutalising effects of mass suffering and was appalled that the pestilence was 'making us more cruel to one another than if we were dogs'. And, as always, he felt drawn to witness events for himself. One day he went over to Moorfields 'to see (God forgive my presumption) whether I could see any dead corpse going to the grave; but as God would have it, did not'. The sense of London-wide agony was appalling. How this once bustling city was reduced! 'Everybody's looks and discourse in the street is of death and nothing else, and so few people going up and down, that the town is like a place distressed – and forsaken.' In his correspondence Pepys was even more eloquent and wrote of:

> . . . having stayed in the city till above 7400 died in one week, and of them above 6000 of the plague, and little noise heard day nor night but tolling of bells; till I could walk Lumber Street [Lombard Street] and not meet twenty persons from one end to the other, and not fifty upon the Exchange; till whole families (ten and twelve together) have been swept away; till my very physician, Dr Burnet, who undertook to secure me against any infection (having survived the month of his own being shut up) died himself of the plague; till the nights (though much lengthened) are grown too short to conceal the burials of those that died the day before,

> people being thereby constrained to borrow daylight for that service; lastly, till I could find neither meat nor drink safe, the butcheries being everywhere visited, my brewer's house shut up, and my baker with his whole family dead of the plague.[3]

Pepys's *Diary* was the recipient of his more prurient secrets: his fondling his maid Susan's breasts one Sunday morning when she was combing his hair, his love-making with Mrs Bagwell, his attempt to seduce the married daughter of an elderly waterman, and his erotic fantasies about Lady Castlemaine. The image of this aristocratic whore continued to stalk his dreams. Indeed, she provided him with the best dream he ever had, 'which was, that I had my Lady Castemaine in my arms and was admitted to use all the dalliance I desired with her, and then dreamed that this could not be awake but that it was only a dream'. But even reverie was underscored by death. 'Since it was a dream,' Pepys wrote, 'and that I took so much real pleasure in it, what a happy thing it would be, if when we are in our graves (as Shakespeare resembles it), we could dream, and dream but such dreams as this – that then we should not need to be so fearful of death as we are in this plague-time.'

The remaining officers of the Navy Board begged that their meetings might be held in the relative safety of Deptford or Greenwich, for they had much to attend to. Hostilities against the Dutch were to continue, and Sandwich and Sir William Penn were despatched to intercept the Dutch Atlantic fleet and seize the rich cargoes of their East India ships. The upshot of both plans was disastrous. Sandwich failed to engage with the Atlantic convoy. Worse, when he tried to corner the East India merchantmen, a misunderstanding resulted in his being fired on by the supposedly neutral Danish guns in the port. While the Dutch delighted in a new surge of confidence, the English limped home in ships disgracefully lacking in victuals. Everything was done to make good this latter defect and Sandwich was again despatched to chase de Ruyter as he sailed out to escort his countrymen home. Days of tension followed until finally the news came through that Sandwich had met with part of the Dutch Atlantic fleet and captured two valuable prizes and a number of lesser vessels. Pepys was overjoyed. Money for the board and security for himself again appeared to be assured. He celebrated at an evening party held in Captain Cocke's house.[4] It was a delightful occasion attended among others by Lord Brouncker and a comparatively new acquaintance of Pepys's – John Evelyn.

Evelyn was a figure who was to exert a profound and civilising influence over Pepys. The sheer delight Pepys took in his company is suggested by the pleasure he and the rest had while Evelyn made up nonsense verses with the utmost dexterity as the party got into its stride. All of these serious and high-minded men were in unbuttoned mood, relaxing after days of tension, and so relieved to be sharing each other's company that Pepys counted the evening 'one of the best times of my life wherein I was the fullest of true sense of joy'. But it was not only laughter that Evelyn brought Pepys. This great virtuoso – an amateur of art and gardening, books and prints, science and public life – was a 'very fine gentleman' and as generous with arcane information and scholarly advice as he was efficient in fulfilling his duties as commissioner of the sick and wounded in the current war. Together, Pepys and Evelyn would plan for the building of the great naval hospital at Greenwich (one of the supreme achievements of Restoration architecture) while Evelyn also fostered Pepys's innate tastes as a scholar and connoisseur. The two men were, in a sense, complementary opposites. Pepys was extrovert, professionally committed to public affairs, and saw culture largely as an activity for his leisure hours. Evelyn, by contrast, was more withdrawn, scholarly, and motivated by a gentleman's desire to do his bit for the public good. Each needed the other, and there grew up between them a tender and lasting friendship.

Meanwhile, for Pepys at least, there were more strenuous matters to deal with.[5] Rather than mounting a comprehensive attack on the Dutch, Sandwich had sailed with his prizes for home. Tactically, this was a sensible move, but the nearly £500,000 worth of stolen spices now making for the English coast were an irresistible temptation to him and his fellow officers. They all knew that they were supposed to await the decision of the Royal Commission for Prizes before enriching themselves with booty, but at a hurriedly called conference in Sandwich's cabin a number of the flag-officers resolved on immediate action rather than waiting on the ponderous but proper course of events. That Sandwich himself was deeply in debt was no doubt a spur to his greed, but what followed was the disgraceful spectacle of senior officers ransacking the holds of the Dutch ships and seizing plundered goods worth anything up to £4,000 a man. Having thus illicitly lined their own capacious pockets, the still rich East Indiamen were then directed to Erith and the less rapacious hands of the prize commissioners.

Pepys himself, accompanied by Lord Brouncker and Captain Cocke, came down to view the newly docked flotilla and declared it 'a very fine thing to behold, being above 100 ships, great and small, with the flag-ships of each squadron, distinguished by their several flags of their main, fore or mizzen masts'. Sandwich, still dressed in his nightgown, received Pepys and his companions politely while muttering complaints about the lack of victuals that had forced him to turn for home. Soon this appeared a small poverty compared to the immense riches stuffed in the holds of the Dutch ships, and Pepys, ever the businessman, saw an irresistible opportunity to enrich himself. He swiftly secured a loan of £500 from the Admiral's deputy treasurer and then, in partnership with Captain Cocke, bargained for £1,000 worth of spices.

He surely knew that he was in danger of breaking the law, and knew, too, how desperately every last penny of prize-money was needed for a navy ruinously starved of cash. He was determined to enrich himself all the same, and if he had doubts at all it was not about his own actions but about the probity of Captain Cocke. As Pepys bought another £1,000 worth of booty from a compliant Sandwich, so he warned My Lord against the captain with whom he prepared to buy yet more of the spoils. Pepys began to feel guilty all the same. He knew he had to cover his back and he sought Sandwich's assurance that My Lord had the King's own permission to 'break baulk' and sell off the booty in this way. Pepys would be aware soon enough of the perilous position in which he had placed himself. Already there were mutterings among more virtuous men, and then he learned that Captain Cocke's share of the prizes had been seized by the King's officers. Soon Pepys, too, would be visited by the law.

The officers arrived on the evening of 7 October. Pepys himself was busy dealing with two wagon loads of prize-goods, which had just arrived at Greenwich when the customs men demanded their surrender. He protested in vain, and the goods were impounded. A few days later, four more of his wagons were arrested in front of Greenwich church, and serious worry compounded his embarrassment when he learned later that evening that the King and the Duke of York were furious at what Sandwich had done. Pepys might hope that 'there be no foul meaning towards your Lordship', but he soon found that matters were far more serious than he feared. The temper of the commissioner for prizes was now 'mighty high', and Pepys learned that the King himself had given orders that all the booty illicitly taken from the Dutch ships should be investigated, that warrants were out for the seizure of these goods, and that Captain Cocke's had already been distrained.

The whole matter was now common knowledge and the public mood was ugly. The people knew as well as Pepys that 'prisoners and sick men that are recovered' were lying destitute before the Navy Office gates night and day. There was no money to relieve them and it was not enough that Pepys should try to fob them off with the small change from his own pockets. Violence and anger were seething everywhere, and Pepys wrote to Coventry to tell him that 'the whole company of the *Breda* are now breaking the windows of our office . . . swearing they will not budge without money'. Debt, destitution and angry despair were all around him. The stolen booty was the only hope of salvation for the navy, and that booty had been plundered a second time by those who knew better than anyone how badly it was needed.

Events were now starkly to show how true this was. The Dutch fleet had put out to sea and it was necessary for the English to pursue it once more. Urgent orders were received from Albemarle to ready the fleet, but only a third of the ships had men and victuals sufficient to sail. Sandwich became the enemy of the moment. My Lord was the admiral who had failed to annihilate the Dutch and was now the man who had deserted the fleet for Oxford, where he was pleading his case before the King. Above all, Sandwich was the man who against all the rules had 'broken baulk' to enrich himself at the expense of a desperate nation. His delighted enemies waited for his fall, and Pepys, his fearful client, resolved to save his own skin. It was with 'extraordinary inward joy' that he sold out his entire interest in the booty to Captain Cocke for a profit of £500. A deal with Denis Gauden the victualler secured him a similar amount and, by carefully tending the garden of his perquisites, Pepys found himself, at the end of 1665, worth something over £4400. 'I have never lived so merrily (besides that I never got so much) as I have done this plague time,' he wrote in his *Diary*, and while

Sandwich was pardoned by the King then sent as Ambassador Extraordinary to Spain, Pepys himself glowed in the royal favour as Charles gave him 'thanks for your good service all this year'.

That service was now to be redoubled, for the recent engagements had shown that the navy suffered from two crippling disabilities: want of victuals and lack of money. The first problem called forth one of Pepys's most sterling sentences. 'Englishmen, and more especially seamen,' he wrote, 'love their bellies above everything else, and therefore it must always be remembered in the management of the victualling of the Navy that to make any abatement from them in the quantity or agreeableness of the victuals is to discourage and provoke them in the tenderest point, and will sooner render them disgusted with the King's service then any one other hardship that can be put upon them.'[6] Clearly something had to be done to cure the victualling problem, and Pepys's solution called forth all that was most characteristic of him: his energy, his mastery of detail and, above all, the incisiveness and creativity of his intellect. While the virtuosi gathered in the Royal Society were laying bare the secrets of the natural world, Pepys was discovering important rules in the human world of administration and, in particular, the need for a balance between strong central authority and delegated responsibility.

It was necessary to see first of all why things had gone wrong. It would have been easy enough to blame the shortage of victuals on the monopolist Denis Gauden – easy but unfair. Unjustified criticism would not solve the problem and Pepys had the sort of intelligence that looked deeper than personalities and probed structural faults instead. This was where the changes had to be made. It became clear to him that Gauden's outfit was more or less competent to victual the navy during peace-time but that it was quite impossible for him to raise the required credit adequately to feed and water the 30,000 men required in time of war. Carefully marshalling his facts, Pepys tabulated how Gauden had been unable to supply victuals to the level he had estimated. It was unrealistic to suppose that he could, and dangerous to continue with a system where the 'honour and wealth of King and kingdom depend without check upon the understanding, credit, diligence, integrity and health of one man, whose failure in any of these five circumstances inevitably overthrows all'. This, when pointed out, was self-evident, but to isolate a problem was not to solve it. The Duke of York made the common-sense suggestion that other merchants should combine with Gauden. Pepys dutifully sought out likely candidates, but they all replied that the risks were too great. A Royal Commission was then proposed, but Pepys was no more enamoured of this. For all his shortcomings, Gauden had proved himself more efficient than earlier committees set up to do his job, and who was to say that men suitable for such a committee could be found anyway?

'My own proposition,' Pepys wrote, 'is that a person should be established in every victualling-port, on behalf and at the charge of His Majesty, as a Surveyor of the Victualler's action in that port.' These regional officers would then report back to a central figure, who would thereby know and have overall responsibility for the state of victualling of the whole navy at any one time. It is not difficult to guess whom Pepys had in mind for this vitally important role. He had already drawn up a scale of pay for the regional surveyors and suggested that the surveyor-general should be paid the generous sum of £300 a year. It would mean a lot more responsibility but it would also make Pepys's job easier and, above all, the post would secure him a rich and reliable reward. He argued his case for a new approach to the victualling problem so thoroughly that a relieved King and council willingly approved it, while Pepys also recommend himself so adroitly for the job of surveyor-general that, on 27 October 1665, he was appointed to it.

Among other matters, he had now to deal directly with that most arcane of civilian naval trades: the business of the pursers.[7] The responsibilities of these men were wide-ranging and lucrative, while their methods were almost invariably dishonest. It was a purser's task to muster the ship's company every ten days, to get the clerk of the cheque to issue dockets for victuals, to countersign pay and discharge tickets, keep accounts of all on-board expenses and records of the 'slops' or items of clothing sold to the ordinary seamen. Since these last were known to be a breeding-ground for typhus, the sale of slops was tightly regulated. Blue shirts cost 3s. 6d., red caps 1s. 1d., cotton trousers 3s., yarn stockings 3d. and neats' leather shoes 3s. 6d. These items were sold weekly at the main mast and in the presence of the captain but, as Pepys soon discovered, there were numerous secret arrangements between captains and pursers that worked to their mutual advantage and against the interests of the Crown.

Each officer regularly connived at the other's malpractices with the result that 'comes an extra provision of great candles, white biscuit, Cheshire cheese (and it may be Parmesan), butter, strong beer, wine, poultry, fresh meat, and what not, for the Captain's table'. The system was so complex that Pepys at first doubted his ability to understand it, but eventually he felt sufficiently confident to assert that the current way of doing things encouraged dishonesty since, if he were to make a profit at all, the purser was bound to use 'all the artifices he can . . . to find ways of charging the defects of provisions upon the King'. Pepys was determined to root out such abuses and, in the great memorandum on the subject that he drafted for William Coventry (it says much about both men that Pepys intended it as a New Year present for his friend), he made his plans clear. While it would be unwise to make radical changes in the present climate of war, he asserted, it would surely be better to give the pursers a budget designed to cover all expenses for the time the ship was in service. Excess spending would have to be made up by the pursers themselves while any profits they made would be theirs to keep. It was a shrewd idea and one that embodied Pepys's belief that 'the expectation of profit will have its force and make a man the more earnest'. It was a truth he had tested on his own pulses.

The financial problems of the navy remained embarrassingly obvious. Debts were accumulating at the terrifying rate of £23,000 a week, the increased cost of running the fleet was over £1 million a year, and although Parliament had voted generous supplies it was quite another matter to collect them from a severely depressed economy. By the autumn of 1665 the position had become starkly clear. The navy's credit was near to exhaustion. Merchants were now unwilling to provide clothing for the seamen until their enormous arrears were covered. One family of slop-sellers had supplied goods to the value of £24,000 but, having received a mere £800 in payment, now feared bankruptcy. A shipbuilder in Bristol wrote, 'I have so disabled myself in the relief of poor workmen that I am now out of a capacity of relieving mine own family: I have disbursed and engaged for more than I am worth.'[8] Ships' surgeons complained to their livery company that they had not been paid while that immensely wealthy body itself was owed £1,466. 6s. 10d by the board.

No one who had trusted their money to the war effort was safe, and a letter from a poor widow complained that she was so broke that she had neither coals nor wood to light a fire. Dreadful as all this was, however, it was but a symptom of an altogether more awful possibility: that the nation might not be able to send out a fleet at all and would therefore be unable to defend itself. It was now more than ever essential that abuses be checked and Pepys, as the new surveyor-general of victualling, had special responsibilities in this area. His burdens were considerable and sometimes depressing. Huge amounts of figures had to be prepared, inefficiency and corruption remained enemies, while a deepening disillusion and bitterness in the public sphere added to the sense of pessimism.

The court in particular was attracting ever more widespread criticism for its profligacy. Pepys and Evelyn, riding together in a coach to Clapham, passed the journey 'talking of the vanity and vices of the court, which makes it a most contemptible thing'. The political influence of the royal mistresses was especially feared, a concern shared by Pepys. Castlemaine might provide him with the most intense erotic dreams he had ever had, but when he woke she was a figure to be loathed. Nor was it only shc whose presence was despised. Charles's open erotic servitude to *la belle Stuart* also brought him into contempt, even with Pepys, while Catholicism in royal circles was yet another cause for concern. In a devoutly Protestant country an irrational fear of popery was tightening its grip. The Duke of York was already under suspicion, and a long conversation with Sandwich on 25 October 1665 confirmed Pepys's worst fears. It seemed that moral decay was rotting the highest echelons of society. 'Nothing at court is minded but faction and pleasure,' he concluded, 'and nothing intended of general good to the kingdom by anybody heartily.' He believed that 'in a little time confusion will certainly come over all the nation'.

As so often, Pepys sought release in the company of his women friends, old and new. Among the new were Miss Tooker, with whom he could spend time 'dallying' and 'doing what I would with my hand about her – and a very pretty creature it is'. Mrs Pennington, by contrast, was 'a very fine witty lady, one of the best I ever heard speak – and indifferent handsome'. She was also rather more interested in Pepys than he had supposed. On 13 November he found her 'undressed in her smock and petticoats by the fireside; and there we drank and laughed, and she willingly suffered me to put my hand in her bosom very wantonly, and keep it there long – which methought was very strange, and I looked upon myself as a man mightily deceived in a lady, for I could not have thought she could have suffered it, by her former discourse with me – so modest she seemed, and I know not what'. By the end of the month she was 'suffering me a hazer whatever ego voulus avec ses mamelles – and I had almost led her by a discourse to make her tocar mi cosa naked, which ella did presque and did not refuse'.* But soon Pepys was 'almost cloyed with this dalliance'. He continued to see Mrs Pennington, but another woman had now entered his life.

Mrs Knepp was an actress whose company delighted Pepys.[9] She was open, sexy and talkative, a woman who was part of a world that rarely failed to allure him. She could tell him 'the whole practices of the playhouse and players, and is in every respect most excellent company'. Pepys came across her at Lord Brouncker's and he travelled back from there in 'the coach where Mrs Knepp was, and got her upon my knee (the coach being full) and played with her breasts and sung; and at last set her at her house, and so goodnight'. Her 'surly husband' could easily be ignored while Pepys delighted in, among other things, Mrs Knepp's trained and excellent voice. At Lord Brouncker's party they had sung together and she performed for him 'her little Scotch song of "Barbary Allen"'. Soon she was signing notes to him under this sobriquet and he was replying as 'Dapper Dicky' – an irresistible nickname. It was part of Dapper Dicky's appeal that he could compose as well as sing, and in December 1665 Pepys had 'spent the afternoon upon a song of Solyman's

* 'allowing me to do whatever I wanted with her breasts – and I had almost persuaded her to hold my bared thing which she almost did and was not averse'

words to Roxolana', a declamatory piece of which he was enormously proud. He had taken the lyric from Davenant's 'The Siege of Rhodes' (a work that held a fascination for him out of proportion to its merit) and, as 'Beauty Retire', the song has become Pepys's best-known composition. Mrs Knepp was soon singing it and making it 'go most rarely', so that a proud Pepys could declare 'a very fine song it seems to be'.

Despite these pleasures the man of duty and the Puritan in Pepys fought back. Beauty had indeed to retire when the office called. 'But, Lord!' Pepys wrote, 'what a conflict I had with myself, my heart tempting me a thousand times to go abroad about some pleasure or other, notwithstanding the weather foul. However I reproached myself with my weakness in yielding so much my judgement to my sense, and prevailed with difficulty and did not budge, but stayed within and to my great content did a great deal of business.' It was as well that he did, for it was Pepys's work that was preparing for the ominous days of early June 1666, when the fleet would at last put out to sea again. It did so amid confusion, division and a frightening escalation of the scale of hostilities.

The death of King Philip IV of Spain had brought the French into the war since Louis XIV, who was seeking to wrest parts of the Spanish Netherlands from Spanish control, had signed a treaty with the Dutch and looked on their leader de Witt as a vital ally. De Witt himself, a man of extraordinary personal magnetism, believed that the survival of his nation and its trade largely depended on his own leadership in the struggle against the English and he determined to sail with his fleet as commander in all but name and to rely for practical advice on one of the greatest of his admirals, Michael de Ruyter. All of these men recognised that the defeat of the Dutch off Lowestoft had shown that their mighty navy was not invincible, and what they feared was that another English victory – a decisive one this time

– would see the fall of the Dutch republic and the House of Orange returned to lead a country that would then become merely an English protectorate. The Dutch were fighting for their lives, the French for their glory, while the English were divided among themselves.

The old struggle between gentlemen and tarpaulins had reached a new stage and, with the rise of Prince Rupert especially, the gentlemen were in the ascendancy since the honour and courage they supposedly had by birth were surely the values the country most required. The fallacy of such thinking was soon made clear. Entirely false reports reached London that the French fleet was about to enter the Channel. The fiery Rupert was at once despatched with twenty ships to fight an illusory enemy while the elderly Albemarle was left to face the Dutch. As eighty-four of their great ships hove into view there were those among Albemarle's divided officer corps who counselled him not to fight. He brushed aside their objections and headed for the enemy fleet. Soon he was sandwiched between two lines of fire with consequent terrible losses of men and *matériel*. The *Swiftsure*, the *Seven Oaks*, and the *Loyal George* were all lost as Albemarle tried desperately to break the enemy line. Night fell, much-needed repairs were desperately made but, as dawn rose, Albemarle realised he would have to head for the English coast. The Dutch pursued him through the night, but by the following afternoon Albemarle had reconnoitred with Rupert's fleet. They resolved on a joint attack the following day.

Fifty-eight English ships faced seventy-eight Dutch. Even though many among the tarpaulins realised that this was the merest folly, there were acts of extraordinary heroism. Sir Christopher Myngs, surrounded by the enemy, continued to shout his orders although part of his throat had been shot away and he was obliged to plug his windpipe with his fingers. Only a bullet through the neck finally ended his life. But such heroism was not enough. 'We are beaten,'

Pepys wrote, 'lost many ships and good commanders; have not taken one ship of the enemy's, nor is it certain we were left masters of the field.' In fact, neither side had won decisively, for neither had achieved an overall strategic advantage. But the cost was terrible. The fleet that Pepys, with prodigious effort, had readied for sea lost two admirals, twenty ships, and some eighty thousand men either killed, wounded or taken prisoner.

Pepys laboured with heroic energy to ready the surviving fleet for one more encounter. Unpaid seamen were now deserting in huge, unruly groups. The press-gangs set about replacing them with savage relish, tearing men from their weeping families and even seizing messengers from the Navy Office itself. Yet, amid this brutality, there were scenes that reduced a sensitive man to tears of pride and pity, Pepys among them. Along with Coventry he attended the funeral of Sir Christopher Myngs and, as he and Coventry were about to depart,

> about a dozen able, lusty, proper men came out to the coach side with tears in their eyes, and one of them that spoke for the rest began and said to Sir W. Coventry: 'We are here a dozen of us that have long known and loved, and served our dead commander, Sir Christopher Myngs, and have now done the last office of laying him in the ground. We would be glad we had any other to offer after him, and in revenge of him. All we have is our lives; if you will please to get his Royal Highness to give us a fireship among us all, here is a dozen of us, out of all which choose you one to be commander, and the rest of us, whoever he is, will serve him; and, if possible, do that that shall show our memory of our dead commander, and our revenge.'[10]

Such fireships were indeed to be the means if not to victory then at least to the salvaging of some security. The hastily patched-up fleet now sailed close inshore along the Dutch coast, and when Sir Robert Holmes led a privateering raid on the island of Terschelling he found a vast flotilla of Dutch merchantmen riding at anchor there. Fireships were launched at once and, in what became known as Holmes's Bonfire, 170 enemy vessels were destroyed, £1 million of damage was inflicted, and a serious depression hit Dutch trade.

For all this, Pepys himself still had to bear the brunt of the English admirals' anger when they claimed that their ships had, yet again, been inadequately victualled. He was able to answer their 'most scurvy letter' before the King and Privy Council by proving that the officers had provided him neither with adequate accounts of their needs nor accurate intelligence of their movements. Pepys was exonerated by his own efficiency and could now turn to the more cultivated pleasures of peace. In particular, he set about attending to his library. On 23 July he was visited by Simpson the joiner and the two men spent the time 'with great pains contriving presses to put my books up in; they now growing numerous, and lying one upon another on my chairs, I lose the use, to avoid the trouble of removing them when I would open a book'. It was time to refurbish his study (always a significant moment in a life) and by the close of August Pepys had began on it. The first two of his magnificent new bookcases had been built* and when Simpson arrived with the second of them he and Pepys 'fell into the furnishing of my new closet, and taking out the things out of my old. I kept him with me all day, and he dined with me; and so all the afternoon, till it was quite dark – hanging things; that is, my maps and picture[s] – and draughts – and setting up my books, as much as we could do – to my most extraordinary satisfaction; so that I think it will be as noble a closet as any man hath, and light enough;

* The complete set is still preserved in the Pepys Library at Magdalene College, Cambridge.

though indeed, it would have been better to have had a little more light.'

It was natural that Pepys should want to show off his new study to his friends, and he arranged for them to come and eat with him on 1 September 1666. What should have been a day of quiet domestic pride turned into one of the great dramatic episodes of English history and one that called forth from Pepys himself powers that even the last few remarkable months had barely hinted he possessed. Pepys had received his first suggestion of what was to come at three o'clock that morning when one of the maids had woken him and Elizabeth 'to tell us of a great fire they saw in the city'. Pepys slipped on his nightgown and looked out of the window but, seeing that the fire was a long way off, went back to bed. Five hours later the danger still seemed remote, but 'by and by Jane comes and tells me that she hears above 300 houses have been burned down tonight by the fire we saw, and that it was now burning down all Fish Street by London Bridge'.

Clearly, the fire was more serious than Pepys had supposed, and he made his way to the Tower of London to get a better view from one of its turrets. The scale of what he saw appalled him, and his first thought was of the danger to his friends living in the area where the conflagration had already taken hold. As he hurried down to the waterside and took a boat, the spectacle of fear and panic moved him to the quick. Everybody was trying to save their goods, flinging them into the river or hoping to commandeer lighters, 'poor people staying in their houses as long as till the very fire touched them, and then running into boats or clambering from one pair of stair by the waterside to another'. And, like the poor, pigeons kept to their nests and 'hovered about the windows and balconies till they were some of them burned, their wings, and fell down'. It was clear that something had to be done, but nobody appeared to be taking an initiative and, as a 'mighty high' wind drove the giant and all-devouring flames towards a city tinder dry after a hot summer, Pepys took a lighter to Whitehall where, relying on his growing prestige, he sent word to the King and was immediately called for.

Mr Pepys was a man whose advice was respected, and he would not have come on a fool's errand. He was summoned before Charles and his brother – Stuarts both, whom nobody told what to do – informed them what he had seen, and added that 'unless His Majesty did command houses to be pulled down, nothing could stop the fire'. The King knew the truth of this. Six months earlier Charles had written to the city authorities warning them of the danger of fires and giving the authorities the necessary permission to pull down buildings and so create fire-breaks. Nothing had been done, and now the troubled monarch commanded Pepys to go at once, seek out the Lord Mayor and present him with the royal command 'to spare no houses but to pull down before the fire every way'. The Duke of York, also rising to the occasion, added that soldiers would be made available should they be needed.

Pepys hurried in a coach to St Paul's as the crowd scurried around him, 'every creature coming away loaden with goods to save – and here and there sick people carried away in beds'. By now the heat of the fire was so intense that the very stones of the churches were cracking and burning, and the Lord Mayor was beside himself. Fires were a fact of life in London, a cheek-by-jowl infinity of timber-framed buildings ensured that this was so, and the Lord Mayor had at first been contemptuous of the panic that this one produced. 'A woman might piss it out,' he had declared. Now he himself 'cried like a fainting woman: "Lord, what can I do? I am spent! People will not obey me. I have been pull[ing] down houses. But the fire overtakes us faster than we can do it."' The exhausted man wandered away to his bed and to ignominy while Pepys walked home seeing people 'almost distracted and no manner of means used to quench the fire'. The clerk of the acts knew that the houses in Thames Street especially were full of pitch and tar, and that the warehouses were stuffed with oil, wines and brandy, which would flame with terrible combustion. The Great Fire was far from over.

By midday Pepys was back in Seething Lane to greet his guests, but this was no longer the occasion to admire the gleam on his new wooden bookcases, the gilded spines of his many volumes, or his rich display of maps and prints. For all that the company had 'an extraordinary good dinner' and were as merry as they could be the sense of catastrophe spoiled all. The streets outside were 'full of nothing but people and horses and carts loaden with goods, ready to run over one another, and removing goods from one burned house to another'. Pepys went out to observe. Spotted by the King and the Duke of York from the royal barge, he travelled with them as far as Queenhithe, noting that 'their order was only to pull down houses apace . . . but little was or could be done, the fire coming upon them so fast'. The Thames itself was now an artery of panic, full of bobbing goods and overloaded boats, and Pepys 'observed that hardly one lighter or boat in three that had goods of a house in it, but there was a pair of virginals in it'.

By now Pepys himself had done as much as he could and, as daylight faded to evening, he met up with his wife and friends and went out with them in his boat on the river and watched the inferno mounting as a great wind blew the insatiable flames across a darkening sky. The appalling, hypnotic beauty of the destruction sharpened Pepys's eye for detail and, as he passed down the Thames with his face in the wind, he was 'almost burned with a shower of firedrops – this is very true – so as houses were burned by these drops and flakes of fire, three or four, nay five or six houses, one from another'. The heat was unendurable, and Pepys's little party went over to a tavern in Bankside to watch. As darkness fell the fire 'appeared more and more, and in corners and upon steeples and between churches and houses, as far as we could see up the hill of the city, in a most horrid malicious bloody flame, not like the fine flame of an ordinary fire'. The great incandescent arch was now over a mile long and it made Pepys weep to see it. The city of his childhood, the city of his life – that great medieval seething city – was being ravished before his gaze: 'the churches, houses, and all on fire and flaming at once, and a horrid noise the flames made, and the cracking of houses at their ruin'.

London was above all a place where people lived, and now the human dimension of the tragedy began to impinge on Pepys. He and his wife returned home to find his luckless clerk Tom Hayter come to them with a few possessions and begging for shelter. This was given to him, but there was little sleep for the poor man since Sir William Batten's carts had arrived from Walthamstow and the great hoard of Pepys's goods in Seething Lane – precious and private – were loaded on to them or hidden in the cellar. Pepys and his servants worked all night, and by four in the morning were ready to ride the loaded cart to a friend's house at Bethnal Green where many of Pepys's things (including his *Diary*) were left. Pepys himself and Elizabeth then returned to their house to pack up yet more goods, which they loaded into a lighter as Lombard Street, Cornhill, the Royal Exchange and all the lovely medieval churches between them flamed and burned to charcoal and ash.

Only now, as Tuesday dawned, did the fire reach its height. The great leaden roof of St Paul's turned to a steaming liquid pool. Salisbury Court, where Pepys had begun his life, crashed down into anonymous flatness, while in the garden of his office he and Batten dug a great hole in which to hide papers, wine and a valuable Parmesan cheese. The Navy Office had at all costs to be spared, and as the pounding roar of the Duke of York and his men blowing up houses on Ludgate Hill reached his ears, so Pepys sent down to the dockyards for men to come and demolish the houses around his place of work. By two that morning the fire had reached Seething Lane and there was no alternative for Pepys but to flee with his wife, his servant Jane, loyal Will Hewer and a great supply of gold.

When he returned from Woolwich where he had left them all, he found that the Navy Office at least was still standing and he climbed to the top of a nearby steeple to survey 'the saddest sight of desolation that ever I saw, everywhere great fires, oil cellars and brimstone'. In fact, the worst was over, but a wasteland of devastation stretched before him, its mantle of ash so hot that it scorched through the soles of Pepys's shoes. Exhausted, he fell asleep but woke at five the following morning to help fight more flames in Bishopsgate before, filthy and exhausted yet again, he made his way to Westminster to buy a shirt and have a shave. His journey along the Thames was an agonising panorama of familiar sights gone for ever. Over 13,000 houses had been destroyed, eighty-nine churches were rubble, forty-four livery halls were ash, and 100,000 people faced a cold, homeless winter.

A scapegoat had to be found since for many it was impossible to believe that the Fire, in the insurers' phrase, was an act of God. Clearly it was the work of some diabolical agency. Ancient, atavistic hatreds were stirred. Frightened vindictiveness focused on the country's small and diminishing community of Roman Catholics. Here was the enemy within. Every good Protestant knew about the evils of popery. In flat contradiction to the sacred authority of Scripture, Catholics believed that by some priestly hocus-pocus the bread and wine of the communion service were turned into the actual body and blood of Christ. Such abominations provoked visceral disgust, and to this was added a fear and loathing of the power of the Catholic Church and the means by which this was promoted: war, absolutist government and the burning of heretics alive. Foxe's so-called *Book of Martyrs* itemised such enormities in lurid and wearisome detail and had for generations been a best-seller. Now the swelling might of Catholic despotic France was showing itself a menace to all that true Englishmen held dear – their Church and their liberty especially. An advance guard of Jesuits was wreaking untold harm. What could be clearer than the fact that these agents of the devil had razed London to the ground? Such suspicions would soon develop into a national paranoia and sweep up even Pepys in their destructive wake. In the meantime, as Londoners set about the immense task of rebuilding their city, an inscription on the Monument raised to record the devastation blamed the disaster squarely on 'the treachery and malice of the popish faction'.

But still the nation's agony was not done, nor Pepys's part in it. As the citizens of London made what shift they could, the Parliamentary Committee of Navy Accounts was now preparing to ask awkward questions in the wake of the navy's expensive defeat. Pepys and his clerks laboured through weekdays and weekends to provide it with figures, fearing all the while that they might easily lose their jobs. In the end they managed to prove that the costs of the war had so far mounted to a terrifying £3,200,000 of which nearly £1 million was still owing. Pepys was faced with the gruelling responsibility of answering the committee's questions, and he did so with the sort of quiet efficiency that was born of his mastery of the facts. The Commons was sufficiently impressed by his performance to vote a further £1,800,000.

The debates on how this vast sum should be raised were of the greatest importance to Pepys for two reasons: first, the discussions were so long spun out that it would not even be possible with the help of bankers' loans advanced against the promised sums adequately to fit out the fleet in time for renewed hostilities; second, the difficulties raised by Members and the divisions between them pointed to future developments of the greatest importance.[11] Those who unquestioningly supported the court believed that the money should be raised by a general excise that would continue after the war. Many others believed that this was a ruse to lessen the Crown's dependence on Parliament for an opposition was beginning to form, a group that stood firmly for the country rather than the court, for the Anglican Church rather than religious sects and for Parliamentary privilege rather than the royal prerogative alone. For the moment, such men formed a loose grouping rather than a coherent party. Among their number were the Presbyterians (many of them Members from an older generation) who had a genuine zeal for the Protestant Church and religious reform. Most of them felt their ideals had been betrayed in the years since the Restoration, while they also increasingly believed that their liberties were threatened by the immoral atmosphere that surrounded the court with its evident French bias in matters of culture, religion and politics.

A larger group in the House were traditionalists, men who respected the institution of monarchy and honest administration on the part of the King's ministers and civil servants. They believed also that Parliament should be consulted in great matters, and were firm in their desire for financial probity and restraint. To such men as these, the advancement of trade and the defence of the Protestant religion were matters of fundamental importance, and they were soon to adopt the name of the Country party to distinguish themselves from adherents of the court. One of their most eloquent spokesmen defined them thus:

A gross of English gentry, nobly born,
Of clear estates, and to no faction sworn;
Dear lovers of their King, and death to meet,
For Country's cause, that glorious thing and sweet:

To speak not forward, but in action brave;
In giving generous, but in counsel grave;
Candidly credulous for once, nay twice;
But sure the Devil cannot cheat them thrice.[12]

Here were the men who would eventually play their part in the first stirring of party politics in England and, in the adversarial world slowly emerging, it was necessary for the secure well-being of the Crown that its officers show them that they themselves were honest, competent and trustworthy – that, given the circumstances, national security was safe in their hands.

Pepys was acutely aware of this, writing in his *Diary* on 5 November that 'all the country gentlemen are publicly jealous of the courtiers in the Parliament, and that they do doubt everything they do propose'. This division was to widen and eventually to threaten the very life of Pepys, the confirmed King's man, but for the moment all he knew was that the promised money for the navy would come in slowly and incompletely, and that the financial problems of the Navy Board were far from over. In April 1667 he was obliged to write to a merchant in Hull that 'you may be confident that all the care that can be shown by people without money you shall find used by this Board, and particularly myself'. This was cold comfort, but Pepys did not really know what else he could say 'having no commission to discourage you by saying there will be no money, nor being otherwise willing to mislead you into an expectation of it'.

Appeals to the Treasury proved bleakly unsatisfactory and the Navy Board in its desperation resolved to ask the King and the Privy Council for funds. So daunting was the prospect that when he arrived for the meeting Pepys discovered that none of his colleagues had readied themselves to present their case, 'so I was forced immediately to prepare in my mind a method of discoursing'. Pepys decided that truth had its own eloquence and, in what he prided himself was a 'good speech', he made plain to the assembled grandees 'the ill state of the Navy – by the greatness of the debt – greatness of work to do against next year – the time and materials it would take – and our incapacity, through a total want of money'.

This calm and brave statement of the facts roused Prince Rupert to apoplectic fury, his usual manner of dealing with most problems. He launched himself on a tirade in which he declared that 'he had brought home his Fleet in as good a condition as ever any fleet was brought home'. All he needed was twenty ships for a new campaign. Pepys stood his ground until the tirade finished, whereupon he quietly said that he 'was sorry for his Highness's offence, but that what I said was but the report we received from those entrusted in the fleet to inform us'. Rupert scowled, muttered, and remonstrated as angrily as before. As he ended, a dead silence fell in the Green Room where they were all met. Not a grandee came to Rupert's aid, not even Albemarle. Mr Pepys's facts were decisive and there was no more to say. Pepys himself withdrew, his mind beating in an agony of fear. There were quick, whispered conversations about how the princely face might be saved, but the bankruptcy of the court was such that the Navy Board was informed 'that after all this pains the King hath found out how to supply us with 5 or £6000, when £10,000 were at this time but absolutely necessary, and we mentioned £50,000 – this is every day a greater and greater omen of ruin – God fit us for it'.

The cry of despair was justified, but it hid the more subtle, and ultimately more important, historical forces that were at work here. The problem was not only the financial bankruptcy of the Crown but its intellectual poverty as well. Paralysis at the top meant that Parliament could take on itself an ever more powerful role and become not just a legislative assembly but a body that, because of its financial powers, could increase its influence over royal policy. There were those who had hoped the war would free the Crown from its dependence on Parliament, but lack of an outright victory at sea had brought about the reverse and now the fleet was rotting.

Why bother? Why slave night and day in a hopeless cause? There was nothing Pepys could do, 'the business of the Navy standing wholly still. No credit. No goods sold us. Nobody will trust. All we have to do at the office is to hear complaints for want of money.' And on the streets outside the effects were clear and frightening. 'The seamen grow very rude,' Pepys wrote, 'and everything out of order – commanders having no power over their seamen but the seamen do what they please. Few stay on board, but all coming running up hither to town; and nobody can with justice blame them, we owing them so much money, and their families must starve.' Would it not be better to resign and settle down in Brampton 'where I might live peaceably and study, and pray for the good of my King and my country'? These were fantasies, and Pepys, the great edifice of his professional ambition having apparently crashed, sought other distractions. He played his music, he entertained his friends, 'eating in silver plates and all things mighty rich and handsome'. There was a certain self-satisfied pleasure in knowing that he had made himself so comfortable and, when opulent displays cloyed, there were always his women friends. Pepys's sex life at this time became compulsive, not just a matter of furtive pleasure and release, but of conquest – desperation almost – as if he were trying to fill up the great chasm that had opened in his life.

He had Mrs Bagwell 'con much voluptas'.* He had Mrs Martin too, and when that easy lady fell pregnant by another, he turned to her obliging sister Doll Lane. Mrs Burrows, the navy widow, he had in Mrs Martin's lodgings. Mrs Daniel he fondled in his office. One week in December saw Pepys

* 'with much desire'

having sex with Doll Lane, Mrs Martin and Mrs Daniel in quick succession. Mrs Knepp was still available too, and he threw a dinner at home for her (Elizabeth was supposedly appeased by the presence of the egregious Pembleton who led the dancing), and when *la* Knepp took a bad turn and felt she had to go upstairs, Pepys lay on the bed with her singing a song and fondling her magnificent breasts. There was another woman, too. Pepys had known Betty Mitchell since her girlhood days in Westminster Hall when he had called her his 'wife' because she looked so much like Elizabeth. Now she teased him with a disingenuous modesty, let him kiss her, stood him up, played with him in a coach and then, one moonlit evening in another coach, 'she making many little endeavours para stir su main . . . yielded'.*

These long hours of pleasure did not distract Pepys from his more serious duties. He remained the loyal brother and dutiful son. When his mother died in the spring of 1667, saying as her last words 'God bless my poor Sam!', he wept heartily and gave her an expensive funeral, priding himself that he could easily afford to do so. His poor passive father moved his pity too, and Pepys bought him a horse and made up his income by £30 a year. He provided a dowry and tried to find a husband for difficult, plain Pall, and even Balty, who had distinguished himself in the Duke of York's eyes as the best muster master in the navy, was made its deputy treasurer through Pepys's agency. Only Elizabeth failed to profit from his charity. When she tried to impress him with her singing, Pepys lost patience and knew that he made matters worse because his temper scared her.

Nor, in this dead and depressing time, did Pepys neglect his own business. Sleaze and corruption were now endemic in the atmosphere of bankrupt hopelessness and Pepys himself was not above having one of the King's ships go about Captain

* 'she, making many little hand gestures . . . yielded'

Cocke's business for a handsome commission. Pepys and other members of the Navy Board also borrowed a royal ship so that they could hire sailors to indulge in a little privateering. Pepys himself broke with Warren when he realised he could not monopolise that merchant's favours but, as surveyor-general of victualling, he found Gauden more than willing to pay for his friendship. Pepys continued to grow rich, 'for which the Holy name of God be praised', while the navy grew poorer still. Just how poor Pepys made clear in a letter to the Duke of York. The Navy Board had received considerably less than 1 per cent of the money required to discharge its debts. It was all but impossible to make substantial contracts, and £500,000 was needed at once if the fleet were to sail again. The money was not to be found, the ships were laid up in the Medway, and a boom was put across the river while the coastal forts were strengthened. Even the readying of these last, pathetic defences of the realm was disgracefully mishandled. Meanwhile, the half-starved families of the unpaid seamen cried aloud for bread and dockyard labourers laid down their tools.

But even at this most desperate time important initiatives were being taken elsewhere. While the neglected and rotting fleet strained on its frayed ropes with the Medway tides, changes were taking place in the Treasury that would soon rouse Pepys to his familiar professional vigour. With the death of Lord Treasurer Southampton the Treasury itself was put into the hands of commissioners.[13] Clarendon, with the fixed, backward gaze of an ageing conservative, complained that the men appointed had insufficient social standing to merit the places offered them, but King Charles and his brother were making a move of the most profound importance by employing men whose proven ability was more important. Pepys had worked with two of them: Sir George Downing and Sir William Coventry. He was delighted. Men of his own way of thinking were taking over affairs of the greatest importance 'and my heart is very glad of it; for I do expect they will do much good, and that it is the happiest thing that hath appeared to me for the good of the nation since the King came in'.

The commissioners rapidly made their presence felt. They were determined that all departments should know that they were the real and effective centre of government finance. Orders were issued making this clear and even the King could not sign warrants for money without the commissioners vetting the warrant first. Further, they had a discretionary power over all departmental spending on specific projects and gained powers at the expense of the secretaries of state. Discipline, authority, a strong measure of central control, rigorous analysis and scrupulous bookkeeping became the order of the day. The whole amounted to a cultural innovation that was profoundly to influence Pepys – as well as keeping him very busy – and even now, at the end of May, Coventry had a word with him and 'desired that I would be thinking of anything fit for him to be acquainted with for the lessening of charge and bettering of our credit'.

Pepys complied with alacrity, but paper alone was no defence against disaster. On 8 June news came in that the Dutch were at sea. The States General had secretly resolved to attempt 'something notable'. Their spies had familiarised them with the treacherous channels of the Medway and they were riding a spring tide. Pepys busied himself ordering fireships, but he was soon to discover that all defence was vain. On the night of 7 June de Ruyter read out his secret instructions, divided his fleet and sent a convoy of seventeen warships and twenty-four auxiliaries and fireships up the river. For a few days they were delayed by contrary winds but the English lacked the *matériel* and organisation effectively to repel them. There were few guns at either Tilbury or Gravesend. There was panic at Chatham. Ships were eventually sunk on either side of the chain, but when

Albemarle tried more active forms of defence he found that the mountings for the guns had been stolen and replaced with cheap wood. The guns, when fired, sank into the mud.

The English fleet was defenceless and the imperious enemy convoy sailed on virtually unopposed. As the Dutch vessels moved in arrogant assurance up the river, so the unpaid seamen and the dockyard workers watched or cheered them on. English crews deserted, English ships surrendered, and ineffective English fire was a derisory response to the humiliation. Then came the final insult. The Dutch, with a mere one boat and six men, started to tow away the *Royal Charles* through the thick smoke of the smouldering fleet. The pride of the nation was in tatters and the work of the Navy Board was in ruins. When the news reached a panic-riven London it struck the clerk of the acts 'to the heart', but even in this anguished moment the spirits of malevolence had not yet finished with Mr Pepys.

CHAPTER EIGHT

Perpetual Trouble and Vexation

Pandemonium engulfed the city in the wake of the Dutch attack. News and rumour whipped up a witch's brew of fear as people said that the humiliations had only just begun. The fall of the country was imminent. The Dutch would sail up the Thames and wreak revenge for Holmes's Bonfire. The French would launch an invasion from Dunkirk. Even the last-minute desperate steps taken to defend the capital were hopelessly ineffective. When ships were sunk off Woolwich and Blackwall to block the river it was discovered that they had been laden with badly needed supplies. Everybody feared that the crews would mutiny, while the seamen's wives shouted in Wapping streets that all the horrors about to descend on the country were due to the failure to pay their husbands. A horrified Pepys listened while visitor after visitor to his office told him that treason was being openly talked as people gave it out as their opinion that 'we are bought and sold and governed by Papists and that we are betrayed by people about the King'. Fear of popery in high places gripped the nation and combined with contempt for the court's lascivious way of life. After all, 'the night the

Dutch burned our ships, the King did sup with my Lady Castlemaine at the Duchess of Monmouth, and there were all mad in hunting of a poor moth'.

Pepys took immediate emergency measures to protect himself. He rightly foresaw a run on the banks, and his father and Elizabeth were hurried off to Brampton 'with about £1,300 in gold in their night-bag'. Pepys himself remained in London, constantly worried that he had had to trust so much of his wealth to two such ineffectual people and wondering what he could do with the rest of his money. Should he fling his silver into the Navy Board's 'house of office'? It seemed a good idea, but then he realised he would probably not be able to retrieve it if he were to lose his job. Fearful of what might happen, he wrapped a further £300 in a girdle round his waist so 'that I may not be without something' in case he should be surprised by cut-throats seeking to avenge the nation's wrongs. A messenger was then despatched after Elizabeth and his father to check on their safe progress to Brampton, while cousin Sarah and her husband were sent in the same direction with a chest of Pepys's private papers, among which were the volumes of his *Diary* 'which I value much'. Finally, yet another messenger was sent off to Brampton with a thousand gold coins under cover of an official express to the admiral in charge of those remaining parts of the fleet anchored off Newcastle. Pepys had done what he could, and now he sat 'alone here at the office; and the truth is, I am glad my station is to be here – near my own home and out of danger, yet in a place of doing the King good service'.

He was not as comfortable as he supposed. Elizabeth returned to London with a stuttering story about how she and her father-in-law had buried Pepys's gold 'in open daylight in the midst of the garden, where for aught they knew, many eyes might see them'. Pepys was so worried and so angry that he refused to sup with his wife or even to speak to her. But his troubles were far from over. That morning he had been ordered to attend a meeting of the Privy Council. He was so gravely concerned that the grandees gathered there would blame him for the nation's ills that he gave his clerk his closet key and told him where he could find £500, which the man was to remove 'in case of any misfortune to me'. It seemed that Commissioner Pett was to be the real victim of the enquiry. After all, had not Pett at the time of the Dutch attack busied himself removing his precious models of ships rather than moving the ships themselves up the river to safety?

Pepys, as always, was admirably briefed for the occasion and acquitted himself well. He was determined all the same that he should not shoulder the responsibility for the recent disaster and he spoke harshly against Pett, 'for which God forgive me'. Pett himself was returned a prisoner to the Tower and Pepys, as he made his way past the inquisitive eyes of the courtiers gathered in Whitehall, smiled and greeted those people he knew to show them that he at least was a free man. For all that, he still dreaded meeting his colleagues, and when he ran into Coventry a fortnight later the two men could scarcely look each other in the eye. But Pepys alone of all the Navy Board was not mired with disgrace, and the rest knew it. When he said to one that he would not mind being sacked, provided the nation was safe, he was laughed at: 'That is a good one, in faith! For you know yourself to be secure in being necessary to the Office.'

Such indeed proved to be the case and Pepys, relieved but exhausted, decided he had earned himself a rest. He attended the theatre voraciously (in one week he went six times) and laughed himself sore at the antics of *Sir Martin Mar-all*. He also made a rare expedition into the countryside for pleasure. With loyal, kindly Will Hewer as a companion for himself, and pretty Miss Turner as a friend for Elizabeth, Pepys took an early-morning coach to Epsom. The sense of relief after so many weeks of anxiety called forth one of the loveliest and most unusual passages in the *Diary*. The party went sightseeing, visiting, and Pepys at least took the waters 'and had some very good stools by it'. After lunch and a nap, 'the day being wonderful hot', the inveterate townsman took his party for a walk in the woods, got lost and sprained his ankle while trying to get out. Eventually the Londoners found themselves on the Downs:

> where a flock of sheep was, and the most pleasant and innocent sight that ever I saw in my life; we find a shepherd and his little boy reading, far from any houses or sight of people, the Bible to him. So I made the boy read to me, which he did with the forced tone that children do usually read, that was mighty pretty; and then I did give him something and went to the father and talked with him; and I find he had been a servant in my cousin Pepys's house, and told me what was become of their old servants. He did content himself mightily in my liking his boy's reading and did bless God for him, the most like one of the old Patriarchs that ever I saw in my life, and it brought those thoughts of the old age of the world in my mind for two or three days after.[1]

But Pepys being the man he was could not rest content with dreaming. The vivid physical presence of the old man sharpened his curiosity. He noticed the shepherd's hobnailed boots and, intrigued by anything special to a particular trade, asked him about them. '"Why," says the poor man, "the Downs, you see, are full of stones, and we are fain to shoe ourselves thus; and these," says he, "will make the stones fly till they sing before me."' They then talked about the man's highly trained dog, which helped him to control the '18 score sheep in his flock'. For this work the man earned four shillings a week and so was 'mighty thankful' for the tip Pepys gave him. With that they parted, but for all the delight of the day, the delicious milk drunk in Epsom on their journey home and the glint of glow-worms in the dark, the countryside was not Pepys's terrain and he knew it. His twisted ankle was hurting badly now and he made a resolution 'never to keep a country house, but to keep a coach and with my wife on the Saturday to go sometimes for a day to this place and then quite to another place; and there is more variety, and as little charge and no trouble, as there is in a country house'. The Londoner was a Londoner through and through.

The greater part of the city of his youth and early manhood had been burned to the ground, and the London that Pepys knew for the next decade was a vast and busy building site, eventually dominated by Wren's St Paul's, which was not completed until 1711, eight years after Pepys's death. Immediately after the Fire the King had issued a proclamation requiring 'a much more beautiful city than that consumed', and a number of steps were taken to ensure that this plan proceeded as smoothly as possible. Fire courts were set up to deal with the innumerable legal problems that arose, while a rebuilding Act set out clear guidelines for the types of dwellings that were to be erected. This made adequate guttering compulsory and thereby helped to create cleaner streets than Pepys had known before. The old practice of building storeys that jutted out beyond the foundation lines was expressly forbidden, which helped to make the new streets brighter. By April 1667, the lines of these streets had been staked out and soon the required stone or brick façades were rising along them.

Pepys was well aware that a few would make considerable sums of money from this ferment of activity. He himself lent a cousin £350 to construct one of the regulation three-storey buildings, but he noticed how speculators like Mr Jaggard were erecting 'many brave houses', while the immensely wealthy Alderman Blackwell showed him 'the model of the houses he is going to build in Cornhill and Lombard Street; but he hath purchased so much there, that it looks like a little town, and must have cost him a great deal of money'. Despite such initiatives, a property boom did not take place. Seven years after the Fire a thousand plots were still empty, and over 3,500 newly built homes were still unoccupied: many people had begun to prefer the suburbs.

The relative anonymity of the new city allowed Pepys to pursue his numerous affairs with a degree of ease. Perhaps this was just as well, for worry and sordidness alternated with the pleasure he found. On 3 July 1667, he visited Mrs Martin and found her 'all in trouble'. She believed she was pregnant and that Pepys was the father of her child. Pepys himself was equally sure that he was not but he was gravely worried until he met her again three days later in Westminster Hall where she greeted him with 'the good news que esta no es con child, she having de estos upon her'.* In his relief Pepys sent her sister off for a bottle of wine, but when Doll returned she was in a terribly agitated state which, for Pepys at least, was merely an 'instance of a woman's falseness'. What had happened was that Doll had caught the eye of the Dutchman who worked at the wine store and so roused him that he 'pulled her into a stable by the Dog tavern and there did tumble her and toss her'. To Pepys, Doll's tears and outrage were the merest hypocrisy for, after all, 'she knows that ella [she] hath suffered me to do anything with her a hundred times'.

Other women were not so compliant to his demands. One Sunday in the following month when Pepys was at church he managed to stand by 'a pretty, modest maid, whom I did labour to take by the hand and body'. She wanted nothing to do with him and as Pepys continued to press his suit she tried to get further and further away from him. Still he believed she would yield but 'at last I could perceive her to take pins out of her pocket to prick me if I should touch her again'. He

* 'the good news is that she is not with child, she having those [i.e. her period] upon her

gave up, listened to the sermon for a few minutes, and then started 'upon another pretty maid in a pew close to me'. She seemed to respond and Pepys took hold of her hand. For a few pleasant seconds the girl let it rest there but after a little while withdrew it and 'so the sermon ended and the church broke up, and my amours ended also'.

In fact, his problems had only just begun. Elizabeth, not surprisingly, was feeling neglected and there were perhaps grounds for Pepys's jealousy when he received a letter from his father informing him that on the coach journey to Brampton with his gold she had fallen in with an 'idle companion' called Coleman, then travelled back to London with him. Pepys was determined to put a stop to the matter before it went any further, and relations between husband and wife again reached a low ebb. Small incidents sparked savage rows. For instance, early in July 1667, Pepys failed to turn up for lunch at home, and when he finally got back, he found his wife in a 'dogged humour'. The nastier side of his nature was immediately stirred and he gave Elizabeth 'a pull by the nose and some ill words'. A shouting match followed and was so bad that Pepys felt he had to return to the office to escape it. Elizabeth followed him there 'in a devilish manner', and it was only with the greatest difficulty that Pepys eventually persuaded her out into the garden where he gradually quietened her down away from the public gaze. That evening he stayed in the office until 'pretty late', but eventually the quarrel was patched up 'and so to supper and pretty good friends; and so to bed – with my mind very quiet'.

Elizabeth's frustrations continued to plague her all the same, and one day the following month, angry with premenstrual tension and what she supposed were her husband's suspicions of her, she told him in no uncertain terms of her physical state. 'I asked her why, and she said she had a reason. I do think by something too she said today that she took notice that I had not lain with her this half-year, that she thinks that I have found out that she might be with child by somebody else, which God knows never entered my head.' Pepys was being extraordinarily insensitive and, as so often when in this state, priggish too. 'I do not do well,' he wrote, 'to let these beginnings of discontent take so much root between us.' Far worse was to come, however, since in the effort to allay Elizabeth's bad temper, Pepys had agreed she should once again have a lady companion.

Her name was Deborah Willet and she was, according to Elizabeth, a pretty little thing, 'extraordinary handsome' even. Pepys first saw her on 27 September 1667, and was at once intrigued while sensing danger. Deb, as she soon came to be called, was demure, courteous and petite. If she was not quite as pretty as Pepys had been led to imagine then there was in her falling short of his ideal something that roused a tenderness far too close for comfort to desire. Deb was, besides, tractable, dependent and perilously young. Part of Pepys hoped that she would not accept a post in his house 'lest I may be found too much minding her, to the discontent of my wife'. Then, in his next sentence, he wrote, 'she is to come next week'. Pepys was delighted, and when the interview was over he went back to the office, his mind running over with thoughts of the girl.

By the middle of the following month the first signs of danger were all too apparent. Quite why Elizabeth had chosen Deb in the first place it is impossible to say, but now, on 15 October, as all three of them sat in the theatre, Elizabeth explored the possibilities for whining and suspicion with which the girl provided her. She complained about her 'sitting cheek by jowl with us', which was so patently absurd that Pepys himself was obliged to call it 'a poor thing'. Elizabeth was clearly trying to be petulant about her status, but worse than this was the fact that Pepys perceived she was already so jealous of his 'kindness' towards Deb that he began to fear the girl 'is not likely to stay long with us'. For the moment his worries were unjustified. Deb survived November, and when her aunt came to visit in early December she was firmly established in the household. The aunt, who was something of a *grande dame*, was clearly satisfied and was even led to comment, 'which was pretty odd', that since her niece had entered Elizabeth's service 'her breasts begin to swell, she being afeared before that she would have none'.

The rounding out of Deb's little body had not been lost on Pepys. The girl was deliciously on the verge of womanhood and irresistible. On the last Sunday in December, when Pepys was going through his accounts, she came into his office with a message from Elizabeth 'and this first time I did give her a little kiss, she being a very pretty-humoured girl, and so one that I do love mightily'. Now Pepys watched her with increasing delight and took a special pleasure in those more intimate duties that a serving-girl was required to perform. The start of 1668 saw him recording in his *Diary* how, after supper, he sat by the fireside 'to have my head combed, as I now often do, by Deb, whom I love should be fiddling about me'. For the moment at least this was enough.

Besides, the would-be philanderer had altogether more serious responsibilities, which drew on all his resources of self-discipline. Parliament was now insisting on a most rigorous investigation of the débâcle in the Medway, and Pepys was to answer for the Navy Board. Retrenchment, accuracy and courage were the watchwords of these anxious months, and in line with the first Pepys surrendered his post as surveyor-general of victualling and, on a repeated hint from Coventry, lent the King some of the profits he had made from his privateering ventures. Then, despite his aching eyes, he threw himself with gusto into the enormous amount of work there was to do. He was determined to hold hard to the principle that the Navy Office could not be held responsible for failing to do what it had not been given the means to achieve, a task made the more difficult by the atmosphere of mutual recrimination raging about him. 'I see everybody is on his own defence, and spares not to blame another to defend himself.'[2]

In this time of dog-eat-dog, Pepys would do the same, but he would also be zealous in presenting and defending arguments of real quality. The thought of what he had to do turned his bowels to water. He knew that nature had not cast him in a heroic mould and he confessed as much to his *Diary*. 'I am not a man able to go through trouble as other men are,' he wrote, 'but that I should be a miserable man if I should meet with adversity, which God keep me from.' Method would have to be his shield, his clerks his men-at-arms. They laboured prodigiously and Pepys, ever the innovator, took to inviting them home to lunch, 'by that means I having opportunity to talk to them about business, and I love their company very well'. In such ways Pepys prepared himself to face the hostile Committee of Miscarriages' questions on two great issues: the defence of the Medway and the vexed matter of issuing discharged sailors with redeemable tickets rather than paying them in cash.

The tickets issued to sailors were often bought at far less than their face value for badly needed ready cash and this, like the press-gang, was an abuse that troubled Pepys deeply.[3] He knew that 'seamen are the most adventurous creatures in the world, and the most free of their money after all their dangers when they come to receive it'. That they were often tardily paid or paid by ticket was a disgrace attendant on the navy's chronic shortage of money. Now that the wages bill had increased tenfold the situation was desperate and alarming. Worried officers had begged Pepys and his colleagues to send ready cash at once 'to stop the bawlings and impatience of these people, especially of their wives, whose tongues are as foul as the daughters of Billingsgate', but the money was simply not available. The wages of some crews were as much as fifty-two months in arrears.

Men, women and children were naked, starving and ill, and many sailors were deserting with angry mutterings about the service of the King being 'worse ten thousand times than to die by the hands of the enemy'. Others resorted to different types of direct action. When Pepys left the office for his lunch 'a whole hundred followed us, some cursing, some swearing and some praying to us'. Others hurled stones at the windows and the frightened inhabitants of Seething Lane asked to be sent 'twelve well-fixed firelocks with a supply of powder and bullets for the defence of the said office'. The whole situation was both frightening and pitiful, but the compassion Pepys felt for the 'poor wretches' would fill no stomachs. Nor was it an adequate response to the angry murmurings in Parliament.

Tuesday, 22 October 1667, was the much feared day of reckoning. Pepys slept badly the night before and rose early and anxious. The morning was spent readying his information and then, around two in the afternoon, he and his colleagues set off for the Commons. After a little wait they were ushered in and it was Pepys who spoke for them all. Despite his nervousness, his presentation was masterly. The facts were at his fingertips, literally so, since he called for a chair on which to lean his papers and for candles when it grew too dark to read them by daylight. He gave the Committee of Miscarriages a full and orderly account of the whole manner in which the defence of the Medway had been handled and then 'answered all questions given me about it'.

Pepys did well and he knew it. He could sense that his inquisitors were 'fully satisfied' with him, a compliment he could not return. His forensic skills were such that he had been obliged to listen with contempt to the coarse lack of method revealed by the MPs. 'But Lord', he wrote afterwards, 'what a tumultuous thing this committee is, for all the reputation they have of a great council . . . there being as impertinent questions, and as disorderly proposed, as any man could make.' Real politics ruffled the civil servant. There was danger here all the same and, despite the congratulations offered him by some of the Members and the obvious relief of his colleagues who were 'all very brisk to see themselves so well acquitted', Pepys tempered his natural feelings of pride with the suspicion that 'we may yet meet with a back-blow which we see not'. Certainly this was one danger, but inexperience was another. Pepys had the strength of personality to put Sir Robert Brooke, the young chairman of the Committee of Miscarriages, in his place, but the very force of his conscientiousness exposed him to unforeseen difficulty. Pepys was a mandarin confronted with a blunt, crude instrument, as his account of being questioned about the seamen's tickets suggests:

> . . . they fell to the business of tickets; and I did give them the best answer I could, but had no scope to do it in that methodical manner which I had prepared myself for, but they did ask a great many broken rude questions about it, and were mighty hot whether my Lord Brouncker had any order to discharge whole ships by ticket; and because my answer was with distinction and not direct, I did perceive they were not so fully satisfied therewith as I could wish they were: so my Lord Brouncker was called in, and they could fasten nothing on him that I could see, nor indeed was there any proper matter for blame. But Lord, to see that we should be brought to justify ourselves in a thing of necessity and profit to the King, and of no profit or convenience to us, but the contrary.[4]

Here speaks the civil servant and royalist about an institution he feared and in large measure despised but, for the moment, he had to attune himself to the most basic practices of the

House and confine his exasperation to his *Diary*. 'Comes a damned summons to attend the Committee of Miscarriages today,' he wrote on 11 February 1668, 'which makes me mad, that I should be by my place become the hackney of this Office, in perpetual trouble and vexation, that need it least.'

Meanwhile, the personnel of the Navy Office itself was changing. Carteret had resigned as treasurer and Batten died in October. Coventry resigned his position as secretary to the Duke of York and, for a while, Pepys thought he might be appointed in his place. What he gained in fact, was not his ally's position but his advice. Coventry told him in particular how to handle a Parliamentary committee. With the insight of an adept and ambitious man, Coventry suggested that when answering questions Pepys be 'as short as I can, and obscure, saving in things fully plain; and that the greatest wisdom in dealing with Parliament in the world is to say little, and let them get out what they can by force'. Such a lesson was extremely valuable for, at the start of 1668, the Committee for Accounts set about its business of examining the Navy Board's huge expenditure with a vengeance.

This was a deeply threatening situation, for the King's servants were an obvious target for the Members' wrath and, in order to vent their fury in a constitutional manner they dug up an old precedent whereby the House could demand both 'appropriation' – in other words, an investigation to determine whether the money they had allocated had been spent on the purposes for which it was intended – and an audit of accounts. The danger that Clarendon had foreseen was now emerging. Parliamentary scrutiny of royal plans and spending was tightening its grip. It was doing so in an increasingly poisonous atmosphere. So crushing had the humiliation by the Dutch been that changes at once acrimonious and subtle were taking place in the nation at large. A people that had welcomed the restoration of

Charles II with unexampled joy were now disillusioned to a dangerously divisive degree.

In the strife that divided the country, many people united against the policies of the Crown. The narrow streets of London echoed with political discontent as people openly blamed national disgrace on the 'debauchery and drunkenness at court'. Nor was this merely moral censoriousness. To a people reared in the belief that Protestantism, for all its snarling mutual antipathies, was self-evidently superior to the superstitious pomp of the Catholic Church, the popularity of Rome in royal circles was a cause for deep alarm. Of course the nation had been dishonoured, but then 'no better could be expected when the Popish and profane party are in such credit', particularly as it seemed with the Duke of York. Time would magnify these fears until the nation was gripped by an all but universal paranoia, a nightmare of unreason in which Catholics not only threatened true religion but supposedly plotted to overthrow the English way of life and impose the sort of arbitrary tyranny under which so many people on the Continent laboured.

Once again Pepys was to be his office's principal spokesman to a House deeply troubled by such thoughts, but this time his anxiety was all the greater since he might also have to speak in his own defence. The Committee of Accounts might very well examine the grey areas of his and his colleagues' private dealings and do so under oath at the Bar of the House. Even the upright Coventry was concerned, and in the guilty and panic-ridden atmosphere that now swirled about him Pepys was distinctly uneasy. Gossip fed his fears. He heard that he might be accused of taking a £50 sweetener from Mason the timber merchant 'though the thing is to my best memory utterly false'. It was troubling all the same 'to have my name mentioned in this business, and more to consider how I may be liable to be accused where I have indeed taken presents, and therefore puts me on an inquiry into my actings in this kind and prepare against a day of accusation'. Just as serious was Pepys's involvement in his colleagues' privateering exploits. 'Our business of the prizes' preyed on his mind, and he eventually decided that the best thing he could do was make a clean breast of the affair rather than 'be forced at last to do it and in the meantime live in pain'.

Nor was this all that worried him. Pepys felt he had quite as much to fear from his dealings with Sir William Warren, particularly as he had fallen out with him, and on 17 February, chancing to meet the man in Fleet Street, he took the opportunity of taking him to lunch. The conversation was distinctly edgy, for Warren too was running scared and had half decided that attack was his best means of defence. He was 'very high' in his resentment of the Navy Board and made some worrying observations on Pepys's recent coldness to him. Both men knew they could do each other great damage and they managed to patch together a mutually convenient conspiracy of silence. 'I do find that he is still a cunning fellow,' Pepys wrote of Warren, 'and will find it necessary to be fair to me; and what hath passed between us of kindness, to hold his tongue – which doth please me very well.' That, at least, was settled.

Having secured his back, Pepys also had to prepare for his frontal assault – his defence of the Navy Board before the House of Commons.[5] He would, with his utmost ability, justify what he and his colleagues had been able to achieve under the most difficult circumstances. This required an enormous amount of work and the co-operation of a devoted team. The loyal Will Hewer in particular was a stalwart, and Pepys, his mind 'mighty full of trouble', discussed 'the business of the office' with him in the privacy of Seething Lane. This was a help, for Hewer 'doth well understand himself and our case, and it doth me advantage to talk with him and the rest of my people'. The bond between the two men was strengthening into a deep friendship. 'My head is full of care and weariness in my employment', and even collecting a beautifully bound copy of a musical work from his booksellers could not give Pepys the usual delight. All he felt he could do was shut his office doors and fall to work with his clerks as he prepared a defence of himself and his worried, suspicious colleagues. Lord Brouncker in particular 'looked mighty dogged' at Pepys's efforts and could not conceive that the clerk of the acts was actually labouring to save him along with the other commissioners.

It was a dreadful time. The volume of work was tremendous, the detail proliferated endlessly, the atmosphere was sour, while the thought of an inquisitorial House of Commons stirred fear and fatigue in equal measure. The candles burned in Pepys's office until ten at night and, as the papers piled up on the tables in front of his painful, failing eyes, so he grew ever more vexed and tired until he knew that he had to go home 'in full discontent and weariness'. He was too exhausted and worried even to eat. He went straight to bed but got no more than three hours' sleep. The long, hag-ridden hours after midnight slowly passed and, by six in the morning, his torment was unendurable. He desperately needed someone to hold him, to comfort him, to show him that there was a world beyond his own whirling thoughts. He sent for Elizabeth and 'at last' she came 'and made me resolve to quit my hands of this office and endure the trouble [of] it no longer than till I can clear myself of it'. Here, at least, was 'some ease' and now, enervated but not wholly in despair, Pepys trudged back to the office for one final attempt at marshalling his defence.

By nine o'clock on Thursday 5 March he had done all he could. He went down to the Old Swan to meet with his senior clerks Hayter and Hewer and travelled by boat to Westminster with them. There his colleagues on the board were assembled, but their anxious and suspicious company was not agreeable. Pepys's mind was overflowing with the same worries as theirs – the thought that in a few moments they would all be summoned before the assembly of the nation to justify their part in that nation's crippling humiliation – but Pepys had (as they had not) his marshalled phalanxes of facts, figures and arguments to ponder. He went to the Dog for half a pint of mulled sack and then, returning to Westminster Hall, took a dram of brandy at Mrs Howlett's stall. It made him feel better, 'truly'.

Towards midday Pepys and the rest of the Navy Board were called into the House. To fit with the full solemnity of the occasion the mace was borne before them, and, as Pepys entered the chamber and made his way to the Bar, he could 'perceive the whole House was full, and full of expectation of our defence what it would be, and with great prejudice'. The speaker expressed the House's dissatisfaction with what Members believed was the Navy Board's incompetence. The report confirming their beliefs was read out, and then it was Pepys's turn to speak. He rose like a man inspired. For three hushed and spell-binding hours – smoothly, agreeably, with ample detail and sound ideas – he defended his colleagues' behaviour and his own. His arguments sailed before him in well-disciplined squadrons and each argument destroyed an error, a prejudice, an enemy. The silent speaker and the silent House (or those Members, at least, who had the powers of concentration to attend) listened with deepening admiration. Who had ever spoken like this before or shown himself so fluent and so well informed? The mind of the clerk of the acts was capacious, nimble, remarkably clear, and as was the mind so indeed was the man – the King's man.

When Pepys had concluded his case he withdrew from the chamber. His colleagues gathered about him in overjoyed relief while other men cried up the speech 'as the best thing they ever heard'. Reason, it seemed, had driven out prejudice – quite literally so, for during the course of Pepys's speech a considerable number of hostile Members had slipped away from the House aware that they had made a tactical blunder in thus attacking so able a servant of the Crown. Many had got drunk over lunch and those who now returned, stumbling and aggrieved, resolved to try to limit the damage and reopen their campaign by advancing on a different flank. Since the House was no longer full it would be highly improper, they said, to vote. They would postpone the matter. They had far more important considerations. They were due to attend the King that afternoon 'about the business of religion' and inform him of their earnest desire that the Penal Laws against Catholics and Nonconformists be prosecuted with the utmost rigour. Pepys was too shrewd and too relieved to be offended. 'It is plain we have got great ground,' he wrote, 'and everybody says I have got the most honour that any could have had opportunity of getting.'

The following days made this ringingly clear. '"Good-morrow, Mr Pepys, that must be Speaker of the Parliament-house,"' declared Coventry. Someone else told him he could earn himself £1,000 a year by putting on a gown and pleading at the Chancery Bar. The reported phrases of the solicitor-general were sweet in Pepys's ears. The Duke of York, preparing for his morning walk, allowed him to know that he was greatly pleased. In St James's Park the King graciously declared his content too: '"Mr Pepys, I am very glad of your success yesterday."' A chorus of lesser men sought to outdo each other in hyperbole. Some swore they would walk twenty miles to hear such a speech again. Pepys was called 'another Cicero'. He was told that 'the kingdom will ring of my ability'. Senior Parliamentarians said they had not heard such a speech in a quarter of a century, and Pepys's fame echoed in the measured talk of the great merchants in the City.

It was all enough to turn a man's head, but Pepys, with the piety and pragmatism that together made up his Puritan second nature, merely totted up the praise 'for which the

Lord God make me thankful and that I may make use of it not to pride and vainglory'. Only once did he fear that he might have been carried away. One afternoon in April, passing the Privy Stairs at Whitehall as his boatmen rowed him to the House of Commons, the affable King called out to ask where he was going. '"To wait on our masters at Westminster,"' was Pepys's quick response. He wondered later if he had gone too far, but the royal laughter that greeted his wit was enough to reassure him of his safety and his prestige. In royal circles, at least, Mr Pepys was a valued man, but his duel with Parliament was far from over.

CHAPTER NINE

Darkness

When Parliament was prorogued in the hope that Members would become more accommodating, Pepys could at last relax. The recent months of work had placed an enormous strain both on his powers of self-discipline and on his eyesight. Now he could rest both. Music and the theatre beckoned, as did the altogether more furtive delights of sex. The prospect of these last was made easier because Elizabeth and Deb were about to take a holiday in Brampton, but just before they departed two incidents occurred that pointed to future troubles. Unwilling to believe that Elizabeth was able to organise her departure for herself, Pepys 'called Deb to take pen, ink, and paper and write down what things came into my head for my wife to do, in order to her going into the country'.[1]

The girl stumbled over Pepys's dictation, began to cry and, being found in this tearful state by her mistress, was told that she was merely being sullen. Pepys too 'seemed angry' with her, but the rather cruel little scene had stirred him all the same and that night, on his going to bed, he had Deb help him undress. As he gave the still weeping girl some advice about how to handle her mistress, so he began first to kiss her and then to put her on his knee and brush her breasts and thighs with his hand. He went no further for the moment, but the following morning, calling in the girl to dress him, he petted her and then 'would have tocado su thing; but ella endeavoured to prevent me con much modesty by putting su hand thereabout which I was well pleased with and would not do too much, and so con great kindness dismissed la; and I to my office'.*

Deb and Elizabeth departed for Brampton the following day and Pepys turned his attentions elsewhere. In particular, he recalled the delights of the actress Mrs Knepp and, throughout much of April and May 1668 pursued her with a vicarious combination of lust and fear, curiosity and revulsion. He kissed her but winced at the thickness of her makeup. He took her to see the sights of the Tower, to eat lobster in the Temple, and to Vauxhall where he touched her all over 'but did not offer algo mas'.† Her evident sexuality thrilled and frightened him in equal measure and there are hints in the *Diary* that suggest Mrs Knepp herself was perhaps a little disappointed that a man so famous for subduing the House of Commons failed to master her.

By the beginning of June, Pepys's inconclusive fumblings had come to a close. He was badly in need of a holiday and, having been granted a week's leave of absence by a grateful Duke of York, he set out first for Brampton and from there with Deb and Elizabeth on a twelve-day jaunt through Oxford, Abingdon, Hungerford and Salisbury. From there the party went on to Bath and Bristol. Pepys derived a great deal of pleasure from the trip, nowhere more so

* 'would have touched her thing, but she endeavoured to prevent me with much modesty by putting her hand thereabout which I was well pleased with and would not do too much, and so with great kindness dismissed her; and I to my office'.

† 'but did not offer anything more'

than in Bristol, which was Deb's birthplace. The pretty, tempting little girl had been almost continuously at his side throughout the journey, and her reception by her Bristol relatives provided the high point in the diary notes Pepys made of his expedition and pointed to the direction in which his thoughts were now running.[2] The party was shown round the city by Deb's uncle, and while Pepys was impressed by the sights he saw what really moved him was the affection so openly showered on Deb. 'But Lord!' he wrote, 'the joy that was among the old poor people of the place to see Mrs Willet's daughter: it seems her mother being a brave woman and mightily beloved.' One of these poor women greeted the girl with weeping, speechless rapture, and Pepys himself was so moved that he, too, was unable to speak. Deb's innocence was at once infinitely valuable and all but unbearably tempting.

Only the presence of Elizabeth served to exasperate Pepys and remind him that he was chained to a responsibility he increasingly regarded with contempt. He had married his wife when he was a sexually infatuated young man and it seemed there was little enough to support their relationship now that the sex was all but dead. By way of compensation, Pepys expected freedom for himself and obedience from her. This was the way of his world and he had taken his pleasure with a dozen compliant women. Now the childlike innocence of Deb was stirring ambivalent feelings, which made the behaviour of his all-too-neglected wife seem, by contrast, merely irksome. That Elizabeth was unhappy and needed his attention never occurred to Pepys, and the way she expressed her resentment could almost have been designed to push him further from her. She was by turns lost in a vague sulk or stupidly demanding in the pettiest matters. Pepys's response was to find her contemptible and to blame himself for giving her too much freedom, 'which she is never to be trusted with; for she is a fool'.

His disillusion deepened after they returned to London. They had barely arrived back in Seething Lane before Elizabeth somehow found out what her husband had been doing in her absence. He found her 'in a fusty humour and crying'. Elizabeth was probably frightened to challenge Pepys directly (she knew that her husband could be physically violent) and instead she turned her weakness against him and obliged him slowly to force out of her all she knew. If she hoped in this way to make him feel guilty she failed. Pepys's self-esteem was at stake and he prepared himself to outstare the storm he knew his wife was sure to raise. It began to break just after one the following morning. Elizabeth, powerless and in anguish, went crying to Deb's bed. A troubled Pepys did nothing. Elizabeth returned to him, still crying. Pepys felt that if they talked perhaps things would be better. He was prepared to talk all night if needs be but Elizabeth, longing deeply for peace and mistrusting words, suggested they go to bed. They did so and fell asleep.

They were woken by a fire. Dreadful memories from two years earlier shattered all hopes of intimacy – the sleep in each other's arms, the morning kiss. Thoughts of his gold, plate and papers leaped into Pepys's mind. He rushed outside to see the damage the fire was doing and, relieved that it was slight, talked to his neighbours before returning to bed to sleep 'pretty well'. But Elizabeth had failed to get what she most craved. The tenderness in which she had placed her trust had been snatched from her and, as Pepys once again awoke, she broke down in tears. In a desperate, pathetic demand for love she begged him to let her go and live in France, out of the way. Then, with the courage of her wretchedness mounting, all her resentments began to spill out – the resentments of a bullied, deprived, foolish, bruised and frightened woman, whose husband 'loved pleasure and denied her any' and whose father-in-law, it now appeared, had treated her to savage lectures on her duty to his son.

Pepys silently resolved to put a stop to these at least and, chastened, 'said nothing; but with very mild words and few suffered her humour to spend, till we begin to be very quiet and I think all will be over, and friends'. With that he left for the office.[3]

There further trouble awaited him. Lord Anglesey, the new treasurer of the navy, suggested to Pepys that his holiday had overrun its permitted limits. Pepys himself, made confident by his recent achievements, told his *Diary* that 'I care not a turd' and proceeded to settle to work. There was much to do. Coventry had informed him that he was having the utmost difficulty raising money for the navy, his colleagues at the Treasury 'being all concerned for some other part of the King's expense'. He suggested that Pepys write a 'smart letter' to the Duke of York, who had shown himself 'very hot for regulations in the Navy', and with this in mind, Pepys left Coventry's office much impressed both by his friend's concern and by the new circular desk Coventry had had made so that he could sit in the middle of it entirely surrounded by his papers.

On 23 July, Pepys had a private conference with the Duke about the constitution and working of the Navy Board. Theirs was a grave and important discussion about reform. The recent disasters had made it abundantly clear that the Navy Board would have to put its own house in order if it were to function with any degree of efficiency and stave off criticism from the Commons. Pepys's ability to defend the board had been amply displayed in the House itself and now the Duke wondered if he could exercise critical rigour as a prelude to reform. 'I did long and largely show him,' Pepys recorded, 'the weakness of our office, and did give him advice to call us to account for our duties.' The Duke, already considerably impressed by Pepys's abilities, listened to what he had to say and took it 'mighty well'. A relationship of the greatest importance to both men was deepening and, keenly aware that something needed to be done, York asked Pepys to draft him the letter that he should write to the Navy Board. In this he would 'lay open the whole failings of the Office, and how it was his duty to find them and to find fault with them'. Much of August was given over to this onerous business as Pepys and his clerks, working late, made clear the principles on which the office should operate, examined precedents, drew up long lists of failings and made recommendations for better practice in the future.

The memorandum was a searing indictment of inefficiency since Pepys was fully aware that 'the pest of this office has all along been an indifference in some of the principal members of it in seeing their work done, provided they found themselves furnished with any tolerable pretence for their personal failures in the doing of it'. As early as August 1666 Pepys had intimated to Coventry his concern about 'personal and particular failings' at the Navy Board and, as his mind dwelt on these, so the Puritan in him rose to castigate the incompetence around him. A solitary walk in early June 1667 had seen him 'reflecting upon the bad management of things now, compared with what it was in the later rebellious times, when men, some for fear and some for religion, minded their business, which now none do, by being void of both'. But moralising was not enough. Castigating the follies of the age was insufficient. Such methods were for preachers, and Pepys was a civil servant. The Navy Board needed the sort of thorough overhaul Downing, Coventry and other colleagues had given to the Treasury.

Pepys needed to proceed by detailed factual analysis of functions and performance and now, as he prepared his charges, he based his criticisms on the Navy Board's failure to fulfil the Lord High Admiral's Instructions of 1662. He moved from the general to the particular, and drew up his indictment with admirable order and method. He did not spare individuals. The treasurer was charged for his irregular attendance at meetings, especially when these concerned contracts and estimates. Pepys wrote that his accounts were usually at least two years in arrears and were always incompetently presented. The accountancy techniques of the Comptroller were similarly remiss, and his officials had singularly failed to audit the victuallers' and storekeepers' books. The surveyor had omitted to submit annual reports on the state of the ships and the dockyards.

This was a comprehensive indictment of inefficiency, and only the clerk of the acts escaped from Pepys's damning charges. That these would soon make enemies of his colleagues was inevitable but Pepys forged ahead and, by Sunday, 23 August, the great document was ready to deliver to the Duke at four o'clock in the afternoon. Pepys was ushered into the royal presence and presented his memorandum. Having read it through, York declared himself extremely pleased with it 'and did give me many and hearty thanks, and in words the most expressive tells me his sense of my good endeavours, and that he would have a care of me on all occasions'. Bidding Pepys farewell, he told him that he would have his memorandum transcribed and sent to the office forthwith.

Such professional success was pleasing but it had been bought at a high price. Pepys's eyes were now in a desperate state. Rest and a holiday had not cured them and the recent strain appeared to have caused them to have deteriorated further. The fear that he was going blind was now real. Pepys made strenuous efforts to get such professional advice as was available to him. He consulted Dr Turberville and 'did receive a direction for some physic, and also a glass of something to drop in my eyes; which gives me hopes that I may do well'.[4] There was no improvement. By the close of June, Pepys was worried and depressed. He noted in his *Diary* how he could read for small periods at a time without much difficulty but then his eyes would give way until tiny letters especially became a blur. There were moments when he thought things were getting better, as when some pills Dr Turberville prescribed for him 'wrought pretty well most of the morning'. He had a surgeon bleed him of fourteen ounces of blood in the hope that this might improve matters, but by the end of July he was desperately seeking any relief he could find. 'The month ends mighty sadly with me', he wrote, 'my eyes being now past all use almost; and I am mighty hot upon trying the late printed experiment of paper tubes'.

It was with the help of these cumbrous spectacles that Pepys drew up his great memorandum for the Duke of York. At first he was 'mightily pleased' with the help they seemed to offer, and he was delighted that 'my paper tube' allowed him to read through the lengthy document 'without pain to my eyes'.

Pepys's colleagues at the Navy Board soon had cause to regret that he had laboured so hard and with such difficulty. The office was already rife with rumour, but when the document Pepys had composed for the Duke was read out, its searing criticism of numerous incompetencies was all too clearly Pepys's work. His fellows were naturally hurt and angry, but Pepys did not care. He had laboured hard in an affair of the utmost importance, ruined his eyes (as it seemed) in the process and had come to realise that he might have to accept a life of darkness and retirement. What did he care about the bitterness of his colleagues in circumstances such as these? Even an angry peer failed to intimidate him. 'I met with Lord Brouncker,' Pepys wrote, 'who I perceive, and the rest, do smell that it comes from me, but dare not find fault with [it]; and I am glad of it, it being my glory and defence that I did occasion and write it.' The memorandum stood on its own merits and, in this mood, Pepys was not prepared to be browbeaten either by a peer or by such rising Treasury officials as Sir Thomas Clifford, who sought to make difficulties about the victualling of the fleet.

Pepys told the great man that his objections were based on misinformation and proceeded to get on with his business, writing that he knew he had 'done the King and myself good service in it'.

As so often, Pepys sought relief from his burdens in compulsive sexual activity. A visit to Bartholomew Fair ironically indicated his state of mind, for one of the showmen there had a knowing horse who, when bidden to find the most amorous man in the crowd, made straight for Pepys. Taking a coach home, Pepys paid a prostitute a shilling to play with him and, as the month progressed, tried his luck with a whole succession of women, including his neighbour Miss Turner and, eventually, with little Deb. On 10 October he had the girl comb his hair and again let his roving hands explore her. The pleasure was repeated on the evening of 25 October, but such careless pleasure was brought to a sudden and terrible end by Elizabeth entering the room as Pepys was 'embracing the girl con my hand sub su coats; and indeed, I was with my main in her cunny'.*

Husband and maid were horrorstruck as Elizabeth, mute at first, grew suddenly and screamingly angry. Pepys sloped off to bed but was woken at about two in the morning by a hysterical Elizabeth. Allying herself to the nationwide paranoia about papists, she declared she had become a Roman Catholic and received the sacrament. If true, this would do Pepys immense harm. He was troubled but took (or pretended to take) no notice and allowed her to dart desperately from one subject to another 'till at last it appeared plainly her trouble was at what she saw'. Not knowing quite how much she had indeed seen, Pepys kept silent while Elizabeth cried and reproached him 'with inconstancy and preferring a sorry girl before her'. Eventually she quietened

* 'embracing the girl with my hand under her dress; and indeed, I was with my hand in her cunt'.

down, and Pepys was able to get some badly needed sleep, for the following morning he had a high level conference with the Duke of York.

The aggrieved members of the Navy Board had now written their replies to Pepys's great memorandum and York urgently needed advice as to how he should reply. He was feeling threatened, for it appeared that moves were being made by members of the Treasury to place the running of the navy in the hands of his enemy, the Duke of Buckingham. Pepys agreed to draft replies and, burdened by these responsibilities, returned to a home brooding with discontent. Nothing was said until night fell when Elizabeth launched her second attack, saying that she had seen her husband hugging and kissing Deb. Pepys confessed to the first but not to the second and, harassed and guilty, bowed before Elizabeth's wrath and promised he would see no more of his other women friends. Sensing victory, Elizabeth exulted in her power and determined to display it. When Pepys returned weary from an anguish-ridden day at the office, she waited until bedtime before she once again flew into a rage, raving at him and threatening to publish his shame.[5]

Elizabeth called for a candle to be lit and continued ranting by its light. Eventually the storm appeared to blow itself out, Pepys went to bed, and the following morning, in an abject mood, he wrote a hurried note to Deb to tell her just how much of their relationship he had been obliged to confess. The thought that the girl would be dismissed and thereby ruined harrowed him and, over the supper table through the following nights, Pepys was aware of a vengeful-eyed Elizabeth watching to see if he stole as much as a glance at the girl. It was ghastly, for Pepys could not but look at Deb 'now and then, and to my grief did see the poor wretch look on me and see me look on her and then let drop a tear or two, which do make my heart relent at this minute that I am writing this with great trouble of mind, for she is indeed my sacrifice, poor girl'. Eventually, when Elizabeth decided that Deb should indeed leave Seething Lane, Pepys did not dare ask when or where she was to go but meekly submitted as Elizabeth, in her Juno-like wrath, made sure he dressed and undressed himself without the poor girl's help. All he was able to do was throw Deb a hurried note begging her not to confess to anything and deny that he had ever kissed her. But underneath the humiliation his desire burned on. 'The truth is,' he admitted to himself, 'I have a great mind for to have the maidenhead of this girl, which I should not doubt to have had if je could get time para be con her.* But she will be gone and I know not whither.'

Before she left, poor Deb – harassed by her mistress and apparently ignored by Pepys himself – made a fatal mistake. She confessed to everything that had happened. Elizabeth's anguished fury knew no bounds. She had experienced her power over her husband and now she was determined to humiliate him utterly. She told a weeping Pepys that she had been wholly faithful to him, for all that she had had offers from elsewhere. The storm continued through the night with tears on both sides until Elizabeth managed to get her husband's promise that he would himself dismiss Deb and, more cruelly still, express his dislike for her.

On Saturday, 14 November – the day on which Deb was due to depart – Elizabeth prevented Pepys even from handing her a note and a little money. She forbade her husband to go into the kitchen where the girl was, and when he answered her angrily she flew into a rage, 'calling me dog and rogue, and that I had a rotten heart'. Pepys, knowing that he was in the wrong, bore with it all and then, 'word being brought presently up that she was gone away by coach with her things, my wife was friends; and so all quiet, and I to the office with my heart sad, and find that

* '. . . if I could get time to be with her.'

I cannot forget the girl, and vexed I know not where to look for her'.

The guilt of harming the child weighed on Pepys, while the dreadful realisation dawned that his wife would now for ever have the upper hand. The only hope seemed to lie in that he believed Elizabeth would endeavour to please him all she could 'to keep me right to her'. He squirmed with compromises. For his part he would try to behave himself from now on 'for she deserves it of me, though it will be I fear a little time before I shall be able to wear Deb out of my mind'. This last was certainly true. The weekend passed and Pepys knew that he could not simply forget the girl. He desired her and, in his feelings of guilt and anxiety, realised that he loved her too. No hint of her escaped his notice. Elizabeth accidentally let slip that Deb was now lodging with a certain Dr Allbon in Whetstone Park, an area on the south side of Holborn and notorious as the haunt of prostitutes. Much troubled 'that the poor girl should be in a desperate condition forced to go thereabouts', Pepys made his way to Whetstone Park but could gather no news about Allbon at all. Then he remembered that Elizabeth had also said something about the man living in Eagle Court and he sent a boy over to find him there. When the lad returned, Pepys was told that Allbon was a debtor and 'a kind of poor broken fellow that dare not show his head or be known where he is gone'.

This, awful as it was, was a lead and Pepys was 'at mighty ease in my mind, being in hopes to find Deb, and without trouble or the knowledge of my wife'. He set about trying to contact her. He found a porter who had once delivered a chest of drawers to Allbon's lodgings and persuaded the man to take a message to Deb. This the porter eventually did, returning to say that Deb was well 'and that I may see her if I will – but no more'. Even the girl's reported words were irresistible. 'I could not be commanded by my reason, but I must go this very night; and so by coach, it being now dark, I to her, close by my tailor's; and there she came into the coach to me, and yo di besar her and tocar her thing, but ella was against it and laboured with much earnestness, such as I believed to be real; and yet at last yo did make her tener me cosa in her mano, while mi mano was sobra her pectus, and so did hazer with grand delight'.*

Even in the midst of this despicable scene the Puritan in Pepys was roused to a display of hypocrisy. Having had his pleasure with a frightened and reluctant girl whom he had driven into destitution, Pepys counselled her 'to have a care of her honour and to fear God' and to let no other man play with her as he had done. Perhaps he felt better for this. Certainly, Deb herself promised to obey and Pepys gave her twenty shillings. If she needed to get in touch with him at any time, he added, she was to leave a sealed note for him at his bookseller's. With that he bade her goodnight 'with much content to my mind and resolution to look after her no more till I heard from her'. Pepys then went home, lied to his wife about how he had spent his time, had supper and went to bed. He noted in his *Diary* how Elizabeth had been busy all day getting the house ready for the men who were to come the following morning to hang tapestries in the best chamber.

If Pepys thought he was free of trouble he was wrong. When he hurried back from the office to lunch the following day he found Elizabeth sitting sadly in the dining room. He asked her what the matter was, and once again the thunder of her anger was let loose as she called him a false and rotten-hearted rogue. It seemed that Elizabeth had somehow discovered what Pepys had been doing the previous day and,

* '. . . and there she came into the coach to me, and I did kiss her and touch her thing, but she was against it and laboured with much earnestness, such as I believed to be real; and yet at last I did make her take my thing in her hand, which my hand was under her breast, and so did indulge myself with great pleasure'.

although he assumed for a while that she was bluffing, he eventually confessed all. The rowing couple were in their bedroom as Pepys was subjected to Elizabeth's threats, vows and curses. So vindictive was she that she promised she would herself go and find Deb and slit the girl's nose. Then she said she wanted a separation and demanded three or four hundred pounds 'that she might be gone without making any noise'. It was all searingly ghastly and exhausting, 'the greatest agony in the world'. Eventually, unable to support Elizabeth's rancour any longer, Pepys sent for the one man he believed might stand by him – his clerk Will Hewer.

The loyal secretary burst into tears as his master made him privy to his shameful secrets, but Hewer at least could view the situation with an independent eye and a natural gift for diplomacy. He eventually persuaded Elizabeth to forgive her husband, provided that Pepys himself would promise in writing never to see Deb again. For the moment, and beyond all Pepys's hopes, there was peace. That night husband and wife made love and Pepys, for the first time in a long while, prayed – that 'God will give me the grace more and more every day to fear Him, and be true to my poor wife'. The storms of the past week had shaken him to the core. He felt he must strive to be no longer the arrogant and self-indulgent amorist seizing his pleasures where he would. He had been humbled, utterly humbled. He had not realised the anger Elizabeth was capable of. He had not sensed how he had hurt her and, in damaging her happiness, had threatened his own. He knew now that there was 'no curse in the world so great as this of a difference between myself and her'. God would help. He would change.

Elizabeth ensured that this was so. She was determined to watch her husband's every move and, to guarantee that she could do so, she insisted Will Hewer accompany Pepys everywhere he went. This was humiliating, but still she was not satisfied. Elizabeth wanted vengeance on Deb. Pepys returned home from the office to find Elizabeth once again in a terrible mood. She called him names, she pulled his hair, she hit him. He took it all in new-found humility, but although he managed to quieten her down she flared again after supper and Will Hewer had once again to intervene. The whole situation was desolate and, in his anguish, Pepys threw himself on his bed while his wife and his clerk spoke together in the next room. Eventually they came to tell him that he would only be fully forgiven if he would write to Deb and call her a 'whore'. The cringing man protested but Elizabeth was firm in her resolve, and it was only the shrewd Hewer who saved the day by winking at Pepys, thereby suggesting that although the letter should be written he would never deliver it. The wretched note was indeed scribbled out, but Hewer was as good as his word while Pepys, finding strength in his Puritan side, promised Elizabeth that he would never again go to bed without praying on his knees, comforting himself with the fact that 'I do find that it is much the best for my soul and body to live pleasing to God and my poor wife'. Morality, he decided, would give him an easy life and stop him wasting money besides.[6]

The Puritan had won and Pepys was able once again to turn his full attention to his work, Will Hewer still acting as Elizabeth's watchdog 'but yet with great love'. He continued with much-needed exercises in cost-cutting. He looked into the purchasing of such small items as nuts, bolts and glue with cash rather than by credit. Having proved that great savings could be made in these areas, he examined ways of dealing more equably with suppliers so as to avoid 'sacrificing our own content and good names by the ruining of private men'. Larger-scale projects also absorbed him. The annual navy budget had now been fixed at £200,000, and Pepys costed out the possibility of keeping a number of ships in harbour while still sending out winter and summer fleets of ten and twenty-four ships respectively. Unbeknown to him, this would soon become a matter of the utmost importance, for in the canny recesses of his mind Charles II was planning a new war against the Dutch.

The King's reasons were as clear as his methods were devious. The political price of the recent disasters had been paid by Clarendon with his fall and exile. With that steadying influence at long last removed, Charles wanted to be one of the major players on the European scene and to become so by asserting the prerogative rights of the Crown and freeing himself from what he conceived of as his humiliating dependence on Parliament. In order to achieve these aims he began to shape a policy known as the Grand Design.

Everybody knew that the conduct of foreign affairs was the exclusive right of the Crown, but few indeed were privy to the guile of the man who wore it. In order to bamboozle the greater part of his subjects, Charles entered a Triple Alliance with his Protestant neighbours. Having publicly declared his religious credentials, he then resolved to free himself from the Anglican majority by offering religious toleration to his Catholic and Nonconformist subjects and to secure his back by opening secret negotiations with Catholic France. Charles and Louis XIV agreed they would wage war on the Dutch and so win for themselves a great share of the world's trade. The resulting prizes and the increase in tax revenue would (as the Duke of York had once hoped) free Charles from his subservience to Parliament, while victory at sea would also redeem the tarnished reputation of the Crown. What was needed to ensure success was a strong navy, and Mr Pepys was the obvious man to consult on this all-important matter. There was no reason to make him privy to the details of policy. They were none of his business. The readiness of the navy was, however, and, on Sunday, 24 January 1669, Pepys was summoned before the King to answer Charles's questions about how soon his ships could be put to sea. Contrary to the advice of others, Pepys believed that the fleet could be readied by the following summer, provided always that sufficient money was available. 'I see,' he wrote of his royal masters, 'that on all these occasions they seem to rely most on me.'

Pepys knew that if he and his colleagues were really to be relied on then the manifest defects of the Navy Board would have to be sorted out once and for all. A clear statement of aims and purposes was required, and Pepys now applied his great talent for research to investigating the historical background of the board and clarifying its functions and responsibilities in the light of this. With the regularity and method that were second nature to him, Pepys divided the board's duties under five heads. His style was a model of condensed, precise English and was a world away from the ebullience of the *Diary*. Instead of a sense of almost endlessly proliferating life, here was official English at its most elegant. For example, the first duty of the Navy Board was described as 'the well and husbandly building, equipping, manning, victualling, safe mooring, repairing, and preserving in harbour His Majesty's ships'.[7]

A vast responsibility is here encompassed in a single, comprehensive sentence, and the same mind can be seen at work as Pepys set out the board's other responsibilities: the management of stores and money, the regulation of personnel and the prompt execution of royal commands. There then followed several paragraphs that deftly summarised the history of naval administration and focused especially on the three most salient points: the innovations brought in by Henry VIII, the changes wrought 'upon the rupture between his late Majesty and the Parliament', and the appointment of assistant commissioners to the board subsequent to the Navy Office's return to traditional forms after the Restoration. Pepys then carefully paid tribute to the Duke of York's attempts to systemise 'the rule by which the hands thus entrusted are to govern themselves' then moved on to his familiar argument: the fact that the work of the Navy Board was hampered by a lack of adequate funding and the shifts and corruptions consequent thereupon.

Pepys felt that he needed to run so important a document past other minds and went to call first on Coventry, whose professional acumen he always regarded with the highest respect. To Pepys's relief, Coventry liked the document 'very well'. He then made his way to Whitehall and an interview with the Duke of York, who took Pepys into his closet 'and there did hear and approve my paper of the Administration of the Navy; only bid me alter these words, "upon the rupture between the late King and the Parliament" to these, "the beginning of the late Rebellion" giving it me as but reason that it was with the Rebellion that the Navy was put by out of its old good course into that of a Commission'. The suggested emendation shows York both as an administrator with an eye for detail and a man of some political discernment in matters on this scale at least. Having received the Duke's approval, Pepys had his memorandum fair-copied then listened as it was read out to the grandees of the court. When this had been done the document was left with Lord Arlington for any of the other lords that had a mind to read it 'and to prepare and present to the King what they had to say in writing to any part of it; which is all we can desire'. The civil servant's duty had been done.

Very gradually the orderliness of Pepys's professional life was matched by a calming of his domestic circumstances too. Peace with some measure of dignity was hard won. Elizabeth was still suspicious of her husband and easily moved to outbursts of anger. Even the sleeping Pepys did not escape her surveillance. 'Up, after a little talk with my wife which troubles me,' he wrote on 5 December, 'she being ever since our late difference mighty watchful of sleep and dreams, and will not be persuaded but I do dream of Deb, and tells me that I speak in my dream and that this night I did cry "Huzzy!" and it must be she.' Pepys was genuinely troubled by this, for he was unsure whether he did dream of Deb or not, but he knew that he thought of her sometimes and was well aware of what would happen if he were ever caught loving anybody but his wife again. He was fearful of Elizabeth now, but time, he believed, was healing the breach between them, and on the last day of December 1668 he could write: 'blessed be God, the year ends, after some late very great sorrow with my wife by my folly; it ends, I say, with great mutual peace and content – and likely to last so by my care, who am resolved to enjoy the sweet of it which I now possess, by never giving her like cause of trouble'.

Such moments of hope were over-optimistic for there were times when Elizabeth still showed herself half crazy with jealous insecurity. Barely had the New Year started than one of the most frightening and melodramatic of all the scenes between them occurred. Things had been bad between them for most of 12 January, and when Pepys finally asked Elizabeth to come to bed 'she fell out into a fury, that I was a rogue and false to her'. As her temper rose so Elizabeth invented a story of having heard that Pepys had been seen with Deb in a hackney coach. He knew that he was innocent, but his protestations availed him nothing and, 'mightily troubled', he went to bed. Then the storm broke again:

> At last, about one a-clock, she came to my side of the bed and drew my curtain open, and with tongs, red hot at the ends, made as if she did design to pinch me with them; at which in dismay I rose up, and with a few words she laid them down and did by little and little, very sillily, let all the discourse fall; and about 2, but with much seeming difficulty, came to bed and there lay well all night, and long in bed talking together with much pleasure; it being, I know, nothing but her doubt of my going out yesterday without telling her of my going which did vex her, poor wretch, last night: and I cannot blame her jealousy, though it doth vex me to the heart.[8]

The tenderness here and the forbearance are a truly moving tribute to a changed man, and slowly things began to right themselves.

This was helped by conspicuous expenditure on Pepys's part. January 1669 saw a number of lavish dinner parties in Seething Lane. On 3 January, members of the family were entertained to 'a good dinner and all our plate out, and might fine and merry'. It was surely comforting to Elizabeth that six days later they had another 'neat dinner, and all in so good manner and fashion and with so good company and everything to my mind, as I never had more in my life – the company being to my heart's content, and they all well pleased'. It was 23 January, however, that saw this entertaining reach its apogee.

The Pepyses' guests on this occasion included Lord Sandwich (newly returned from his Spanish embassy), his son Hinchinbrooke, Lord Peterborough, Sir Charles Harbord, Sidney Montague and Sir William Godolphin. A dinner of some six or eight dishes had been prepared for them, each being brought up separately and all of them 'as noble as any man need to have I think – at least, all was done in the noblest manner that ever I had any, and I have rarely seen in my life better anywhere else – even at the court'. There was, too, an excellent variety of wines to accompany the feast and Pepys, for all that he was itching with the twenty or so lice that his wife would find on his body after the guests had gone, was in high good form. When the meal was over the aristocrats betook themselves to cards, 'and the rest of us sitting about them and talking, and looking on my books and pictures and my wife's drawings, which they commend mightily'. Elizabeth surely was in her element, and as if this were not enough, she and her husband were now the owners of a magnificent new coach.

Pepys had prepared to buy this statement of social status prior to the dreadful revelation of his affair with Deb. As early as 24 October 1668, he had agreed to have a coach built and to acquire the necessary liveried coachman. The elegant Mr Povey managed to convince him that the choice he had made was quite hopelessly old-fashioned and that only the latest model – light, leather-lined and seating four – would do. A new order was placed, and on 28 November the coach arrived, Pepys declaring it to be 'mighty pretty'. The following day the coachman's livery of green lined with red was delivered, and on the last day of the month Elizabeth Pepys was driven out 'to take the maidenhead of her coach'. The equipage was finally completed when the original horses were replaced with a proud pair of black ones – 'the beautifulest almost I ever saw'.

There were jealous murmurings, of course, as Pepys and his wife no doubt hoped that there would be, but May Day 1669 saw the couple riding in triumph through the capital. Elizabeth was dressed in a 'flowered tabby gown', which she had garnished with new lace, while Pepys was wearing his finest suit, 'and so anon we went alone through the town in our new liveries of serge, and the horses' manes and tails tied with red ribbon and the standards thus gilt with varnish and all clean, and green reins, that people did mightily look upon us; and the truth is, I did not see any coach more pretty, or more gay, than ours all the day'. The occasion was marred by little squabbles and poor weather, but to the many that looked upon them the Pepyses must have surely seemed a happy pair. Their marriage had been saved, Pepys had discovered a new personal maturity and Elizabeth was content. They had a beautifully furnished house, a marvellous coach and horses, and Pepys himself felt that he was in 'the greatest condition of outward state that ever I was in, or hoped ever to be, or desired'.

His happiness was far from undiluted. Even as he counted his blessings he knew that one terrible threat blighted all he had achieved. 'My eyes are come to that condition that I am not able to work,' he wrote. He laboured as best he could (which was mightily) but he could no longer sit in his office facing the window, while the lights in the theatres scorched his eyes. Peering at white paper was an agony and, as his *Diary* entries became shorter, it gradually became clear to Pepys that he would have to cease keeping it altogether. On 31 May 1669, he took up his pen to write in the final volume for the last time. His concluding paragraph was suitably, gravely elegiac, and yet uniquely personal all the same. For the better part of a decade, day by day, the matchless candour of his entries had provided a unique picture of the private and professional man, the individual and his times. Now that vision was threatened by an occluding darkness. Sincerity, regret and a sense of life diminishing beat through every syllable, every clause:

> And thus ends all that I doubt I shall ever be able to do with my own eyes in the keeping of my journal, I being not able to it any longer, having done now so long as to undo my eyes almost every time that I take a pen in my hand; and therefore, whatever comes of it, I must forebear; and therefore resolve from this time forward to have it kept by my people in longhand, and must therefore be contented to set down and no more than is far for them and all the world to know; or if there be anything (which cannot be much, now my amours to Deb are passed, and my eyes hindering me in almost all other pleasures), I must endeavour to keep a margin in my book open, to add here and there a note in shorthand with my own hand. And so I betake myself that course which [is] almost as much as see myself go into my grave – for which, and all the discomforts that will accompany my being blind, the good God prepare me.[9]

Pepys initialled his *Diary*, dated it and closed it for the last time.

This was a moment of the gravest private significance, but

the public duties of the public official could not so easily be put aside, nor would Pepys allow them to be. For the following two months he laboured hard and in ever more painful circumstances. The commissioners of accounts still had to be satisfied and there were questions about his own dealings in supplies to the navy that had to be answered. He still fought with his colleagues too in the attempt to improve the professionalism of the Navy Board. And even amid these tribulations Pepys's ambition was undimmed. In order to represent the Navy Board in the House of Commons he sought to enter Parliament as the Member for Aldeburgh and worked hard to win the electors' support. Aldeburgh was a coastal seat and Sandwich, Coventry and even the Duke of York were all enlisted to persuade the local people how useful the Navy Board would be to their interests. They remained unmoved. The burghers would not vote for a stranger, and all that Pepys derived from his campaign were worrying accusations about him being a papist.

Such allegations were as dangerous as they were absurd (as well as being a taste of things to come), but the deterioration of Pepys's eyesight was more immediately worrying. He was stoic in the face of near despair and desperately hoped that a holiday might bring relief. Permission for this was readily given and in August, having reckoned up his accounts, ordered his papers and sought the advice of John Evelyn and others as to what he should see in France, Pepys, Elizabeth and Balty crossed the Channel. They travelled for two months, visiting the Low Countries and Paris, enjoying and refreshing themselves in a manner which, as Pepys was to write years later, brought him 'a degree of satisfaction and solid usefulness that has stuck by me through the whole course of my life'. But there is no *Diary* to record these incidents nor any personal testimony to the tragedy that now befell. The party were in Brussels when Elizabeth fell ill, and by the time they had returned to London her fever was mortal. On 10 November 1669 she died, and Pepys was left alone in a world darkened by his grief and his failing eyes.

CHAPTER TEN

An Encirclement of Enemies

Pepys buried Elizabeth beneath a fine, flamboyant tomb in St Olave's church, Hart Street, then turned to his public duties. The *Diary* was closed and there would be no private record of his feelings, no expression of his emotions whether of grief or guilt or loneliness. From now on Pepys emerges only – but often magnificently – as a public man, an individual ever more closely and impersonally identified with his work. Indeed, work was as always his salvation and there was much for him to do. Even as he was bringing home his dying wife Pepys knew that the commissioners of accounts were waiting to interrogate him about the Navy Board's efforts during the Dutch war. The Parliamentary principles of appropriation and audit were being applied ever more firmly and, in preparing a defence, Pepys built a bulwark against despair. He also fashioned a new persona: he would become the great civil servant.

His labours were a triumph of will-power, for his holiday had done nothing to alleviate his eyes and his vision brought him almost continuous pain. Worse, he believed that it was just the sort of effort he now felt compelled to make that was the cause of his trouble. For years Pepys had often worked an eighteen-hour day, toiling by the smoky light of candles as he drafted interminable papers, many of them in shorthand. Sometimes the problems with his sight were so severe that he could only just see his way out of his office at night, and always he was aware of 'a constant redness and issuing of a waterish humour' from his eyes.[1] He believed, as the state of medical science prompted him to, that it was precisely such 'moisture', which was the physical origin of the problem and he sought to alleviate the symptoms every morning by spitting repeatedly and blowing his nose. That done, he could make his way to his office where his clerks took down instructions as he dictated them, unless the matter was so confidential that only Pepys himself could commit the words to the sheets of white paper glaring before him on his desk.

The commissioners of accounts had marshalled their criticisms under eighteen heads and Pepys was resolved to demolish them all. He did so with an admirable combination of fact and strong argument. He conceded that there had indeed been problems with subordinate officers but claimed that he and his colleagues could not be expected to shoulder the responsibility for them. As for the Navy Board paying excessive prices for goods, this had been forced on them by a Parliament that had refused an adequate supply and so obliged the board to make purchases on credit. Allegations of corruption were dismissed with contempt, and throughout Pepys was careful to illustrate his arguments with historical precedents, sarcasm when he thought it was called for and an occasional personal reference to 'the sorrowful interruption lately given me by the sickness and death of my wife'. In such ways a great memorandum of some fifty pages was prepared in barely a month and, once he had run it past the Duke of York, Lord Brouncker and the invaluable Coventry, Pepys had a fair copy delivered to the commissioners at Brooke House.

Meanwhile, the King had decided that the matter would be heard before himself. Pepys would have to appear personally as his defence and together they would defend the Restoration regime. They made a powerful team: the short, energetic, endlessly informed Pepys and his master with the pencil-line moustache, hiding his sharp and cynical political intelligence behind a wet, sensuous smile. Theirs was a relationship constructed on the basis of strict professionalism, as all Pepys's relationships would be from now on. The secret shorthand entries in Pepys's *Diary* show that as a private man Pepys harboured severe reservations about Charles and the moral atmosphere in which he moved. Now, in the long-hand journal of the Brooke House meetings kept for him by his clerks, Pepys carefully portrayed himself as an unswervingly loyal civil servant whose powers were entirely given to supporting the monarchy.[2] Henceforth, even his private memoranda would show him as a fully public figure. The artist had, perforce, given way to the bureaucrat.

The Brooke House commissioners began their interrogation of Pepys on 4 January 1670. It was already clear to Pepys himself how much trust the King had vested in him. One of the chief accusations levelled against the conduct of the war was the commissioners' insistence that Charles had squandered the supply voted by Parliament on 'uses of pleasure or other private respects'. Pepys was charged with the responsibility of answering a false but widely believed accusation that threatened the very foundations of the monarchy's credibility. This was an awesome task. His old boss, Sir George Downing, asked him to prepare a written answer, officials at the Treasury provided him with details, and when the commissioners at Brooke House opened their attack, Pepys was able to show that previously and in private the committee had accepted that the money voted to Charles by Parliament had been properly spent. The commissioners' effrontery was thereby exposed and they were made to look more ridiculous still when Pepys proved that the King had spent a further £300,000 of his own money on the campaign against the Dutch.

So far, so good. These were important victories, but if the bias of the commissioners had been made public this did not mean they were fools. Pepys was well aware that two of these men in particular were figures of high calibre. The chairman of the Brooke House committee, Lord Brereton, was a virtuoso of recognised achievements and a founder member of the Royal Society. Colonel Thomson, easily ridiculed as an old fool with a wooden leg who forever harped on about the glories of the Commonwealth navy was, as Pepys recognised, well placed to ask embarrassing questions about why Cromwell's ships had won famous victories at apparently less cost than the recent expensive defeats.

As a result, it became one of Pepys's principal aims to re-establish the honour of the Navy Board 'by letting the world see that . . . matters in the Navy have been at least as well or rather much better than in the time of the usurpation'. In letters to the King and the Duke of York, Pepys showed that his extensive researches proved beyond doubt that the Cromwellian victories at sea had not been based on sound financial management but on wholly ignoring 'considerations either of thrift or method'. The real problem thus lay not with the Navy Board but with a Parliament that voted inadequate supplies and thereby inflicted on Pepys, his colleagues and the nation at large what Pepys called 'the costliness of poverty'.

The King was delighted by Pepys's performance, brushing aside Pepys's own concern that he had been too assertive, thanking him and, in a manner typically combining ease with guile, apologising for the rudeness repeatedly shown by Lord Brereton. Pepys glowed in his master's favour, but he was still half minded to write to Brereton testifying to his resentment. He wisely thought better of this and, instead, drafted 'a particular defence' of his own conduct. This showed him in an altogether less pleasant light: smug, superior and occasionally untruthful. Pepys was under attack, and he was determined to appear a paragon of virtue, sparing no efforts in proving the 'diligence of my attendance, effects of my performance and uprightness'. He alone, he asserted, had laboured for the Navy Board 'even under the terror of the plague itself'. The result had been 'that untimely ruin of my eyes . . . which renders the remainder of my life of much less content or use to me than can be supplied by any other satisfaction than what flows from the consideration of that duty to His Majesty to which I sacrificed them'. This was a shrewd expression of loyalty, but as for lining his own pockets, Pepys swore that 'in exchange for ten years' service and these the most valuable of my life, I find not my estate at this day bettered by £1,000 from all the profits, salary or other advantages arising from my said employment beyond what it was known to be at my admission heretofore'.

The commissioners were less than convinced. It would be useful to them if they could prove that a man so dangerously able and so loud in the assertion of his own virtues was in fact no better than anyone else. Eventually they believed they had the evidence to do so. The business of paying seamen by ticket rather than in cash (a practice Pepys deplored) appeared to provide them with their weapon. A clerk Pepys had had sacked for dishonesty swore an affidavit to the effect that Pepys had indulged in the common crime of buying tickets from seamen at a fraction of their face value then cashing them in for their full worth. Pepys denied the accusation, but a jubilant Lord Brereton thought he had him cornered. '"How, Mr Pepys, do you defy the whole world in this matter?"' Pepys replied that he did indeed defy the whole world – and Lord Brereton in particular.[3]

The peer was 'struck dumb', but a week later he produced what gave every appearance of being an incriminating ticket valued at £7. 10s, which had seemingly passed through

Pepys's hands. This was an anxious moment. The ticket was passed round the room. The King examined it. The Duke of York examined it and, as it was handed to a worried Pepys, so Colonel Thomson told all those present that he would not have troubled His Majesty with such a trifle but that Mr Pepys was so positive about his own virtue. It was time for Charles to save the man who was saving him. With the quickness and lightness of touch that was his to command, the King smiled, shook his head and said that 'he thought it a vain thing to believe that one having so great trust, and therein acting without any exception in matters of the greatest moment, should descend to so poor a thing as the doing anything that was unfit for him in a matter of £7. 10s.'. After that, the matter was dropped.

Such moments showed that together Charles and Pepys made an excellent team, the embattled civil servant being the master of detail while the dark, quick-witted King appeared as the suave voice of common sense. Both men knew the value of irony and recognised that points might occasionally be won by laughter. For all the high seriousness of the matters before them, it was sport to trap a man like Thomson in his own bluster. When, for example, the colonel began 'with some insultingness' to praise the virtues of 'good English plank' over cheaper foreign imports Pepys realised that he could nail his man. He replied that he and the Navy Board 'were as much in love with English plank' as the colonel was 'and should give him thanks to direct us where, for a considerable advance of price, we might be furnished with 2,000, or but 1,000, or 500 loads at this day of English plank'. The colonel, of course, could not answer and his mouth, in Pepys's expressive phrase, was 'stopped'.

Not all Pepys's victories were so easy. The commissioners rightly had suspicions about the profits his friend Sir William Warren had made from supplying masts, and they pressed Pepys 'very earnestly' on the subject. He needed to defend himself and did so by resorting less to humour than to a hammeringly technical argument (a favourite ploy) about the terms and history of advance payments made to suppliers like Warren. This left the exhausted commissioners floundering, and Pepys then showed them not only that the deals struck with Warren had been legitimate but that the international market in masts was so difficult that the English had been lucky to obtain any at all in the face of stiff foreign competition.

Still the commissioners were not satisfied. They urged that Warren's rivals could have supplied the navy more cheaply, and it fell once again to the King to come to Pepys's defence. It was true, Charles conceded, that these rivals of Warren's might have been able to supply cheaper masts to the navy but they were only prepared to do so on the condition that they could secretly supply them to the nation's enemies as well. The commissioners were once again struck dumb and sought other lines of attack. This was a tactical blunder, for if matters went on like this then it was clear that the Brooke House Committee would be obliged to sit for ever. Pepys carefully played on the King's mounting impatience. Raillery being ever the way to win Charles's attention, he 'plainly told His Majesty my work must be to get a son and bring him up only to understand this controversy between Brooke House and us and that His Majesty too should provide for successors to be instructed on his part in the state of this case'. The smiling King agreed. The onerous hearings came to an end, the objections of the Parliamentarians having been smothered in the wealth of technical detail only a professional servant of the Crown like Pepys could muster.

Thus 'the ridiculous success of that terrible Commission', Pepys wrote. But far more had been achieved than perhaps he knew or even supposed. At an increasingly perilous personal cost the navy was coming to replace all Pepys had lost, all that he had never had. An institution was becoming his family: a source of achievement, exasperation, solace, purpose and – ultimately – disappointment. For now Pepys had sunk private grief in public duty and was emerging as what for the rest of his career he would so conspicuously be: the great bureaucrat, the champion of the Stuart cause, the unquestioning servant of monarchy rather than Parliament, and the one man who could ensure that the country's greatest fighting force would be wholly and efficiently devoted to the policies of the Crown, however devious those policies might be.

The full extent of his master's guile was probably never clear to Pepys, but for his own part Charles had secured his man at the Navy Board and was now pursuing those tortuous elements in the Grand Design by which he hoped to assert the prerogative powers of the Crown over the influence of Parliament. The dangers to Charles himself were enormous. His alliance with Catholic France could only strike the greater number of his subjects as abhorrent, and their wrath would be increased when they realised that its real purpose – the augmenting of royal power at the expense of Parliament – was all too clearly reminiscent of the events that had led to the civil war. Charles had no substantial army to protect him from the extremes of his people's anger, nor any guarantee that Louis would stick by him in the long term. It was essential therefore that he tie the French king down by some ruse, and he found his answer in an arrangement of breathtaking cynicism. In return for two million badly needed *livres tournois*, Charles declared that he was now 'convinced of the truth of the Catholic religion' and was 'resolved to declare it and reconcile himself with the Church of Rome as soon as the welfare of his kingdom would permit'. What Charles was gambling on was the hope that if things went badly wrong at home then he would convert (or appear to convert) to Catholicism and so oblige Louis, *le roi très chrétien*, to come to his aid for the honour of Catholic Europe.

In the meantime, Charles would rely on his navy and the efforts to ready it being made by the industrious Mr Pepys. There was no reason why Pepys himself should have been in the know about the terms of the so-called treaty of Dover signed between Charles and Louis on 22 May 1670. Indeed, it was probably better for all that he did not. Instead, he laboured to prepare the navy that would execute it. Debt, as always, was the crippling problem. Attempts to retrench by limiting the number of ships at sea proved unsuccessful, nearly £500,000 was still owed, while a nearly comparable sum was required to fit out and man the ships during 1670. It was the familiar problem.

Pepy's own financial position, by contrast, appeared distinctly healthy. Will Hewer, in particular, was helping him acquire large sums from the perquisites of his office, and by the start of 1671 Pepys had a balance on his account at Alderman Blackwell's of £6,855. Such sums allowed him to maintain an extremely comfortable lifestyle amid the orderly sumptuousness of his house in Seething Lane, with its tapestries, silver plate and ever-growing collection of beautifully bound books. But it was not money alone that allowed Pepys to lead a full and satisfying social life. Despite his problems with his eyes, his company was always marvellously stimulating and it won him the friendship of some of the most brilliant men of his day.

Pepys and Evelyn, for example, remained firm friends. The virtuoso continued to inspire the bureaucrat, and it was in Evelyn's company – along with Christopher Wren – that Pepys was first shown the work of Grinling Gibbons and introduced to the brilliant young wood-carver who had just completed a sculpted version of a painting by Tintoretto.[4] The city, too, offered Pepys the friendship of wealthy, cultured merchants, such as Sir John Banks who, like Pepys himself, had risen from obscure circumstances and now commanded a considerable fortune. Banks was a Member of Parliament as Pepys wished to be, a fellow of the Royal Society, while in 1673 the prestige of his business interests was such that he was made governor of the East India Company. Banks had fine homes both in London and the Kentish countryside, and a happy, intelligent family to whom the widowed and childless Pepys was much attracted. Others of his merchant friends included the Houblons, a large family of high and open-minded people, cultured, modern and intensely competent. Sir James Houblon in particular, who lived in some considerable style in Great Winchester Street, was a devoted friend of Pepys and not only offered him invaluable advice on trade and shipping but would soon stand by him in the difficult times to come.

By contrast, almost nothing is known of Pepys's particular women friends at this time. The astonishing revelations of his private life closed with the *Diary* and it is impossible to say if he sought solace with old acquaintances or submerged his grief entirely in his work. Certainly, he never married again, but he was not entirely without female companionship for eventually he formed a relationship with a young woman called Mary Skinner.[5] She hovers tantalisingly in the penumbra of his life, a benevolent but barely perceptible presence. It is known that she was the daughter of a London merchant and that she was younger than Pepys. It is known, too, that there was a dangerous family connection with the great poet and republican John Milton. Milton had addressed a complimentary sonnet to Mary's uncle and her brother at one point sought to publish some of Milton's prose works. He was persuaded to abandon this project, but to a deeply conservative figure like Pepys the association was potentially embarrassing.

Nor were his attentions to Mary at first welcomed by her family. That so substantial a man should apparently be leading their daughter astray was a point of bitter contention.

There was a period of distance between the parties and then, it appears, a reconciliation. Perhaps the gravitational pull of Pepys's personality and position had much to do with this. He became a patron of the family and a friend of the mother. Above all, he was the recipient of Mary's devotion. She eventually managed his house for him and, in the polished sophistication of late-seventeenth-century London, was accepted as his companion. Evelyn respected her as such and the great scientist Robert Hooke even thought she was Pepys's wife. To Pepys himself, Mary Skinner was to the end his 'dear child'.

Other members of his family were also the recipients of Pepys's bounty. Balty wrote thanking him for his goodness both to himself and to his 'poor drooping mother'. He named his son Samuel in Pepys's honour and, in a charming postscript to his letter, wrote how the boy, who was just learning to speak, 'desires to have his most humble duty presented to his most honoured uncle and god-father'. John Pepys, too, rose through his brother's influence. As a younger Brother of Trinity House, Pepys was in a position to do the man a kindness and he set about this with his usual efficiency. He wrote to Sandwich, to the Duke of York, then explained his purpose to Evelyn's influential father-in-law. 'I have a sudden occasion offered me of asking your friendship,' he declared. ''Tis this', he went on. 'Mr Askew, Clerk of Trinity House is dead. I have a brother of my own, whose relation to me could not tempt me to this motion, were it not that his sobriety, diligence and education . . . doth lead me to think it a service to the Corporation to offer him to them.' The wheels were set in motion and Pepys wrote to his brother telling him that 'something hath offered itself which may prove of advantage to you, that makes it necessary for me to have you here on Tuesday night next'.[6] John, who was then living with his father at the now-married Pall's house near Brampton, hurried to London and found that the post of clerk to Trinity House was indeed his, as Pepys had 'for some time designed'.

Such were the workings of influence, but nepotism was not Pepys's only concern. It is profoundly touching to find amid a great bureaucrat's voluminous correspondence testimonies to the time he took in attending to the needs of little men. One of these was the good Captain Guy, who wrote to Pepys with more gratitude than grammar to say how 'my wife and children and I am bound to praise God that hath sent us such a friend'. A relieved widow sent Pepys a pair of china flower-pots. A distressed wife whose husband had lost his pay ticket came to beg his help, while aged and invalid sailors too felt the effects of his competence and goodness. We have seen that Pepys had known for years that the Chatham Chest, which had been set up for the relief of poor mariners by the great Elizabethan sea-dogs, had been a source of scandal.* Batten had sunk his rapacious hands deep into its contents, as had the erstwhile Navy Treasurer Lord Anglesey. Poor men dragged themselves from the ends of the country to apply for the dole only to be disappointed of their rights. Morals and morale alike suggested that something should be done and Pepys, having written a letter so scrupulously ironic in its politeness that even Lord Anglesey was discomforted, had the reward of seeing the abuse at least temporarily checked.

Such kindnesses were carried out amid exhausting preparations for war. To this end, Pepys and his colleagues from the Navy Board made an expedition to inspect the timber in the Forest of Dean. What they discovered there gave them little encouragement. Less than a tenth of the oak trees were fit for use by the shipwrights, the beeches were suitable only for planking, while some of the felled timber was in danger of rotting on the ground where it lay. Back in the capital, things were no better for suppliers were all but bankrupted

* see p. 92

by the Navy Board's inability to pay them. By the start of 1672 Pepys had calculated that £1,337,292. 9s. was needed to settle arrears and ready the navy for eight months of active service. This dire financial situation was slightly alleviated by the money that now began to come in from France as a result of the secret treaty of Dover, but the King recognised that more drastic measures would have to be taken if he was adequately to fund his war. These he now put into action.

Over recent years Sir George Downing had considerably developed his initial scheme for raising money against promised tax revenues by the creation of printed certificates or 'treasury orders'. Charles decided now to renege on these and thereby free up his annual income from its burden of debt repayment. The inevitable result was havoc among the country's financial community and such irreparable damage to the Crown's personal credit that it was no longer possible readily to identify the nation's financial interests with the personal conduct of the monarchy. But the Stop of the Exchequer was not the only cynical move that Pepys's master made at this time. In the effort to free himself from the dominating influence of the Anglican gentry in Parliament, Charles issued in March 1672 a Declaration of Indulgence, which suspended the Penal Laws against religious minorities. By permitting Catholics to celebrate in private houses and Nonconformists to worship at authorised public meetings, Charles hoped to secure the allegiance of what he believed would prove large and grateful minorities across the country. It would soon become clear that rather than winning allies he had exposed himself to attacks from enemies on several fronts, enemies who would soon also be planning the downfall of Pepys.

Fear and detestation of Catholicism reached a new pitch, while the means the King had employed to get his way sent shudders through the majority of thinking people. Pepys's master was alienating himself from his subjects. Charles himself claimed that in issuing his Declaration of Indulgence he had acted according to the law, that he was exercising 'that supreme power in ecclesiastical matters which is not only inherent in us, but hath been declared and recognised to be so by several statutes and Acts of Parliament'.[7] There were many, including the judges, who denied that Charles possessed the power he claimed and, as they muttered against what they sincerely believed was the international threat of popery, so they also convinced themselves that the country was being bullied into submission by a ruler who aimed at nothing less than the sort of absolute power exercised by Louis XIV in all-powerful Catholic France.

Such was the reputation of the King Pepys was labouring to serve by a remorseless attention to detail. He was constantly harassed by complaints and demands. The commissioner of the Portsmouth shipyard wrote to him saying that he had no flags, cotton or kerseys in store. The ships had been obliged either to sail without them or fly flags that were so rotten they would hardly stay on the mastheads. Despite such problems, a joint English and French navy of some 98 warships, 6,000 guns and 34,000 sailors was eventually readied for war. The fleet was 'a goodly but terrible sight'. However, hostility against the Dutch was matched by rivalries between the allies. The French admiral was under orders to enhance his master's *gloire* wherever possible by revealing superior courage and expertise. Meanwhile, an equally destructive pessimism clouded the minds of other men. Sandwich, the vice-admiral of the fleet, foresaw only disaster and, in his despair, dwelt constantly on thoughts of his own death.

Pepys had done all he could, but eventually, as the enemy forces met off Southwold Bay, the allied navy's confidence in their superior forces of men and *matériel* proved to be unfounded arrogance. The French misread the Duke of York's signals, with the result that the joint English and French fleet divided as the Dutch themselves, knowing that they were fighting for their very existence, bore down on them. The resulting carnage was appalling. English casualties amounted to some 2,500 men, including the doom-burdened Sandwich. Pepys's erstwhile patron had fought heroically amid the all-obscuring fire and smoke until his flagship was blown to pieces and the little boat in which he escaped capsized in the water. He was drowned, and his swollen, mutilated body was found a few days later, the Garter star glinting futilely on his breast. The mangled corpse was eventually brought back to Westminster and, as the guns sounded in funeral salute, Pepys's first master was borne in solemn pomp into the Abbey accompanied by the peers of England and the mourning clerk of the acts himself, whose first steps Sandwich had so generously guided.

It was a sad moment and pointed to the fact that Charles's war had gained him nothing. Pepys's enormous efforts had been to no avail. The allied navy had been prevented from gaining mastery of the North Sea and the Dutch still had their fleet. On land, however, they faced imminent annihilation. Their army, pursued by Louis XIV, had been obliged to fall back on the state of Holland itself and, in an act of heroic resolve, the people breached the dykes and flooded their land before vainly suing for peace. The leaders of the republican party were chosen as scapegoats for national disgrace and Charles's nephew, William of Orange, the general of the Dutch forces, was declared stadholder, or hereditary ruler. Another figure who was to be of the greatest importance to Pepys was emerging on the European scene, and now it became apparent that the 'very pretty boy' Pepys had first glimpsed when he sailed to return Charles from exile had matured into a man of outstanding courage and considerable guile. For all the seeming hopelessness of his military position William refused to surrender and he also resolved on a sophisticated propaganda campaign by which he hoped to isolate his uncle from the growing number of Englishmen who detested the war against Holland. He would persuade them that it was the Catholic French rather than the decent, Protestant Dutch who were their real enemies.

As the international situation became more tense, the affairs of the English navy continued to take up the greater part of Pepys's time but, for all that he laboured to put the fleet to sea again, it was clear by the end of August that this was no longer possible. Pepys could not get adequate supplies on the Navy Board's overstretched credit, there was a wages bill of over £300,000 to meet, and sickness was endemic among the wounded and exhausted crews. Coping with such situations took up all of Pepys's attention for the next six months. Then, on the night of 29 January 1673, an accident made matters even worse. A fire in Seething Lane rapidly engulfed some thirty houses and the Navy Office itself. The proud and beautiful home that Pepys had created for himself was all but wrecked. The pictures, the tapestry hangings – all were destroyed. Of his most treasured possessions only a number of his books and, above all, the bound volumes of his *Diary*, were saved.

Nor in this painful time could Pepys draw any comfort from politics at Westminster. Enemies abroad were being joined by foes at home. The efforts his royal master had made to secure money and support for his war had rebounded in Charles's face. The King was obliged to summon Parliament to vote him a supply, and his minister Lord Shaftesbury – Charles's 'Little Sincerity' – urged on the House the necessity of destroying the Dutch now that they were apparently down. It was a dazzling performance, but the truculent Members refused to be blinded by its light. For all that they eventually resolved to grant Charles a small supply, they attached the most stringent conditions to it. Once again, the failure of a war designed to free the King from Parliamentary control had resulted in his being ever more dependent on it. The implications for Pepys would be far-reaching indeed.

The King's Declaration of Indulgence had offended the

Members' religious beliefs and their constitutional principles, and now they were determined to protect their Anglican culture, their Anglican Parliament and their Anglican Church. Toleration they saw as weakness, pluralism as cowardice. In this mood of mounting bigotry they framed a Test Act that subjected the nation to the most stringent limitations. Anyone wishing to enter public life or use such public institutions as the courts was required to receive communion according to the Anglican rite. Roman Catholicism – that detested farrago of foreign superstition and tyranny – was driven to the extreme margins of national life as the gentry of the Church of England sought to assert their power. A cornered Charles could do nothing. Louis XIV refused to bail him out and, as the Lord High Admiral of England stepped down from his office, unable any longer to deny his Catholic beliefs, there was rejoicing in the streets as institutionalised intolerance became a fact of life.

While the national mood darkened and bigotry tightened its grip, it seemed that a circle of gloom was deepening around Pepys himself. His eyesight was still troubling him gravely. He had lost his home in a terrible fire. His work for the Dutch war had ended in ignominy. He had recently been unsuccessful in yet another attempt to enter Parliament. He had also failed to be promoted as comptroller of the navy (a post he coveted and which went to a nonentity) or to become secretary to the Duke of York. Now that great patron himself was a widely loathed man who was openly allied to the most abhorred religious minority in England. York's duties as Lord High Admiral passed for the moment to Prince Rupert, but that hot-headed, brilliant man was a constant burden to Pepys too. When Rupert was sent out with the French fleet to harass the Dutch once again, he quarrelled with his fellow officers, wrote letters complaining of royal interference in his plans, and so successfully blamed the French for everything that went wrong that public opinion swung ever more vehemently against the nation's allies, as William of Orange's propaganda campaign stoked the fires of anti-popery to a white heat.

King Charles, it seemed, was hopelessly beleaguered, but the great survivor was not easily subdued and he still had plans for those, like Pepys, who were unquestioningly loyal to him. Parliament might have exposed the fallacies of his foreign policy and ridiculed his efforts to seize Dutch trade as naïve, the cabal of his ministers might have fractured beyond repair, leaving Shafesbury to make overtures to an ever more articulate opposition party, his brother might be the most hated man in England, but Charles still had his navy and he still had Pepys. He would play these cards with all the skill he possessed. Fifteen of the greatest men in the land were chosen to execute the Lord High Admiral's duties. Among these was Pepys himself who suddenly, amid the apparently all-encircling gloom of his life, found himself appointed to the immensely prestigious position of secretary to the office of the Lord High Admiral of England. Here was real power.

The position of secretary had been created with the Restoration in 1660 and the early holders of the office had acted largely as the private amanuenses to the Duke of York. Pepys, with his enormous energy and driving ambition for order and regulation, was to recast his new role into something altogether more influential. It was an extraordinary opportunity. He was, first of all, the man responsible for garnering all information concerning the present state of the navy, the civil servant who would always be comprehensively informed.[8] When added to his regulation of the Admiralty's business, he would effectively concentrate the administration of the navy in himself, ensure the common execution of policy throughout the service, and not only give the policy-makers a stable organisation with which to work but, by the sheer stature of his presence, have a considerable effect on policy-making itself. Just as the reorganisation of the Treasury under the commissioners appointed by Charles II in 1667 ensured that the tentacles of that mighty department reached out to embrace virtually all aspects of public spending, so Pepys at the Admiralty would aim for a similar authority. He was of a new breed of senior civil servant, a small oligarchy of professional administrators who, with direct access to the King and full responsibility under the royal will, combined in themselves a heady mixture of administrative power and political influence.

In order to secure this last, Pepys was determined to be the navy's spokesman in the House of Commons, and to this end he stood as an electoral candidate for yet a third time. There had been, he wrote, 'too many instances' of the 'prejudices and disadvantages' of the navy not being represented in the House, and Pepys believed that 'a few hands in Parliament thoroughly conversant with these affairs' might easily amend matters.[9] The seat at Castle Rising had fallen vacant and Pepys wrote careful letters to Lord Howard, the local magnate and a known Catholic, delicately pointing out the wishes of the King and the Duke of York in the matter. He received a favourable response and was told that he may 'depend upon it as done'. Howard's confidence was misplaced. The growing atmosphere of confrontation in the House of Commons meant that matters could not so easily be settled as he supposed and Pepys himself was, by the very competence he had shown, a prime target for the opposition to royal policy and its leader, Lord Shaftesbury.

Before Pepys left to fight the seat, the wily Shafesbury wished him well but, once Pepys had arrived in Castle Rising, opposition soon emerged in the disreputable form of one Offley who appeared on the scene with sufficient cash and plausibility to turn the tipsy electorate against Pepys in the most dangerous way imaginable. Was not this unknown Pepys a follower of the Duke of York, and was not the Duke himself a known Catholic? Did Pepys not also have the Catholic Lord Howard's favour? Tremors of fear and disgust ran through the voters' solid rural minds. This man Pepys was alien and a danger. The voters were easily persuaded of the threat to their moral and spiritual lives, and by the time Offley had done his work they were convinced that 'Mr Pepys was a bloody papist'. When Pepys himself arrived in person, the rabble came out to jeer at him and only a letter of recommendation from Howard, along with the written assurances of the surrounding clergy, persuaded the men of Castle Rising into voting Pepys a Member of Parliament by a majority of twenty-two.

But the threat of popery would not go away. Popery was a menace, both to true religion and to the constitution, and national events now seemed to conspire to suggest that it was rousing itself for a full-scale attack. Not content with publicly declaring himself a Catholic, the now widowed Duke of York was looking for a new wife. He eye eventually alighted on the fifteen-year-old Mary Beatrice of Modena, a raven-haired Catholic with strong French connections. When the nation learned that Pepys's erstwhile patron was to marry 'the daughter of the Pope', there was outrage and a great revival of pope-burning ceremonies. It was clear to all that York's marriage was a manifest design to subvert the nation for, his brother the King having no legitimate children, any son born to him would not only be educated as a Catholic but would be the heir apparent to the English throne.

The spectre of Antichrist loomed across the popular imagination and neither the King nor York did anything to deflect it. Royal marriages, they believed, were a royal matter and both men held hard to the belief that any criticism of them was an attack on their prerogative powers. Once again, popery and absolutism appeared to go together ever more closely, and while many people turned their eyes and hearts to Charles's eldest illegitimate son – the glamorous, foolish, Protestant Duke of Monmouth – the now disgraced Shaftesbury inveigled his way into the leadership of the ever more disenchanted anti-court and anti-papist groupings in the House of Commons. He was the opposition, and the newly elected Pepys – the King's most loyal and able civil servant and the man responsible for the country's most prestigious and expensive institution – was a prime target for his machinations. To destroy Pepys by showing him to be a corrupt servant of the Crown would seriously weaken the royal cause.

As Pepys took his seat on Wednesday, 7 January 1674, a paper protesting at his being voted a Member at all was passed to the Committee of Elections and Privileges. While the committee pondered the matter, the opposition opened up its other line of attack. They would show that Pepys was corrupt. The Navy Board's conduct of the recent war once again became an issue and questions were asked about the supply of stores to the French from depleted English resources. Pepys managed to answer effectively, and the opposition then turned to the altogether more vexed matter of the press-gangs. Instances of the alleged illegal impressment of men were raised and Pepys countered them hotly, saying that no fleet could be sent to sea at all if the old methods of recruiting men were abandoned.

The debate became acrimonious and Pepys did nothing to cool it. His answers were truthful, he knew he was right, he could prove it and was prepared to be accountable. His was a strong but hardly a shrewd performance for it made clear to every Member present that the nimble-witted, well-briefed civil servant who had routed the commissioners at Brooke House was not inclined to be any more conciliatory in Westminster. Pepys was the spokesman for the King's navy and the House should know it. That being the case, it became the opposition's aim to remove Pepys from their debates altogether. A month after he took his seat, the Committee of Elections and Privileges declared it their opinion that Pepys had not been duly elected for Castle Rising. Catholic influence had been at work to promote him. The rumour now ran around the House that Pepys was merely the puppet of the Catholic Duke of York, that he was himself a secret papist, that he had converted his wife to his confounded beliefs and that – most horribly – such papist trash as crucifixes and altars were openly displayed in his home and that he had declared how the Protestant religion had 'come out of Henry VIII's codpiece'.[10] The allegations were as dangerous as they were absurd for, Elizabeth being dead and Pepys's house in charred ruins, they could be neither easily verified nor contradicted.

The opposition was proving how adroit it could be in manipulating an atmosphere of suspicion and Pepys was put on his mettle. To be proved a Catholic was to be exposed to the full rigour of the law, while to walk away with anything less than a clean name was to learn that mud sticks. Pepys stood his ground. When he was eventually allowed to speak he flatly denied the allegations of his accusers, and the chief of them, Sir Robert Thomas, was told to name and produce those who accused Pepys of popery. This was the last thing Thomas wished to do, but eventually he was obliged to give way. Chief among his witness, he confessed, was no less a man than Shaftesbury. It was Shaftesbury who claimed he had seen the altar in Pepys's house, Shaftesbury who had apparently glimpsed the crucifixes, and it was Shaftesbury who now wanted Pepys out of the way. He was a terrifying enemy, a man 'as proud as Lucifer, and ambitious beyond whatever entered into the designs of any man; impatient of every power but his own, of any man's reputation; false to that degree, as he did not esteem any promise, any engagement, any oath, of other use than to serve a purpose, and none of these of consequence to bind a man further than

Pepys in the middle age by Kneller.

James II, artist unknown.

Anthony Ashley Cooper,
1st Earl of Shaftsbury, artist unknown,
c.1672–3.

William III, artist unknown, c.1690.

John Evelyn by Robert Nanteuil, 1650.

Sir Christopher Wren by Kneller, 1711.

Boat action during the Third Dutch War by Ludolf Bakhuizen.

it was his interest'.[11] Shaftesbury already had the Catholic Duke of York in his sights and was resolved that Parliament should exclude him from succession to the throne. To remove Mr Pepys would be a useful stepping stone on the way.

This was less easy than he supposed. The House resolved that Shaftesbury's allegations against Pepys should be investigated but, as a peer of the realm, Shaftesbury could not be compelled to appear before the Bar of the Commons. A committee (which included Pepys himself) prepared to go to see him. When they presented their case 'Little Sincerity' grew restive. As the most able man in Westminster he was not going to be embarrassed by such a minor business as this. He prevaricated. It was a long time since he had been to Pepys's home, he said. No, he had not actually seen the altar. He could remember something like a crucifix but, in his best memory, he was not sure whether it was painted or carved. He could hardly be expected to give sworn evidence on such flimsy grounds, he implied. It was better he stand down. He did so with the insouciance of a master politician and cracked a joke to laugh it all off: 'Mr Pepys,' he declared, 'the next time we meet, we will remember the Pope!' That, Shaftesbury decided, was the end of the matter. He refused to see Pepys again and was rewarded for his lack of pains with a letter. Composing with all the earnestness and much of the self-righteousness at his disposal, Pepys wrote to Shaftesbury declaring that:

> I do both desire and conjure your Lordship by all that is honourable in itself and just towards me, to perfect your recollections so far as to give the House (in what method you shall think fit) a categorical answer one way or t'other tomorrow morning in this business of the crucifix. Which whether it be Aye or No, I do hereby declare I will hold myself equally (and but equally) obliged to your Lordship for it; as being one who has always directed myself in my duty both towards God and my Master, with such open

> blamelessness, as not to leave either my security or my good name therein to depend upon a single Aye or No of any one, friend or enemy.[12]

No reply was received, of course, and Pepys was left to defend himself before the House. He had regularly attended Anglican services, he declared. He had taken the Test Act, as a public servant must, and had a certificate to prove it. There was no evidence whatsoever that he was a Catholic and, since Lord Shaftesbury himself had wished him well before his election, why should that scrupulously Protestant peer have spoken thus to a supposed papist? Pepys even read out the letter he had written to Shaftesbury. He dwelt on his accuser's silence and much on his own innocence, the openness of his house and the fact that anyone could see there those totems of true Anglicanism – his Bible and Book of Common Prayer. The majority in the House was won round to Pepys's side and it seemed that, in his confrontation with the most prominent and dangerous politician of his day, he had won at least a temporary victory. But, having done so, Pepys would not compromise. He was the King's man and time would show that he would stand by his King and the traditional ways even to the imperilling of his own life.

CHAPTER ELEVEN

At the Admiralty

By the start of 1674 Pepys had moved both the Admiralty and himself into Derby House, a sumptuous building in the heart of Westminster whose grandeur reflected on the status of the navy and Pepys alike. Here, leading off the great gleaming staircase, were the solemn committee rooms with their draped tables and elaborate silver standishes, the office of the principal clerks with its windows looking out across the Thames, and the secretary to the Admiralty's own private apartments. Under one magnificent roof were gathered all the seemliness and order that Pepys craved, the work that defined him as a man, along with the material abundance and the carefully ranged evidence of his intellectual curiosity, which helped to make him so valued a friend. On the surface, at least, everything seemed secure.

The regular ticking of the Tompion clocks measured out Pepys's hours. An apparently 'sober and virtuous' housekeeper, well bred but 'as humble as the meanest servant', saw to his daily wants, while a butler presided over the hierarchy of the servants' quarters and the discipline of the cook, the maids, the footman and the little black pageboy.

Yet all was not as decorous as it appeared, for one of the men Pepys employed as his butler – a certain John James – was found in bed with the housekeeper at three o'clock one Sunday morning and, having been summarily dismissed without a reference, was to become one of Pepys's bitterest and most dangerous enemies. Later Pepys claimed that he was indeed most unlucky in his servants but, in the meantime, gardeners attended to his carefully sheltered orange trees in the courtyard, and a liveried coachman drove him about town in a vehicle flamboyantly (and to some rather ostentatiously) painted with scenes of war at sea. At other times silent watermen rowed their master along the Thames in his damask-curtained barge.

Such pomp magnified Pepys's status as secretary to the Admiralty, as did the honours that came on his appointment. In 1677, for example, Pepys was made master of his livery company and presented Clothworkers' Hall with a large covered silver-gilt bowl, an ewer and a rosewater dish. He was asked to be steward at the Honorary Artillery Company's annual feast, to become a governor of Bridewell, master of Trinity House, and to contribute to that lovely building in his old college, which now contains his books and bears his name. Such honours and such a way of life were expensive, naturally, but Pepys was now a wealthy man. His promotion raised his salary to £500 a year, the Tangier Committee still brought him dividends, but his real money came from the perquisites of his new office. Pepys was entitled to charge a fee of twenty-five shillings for each English ship given a pass to trade in the Mediterranean. Since at least a thousand a year of these passes were issued, he could comfortably afford the luxuries he felt became his status, but soon his probity in such matters would fall under close and jealous scrutiny.

The public man was a grand and conspicuous figure while the friend of the great was a virtuoso of discernment. The merchants and intellectuals of the day who visited Pepys at

Derby House might, after a decorous meal enlivened with high and important talk, be invited to view his collections and curiosities. Engraved maps gathered by a French acquaintance from the booksellers of Paris lined the walls and filled his portfolios. Exquisite medieval manuscripts, rare and lovely in their jewel-like brilliance, were opened for admiring and sometimes envious eyes. Sheafs of black-letter ballads were also accumulating, while a wealth of original documents was being catalogued in preparation for the history of the navy that everybody knew would one day make Pepys famous, his never-to-be-written *Navalia*. Meanwhile, his library continued to multiply and his lovely bookcases to fill with beautifully bound volumes, each of which was adorned with its owner's symbol, two crossed anchors with elegantly intertwined ropes surmounting his motto: *mens cujusque is est quisque*. As was the mind, so indeed was the man. Pepys talked much about his books and, as his guests admired and talked in their turn, so his beloved canaries pecked at their seed and chirped. Later, and sometimes in consort with his women friends, music of an altogether different kind might be provided by Cesare Morelli, the young resident Flemish lutenist, who sang in the latest Italian style and was wont – all innocently – to practise his papist trills in the garden of Derby House.

On other occasions, when Pepys lacked company, he would have his clerks read to him. His eyes were still troublesome, as occasionally was his old complaint of wind colic and the muscular aches he associated with the damp and the cold. However it was reading and writing that caused the greatest difficulties. Neither glasses nor cardboard tubes had eased Pepys's headaches and inflamed eyes, although it is possible that he derived some comfort from the four or five drops of distilled green hazelnuts and '*lapis caliminaris*' with which he bathed his eyes night and morning. In such trying daily circumstances as these an amanuensis was essential for all but the most confidential work, and clerks like young Sam Atkins soon came to appreciate – if they did not know already – that the 'Squire' of Derby House, as they called him, was an awe-inspiring figure indeed.

Discipline was all and lapses were not lightly glossed over. 'Mr Pepys,' as Atkins was to declare, 'is the severest man in his house in the world, and whoever serves him laudably for seven years, for an hour's absence from his business without his knowledge shall lose his favour'.[1] The young man was speaking from experience. Atkins liked his pleasures, was known to stay out late, and he had already been warned about this a couple of times by Pepys when he felt he had to write a cringing note promising that 'upon my first ill comportment on being (on any occasion) found a minute out of your house without your leave, I willing lay this at your feet as my own act to banish me forever your service, favour or countenance'. The Puritan in Pepys had triumphed over the hedonist but, if he was not minded to make concessions to weakness, Pepy's rigour earned him a respect that ran deep. Certainly it did so in Atkins, and in a few years' time the young man's regard for his master (preserved amid the most trying circumstances) would help to save Pepys from the direst peril.

The moral tone Pepys set at Derby House was a result of his own maturing conservatism and his wholesale subduing of himself to his task. The conduct of affairs at the Admiralty was largely in Pepys's hands, and from his energy, his desire for order, his experience and innovation all else would flow. Pepys would make the Admiralty into the unique, ruthlessly controlling force of the entire naval service. To this end he instituted unprecedented procedural discipline. Henceforth his erstwhile colleagues at the Navy Board would attend meetings at Derby House every Saturday morning at eight o'clock, and he required of them reams of statistics: accounts of stores, wages, debts and an accurate picture of the number of men genuinely in service. The first necessity, as always, was to save money and to attend to what Pepys called 'the cutting off of the growing charge upon seamen's wages'. By the summer of 1674 the fleet had been reduced to 8,200 men, and if the old ideal of reducing annual running costs to £200,000 (proposed by the recently ennobled Danby, the new treasurer of the navy) proved as illusory as ever Pepys was at least gratified by the King's interest in economy and 'the thoughts he is now under of stopping all things that look like occasions of laying out money'. From now on there would be order, economy and system everywhere.

Such matters were deeply pleasing to Pepys in his love of detail and factual scrupulousness, and to watch him at work is to see a great administrator giving his whole attention to even the slightest matter. A single day might see him writing to the Navy Board about intelligence ships then despatching letters to the captains of a fireship, a privateer and a pink, variously to encourage, to warn or to settle bills. The excuses given by the captain of an escort vessel for coming into port without orders had been accepted Pepys wrote, but the man was advised not to take too independent an attitude to his command. Pepys then informed a fellow escort officer that allegations of cowardice he had made to the Admiralty would be investigated by the King himself, and letters followed to the governor of Plymouth about the storm-damaged Virginia fleet and to the commissioner at Portsmouth concerning problems in organising a court martial. Such day-to-day detail was, of course, very important, but Pepys rarely let it cloud his view of essentials and his wider plans.

Every aspect of his new responsibilities interested him. For example, he was determined to help change the nation's reluctance to breed men for the sea and looked to vocational training to remedy this. To this end, he persuaded Charles to found and partly fund 'a nursery of children to be educated in mathematics for the particular use and service of navigation'.[2] Forty boys from Christ's Hospital were selected for this Mathematical School and a teacher chosen by the Royal Society was appointed to instruct them. In such ways might the future be provided for. Meanwhile, abuse was legion in the service and firmly disciplined central control was essential to root it out. Pepys tried to ensure that chaplains should be subject to greater scrutiny before they were appointed. It troubled him that few commanders bothered to take a chaplain with them and that when they did they made an 'ill choice' of ignorant debauchees 'to the great dishonour of God and the government, and the encouraging of profaneness and dissolutions in the fleet'.[3] In 1677, Pepys tried to institute a procedure whereby the irritable and obstructive Bishop of London would propose candidates to whom he had given a certificate vouching for their piety, learning and sturdy Anglicanism. The whole perfectly reasonable plan was beset with difficulties, and even when Pepys had made his best efforts he knew that the navy still employed chaplains who were barely literate and wrote out their sermons 'with so many blots, interlineations, false spellings and wrong pointings' that their efforts did them little credit.

Senior officers would likewise have to learn that they were now under the direct supervision of the Admiralty and were not free to follow their own profit and whims. In particular, Pepys fought a long and not always successful battle against those captains who were tempted by the considerable profits they could make from 'good voyages' or the illicit transportation of bullion and commercial goods. Discipline collapsed under such golden caresses, but while some officers were prosecuted successfully for this offence, sentenced to six months' imprisonment and an order to pay their profits to the King, others relied on their connections to get them out of trouble. The gentlemen officers still had their privileges, which caused problems. For example, it was all very well for Pepys to write a magisterial letter of rebuke to Captain Priestman when he caught him 'sauntering up and down Covent Garden' when he should have been with his ship in Portsmouth, but Priestman was a royal favourite and survived the incident unscathed.[4]

While loitering amid the delights of London was one temptation, loitering in the more remote and balmy ports of the world was another. Captain Poole, commissioned to accompany a new governor to Barbados, decided to remain there for six months 'without one hour spent in the service of the King'. Pepys was furious. The result of such casualness and self-indulgence must surely be the 'irrevocable ruin' of the navy. How could a fleet be run efficiently if those in whom the greatest trust was placed sunned themselves in a tropical paradise to the detriment of 'His Majesty's honour, service, and treasure'? But King Charles yet again proved himself altogether less concerned than Pepys supposed he should be. Poole was another royal favourite and, obliged to do something, the King gave him the easy choice of a court-martial or forfeiting his pay.

If discipline was difficult to impose when erring captains were idling in the sun or had returned to their home ports, it was even more so when they were at sea. All manner of vices might rapidly become the rule once a ship had sailed beyond the eagle-eyed vigilance of the Admiralty, and his friend James Houblon voiced Pepys's own thoughts when he wrote how he wished that 'all drinking, swearing and gaming and expensive and sumptuous eating may be banished the Fleet, and particularly that the King's ships may not be made bawdy-houses nor the captains publicly carry and entertain their whores on board as some of them have formerly done . . . to the great scandal of our religion and government both amongst Turks, Jews and Christians'.[5]

Alcohol had a particularly bad effect. Certainly it did aboard the *Sweepstakes*.[6] The chaplain of that ship was disgustingly drunk before setting sail from Portsmouth, but once in Dublin he slipped ashore and become so riotous with the bibulous residents of Trinity College that he rushed outside, stripped off all his clothes and swore 'God damn him he was a man of war'. The local people had 'much ado' to get him back inside, and even after they had succeeded in preventing him from parading his shame in the streets he 'did get from them and leapt over the wall and tore his shirt almost from his back'. Matters were hardly helped by Captain Roydon, nominally in charge of the *Sweepstakes*, who was likewise an alcoholic. By the close of October 1677 the ship was anchored in calm seas off Kinsale when, at one o'clock in the morning, Roydon staggered aboard 'crying a huge storm, calling for the Master' and swearing that he should be dragged out from wherever he was if he did not appear at once. '"A rogue! What! Not come and save the King's ship?"' The drunken spree continued for several days until Lieutenant Alymer, who had been repeatedly struck with the captain's cane, slipped away to beg refuge in Dublin Castle 'by reason of his Captain's usage'. The Duke of Ormonde took pity on the poor man and waited on instructions from the Admiralty. By July of the following year, Pepys had decided to convene a court-martial to examine Roydon's behaviour and his allegations that his lieutenant had 'absented himself for several months from his ship'. The wretched truth of the affair eventually emerged and, while the drunken chaplain was dismissed the service, Roydon was relieved of his command.

Such appalling scenes made clear that adequate supervision of the appointment of commanding officers was important, and the care and subtlety with which Pepys approached it showed him at his most adept. His position at the Admiralty was such that, although the power of appointing officers was vested in the King, Pepys himself could have a considerable say, especially in the appointment of men he thought particularly suitable. A procedure altogether more rigorous and uniform was clearly needed and Pepys set about devising this. With characteristic incisiveness he saw to the heart of the problem, realised that it exposed a serious difficulty, and set about getting his way with tact, slowness and guile. He was all too familiar with the points at issue: the old rivalry between gentlemen and tarpaulins and the fact that too many of the gentlemen were amateurs. The lack of professionalism disturbed him. He was painfully aware that 'the general ignorance and dullness of our lieutenants of our ships' was 'a great evil' and now, in one of those passages of serpentine yet pellucid prose that had become the hallmark of his official style, Pepys wrote that these unsatisfactory officers were

> for the most part (at least those of later standing) made out of volunteers, who having passed some time superficially at sea, and being related to families of interest at court, do obtain lieutenancies before they are fitted for it; to which is to be added that the duty and trust of a lieutenant, not being ascertained by standing instructions as those of a commander are, nor no establishment made of the qualifications by which a person is to be judged whether he be fit to be entrusted with the office of lieutenant or not, no man considers of the importance of a lieutenant's duty in the case of the death or disability of his captain; and consequently it is come to pass that no man that can but pretend to have been two or three voyages at sea (nay, some but one) will allow to have it disputed whether he be capable of discharging the office of a lieutenant or not, but expects of course that he will be allowed to do so.[7]

Pepys wanted to do away with such abuses altogether, and of the divide between gentlemen and tarpaulins he wrote that it was a 'distinction I am both ashamed and afflicted to mention, and should be more, but that among other good ends of what I am now doing the removing of that distinction will be one'. His efforts were not an attempt to deny the existence of social differences. Pepys had all the respect his age gave to birth and he feared that the navy lacked social prestige. 'Observe,' he wrote, 'the maliciousness of our English proverb towards the service of the sea, viz. that the sea and the gallows refused nobody.' The low esteem of the navy was then reinforced by 'our practice of sending none thither but the vicious or poor'.[8] Pepys thought it 'very desirable' that new recruits should be gentlemen, but that was not enough. 'As no man living', he wrote, 'can be more inclined than myself to favour a gentleman that is a true seaman, so neither is there any man more sensible than (after many years' observation) I am, of the ruinous consequences of an over-hasty admitting persons to the office and charge of seamen upon the bare consideration of their being gentlemen.' What the ideal well-bred candidate needed was the seasoned seamanship of the tarpaulin, the skills of that generation of men who had been schooled to naval combat in the fleets of Blake and Cromwell.

These men were dying out now, and Pepys knew that it was his responsibility to breed a new generation of officers. To do this effectively, he would have to set a new goal: from now on an officer and a gentleman should have the skills of the tarpaulin, just as the tarpaulin should have the articulate authority of a gentlemen. What Pepys wanted, in other words, was a navy staffed by socially respected men of high professional standards. His thoughts on the matter were given clear expression by his friend James Houblon, who wrote to Pepys saying that 'I shall never think the Navy capable of doing any great matters unless officered with sober, discreet and experienced seamen'. What was needed to encourage this was a career structure, a situation from which 'men may see advancement plain before them when they deserve it, and that instead of being industrious only to get friends to recommend them . . . the officers and seamen shall be brought to an emulation who shall do best as being sure to be preferred that way and no other'.[9]

How was this desirable state to be brought about? To Pepys, the answer was obvious: prior to promotion every candidate should pass an examination that tested his competence, a weeding-out process that Pepys himself called his 'Establishment for Ascertaining the Duties and Trust of a Lieutenant'. By 1 December 1677, the draft of this historic document was ready for presentation to the Admiralty commissioners. In it Pepys laid down that men seeking promotion to the upper deck should be over twenty and have served for at least three years at sea, including one as a midshipman. The hopeful candidate would then have to produce testimonials from his commanding officers as to his 'sobriety, diligence, obedience to order and application to the study and practice of the art of navigation'. Only when the aspiring officer had satisfied these requirements would he be considered for promotion. Once promoted, he would be required to keep a log that might be inspected at any time. The author of the greatest diary in the English language knew well the self-discipline and self-assessment that keeping a journal encouraged, and realised how these qualities might sustain a man through the many temptations to weakness afforded by navy life.

In such ways as these, the Royal Navy might make a professional fighting force, but a plan so eminently practical as Pepys's was bound, at first, to ruffle the feathers of the merely privileged. It might seem to some that there was an uncomfortable whiff of the radical about it, an uneasy reminder of Cromwell's promotion of ordinary men to leading posts in his New Model Army. Pepys knew all along that to get his way he would have to manoeuvre with care and, rather than firing a broadside, he proceeded indirectly, asking minor, piecemeal questions of the Admiralty commissioners until their answers gradually built up into an overwhelming case in support of his idea. Even then he faced opposition. Prince Rupert, that cynosure of the fighting aristocracy, thought it beneath a gentleman's dignity to have served as a midshipman, and Lord Ossory agreed. Pepys would not concede the point, and the matter was referred to a special committee where both tarpaulins and serving gentlemen could give their opinion.

Both parties wholeheartedly supported Pepys's view, and the aristocratic George Legge was deputed to deliver their verdict. There was one last attempt to block the motion. Had Legge ever served as a midshipman? No, he averred, he had not, but 'it had cost him many an aching head and heart since to make up the want of it'. With that, the issue was unanimously resolved. All would-be officers in the Royal Navy should in future serve at least a year as midshipmen then take an examination. Pepys had got his way and the navy would now become a properly professional fighting force. He was immensely relieved. 'I thank God,' he wrote soon afterwards, 'we have not half the throng of those of the bastard breed pressing for employments which we heretofore used to be troubled with, they being conscious of their inability to pass this examination, and know it to be to no purpose now to solicit for employments till they have done it.'

This was a major victory, but an efficient officer class was not Pepys's only concern. Improving the usually dreadful lot of the ordinary seaman also absorbed his energies. There was little, however, that he could change. The evils of the press-gang could only be contained rather than rooted out, just as the abuses of seamen's pay could only be partially alleviated by punishing those who indulged in ticket brokering. The cause of both evils was the enduring and all too familiar problem of lack of money, and its contaminating influence spread into the vexed matter of victualling. For all that Pepys could specify that sailors were to be provided daily with a pound of the best wheat biscuit, a gallon of good beer and 'two pounds avoirdupois of beef, killed and made up with salt in England, of a well-fed ox not weighing less that 5 cwt' this, since it had to be paid for, was all too often wishful thinking. Frequently sailors had to make do with what one described as 'a little brown bread made from the worst of their wheat, a little small beer, which is as bad as water bewitched . . . and a little old, tough beef, when all the best was picked out, leaving us poor seamen with the sirloin next the horns; and a little fish'.[10]

But there were wider issues to consider. The purpose of a navy administered and at least partly reformed with such effort was to be 'a protection to the nation and a terror to our enemies'. The era of great national fleets had fully come into being and it was on the ever-increasing number of new 'great ships' rather than hastily requisitioned merchantmen that a country's security was now seen to depend. Pepys was fully aware of this and he wrote how naval policy had 'quite changed' from earlier days: 'our neighbours being so much stronger than before, and there being quite a different use and service for men-of-war now than there was then, when merchants' vessels and those of war were the same'.

By the 1670s, merchantmen were carrying a huge range of staples and luxury goods: silks, mahogany, tortoiseshell, chocolate and slaves. Here was wealth, and wealth meant competition. As a result, it was essential that the Royal Navy be sufficiently strong to protect the merchant marine and to keep its rivals in awe. Much needed to be done to ensure that this was so. A score of English ships were in a dilapidated state while the size and strength of the Dutch and French navies meant that an arms race was essential if England were to assert its claim to the sovereignty of the seas. Events were soon to illustrate this point, and when North African pirates, sharking out of Tripoli, began seriously to harass the rich fleets of the Turkey and East India Companies

Pepys believed he had an unanswerable case for demanding more money for the navy. By 24 April 1675 he was ready to face Parliament.

He argued from policy and backed up his contentions with detail. He made it perfectly clear that the English fleet would have to be expanded. 'Our neighbours' strength is now greater than ours,' he declared, 'and they will still be building.'[11] There was already a deficit of ships to be made up and competition in the future would be fierce. The rival vessels were more modern, stronger and better armed than the thirty ships-of-the-line and three dozen or so Fourth Rates available to England. A great drive to rearmament was essential and Pepys demanded two new First Rates, seven Second Rates, twenty-seven Third Rates and four Fourth Rates – some thirty vessels in all. Parliament was not convinced. Increasingly suspicious of royal absolutism and still minded to believe that Charles frittered away his supplies on self-indulgence, they were reluctant to spend money on augmenting his power. They argued that the number of ships was sufficient for what was needed to be done, and one particularly obstinate Member declared with ponderous wit that he would dip his hand in his purse only to make sure that his money stayed there.

Autumn saw Pepys trying again. In the interval between of the two sessions of the House he had prepared his 'Notes for my Discourse in Parliament introductory to the Debate of the Business of the Navy'.[12] These were the arguments of a King's man, and it was as an advocate of the court that Pepys spoke – and spoke with flair, authority and thinly veiled contempt for the opposition, which showed how clearly he understood the widening divisions in the House and the nation at large. It was the King rather than Parliament who was the great patriot, he declared. It was Charles who had kept the navy afloat by his 'personal knowledge and labours in war and peace, and enquiries after everything advantageous to navigation'.

It was royal patronage that had provided new docks and, in them, built those ships that so far outnumbered the vessels the detestable republican regime of Cromwell's men had launched, 'notwithstanding what their public revenues enabled them and the necessities of their violent government urged them to'. It was arrant nonsense to claim that the King had purloined navy supplies for his private ends. Look at what he had done! His present fleet was far stronger than the one he had inherited but still more tonnage was needed since (and here Pepys flourished information provided by the intelligence services) rival fleets were continuing to grow and were now an even greater threat than they had been the last time he spoke.

There were mutters of agreement and murmurings over the cost, which Pepys estimated at £144,016. Should Members vote a sufficient sum for Pepys's proposals or merely a year's supply sufficient for twenty ships? Pepys convinced the House of the absurdity of parsimony. There was a European shortage of seasoned timber. Would Members have an inadequate score of ships built from green wood? This was a long-term project and needed long-term finance. The Members accepted the point, voted funds for the building of two-thirds of the fleet Pepys had asked for, then showed the true bent of their policy at meetings of the Committee of Ways and Means. The money for twenty ships might be forthcoming, but it was altogether more prudent to place it in the careful hands of the mayor and common council of the City of London than the Exchequer of the profligate Charles.

Such a calculated insult to the Crown was a massive affront and indicated the true bias of an increasingly articulate opposition determined to thwart the King wherever they could. Pepys himself argued fiercely and successfully against the move they proposed – who knew the honesty of 'this master of ours' better than he? – and the motion was defeated.

A week of bitter technical debate ensued, but if this concluded with a supply for twenty ships being voted, the illusory cash was at once snatched away by the opposition's insistence that the money be taken from the King's customs revenues. Shaftesbury and the opposition were learning their business. A defeated Charles prorogued the House and Pepys did not get his funds.

While Parliament squabbled over the expense of an adequate navy, the available men and ships were, for the most part, proving their worth. At the start of 1676, Sir John Narborough was involved in what Pepys called a 'great and happy action' against the Bey of Tripoli, a victory that was, he declared, 'perfected with all the acceptable circumstances that can attend any attempt of that kind – namely, the being effectual, speedy and not chargeable to His Majesty in his treasure nor to his subjects in their lives'. Narborough was just the sort of officer Pepys wished for as a model for others to imitate, the type of man for whom he had initiated his reforms. But the Mediterranean also showed precisely the dangers of the sort of ill-discipline that Pepys was also fighting so strenuously to extirpate. In the autumn of 1676, Captain Charles Atkins, his ship laden with illicit bullion, surrendered to pirates and was towed into Algiers. Atkins was eventually and rightly deprived of his command.

Parliament reassembled in February 1677 in an atmosphere of growing tension over international affairs. The might of Catholic France seemed every day more threatening and was a subject of grave concern to all men save the infinitely devious King, who opened the session with a heartfelt plea for money to build the thirty ships required by Pepys. Charles's wishes were echoed by the chancellor and then, on 21 February, Pepys himself rose to give a magisterial account of the needs of the navy.[12] With enormous and characteristic labour, he had mustered ammunition for thirteen salvoes against the opposition and with these he bombarded them into submission.

The Members were an enemy he regarded with suspicion and contempt. Long experience had shown him that they were pitifully ignorant of the practical considerations of naval business 'which was deeply irksome to his professionalism' while he also knew that to this lack of knowledge was added a reckless willingness both to attack those who knew better and withhold essential funds. Pepys would silence such irresponsibility. He would present an unanswerable case. Time and again he insisted on the mighty efforts the King had made to secure the navy as an efficient fighting force. Time and again he dwelt on the dangers of powerful enemies everywhere. He pointed out the superiority of Dutch naval power and, above all, the increasing strength of France. He told the House how the French, in their vastly more capacious harbours, had already built nineteen great ships and were now building an additional seven. Altogether they had two dozen more ships with over twenty guns than the Royal Navy could muster. It was a powerful argument and, as he delivered his case, Pepys was more than ever the King's man arguing the King's cause. Even the abstract of his speech given in Grey's *Debates in the House of Commons* suggests something of the power with which he spoke.

Pepys took the Members back to the time of the Restoration, telling them how 'more ships have been built in these sixteen years of the King's return, than in eighteen of rebellion. In his conscience he thinks this to be truth, and therefore says it; though it has done through as many difficulties as any other management in any age whatsoever.' For all that such an achievement was largely the work of the Navy Board and of Pepys himself he was careful to attribute all success to Charles. 'By the King's personal application to building ships, skill has been advanced beyond the memory of man, and, perhaps, beyond any improvement.' Not only this, 'More docks have been built.' In addition, 'No age, at one time, had so many encouragements for navigation.' Officers were now properly valued and trained while at Christ's Hospital boys were being educated for the service. 'Most august is the King's seminary for seamen. From a little hospital, no charitable foundation is endowed like it.' Now it was essential to ask funds for building 'thirty ships more'. After all, 'the French and Dutch are daily building', and a request for thirty more English ships was no novelty. The figures had been carefully prepared, and so convincing was Pepys's presentation and so tense the international situation that the reluctant Members eventually voted to supply 'His Majesty with a sum of money for building ships not exceeding £600,000'.

This was nothing less than a triumph. Pepys had emerged victorious as the King's supporter, but his success marked him out as a dangerous figure to those who had been obliged to submit to his reasoning. Now, as Shafesbury and his cohorts had been unable to defeat his arguments, they were determined to try to sink the man himself. As Pepys himself wrote 'when they found themselves defeated of all just occasions of censure upon me in my public capacity, they were driven to serve themselves with unjust ones in my private'. Ammunition seemed readily available. 'Admiral' Pepys, as the Members sarcastically called him, riding round London in his painted chariot or disembarking from his stately barge at Whitehall Privy Stairs, surely lived the sort of life that could only be paid for by corruption. Obviously he was abusing his office and lining his pockets with ill-gotten gains. Members of the Parliamentary opposition went to consult with their friends in the city and invented the proofs they could not find. As they made public their slanders in the House of Commons so Pepys made shorthand notes of their allegations. He was charging £80 a piece, his enemies said, for passes allowing ships to sail the Mediterranean. He wrote out some four thousand of these a year, they alleged. Others whispered that eight thousand was nearer the mark. All agreed that such passes were an outrage, an abuse of liberty, a restraint on trade.

Pepys was smoulderingly angry for he felt that his honour was at stake. The grey areas of his earlier dealings were a thing of the past and he prided himself now on his probity. He was even rather pompous about it. The days of guineas hidden in a gift of gloves were long gone, and when people had the temerity to offer him a bribe they were apt to receive letters magisterially smug with righteous indignation. 'That which I have reason to take amiss from you,' Pepys wrote to the lieutenant of the *Phoenix*, who was hoping to smooth his way to a small favour, 'is your thinking that any consideration of benefit to myself or expectation of reward from you should be of any inducement to me.' The lieutenant should 'reserve that sort of argument for such as will be guided by it', and realise that 'your meriting well of the King is the only present that shall ever operate with me'.

Now, challenged in the House about his personal probity, Pepys rose no less than three times to defend himself. He was not a profiteer, he said. 'He despises the thought of any undue profit, and of any man that thinks it.' He had actually reduced the cost of passes from what it had been in his predecessor's time 'and his pains and diligence deserve as well, and are equal to any that have gone before him'. He was an honest man who had 'wrote himself blind in the King's service'. It was a complete lie '"that forty shillings a pass hath been taken"'. He would have the matter referred to a committee, for 'he values the reputation of a truth-speaker above all his gains'. Eventually the whole business came up before the Admiralty Board and the King himself. Pepys was defending himself before his allies. Fees from passes were, he insisted, his legitimate perquisite and he argued firmly that the practice should either continue or be compensated for if taken away from him. Charles knew his man and 'was pleased to say that he saw no reason to have it taken away'.

The opposition's attempt to undermine this most articulate of the King's supporters – the French ambassador called Pepys one of the best speakers in England – had foundered on the rock of royal favour, but the duel with Parliament was far from over. As 1677 came to a close an Anglo-Dutch war against the might of Catholic France seemed increasingly likely. Pepys faced the monumental task of readying ninety battleships and some five dozen other attendant vessels. Over a million pounds was needed and, for all their professed Protestant loyalties and the fact that the sum was eventually voted, members of the opposition fought with all their growing mastery of Parliamentary technique to thwart Pepys's efforts at every turn.

It was daily more clear to these men that the passage of events had worn the Restoration settlement to shreds. Tension and mistrust were rampant. In the coffee-houses of London and at meetings of the Green Ribbon Club especially, men argued that 'there has now for divers years a design been carried on to change the lawful government of England into an absolute tyranny, and to convert the established Protestant religion into downright Popery'. To men leading lives of such desperate suspicion, there was one clear answer to their problems: to exclude the Catholic Duke of York from the throne would be to remove all their difficulties and preserve the nation and its religion intact. Only in this way could liberty be maintained and power be vested with those commoners in Parliament who possessed the greatest weight in society. They were the true political nation, sovereignty resided with them, and their interests must take precedence over those of the Crown. To achieve this, means both fair and foul were legitimate, and to thwart the efforts of a Crown servant like Samuel Pepys was but one necessary tactic in a desperate political game.

Members proceeded to ask Pepys to name a precise date by which the fleet would be ready. They raised questions about the use of press-gangs and grilled the harassed secretary about the delays and increased costs that had been brought about by their own refusal to let the navy have immediate and much-needed cash. Of course provisioning the fleet was expensive when the Navy Board had to rely on credit, and 'it will be an unfortunate war', Pepys said tautly, 'if you go not early to market for stores . . . and a contemplation of joy to your enemies abroad'. The barely suppressed annoyance in this last remark sometimes erupted into open displays of anger. Exasperated when Sir John Knight yet again accused him of paying exorbitant charges for goods, Pepys replied with such 'severity' that indignant Members insisted his words be written down and Pepys be made to apologise to the House. He did so, turning to the speaker to say, '"Pray, Sir, forgive me if I was transported to hear the same thing said over and over again here."'[13]

Pepys's had been a lone and exasperated voice. By contrast, many of those who taunted him were encouraged by generous French bribes – often as much as five hundred guineas a head – to 'seek for everything that can give the Court vexation'. One such man was William Harbord who was soon to prove himself a most dangerous enemy. Even now Harbord had readied his first sniping shots of abuse. The real danger, he sorted, was not the enemy abroad but the enemy at home, and he ostentatiously recalled a saying of the great Lord Sandwich's to the effect that it would be perfectly possible to secure the nation against the French, provided someone first secured her against the bureaucrats in Whitehall. Pepys was furious. Such attacks impugned his efficiency as a civil servant and this he would not tolerate. He would let his achievements speak for themselves. 'Some of your ships (that you gave money for at your last meeting) are ready, and will be floating this summer,' he declared. 'Ninety sail of ships may be floating by this summer, by your concurrence for supply, and by God's blessing.'

Far more dangerous than assaults on Pepys's efficiency, however, were allegations that he and the Admiralty were in league with a king who wanted a large navy to help set up an arbitrary government. This was an outrage, a thinly veiled attack on Charles. Who, Pepys asked, was the real promoter of arbitrary government? King Charles, who had, in his wisdom, sought out a great defensive alliance for the sake of his country, or Parliament, which was doing everything it could to prevent this? He answered his own question with a flamboyant display of loyalty to the King that went to the heart of his constitutional thinking and beliefs:

> The best expression of the divinity of a Prince, is to take good council. The King has taken it, and executed it, and it stays with you to enable the King to go through with it. The King has made an alliance as great as with all the world beside. The King has done it, and with great success, and it remains with you to support him in it.

Pepys had once cracked a joke to the King about 'our masters at Westminster'. Now the reality of a highly organised opposition was no laughing matter. He had himself become a Member of Parliament only to serve the King. The royal will was for him the true determiner of the nation's foreign policy and it was now the royal will that, an advantageous peace having been hurriedly patched up with France, the fleet that Pepys had assembled with such efforts should be demobilised. Eighty-nine battleships and more than 15,000 men had been readied in record time and in the teeth of the most vehement opposition. It was a remarkable achievement, it had served its purpose and, at the start of October 1678, with the acrimonious debates at Westminster apparently silenced, the grateful King asked Mr Pepys to attend on him at Newmarket.

CHAPTER TWELVE

Pepys and the Popish Plot

It was lucky indeed for Pepys that he had been invited to Newmarket since, during his absence from London, there occurred a series of events that were to drive to the edge of hysteria a people already agitated by the effects of war, pestilence, fire and their fear of the twin evils of popery and arbitrary government.

Throughout the terrible months of the Plague, Sir Edmund Berry Godfrey, a stalwart London magistrate, had, like Pepys himself, stayed by his post in the anguished city. There, dressed in his black wig and hat with a gold band, he had overseen mass burials and prosecuted grave robbers. For these services he had earned the love of the people and the respect of the King who, when the Plague was over, rewarded him with 800 ounces of gold plate. But Godfrey's place in the public life of the country was not yet over and now, as fears of absolutism and the Catholic menace daily increased, he was approached by two men claiming that they were in possession of the most appalling information and that they wished to swear an affidavit as to its truth. Israel Tonge and the infamous con-man Titus Oates had unearthed a well-planned conspiracy to kill the King, they said, and set up Catholicism across the land. When informed of this Charles himself was sceptical but, while he rode off to Newmarket and his meeting with Pepys, the Duke of York demanded that the matter be investigated by the Privy Council. Herein lay great danger.

Oates was duly summoned before a meeting of the Privy Council and, in his whining, sing-song voice, canted of plots, secret Jesuit armies, and his belief that an erstwhile secretary to the Duke of York had opened up a treasonable correspondence with Louis XIV, concerning the forced conversion of England to Roman Catholicism. The incriminating letters were eventually produced, much to Oates's delight, and 'made as much noise in and about London, and . . . all over the nation, as if the very cabinet of Hell had been laid open'.[1] Astrologers had already convinced the credulous that five recent eclipses and the appearance of a comet with a blazing tail foretold calamity, and now propagandists fanned the flames of fear and suspicion. The Catholic menace, they said, was everywhere. The terrible bonfires of Bloody Mary's reign would surely be lit once more. People went about in terror. All chance of rational proceedings had evaporated and, when the murdered body of Sir Edmund Berry Godfrey was found in mysterious circumstances on a patch of wasteland below Primrose Hill, hysteria gripped the nation. Only Catholics could have committed so heinous a deed, it was said, and soon their invading forces would sweep away every Englishman's liberty and his true Protestant faith.

It was in this atmosphere of terror and suspicion that Shaftesbury and his supporters could best thrive. The so-called 'Popish Plot' was a godsend to them. It did not matter that it was a farrago of the most dangerous lies. Its advantage lay in that people at all levels of society were prepared to believe in its existence and that, by skilful manipulation, their fears could focus ever more sharply on a papist court riddled with Catholic mistresses, Catholic artists, Catholic musicians, Catholic servants and Catholic pimps. Above all, it would direct concentrated hatred on the Catholic Duke of York, and thereby build up what Shaftesbury hoped would be an overwhelming demand for his exclusion from the throne. Every effort was put into achieving this last, and no gambit was too wild or too ridiculous to be refused. Those within the Duke's sphere were inevitably drawn in, and these included Pepys. Was he not 'a known, faithful and professed servant of the Duke of York'? Had not earlier efforts to convince people that he was a 'bloody papist' nearly succeeded? Now these efforts were redoubled as Shaftesbury's agents started to round up and bribe those who might be persuaded to say that the murderer of Sir Edmund Berry Godfrey was none other than Pepys himself.

Ignorant of the horror about to descend on him, Pepys went about his duty. In particular, he was determined to play his part in searching for Jesuits about to flee the country. He had already received orders to close the ports when a letter arrived from Gravesend informing him of the suspicious behaviour of a man calling himself (among other names) Captain Scott. This dubious character evaded capture but his papers were seized and handed to the authorities.[2] The shifty Scott would reappear but, in the meantime, Shaftesbury's men rounded up one of Pepys's clerks – the unhappy Samuel Atkins – and determined to force out of him a confession to the effect that he was privy to Pepys's plan to assassinate Sir Edmund Berry Godfrey.

A net of perjury was drawn tight around the young man as Shaftesbury began his wheedlingly brutal inquisition. '"Did you ever say,"' he asked, '"that there was no kindness (or a want of friendship I think 'twas) between Mr Pepys and Sir Edmund Berry Godfrey?"'[3] Atkins denied the accusation and again remained firm when Shaftesbury told him that they had no option but to commit him to Newgate. Here, remorseless pressure was put on him to confess to having helped Pepys find a killer for Godfrey. Eventually an informant was even found who was prepared to perjure himself by swearing that he had seen Atkins standing over the murdered corpse. But Atkins refused to betray his master, and Pepys worked furiously to clear his clerk's name and his own. As always, detailed accuracy was his strongest weapon, and he produced such overwhelming evidence to prove that young Atkins had been out on a drinking spree at the time of his alleged misdemeanours that, when his case came to trial, the clerk was acquitted. Pepys had turned detective in his own defence, a role that circumstances soon forced him to master.

Against such methodical exactness even Shaftesbury was temporarily powerless and he was obliged to try another approach in his efforts to bring Pepys down. He set about directing his colleagues in the Commons to charge Pepys with issuing Jesuits with passes to flee abroad. Pepys managed to rebut this allegation too and to make his enemies appear ridiculous into the bargain by showing that the issuing of such passes was no part of his job. They tried another tack. The influence of the Duke of York over the navy had been such that surely the whole fleet was riddled with papists. This was certainly the view of Titus Oates, who now gave out that he had knowledge of a Catholic plot to seize every one of the nation's fighting ships. Although it was ridiculous, steps had to be taken to counter his claim and Pepys issued an order to all commanders requiring them to examine their subordinate officers both as to their religion and the occasions on which they last took the sacrament. It was 'a matter of great joy' that the results showed the navy to be solidly Protestant.

There was worse to come for, when an increasingly cornered Charles dissolved the House of Commons, Pepys had to fight an election. Despite his generosity to his constituents in Castle Rising, where he had helped to pay for repairs to the church, agents spread the old rumour that he was a papist.

So effective was this that another seat had to be found, and it was as Member of Parliament for Harwich that Pepys was eventually and all but unanimously returned to a House now full of the King's enemies and his own, who resumed their attack. With that mastery of propaganda by which they made their campaign into an early media war, Shaftesbury's men began to distribute across a London already flooded with scurrilous prints and pamphlets a nasty little piece in which Pepys was attacked for 'Plot, Popery, Piracy'. He brushed it off and got on with his business. Absurd allegations would not distract him from his one real and overriding problem: the navy's familiar, crippling lack of money.

Here again was ammunition for the enemy. The cost of the navy and the duplicity of those running it beggared description, they claimed. The country was paying a shilling for every sixpennyworth of goods received while they still insisted that the Duke of York had filled every available post with papists. This they would prove at the Bar of the House. As part of this attack, Shaftesbury's men focused again on Pepys's relationship with the Duke of York, who was now so clearly the most hated man in England that his brother would soon require him to go into exile. Pepys was firm in his conviction that the Duke was not only a great Lord High Admiral but that he was the only and rightful heir to the throne, for all that his religious beliefs were so unfortunate that Pepys, as he told the House, would give his own life to bring him back to the true fold. In a Parliament bent on excluding York from the throne Pepys was a monarchist through and through. His every action proved it, and some of those actions were not without personal danger, for he kept up a correspondence with the exiled Duke which, had it been discovered, would surely have laid him open to the severest attack.

As it was, Pepys had as much to fear from his allies as his enemies for the King, with that unhesitating *realpolitik* that was his to employ, now took carefully considered steps to establish his own support while appearing to give the opposition a simulacrum of influence. Pepys would be one of his victims. Charles made a clean sweep of his advisers, remodelled the Privy Council so that it appeared to represent the balance of interests in the country at large, and replaced the Admiralty commissioners with members of the opposition. To his utter mortification, Pepys saw such enemies as William Harbord (who already had his eyes on Pepys's emoluments) seated at the tables where he had been wont to get his way. It was ghastly. The enemy had invaded his high, magnificent citadel and cared nothing for the careful plans he had put into execution there. The Admiralty was part of the spoils of party warfare and Pepys, in the words of his friend Sir Robert Southwell, was 'to be pulled to pieces'. He stood it for three terrible weeks then resigned.

But the opposition were far from finished with him. Parliament was their true centre of operations, and a Parliamentary committee was now set up to investigate the supposed Miscarriages of the Navy. As their luck would have it, the notorious Captain Scott had now reappeared on the scene, his often drunken mind running over with hatred for the Stuarts and their parasite Pepys who had tried to have him arrested. Scott easily fell in with his old companions and was eventually to confess to his motives for wishing to destroy both Pepys himself and the monarchy. In so far as the confession of a con-man can be trusted, Scott declared that he was employed by an unnamed rival of Pepys (it was probably Harbord) who wanted his job at the Admiralty and was prepared to kill to get it. As for his political motives, Scott willingly associated himself with men whose 'design was to destroy the government and make themselves kings, or rather tyrants', and to that end 'did all they could to bring an odium and hatred upon His Majesty and family, and by their fictions to delude a giddy and unthinking people'.[4] There was no idealism in either intent or method, and his associates, Scott confessed, were the powerless and the disaffected: 'those that wanted offices and were disappointed, those that were enemies to the government of church and state, and tools that the other two brought over to be of their side'. Their religious motives – their fanning the dangerous fires of anti-popery – were entirely disingenuous. They acted as they did purely because they could imagine no other way 'to destroy or wound' the government.

Proving in Parliament that Pepys was guilty of being a papist, a traitor and, for good measure, a pirate was a useful means to their goal, and Scott and his cronies set about their task with all the brazenness of seasoned con-men, planting their outrageous accusations with just sufficient circumstantial evidence to make them appear credible to those in the House willing to be gulled. A visit made by Pepys's friend Sir Anthony Deane to Versailles, for example, was particularly useful, for on the basis of this known event Scott could build the incredible story of how he had seen Deane handing a packet to Monsieur Pellissary, the late treasurer-general of the French navy. That obliging gentleman had then revealed to Scott how each of the papers in the packet had been signed by Pepys and that they gave information to the enemy about how they could destroy the English fleet in its home ports. An amazed House of Commons was then told that plump and prosperous Mr Pepys had charged £40,000 for this vital information.

It was now clear to his enemies that Pepys was a traitor, but there was more to come, for Scott and his friends had researched their campaign well. They knew of John James, for example, the butler Pepys had fired for impropriety, and had found that they could work on him with ease. With Harbord's gold jingling in his otherwise empty pockets James was willing to use his knowledge of Pepys to do his erstwhile master great harm. It was James 'that first got the merchants together' to make the allegations of piracy that were now being levelled against Pepys. These stories were to the effect that Pepys, his brother-in-law and Deane had fraudulently procured the *Hunter*, provisioned her at the government's expense then used her to prey on English shipping during the Dutch wars.

There had been secret and illicit meetings of some members of the Parliamentary committee investigating the navy at the Mitre in Fenchurch Street to organise these slanders, while it was James who also testified to Pepys being a papist. He seemed in a position to know: he said he had often heard Pepys say that no man would get an appointment in the navy unless he was on the Duke of York's list of approved Catholic candidates. That Pepys himself was a Catholic was perfectly obvious: did he not regularly sing popish music with that known Jesuit Morelli, a man who actually lived in Derby House where his room was full of crucifixes and other Romish trash? In a time of national hysteria these fantasies were given ready credence and, when Pepys rose in the House to speak, he knew that he was arguing for his life.

Pepys addressed the Commons with magnificent self-control, for all that he had been ambushed by such a variety of wholly unexpected accusations. He said he would not complain although in justice he should have been informed of the charges against him before they were levelled. Then, having made it clear that Parliament had acted disgracefully against one of its own Members, he proceeded to rebut the allegations made against him one by one. He denied having been involved with the *Hunter*. He denied any personal knowledge of Scott, beyond having tried to have him arrested and forwarding his treasonable papers to Parliament. As for his own alleged correspondence with Monsieur Pellissary, there was no evidence whatsoever to corroborate it. He then turned to his other accuser. James, he said, had been his butler and had been dismissed under circumstances that Pepys made plain to the whole House. He also believed that James had robbed him. The man was thoroughly unreliable and his evidence against Pepys could no more be relied on than his allegations against Morelli, who was, Pepys declared, a harmless and scholarly musician whose Catholic beliefs were so mild that he had been examined by the Inquisition for his inadequacies.

That should have been enough, but the opposition was in no mood for either reason or justice. A great royal servant was in their grip and his destruction would certainly help their efforts to pass a bill excluding the Duke of York from the throne. The sergeant-at-arms was ordered to arrest both Pepys and Deane as traitors. Two days later they appeared before the House again and were committed under the speaker's warrant to the Tower of London.

Pepys had fallen with sudden and terrible speed to the lowest point in his fortunes, but even in the most dismal place in London (and denied the benefits of the Habeas Corpus Act so recently passed by the Parliament in which he himself had sat) Pepys did not despair. In the furious world outside, Catholic peers were arrested and it was moved in the House that the Catholic Queen should be banished from London too. Parliament attacked Danby, the King's first minister, who only just escaped impeachment. The enemy sights were then levelled at the Duke of York, who likewise barely escaped impeachment. Pepys's friends, meanwhile, rallied around him. Coventry spoke up for him in the Commons. Evelyn visited him in the Tower. Houblon generously offered his help in the mighty campaign Pepys had now launched to clear his name. He was determined to fight for his life and he would do so with the mightiest of his weapons: his ability, honed over many years, to gather massive quantities of information and marshal them into a soundly convincing argument. Scott's lies had sent him to the Tower. Those lies and their fabricator would now be exposed in the minutest detail. 'Such is the credulity of this unhappy age,' Pepys wrote to Balty, 'that no accumulation of evidence can be too much to support the most obvious truth.'[5] Balty himself would soon be part of the most painstaking detective work, as would many others.

Scores of letters, many in duplicate, were despatched across Europe to trace every twist in Scott's remarkable life as a con-man. The English ambassador in Paris, the Duke of York and his secretary in Brussels, friends of Houblon's in Holland and many others were chivvied into finding out 'any part of the legend of this fellow's life'. The most obscure people were tracked down or their families, friends and secretaries traced. Statements were taken, compared and checked until what gradually emerged was the extraordinary tale of Scott's life, and a picaresque extravaganza that almost defied belief.

Scott had been born to poor parents in Kent, travelled early to New England, consorted there with Indians (the women especially) and then, having made enough money to return home, swindled an heiress into buying non-existent American real estate. Back in New York he masqueraded as the heir to the Duke of Buccleuch before making a hurried exit to Barbados and St Kitts, where he just avoided being hanged even as the rope was placed around his neck. Various adventures then took him to Holland where, as Major-General Scott of Scott's Hall, Kent, Shield Bearer and Geographer to the King of England, he won loud acclaim for his republicanism, along with the secret gratitude of the government for what were in fact his appallingly inaccurate maps of the enemy English coast. Fleeing back to England via Flanders and France, Scott was eventually welcomed into that company of footpads and mountebanks who made up the underworld of Shaftesbury's espionage system and who were now trying to bring Pepys down.

The gathering of such a story was a remarkable achievement to carry out in any circumstances and an extremely expensive one. Witnesses and testimonials were collected from across the length and breadth of Europe as Pepys prepared for his trial. But no trial came. The defences he had mustered were so overwhelming, so absolutely certain to expose Scott for the villain he was, that the attorney-general refused to act promptly on the grounds that he had not been able to complete the prosecution case. Still Pepys remained undaunted. He applied for bail and was moved to the Marshalsea as Scott made one more attempt to secure evidence against him. All he found hearsay were statements of the flimsiest kind. Lord Chief Justice Scroggs was appalled, muttering: 'They think to impose any story upon us and would fox us with informations; for my part I am ashamed of it.'[6] As a result, Pepys was granted bail for a staggering £30,000, a third of which he had to provide for himself. But at least he was free and he had his friends. It was a measure of his quality that they were so loyal to him. The gentle, affectionate Morelli had sent him music to soothe his worst hours in the Tower. The Houblons had shown unstinting energy in his cause. Now Will Hewer lent him rooms at his luxurious home in York Buildings. Pepys was deeply grateful. 'I am . . . with Will Hewer at his house,' he wrote to Balty, 'and have received from him all the care, kindness and faithfulness of a son . . . for which God reward him, if I can't.'

This was a move that was to cause both men pain, for the opposition could not let such conspicuous decency pass them by. They turned once again to John James, who wrote for them a venomous screed about Pepys in which 'this tailor-like person' was ridiculed for his birth, his pride and his ailments. It was a shoddy performance and, since this was one of the great ages of English satire and Shaftesbury's men knew the advantages to be gained from a well-written pamphlet, the material was sent to 'Elephant' Smith who reworked it into a ruthlessly clever libel of both Pepys and Hewer. Cast as a dialogue between the two men, it skilfully presents them as rapacious, calculating, dishonest, marvellously adept at dreaming up new schemes to line their own nests, and using the navy purely for their own interests.

> *Hewer*. Sir, there is a boatswain of a First Rate ship is dead.
>
> *Pepys*. Is there so? Of what ship?
>
> *Hewer*. The *Royal*——. Now, Sir, as to this vacancy; if you please to give me leave, we will put a boatswain of a Second Rate into her, into that a boatswain of the Third, and into that Third a boatswain of the Fourth Rate; into the Fourth Rate a boatswain of the Fifth Rate; so that all these shall be advanced; and the Fifth Rate shall be a clear vacancy. So that none of them but will be willing for preferment to give me five or ten guineas, and as much to put a new boatswain into the Fifth Rate. And this amounts to money and makes no notice at all.
>
> *Pepys*. I thank thee, good H., I protest it does; and thus we may run through all the boatswains' and gunners', carpenters' and cooks' employs; which will be considerable in the year, and much more if there comes a rot amongst them. But for the pursers I hope you intend to manage them at a better rate than this.
>
> *Hewer*. O God, Sir, yes, yes.[7]

Pepys – and Hewer too, no doubt – was hurt, but his pain spurred him on to ever greater efforts to clear his name, despite the mounting cost and the fact that many of his best witnesses were Roman Catholics and would not be given a fair hearing. But his was not blind obsession. In addition to being an essential act of self-defence, the whole taxing business was also an aspect of Pepys's loyalty to the King who had treated him so badly. If Pepys could not clear his name in a court of law, he would at least clear it before King Charles, 'whose good thoughts of me I had rather die under than live to have the good opinion of the rabble purchased by one ill deed or thought'.

In fact, it was the so-called 'rabble' who were now to provide him with some of his most useful information. By the greatest good fortune the ever-active Balty had managed to find one John Joyne, an English watchmaker living in Paris, who had a close knowledge of Scott and a grudge against him. Joyne soon introduced Balty to an extraordinary underworld of men who likewise detested Scott and could testify against him, declaring that he had been nowhere near Versailles when he supposedly saw Deane handing over documents to Monsieur Pellissary and could also vouch that he had spoken ill of the King. It was Joyne himself, however, who proved the most useful of these contacts for he was informed, eager and methodical. Here was someone who, by temperament at least, was a man after Pepys's own heart. 'I cannot express the content I have,' he wrote to Balty, 'in the freshness of his report and the ingenuity of his giving it, upon the only consideration of doing right.'[8]

In such ways as these Pepys's case appeared to strengthen amid mounting political crisis. Shaftesbury and his followers were now in full cry against the Duke of York, who had done nothing to ameliorate the situation. Indeed, his Catholic views were hardening. Not only did he refuse to compromise his beliefs, but he made it clear that he considered a Catholic succession entirely legitimate since it would guard against what he considered the deplorable growth of Parliamentary power that had come about from the reign of the Protestant Queen Elizabeth onwards. Such intransigence was a measure of the man and naturally served to worsen the conflict gripping the nation. Shaftesbury became ever more determined to have Parliament exclude him from the throne and had already placed a resolution before the House to the effect that 'the Duke of York being a Papist, and the hopes of his coming as such to the Crown, have given the greatest countenance and encouragement to the present conspiracies and designs of the Papists against the King and the Protestant Religion'.

Any public figure like Pepys who could be rightly or wrongly tarred with the popish brush would be brought down to serve Shaftesbury's ends. He had, besides, a popular and openly Protestant candidate for the throne in the glamorous but gullible figure of Charles's eldest illegitimate son, the Duke of Monmouth, whom Shaftesbury now promoted as the people's darling. What Shaftesbury failed to appreciate, however, was the guile and deep-seated conviction of Charles himself. The King's carapace of self-indulgence hid a political will as flexible and dangerous as a rapier and, with this, he would defend to the utmost his prerogative powers; and his right to settle the succession especially. In such matters as these he would not yield an inch. He proved this when, having recovered from a serious illness, he not only continued to make overtures to the French but sent York to take charge of affairs in Scotland, where anti-Catholic legislation did not apply, then exiled Monmouth to Holland and sacked Shaftesbury from the council. By so doing he was exercising powers that high Tories such as Pepys considered the King's inalienable right – the hereditary rights of the divinely sanctioned Stuart monarchy for which a civil war had been fought and lost and which a grateful people had welcomed Charles back at the Restoration.

But in the streets, at least, high ideas had given way to a bigoted popularism and, as Pepys continued assembling his evidence and waiting for his trial, London became a carnival of protest. Plays performed at Southwark fair showed the Pope seducing a nun. Around the middle of November a great pope-burning procession took place. A bellman strode in front of it crying, 'Remember Justice Godfrey!', the murdered magistrate. A comic Jesuit ran among the crowd selling fake pardons to those who would murder Protestants. An effigy of Godfrey himself was drawn along behind and was followed by yet more Jesuits, 'Popish bishops' and finally the Pope himself in a huge waxen form stuffed with cats that screamed horribly as the effigy was thrown to the flames at Smithfield. Meanwhile, in the coffee-houses of the capital, men were hired to 'ball' the opposition or Whig cause. Playing cards portrayed lurid scenes from the murder of Godfrey, while everywhere those who could read might find 'the noisome excrements of diseased and laxative scribblers'.

One of these satires concerned Pepys. It rehearsed the old charges with a new venom. The usual allegations were made about his corruption and his milking the navy for personal gain, but the most pointed wit was directed to his 'chariot', that all-too-conspicuous coach in which Pepys habitually rode around London with its painted scenes of ships and harbours. It was altogether too flamboyant, too conspicuously *nouveau riche*, too obviously paid for by corruption, popery and absolutism. The satire undermined Pepys's politics and his professionalism but the cruellest jibes were directed to the social origins of this self-made man:

> And now really consider with yourself that you are but the son of a tailor, and wipe out all this presumptuous painting, and new paint it with those things agreeable to your quality. In the first place, paint upon the fore-part as handsome a tailor's shop-board as you please, with the Old Gentleman, your father, upon it at work and his journeymen sitting about him, each man with his pint of ale and halfpenny loaf before him, and the good old Matron your mother and yourself and the rest of your brothers and sisters standing by: this will be agreeable to your qualities. Then behind your coach, paint all the evil deeds of P[epys] and H[ewer] in particulars; also on your right hand, paint your Jesuit, M[orelli], playing upon his lute and singing a Holy Song: on your left hand paint two or three poor cripples, which P. reformed, and giving

> them his charity which he never was wont to do. All this will show P's great humility and reformation and reducement to his right station.[9]

This was a cruel cut indeed: an image of arrogance, cold-heartedness, corruption and treasonable enthusiasms underlined by the rankest snobbery. For all he pretended that he could brush off the attack, Pepys was surely hurt, as he was meant to be, and, once again, the pain caused him to redouble his efforts in his own defence.

As Pepys waited for a trial in which he could prove beyond all reasonable doubt that the allegations against him had been fabricated by such low and pathetic villains as Scott and his cronies, a growing number of level-headed people became increasingly worried that the affairs of the nation were being conducted in such a way and by such people. For older heads especially it was too horribly reminiscent of the civil war and its aftermath: that tumult of Levellers, Ranters and Fifth Monarchy Men who had bellowed through the London of Pepys's youth. The Whigs were coming to be seen as the heirs to these people who had spread anarchy and anguish across the country. The sheer energy of the Whig propaganda machine was undermining the cause it supported and fears of the tyranny of popular government were being revived.

For Pepys himself, this turn in public opinion was matched by a turn in his own fortunes. Those who had connived against him began to divide among themselves. By the start of 1680, Pepys was learning something of this. He was contacted by one of his former Admiralty clerks – a dubious character called Phelix Donluis – who confessed to having been paid by Harbord to provide him with precise details about the fleet. Such a shifty individual was not entirely to be trusted but Donluis had further confessions to make. He had seen, he said, a bundle of forged letters supposedly directed to the Catholic authorities in France and apparently signed by Pepys himself. This faked evidence would be used against Pepys whenever he came to trial.

Just as telling was that John James, Pepys's erstwhile butler, was in desperate straits now that Whig gold had ceased to flow into his pockets and, as a consequence, was willing to divulge secrets. A meeting was suggested and Pepys agreed to see James, provided he could bring Will Hewer as a witness. This was accepted and the men set off. They found James in a sorry state indeed. He was destitute, while the cadaverous symptoms of tuberculosis showed him to be a dying man: excitable, guilty and frightened. He tried to put up what fight he could and then, in Pepys's words, 'he proceeded and told me that it was more in his power to do me right than in any man's in England, for that everything that had been done had passed through his hand'.[10]

James confessed that it was 'men of the greatest quality' among the Whigs who had paid him to collect evidence against Pepys and assured him that new calumnies were now in the making. Slowly the truth was coming to light and ten days later James's conscience was sufficiently troubled to ask for another meeting at which he told Pepys of the occasions when the great and the good of the Whig party had gathered in private conclave at the Mitre in Fenchurch Street to confer with the merchants about Pepys's fall. He even confessed how he himself had been paid by the infamous Harbord to offer false testimony against Pepys. Then, finally, he agreed to tell all. Pepys, accompanied by the ever-faithful Hewer, the sybaritic Mr Povey and a solicitor, hurried to his bedside.

There they took down James's full confession of how he had been bribed by Harbord, attended meetings at the Mitre, provided material for libels against Pepys and generally had done all in his power to harm him. A deeply penitent man now, James signed the deposition and, as he prepared himself for death, Pepys extended to him that charity which, until now, he had denied him: he gave him money and found him a doctor and a priest. For all that James had betrayed him and connived at his being sent to the Tower, Pepys would not deny him: it was his Christian duty to help even an enemy – perhaps especially an enemy – as he sweated and coughed his life away on a straw pallet in a slum.

It remained to be seen if the law was strong enough to protect Pepys himself. Time and again he had suffered from its delay. Time and again he had been refused a trial. The current term was close to its end, the expense to Pepys of supporting the witnesses he had gathered was mounting every day, as were the costs incurred by the immense sums he and his friends had been obliged to provide for his bail. Pepys wrote to the King for his help, but still the attorney-general was not prepared to act. When the court finally met on 12 February, the Lord Chief Justice asked, '"Why, Mr Pepys, would it be much inconvenient to you to appear again here at the next term?"' Pepys replied that it would indeed be very inconvenient and explained why. The judges agreed that, under the circumstances, Pepys's bail should be fully discharged and that he be bound over for £1,000 to appear when required. If the next term were to prove too soon for all concerned, the judge added, his case would be heard 'the first or the last day of the Term following'. It was exasperating. Still there was no guarantee that he would be fully discharged even then. Could not the court give him some assurance that he would be? With 'some fresh expressions of respect', the court replied that it could not, 'but from their present proceedings, we might very well judge what the inclinations of the Court would be'. It seemed that there was nothing more for Pepys to do but send home his expensive witnesses and wait.

But now, across the country at large and in London especially, the mood of the people was changing ever more rapidly. Fear of what the Whigs might do once they gained power was fanned by what had at last become an adequate

Tory propaganda machine. An image of the King was now being promoted that offered the deep reassurances of mythology. Charles II was presented as someone quite other than the cynical philanderer and crypto-papist of popular opinion. He was the Lord's anointed, the father of his subjects and the head of the one, true Anglican Church. He connected the daily with the divine and, serenely above tumult, was 'God's Servant, not the People's Slave'.[11] The latter role was Shaftesbury's. Did not 'Little Sincerity' rejoice in his sobriquet of 'the Tribune of the People'? And who were these 'People'? Tory propagandists would have their readers believe they were Nonconformists, subversives, fanatics and republicans, who sought to inflict the horrors of arbitrary power and the tyranny of popular government. No one needed reminding that that meant civil war, regicide and untold confusion. Fears and memories of such things ran deep and could be skilfully exploited to 'reduce the deluded multitude to their just allegiance'.[12]

It worked and, as the fissures in the Whig resistance began to widen, some of the opposition became increasingly rattled. It seemed that the pathetic creatures Harbord and his cronies had hoped to make their tools were now threatening to undermine them. News of the methods the Whig grandees had employed in their attempt to ruin Pepys leaked out and soon were widely known. Public knowledge of such squalid proceedings was bound to do damage and, while Harbord especially sought to clear his name and bully the dying butler into confessing that Pepys had forced him to tell lies, Pepys himself wisely obtained signed statements from James's family and friends asserting that this was not so. These were but one part of the enormous volume of evidence he had collected in his own defence and, faced with its overwhelming conclusions, his enemies were reluctant to press their attack in court. By 28 June 1680, Pepys was a free man.

His thoughts, as always, returned to his king. The attack on Pepys had really been an attempt to undermine Charles and his brother by men who thought 'no surer aim could be taken at him than through his servants who stood nearest to him, among whom their malice having done me the honour of reckoning me one, they deemed me worthy to be first removed, though at the price of perjury'. In the changing atmosphere Pepys could at last return to the fold and could even attend Charles and the newly returned Duke at Newmarket (where he hoped to settle his arrears of pay) and there take down in his ever-useful shorthand the King's own account of his escape after the battle of Worcester. It was a great honour that the King should trust to Pepys the writing up of the definitive version of this story of royal peril, which he had told so often before – told it, as some of his courtiers might whisper, until they were bored to distraction. Now, in its final version, it was a token that Charles had survived great danger once and might survive again.

It was while he was engaged in taking down the King's dictation that Pepys learned that his father had died, after years of complaining about ill-health. The dutiful son lingered in the countryside through late October and half of November while he sorted out the tangled affairs of John Pepys's mean little estate and, with his clerk Paul Lorrain, worked on the great wealth of material he had gathered on the perfidious Scott. This was eventually copied in fine copperplate handwriting into two great volumes Pepys would call his Books of Mornamont after a castle Scott himself had once laid claim to – a castle in the air. Hewer, in the meantime, sent Pepys news of the great world in letters and news-sheets from London. From these Pepys learned of the progress of the King's duel with Parliament and formed the opinion that he must himself return to the capital, partly, as Hewer suggested, to show that he was not afeared of what might take place in the House. He was also required to give an answer to the King about the vexed question of salutes to foreign flags at sea, Pepys being, in Charles's view, the man 'best able to give satisfaction on that point'. The King wanted him, and his friends and allies wanted him too.

Pepys was aware he owed a debt of gratitude and resolved to send his portrait to Houblon by way of thanks for all he had done. Childless himself, Pepys, in a moment of tender fantasy, imagined Houblon's offspring gathering in front of the picture and asking, 'Was Mr Pepys in those clothes, Father, when you used to go to the Tower to him?' Another who had helped Pepys was also an object of his concern at this time. The loyal Samuel Atkins had lost his job at the Admiralty and Pepys now helped him to a post in Tangier, forwarding him £20 and writing to Hewer that 'his case deserves all manner of compassion, and above all from me, for certainly no youth of his wit and straightness of fortune ever withstood such temptations to have been a villain as that poor creature has done'.

It was proper to pay such private debts but only the King could bring public matters to a conclusion. Shaftesbury had been 'much disconcerted' by a gruelling ten-hour debate in the House of Lords where Charles's position had been ably defended by Lord Halifax, who dwelt on the dangers of excluding the Duke of York from the throne. Attempts failed to force through an Exclusion Bill and, when a newly severe Charles had dissolved the House, he prepared for the most daring political coup of his career. He sought ways to prevent the Whigs from forming a powerful group in his next Parliament and reopened his negotiations with Louis XIV. The French King listened since, for all that he knew Charles himself to be thoroughly untrustworthy, he had faith in his brother and a belief that York might indeed restore a heretic nation to the true faith. He agreed to pay Charles a subsidy that would help to make him independent of Westminster.

Having secured his back, Charles then summoned his

new Parliament to meet in royalist Oxford. The Whigs rode into the city confident of victory and blithely unaware that their king would give them enough rope with which to hang themselves. Charles courted his enemies, declaring that 'no irregularities in Parliaments shall make me out of love with them'. He would show that it was he, and not the Members themselves, who was the true embodiment of a just constitution. Then he let them wrangle interminably about Exclusion until they appeared like men obsessed – dangerous figures aiming for powers they had no right to wield. When their argument was at its height he summoned them to the hall of imperious Christ Church and there, seated in the full panoply of monarchy and certain that he could now do without them, Charles dismissed them. From henceforth he would rule without them. The King and his supporters were safe from attack.

CHAPTER THIRTEEN

The Uses of Adversity

Pepys was safe but if he still hankered for government office he had, for the time being, to find his own employments. Many of these were scholarly or combined his interests as a virtuoso with his administrative powers. His friend John Evelyn was keen to see Pepys use both. During the summer of 1680 Evelyn had encouraged him to take up his old interest in the Royal Society, which, Evelyn feared, was losing its impetus and might even disintegrate. He begged Pepys for 'one half hour of your presence and assistance toward the most material concern of a Society which ought not to be dissolved for want of a redress'. Pepys was the man to set things to rights. 'I do assure you,' Evelyn wrote, 'we shall want one of your courage and address to encourage and carry on this affair.' It would not be too burdensome. 'You know that we do not usually fall on business till pretty late in expectation of a fuller company, and therefore if you decently could fall in amongst us by 6 or 7, it would, I am sure, infinitely oblige . . . the whole Society.'[1] Pepys would indeed do much for the institution, which in its turn would greatly honour him. Even now it provided the intelligent companionship he always so greatly enjoyed, for here were gathered many of his friends: Evelyn himself, Sir William Petty, the pioneer statistician, and Sir Christopher Wren among others. For a while Pepys also toyed with the idea of filling the vacant post of provost at King's College, Cambridge, but the honour had been reserved for another and he withdrew.

There were, besides, his own projects to get on with. *Navalia* was still to be written, and Evelyn encouraged Pepys to turn to it now that he had the leisure to do so. He wrote to Pepys with characteristic amplitude and courtesy of how 'it has been greatly my hopes, and continually my wishes (from some little hints that I have observed sometimes to fall from you) that upon this recess especially, and calm from public business; furnished as you are with a noble library; and instructed by the greatest experience, joined to an industry and capacity (beyond any mortal man that I know) of undertaking so useful and desired a work; that from *you* the learned and curious world, might one day receive that hitherto concealed *Arcano del Mar*,* with the most consummate perfection and advantage'. Such talents should be used. '*Macte ergo vir clarissimum*'.†[2]

There followed letters typical of the style of both men. Pepys bombarded Evelyn with direct and urgent requests for information, drawing on his friend's capacious knowledge of the world's navies both past and present to ask him for 'instances of national mistakes, either new or old, whether at home or abroad, in the over-valuing of their own knowledge or force, or undervaluing those of other countries'. Evelyn's replies were those of the true virtuoso: elaborate, elegant, leisured and running over with that wealth of abstruse knowledge both men wished to collect and organise.

* *The Secrets of the Sea.*
† Go about it therefore, eminent man!'

He told Pepys that a 'volume' might be compiled of navies over- or undervaluing their own and others' forces 'and much more might we have known, had we the writings of Philo-Romanus the Rhodian (as Suidas makes him) which are perished and are supplied to us out of the fragments in Caelius Rodoginus and some few others'. British instances would be sufficient, however. 'As to undertakings upon the opinion of our own dexterity and virtue above our neighbours,' Evelyn wrote, 'I do not see that we have much to boast of, at the foot of the reckoning, when we shall have discounted for the mischief, from the first invasion of the Romans, till our shameful disgrace at Chatham – I need not tell you what the Saxons, Danes and Normans did but you shall find that none of them ever landed on us with any considerable force, but they carried the whole island (if they persisted) unless some unforeseen disaster befell them.'[3] The sharing of such knowledge, serious though its import was, was one of the delights of leisure. None the less, Evelyn's conclusions would, in a few years' time, prove all too true and bring both Pepys's career and his own to their ends.

Evelyn was far from being Pepys's only correspondent: Pepys had become the sort of figure to whom many – fools and wise men alike – sent their thoughts and information, or confided their pet projects. Dr Nathaniel Vincent of Clare Hall, for example, sent Pepys his *Conjectura Nautica*, following it up with an invention of which he was particularly proud: a secret code that could never be deciphered by an enemy since its characters rapidly disappeared after being read. The enthusiastic doctor wanted £1,000 for his discovery and, after a decent interval, Pepys replied, gently pointing out the defects of Vincent's system and informing him that the government service was already supplied with adequate forms of ciphering. More fruitfully, Dr Gale, High Master of St Paul's School, was approached about the proper meaning of the noun '*versonia*' in Plautus, and replied that he conjectured 'that Plautus meant thereby that part of the stem of a ship upon which the stern turneth as a door upon the hinge'. King Charles also proved himself characteristically generous, presenting Pepys with such beautiful naval documents from the royal archive as the exquisitely illuminated Anthony Roll that is still preserved at Magdalene College. Nor was this all. He valued Pepys's practical knowledge and still chose to consult with him on such matters as the Navy Board's curiously inept decision to remove the expensive lead sheathing from the country's ships in order (as they thought) to prevent the rusting over of rudder-irons and bolt-heads.

Such a problem was an indication of the parlous state into which the affairs of the navy had fallen since Pepys's resignation from the Admiralty. He was all too painfully aware of this, and there were times in these bitter, out-of-office years when he was apt in the secrecy of notebooks to blame the King for putting the Admiralty 'into hands he knew were wholly ignorant thereof'. It was irksome indeed that Charles appeared to take pleasure in 'sporting' himself with his appointees' ignorance while turning to Pepys 'to declare to me his dependence was upon my service to keep them right'. But there was little enough, in truth, that Pepys could do. When the new men resolved to spend a vast amount of money on building a wholly unnecessary wet dock for new ships-of-the-line at Chatham he could only write an angry and 'uncalled for' letter on their folly in thus placing so 'essential a share of the strength and security of England within the power of any one villain be he a known enemy from abroad or a false friend (of whatever principles) at home'.[4] Nor did matters improve: £100,000 was squandered on a project in Ireland, convoys failed to defend merchantmen against capture, stores were neglected and corruption was rife. The dangerous practice of 'good voyages' had been resumed, the Chatham Chest was once again an object of abuse, the Admiralty commissioners failed to follow the rules Pepys had so carefully drawn up for the regulation of the service, while the senior officers were 'men either of pleasure or at least generally men of quite another education than that of the sea'.

It was heartrending and proved what Pepys's researches had already shown him: the fact, long recognised by him, that the English had no firm or genuine regard for the navy that secured their coasts and their wealth. Nor, it seemed, were they prepared to change their views. We have seen that in an attempt to breed boys for the sea Pepys had persuaded the King to found his Mathematical School at Christ's Hospital. Now even that institution was failing in its purpose. Pepys complained about 'the ignorance and supiness of its Governors' and 'their frequent objecting to the children's learning Latin, or even more mathematics, or better writing than they say boys abroad do set out commonly with'.[5] Illiterate and innumerate seamen were just what Pepys had hoped to avoid and such neglect was, besides, an insult to the King and 'the charge His Majesty has been pleased to put himself to' to rectify matters.

Something had to be done about Christ's Hospital, and Pepys believed himself to be the man to do it. He determined that he would write a report on the school and this, when completed, laid bare widespread abuse. Dr Wood, the idle and over-qualified master of the Mathematical boys, considered himself far above the humble business of teaching and farmed out his charges to 'a kind of mathematical curate to look after in his frequent absences'. This man, in turn, was an intemperate drunkard who had so entirely lost the boys' respect that, as recent examinations proved, they had learned next to nothing from him, merely acquiring in nine months 'what an indifferently diligent man might have made them learn in one'. When Pepys presented his report it was the unanimous view of the sub-committee of Trinity House responsible for the matter that Dr Wood should be dismissed. Pepys would see to it that he was, 'being unable to suffer the business of the Mathematical School to remain any longer in its present condition without bringing it either to an immediate reformation or finally washing my hands of it'. There followed the matter of finding a replacement for Wood. Pepys prepared a memorandum in which he declared that it would be a mistake to appoint a man who would not consider the post a promotion, while the most desirable candidate would be somebody who had real, practical experience of the sea.

Such a suggestion showed the authentic Pepys, but it was not popular and, when the shortlist of applicants was drawn up, only two men who had any experience of the skills Pepys was hoping the school would impart were placed on it. Neither of them got the job. An altogether more illustrious figure, Edward Paget, fellow of Trinity and protégé of Newton, appeared more acceptable to the governors, especially since his excellent Latin would 'lead the boys to converse with one another here familiarly in that language', while ensuring that they would also be able to speak to fellow mariners from foreign lands. As for a knowledge of the sea, Mr Paget 'could acquire something of practice in navigation by spending now and then a few days at sea in some of the yachts . . . in the Channel'.[6] Pepys gave up in despair and his most lasting contribution to Christ's Hospital was perhaps the flamboyant Verrio painting in the Great Hall of the school in which he and other dignitaries appear beside the Mathematical boys paying their tribute to the Stuarts' benign interest.

Pepys was still most anxious to regain the openly acknowledged favour of the royal circles to which he had devoted his career, and made several efforts to court them. His progress was slow, for the King did not need him urgently as yet. Immediately after Charles's victory at the Oxford Parliament, Pepys secured a Loyal Address from his colleagues at Trinity

House and carefully despatched it to the Duke of York, along with promises of a second Address from the officers of the fleet. The Duke was circumspect – it was still too early to favour Mr Pepys – and he suggested that the proper way for men in the King's pay to express their loyalty was by their service. Not wishing to distance a loyal servant too far, however, the Duke asked Pepys for a copy of the narrative of his brother's adventures after the battle of Worcester, which Charles had recently dictated. It was the second occasion on which the Duke had made the request and Pepys dutifully sent him a transcription not just of Charles's account but of the narratives he had himself collected from others who were involved – a piece of work that has timeless interest and great historical importance.

More had to be done, however, if Pepys was to earn his return to open royal favour and, the following March, he went to Newmarket to pay his respects to the Duke and the King. To his delight he found both men well, and wrote back to his mildly Whiggish friend, the merchant Houblon, a letter of somewhat unctuous monarchical fervour. The Duke, Pepys declared, was looking better than he had ever seen him, 'a thing that I cannot answer for'. But it was not only York's physical health that had improved: 'His political state of body seemed to be much mended too, since his nearer partakings of his brother's sunshine.' The Tory victory was complete and the Stuarts, in Pepys's view at least, were once again the focus of life and light.

He was still determined to have his place in their sun and, to this end, he resolved in the spring of 1682 to accompany the Duke on his voyage to Edinburgh. Pepys had hoped to sail on the *Happy Return* but it was full so he transferred to a little yacht called the *Catherine*. It was fortunate for him that he did so: fog and then gales bore down on the Duke's flotilla, there was a furious row aboard the flagship and, at half past five on Saturday morning, she hit the sands and was holed. Some two hundred people were drowned in the ensuing panic. Pepys, watching from the *Catherine*, was conscious of 'God's immediate mercy' in preserving him from disaster, along with the Duke, who escaped in a small boat.[7] Pepys, ever the curious tourist, decided to make his way home by land, visiting Glasgow, Berwick, Durham and Newcastle. Eventually, he returned safely to London (much to the relief of his friends who had feared for his preservation) but now – suddenly and at little notice – there was another voyage for him to make. The King had resolved, in the interests of economy, to withdraw the English presence from Tangier and Pepys was required to supervise.

He was given two days in which to prepare, and he readied himself in a flurry of activity. He itemised his bills and paid them. He drew up lists of clothes and had them packed: shoes, wigs, worsted and thread stockings, a white hat, a velvet cap, four shirts, eight cravats, thirteen handkerchiefs, a new sea gown and a pair of galoshes. To these he added his toothpick case, a telescope, a silver pen, mathematical tables and his indispensable spectacles. Books on the sea, on fortification, and volumes of music were ranged with spiritual works, some classics and items in Spanish. Arrangements for money and credit abroad were also made. He recruited his friend Dr Ken as chaplain to the expedition's leader, Lord Dartmouth, and then, having made his farewells to his friends, he set off for Portsmouth. He boarded the *Grafton* at Spithead and found that his companions included not only Dartmouth and the sweetly spoken Ken, but the learned Sir William Trumbull, Will Hewer, now treasurer to the Tangier Committee, and the engineer Henry Shere. Quite why they were all going to Tangier was not yet known to them but, as Pepys told Evelyn, he was not greatly concerned. He was at last about the King's official business and

> this only I am sure of that over and above the satisfaction of

> being thought fit for some use or other ('tis no matter what) I shall go in a good ship, with a good fleet, under a very worthy leader, in a conversation as delightful as companions of the very first form in divinity, law, physic and the usefullest parts of mathematics can render it . . . with the additional pleasure of concerts (much above the ordinary) of voices, flutes and violins; and to fill up all (if anything can do't where Mr Evelyn is wanting) good humour, good cheer, some good books, the company of my nearest friend Mr Hewer and a reasonable prospect of being home again in less than two months.[8]

It was only later, when Lord Dartmouth came to his cabin, that the full seriousness of their business, dawned on Pepys. He was to be that peer's sole counsellor in the business of the English withdrawal from Tangier. The admiral's commission and the secret Instructions sent with it confirmed this and, concerned that what he was about to oversee might cause serious anger back home, Pepys resolved to keep a shorthand diary of all that transpired so that he should have an accurate record to show if ever he were called to account.

During the greater part of the passage out the weather was foul. Pepys, now sailing the Atlantic for the first time, recorded his numerous discomforts. On 27 August he wrote that the wind was 'still fresh but against us so we made very little way'. He went to Dartmouth's cabin, the peer having agreed that he would take notes at Pepys's dictation, 'but the motion of the ship was such that I could do nothing there'. He then went up on to the quarter-deck to take the air but the sea continued to run very high with the result that 'my stomach [was] so ill that I could not go down to dinner'. Indeed, the weather was so bad that one of the little attendant yachts had to ask permission to turn back for Plymouth. Yet, despite this, the sailors came up on the deck of the *Grafton* that night to dance and sing.

Pepys stared at the scene with sincere and deeply felt

humility. These were the crews of the ships that he, as sometime secretary to the Admiralty, had commanded with a rigorous eye from his office in Derby House. Now the reality of their existence at sea impinged on him in a way that no paper report could ever suggest. He spoke to the lieutenant of the *Grafton* about their life: their harsh diet and the putrid water, the constant perils they faced, their joy in a good commander and the wretchedness that an ignorant one could so easily inflict. 'I know of nothing,' Pepys would write, 'that can give a better notion of infinity and eternity than the being upon the sea in a little vessel without anything in sight but yourself within the whole hemisphere.'[9] It was from this perspective, his thoughts ever more deeply and angrily stirred by what he was to see and experience, that Pepys's sense of the nation's duty towards its navy was brought back to new and burning vigour.

A conversation a few days later, when the storm had ceased to blow and the sea was 'very smooth and pleasant', helped this process. Pepys went with Will Hewer, Henry Shere and the *Grafton*'s captain Sir William Booth to dine on the *Henrietta* with its commander Sir John Berry. Dinner was followed by music, until the conversation turned to more serious matters. Both Booth and Berry were of the opinion that standards in the service had declined appallingly since Pepys's resignation. The examinations he had so carefully worked for were universally ignored and men wholly incompetent for the commission – footmen of well-born admirals and the like – were regularly appointed. Indeed, the highly born Admiral Herbert, until recently commander-in-chief in the Straits, had given commands to two of his cronies for no better reason than that they shared his numerous vices.

Herbert's name soon figured high in Pepys's rancorous list of naval abuses, and even now he questioned his fellow diners about the old conflict between gentlemen and tarpaulins. Booth, well connected though he was, gave the answer of a man born to the sea: 'I never go out on deck,' he said, 'but I see something or other out of order, either a strap or a rope galled or something else that gives me occasion of giving order for remedying the same. All which a land captain overlooks and never thinks of and so is surprised by an enemy, whereas I always observe that he that seeks his enemy to surprise him, keeps himself always ready and is never surprised but has many advantages above him that is attacked first.'[10] This was the sort of professionalism Pepys admired.

By 13 September, the African coast was in sight. 'Nothing,' Pepys noted, was 'so welcome to a seaman as after being at sea a little time to set his foot on shore, though it be the most barren place in the world'. Such, indeed, Tangier was to prove, for all its colour and exoticism. The battlemented city, with its flat roofs, fortresses and immense and expensive Mole around the harbour, which the engineers in Pepys's party were to dismantle, was at once a pathetic and sinister place. In earlier days, Pepys had profited from it immensely but now that he saw Tangier in its physical reality he could only look upon it with disdain. 'Lord!' he wrote, 'how could ever anybody think this place fit to be kept at this charge, that by its being overlooked by so many hills can never be secured against an enemy?' This was true but, as Pepys was to discover, the real enemy – the real danger – was not the encircling army of waiting Moorish warriors but his own depraved countrymen, who had turned Tangier into a place so morally desolate that discipline had all but collapsed.

It was as well for the English that they were leaving, and Pepys set about discussing with the others in his party the terms of the commission of enquiry they were to set up into the ownership of properties in the place, victualling, and relationships with the surrounding Moors. So much business was sure to be onerous but that night, to make matters worse,

Pepys's sleep was plagued by bed-bugs. Soon he had to wash his skin in brandy to fight the irritation.

A walk round Tangier the following morning lifted his spirits. He found the heat oppressive and the Moors, who even controlled the water supply, a dangerous threat. The woman who ran the public baths told him that all the local females were whores. There were curiosities and spectacles to view, of course – a Moor with five fingers and toes on one foot, for example, and an impressive display from the Moorish soldiers once a temporary truce had been arranged. There were also rare moments of pleasure, such as an evening spent 'listening and dancing to the harp and guitar'. But the most important matter was work.

The proprietors of the city's buildings were summoned to present evidence of ownership, in answers to detailed questions about their rights of tenure, which had been laboriously drawn up by Pepys who now sat in the Town House arrayed in a sweltering gown of scarlet and ermine to adjudicate. Almost no one turned up. The same happened on the following days, and what Pepys had thought at first would be a brief mission easily accomplished began to look like a long drawn-out tedium certain to depress those who had come along with him. His own spirits began to flag as he sat in the Town House from eight till one and then from two thirty till eight at night 'without anything more observable than the slowness of the proprietors coming in with their titles and the infinite unreadiness in those that did to make them good'.

It was exasperating. Even a Sunday visit to church failed to lighten the mood for there were in the congregation 'very few women that appeared gentlewomen' and the governor's wife, Lady Mary Kirke (whom Pepys 'had long admired for her beauty'), appeared to have faded. Indeed, the local wildlife were more interesting. Pepys saw lizards for the first time 'sticking in the windows to bask themselves in the sun'. Later, 'a great locust leapt of a sudden on the table, and this morning in my chamber the most extraordinary spider that I ever saw, at least ten times as big as an ordinary spider. Such things,' he added, 'this country do mightily abound with.'[11] It also, as Pepys rapidly discovered, abounded in vice. This was clear in every rank of society and was most flagrant at the top. Lady Mary Kirke, faded though her looks might have been, had lovers enough to 'play the jade by herself at home', while her husband was brazenly indiscreet. Pepys heard him boast how he had made his wife's sister pregnant and how he would often be 'with his whores at his little bathing house which was furnished with a jade a-purpose'. A disgusted Pepys decided to keep a record of all he heard and carefully wrote down how Kirke had persuaded one of the Tangier prostitutes to help him 'get the maidenhood of a young pretty girl, a kinswoman of this whore's newly come over'.

There was something far more to Pepys's notemaking, however, than curmudgeonly prurience. Rapacious and illicit money-making went hand in hand with promiscuity and both, as Pepys clearly saw, were having a disastrous effect on the morale and discipline of visiting ships. It was this that made his heart ache. Tangier had become a haven for corruption. Kirke himself had borrowed £1,500 from the townspeople and, when asked to pay it back, had merely replied, 'God damn me, why did you trust me?' Gross drunkenness among the forces merely amused him, and the rule of law meant nothing to him. Kirke rounded on the recorder in the local court and publicly told him, 'God damn the law,' and that he would 'stretch' the jury's consciences.

While such swaggering devil-may-care attitudes might have been popular among some of his men, they meant that Tangier was effectively beyond the reach of discipline from London, and had become a haven for all the abuses the undisciplined officers of the navy could practise. Stationed in a distant, sleazy North African port, it was easy for the infamous Admiral Herbert to allow his men to sneak out in their ships and indulge in a little private trading on their own account. Such abuse had become so commonplace as to seem almost their right. Institutional reform and proper pay especially were essential, for Pepys realised that it was impossible to prevent men from indulging in 'good voyages' until 'their lives [were] made comfortable to them by their plain salary, and severe discipline to make them perform their duty for self preservation sake'.

Experience was soon to make him even more convinced of this. By 25 October his work in Tangier was done, and Pepys determined on a well-deserved break in Spain. He was delayed by 'wind, thunder, lightning, rain and hail altogether for eight or ten days' but eventually, on 6 December, the weather had sufficiently calmed for Pepys and Hewer to set sail on the *Montagu*. Thoughts of the ill-disciplined state of the Royal Navy plagued him. He had heard stories of how Herbert and his men had indulged in a month's drunken orgy on the Portuguese coast during which time they 'caused the fleet surgeon to be stripped stark naked with one leg tied by the toe to the cabin roof and exposed in this posture to the mockery of loose women'. Spain showed him far worse abuses.

During the almost six rain-sodden weeks Pepys spent in Seville, for example, the English ex-patriots in the city made him well aware that their standing and credit had been severely damaged by the behaviour of Captains Shovell and Aylmer, who had been loitering in the Spanish harbours for the freight for a 'good voyage' and had only saluted the Spanish flag when obliged to do so at gunpoint. Pepys was furious. 'Here was want of manners and good judgement' and, for all his respect for tarpaulins, he wondered if their behaviour was an argument for 'having gentlemen employed who can better judge of what is fitting'. Pepys saw clearly that a love and need of money was the root of the evil and bluntly declared of such officers that 'it is plain that interest governs them'. With the intellectual curiosity so typical of him, Pepys had gone to some lengths to investigate how the Spanish managed their navy and, for all that he was dismissive of the stultifying rigidity that characterised Spanish administration, he admired the firm rule that forbade any private business being conducted by the King's ships.

Pepys was to have personal experience of the inconvenience caused by English sailors' desire to indulge in this abuse when captains eager for 'good voyages' refused, despite orders, to transport him back to Tangier. Pepys was obliged to linger in Cadiz, were he gathered appalling stories of naval ill-discipline. A violently hungover Sir John Berry told him how, in Pepys's day at the Admiralty, he himself had never indulged in 'good voyages' but now every captain in the Mediterranean was hankering after his share of the profits to be made from shipping bullion to England. Some were so obstreperous in their behaviour and demands that their potential customers preferred to transport their profits in merchant ships, but the amount of money that could be made from illicit dealing was once again confirmed by the conduct of the egregious Herbert. The admiral was a racketeer on a very large scale indeed, and many of his lesser officers were wholly within his grip. In return for a payment of 50 per cent or even 75 per cent of their profits Herbert would issue them with bogus orders to sail to nearby ports. So sophisticated was his operation that he even employed a man to do all his paperwork for him and make up his accounts. Pepys rightly thought that Herbert should be cashiered but the view taken in London was different. Herbert was a royal favourite and was soon appointed a commissioner of the navy and made Rear-Admiral of England. The rot had set in at the top.

It was plain to Pepys that 'this business of money runs through and debauches the whole service of the Navy, and is now come to the highest degree of villainy and infamy'. Worse, 'no one considers it'.[12] He set himself the task of doing so and, during the terrible journey home, clarified his thoughts. The sudden advent of appalling weather showed Pepys scenes at sea he could never have imagined. Amid the near biblical terror, he acquired a new respect for the fleet and the best of those who manned it. Nightfall of 26 February brought a driving south-westerly and by half past four in the morning two of the *Grafton*'s masts had split and the flotilla about her was dispersed. Dartmouth ordered his ship towards Tangier where, as she was being refitted, Pepys looked across at the abandoned ruins of the great protective Mole – that epic and ruinously expensive feat of seventeenth-century engineering whose destruction had been ordered by the King. When the *Grafton* eventually set out once again, Dartmouth and Pepys stood on her quarter-deck angrily discussing the behaviour of men like Herbert and the ruination of the navy. Both men realised that something must be done and agreed that, when they got home, they would insist that the rules be properly enforced.

The return of violent weather only deepened Pepys's resolve. Danger convinced him of the overriding necessity of having trained commanders and rigorous discipline. The *Grafton*'s main yard broke again. This may have been caused by faulty repairs but, as Pepys himself observed, 'no force of timber, plank, iron or cordage is to be relied on against the sea'. Throughout his career these had been items to bargain for – entries on lists, goods to be inspected in the dockyards, necessaries somehow to pay for. Now they were something far more. 'This voyage,' he wrote, 'has shown me at once all the elements dangerous to us, and this in a dark night in danger of famine and upon an enemy's shore.' A man learned quickly under such circumstances. 'Good voyages', ill-discipline, gentlemen captains with no training for the sea, all of these menaced the existence of the navy, all of them threatened to turn to nightmare that vision of maritime supremacy Pepys had first glimpsed in the earliest days of his career and which he had laboured long and hard in an unforgiving world to make a reality.

His old clerk, the loyal Sam Atkins, now a secretary to Lord Dartmouth, provided him with more harrowing details of how the service had collapsed since both of them had laboured together at Derby House. It was common knowledge, Atkins said, that even the most eminent commanders worked hard at securing their fortunes from 'good voyages' so that they need never go to sea again. Were ships' journals kept, Pepys asked. Atkins shook his head and told him that captains these days could not be bothered with paperwork and left the business to their clerks. Herbert in particular boasted that he had never wasted his time with it and, as Atkins listed his seemingly endless shortcomings – his greed, drinking, dicing, whoring and total disregard of even the most basic elements of his profession – so the newly appointed rear-admiral came to personify for Pepys every abuse in the service he had struggled so hard to reform.

He was bitter but he was not despondent and, in conversations with Dartmouth, he began to formulate his plans. The necessity of the country having a strong navy – a navy clean of its current abuses – was clear to both men for they realised that, with the abandonment of Tangier, the French King might easily make himself master of the Mediterranean and even form an alliance with the Moors. Both men considered that Gibraltar might serve as the essential British station to prevent the dominance of any other maritime power, but it was necessary above all to reform the fleet and salvage its morale. There were a number of clear objectives to be achieved. 'Good voyages' would have to be replaced by an adequate salary system. Logs should be kept and regularly inspected. Everything should be done to remove the distinction between gentlemen and tarpaulins, while a Navy

List would make official the precedence between officers. All of this would greatly aid the fleet while at sea but reform at the top was vital too. Men of genuine experience and probity should be commissioners of the Admiralty and members of the Navy Board. There should be professionalism at the highest levels of the service. Men like the repellent Herbert would have to go. This, as both Pepys and Dartmouth realised, was a difficult undertaking and it began to become clear to them that only one man was suitable for heading such reform: the Duke of York. They would present their proposals to him and the King on their return.

Even as they neared the English coast it became obvious that immediate reform was essential. The ships were apparently lost: it was far from clear to any of the navigators in the fleet where they were and every man's opinion differed. To some, the soundings they had taken suggested they were off France. Others believed they were east of the Isles of Scilly. Dawn would show them they were off the Lizard. 'Hence it comes,' Pepys wrote, 'that the science of navigation lies so long without more improvement.' Problems of discipline were similarly obvious. The flotilla had first dropped anchor in Plymouth Sound, but when the signal was given to make for Spithead not a ship followed the *Grafton*. Their captains wanted more time on shore after their terrible voyage and were determined to take it. Pepys was horrified. Clearly something had to be done and Pepys, riding from Portsmouth up the London road, had the answer in his pocket. When he arrived in the capital he requested an immediate audience with the King. He was soon ushered into the presence of Charles II to present him with his memorandum on the deplorable state of his fleet.

CHAPTER FOURTEEN

Return to the Admiralty

The chance to revive the fallen fortunes of the navy came to Pepys with an altogether unexpected suddenness. For a short while after his return from Tangier he had hoped to take the place among the Admiralty commissioners left vacant by the death of Lord Brouncker. To his dismay, he discovered that the infamous Herbert was appointed in his stead, and it seemed that the old rot would eat away at the decaying timbers of the navy with an increased virulence. Then, without warning, the King made a drastic decision: he judged that the time was right to dismiss the men he had appointed in a season of crisis and to begin rebuilding his fleet. He would himself take nominal control, the Duke of York would be restored to his former influence (although not, because of the requirements of the Test Act, to his former title of Lord High Admiral) while effective executive power would be placed in the hands of one man: Pepys. A royal summons was sent out for Pepys to attend on the King at Windsor and there he was informed that his old job was his again and that he was secretary for the Affairs of the Admiralty of England with a salary of £2,000 a year granted to him this time under the terms of letters patent under the Great Seal.

Pepys was now a mature and energetic man of fifty-one, and he set about his task with becoming gravity. He was determined to have a full understanding of the damage that had been wrought by incompetence, frowsty inefficiency, cover-ups and naked abuse, and to this end he required the Navy Board to present him with a 'true and strict report of the state of the Navy'.[1] Members of the board were to work 'without intermission' until they had produced a fully documented account of all that concerned them: the state of the ships and repairs to them, the numbers of dockyard workers, the provision of stores and the burden of debt. As the intolerable summer heat of 1684 gripped London, Pepys returned to the splendours of Derby House. The purchase of a gold pen, a silver ruler and an elaborate standish were pleasing symbols of new authority on his old desk from which he now sent out a series of letters in his most majestic style to rebuke shortcomings great and small.

He required a would-be young lieutenant to be examined for his promotion, wrote granting or withholding officers' leave, appointed accredited chaplains to every ship about to sail, attended to the negligence of a purser who was withholding £10 from a creditor, and ordered a captain who was defaulting on a debt to 'one Anne Laycock' to give him a full account of the matter 'that in case she should petition His Majesty or Royal Highness for leave to arrest you, I may be able to do you and her right by them'. He sought to limit drunkenness in the navy by fining the guilty, presenting the money gathered to the Chatham Chest and dismissing repeated offenders. He was severe but rarely cruel. There was surely a secret pleasure in bringing Herbert to account for his abuses in Africa (he had, as Pepys knew, been slave-trading there and starved many of his victims to death) but there was a warm feeling to be experienced also when the busy bureaucrat found time to write a note to Spithead asking a captain to find a berth for a lad who had been held up because he lacked funds to reach his ship on time.

Even a disastrous fire at Hewer's house in York Buildings and the fact that, in the ensuing pandemonium, many of Pepys's papers had been thrown into confusion failed to daunt him for long, and he was soon chivvying the members of the Navy Board into completing their report. These sometime somnolent men found themselves constantly called before Pepys and the royal brothers, who interested themselves in every aspect of his work. Gradually the depressing facts emerged. When he had resigned his post five years before, Pepys had left the navy with seventy-six ships in commission, 12,000 men and stores sufficient for any emergency. Such had been the fruit of his great campaign, waged in Parliament, to build thirty new vessels. Now, although the navy debt had risen by almost 30 per cent, 3,000 men were employed on a mere twenty frigates while the rest of the fleet was rotting where it rode. A visit to the dockyards made by Pepys, York, the Prince of Denmark and Lord Dartmouth at the start of August 1684, proved beyond doubt that the English fleet could no long play an international role. Visits to other yards confirmed the same sorry story of waste and decay.

The embarrassed members of the Navy Board – their incompetence clear for all to see – decided that attack was their only means of defence and, stirred to unwonted activity, laid the blame fairly and squarely on Pepys. Of course the navy was rotting: what else could be expected when Pepys in the days of his former glory had decided that the new vessels should be built of foreign timber? That there was insufficient English oak of adequate growth ready to be felled for a vast programme of marine expansion was beside the point. Pepys, as always, countered a bludgeoning and emotive attack with detail: he called the expertise of the shipwrights to his defence and, having intimated the conclusions he had drawn to the King, had his report on 'The State of the Royal Navy of England at the Dissolution of the late Commission of the Admiralty' imperiously bound in black morocco leather and presented to the Palace.[2]

He was too late. Charles was mortally ill. Although the King recovered from his first apoplectic fit he did not survive the ministrations of his doctors as, watched by Pepys himself and a throng of the great and the good, they dosed him with enemas, placed red-hot irons on his shaven skull and muttered to each other as they examined his scalding urine. Pepys was moved by what he called the King's 'lamentable condition' and thought him 'less happy than any his meanest subject'. The monarch he had served with unquestioning loyalty throughout his career was dying, and his suffering reminded Pepys of nothing more strongly than the navy, harassed as it was to the point of extinction by those who would use it as a massive swindling operation. Surely the Duke of York, soon to succeed Charles as James II, would support Pepys's endeavours to set things to rights.

The succession of a Catholic King was a cause for the greatest apprehension. The ports were closed, the army was readied, but it was perhaps the greatest of the dead king's many political coups that the country was prepared and, for the moment at least, pacific. Meanwhile, in the rooms of state, the unseemly scurry for high office went ahead, Pepys almost alone of the great servants of government remaining confidently at his post, so assured of his own merit and the new King's favour that he did not even bother to have his patent renewed. There was work to be done and a new regime to establish. Twenty-five years earlier Pepys had been an enthusiastic young man on the outside of things pushing himself to the front. He had risen early to try to get a place in the Abbey to watch the coronation of Charles II. He had glimpsed the grandees of the establishment in their pomp.

Now he was one of the grandees, the foremost Baron of the Cinque Ports, which medieval title gave him the right to carry one of the poles with jingling bells that bore the royal canopy over the King as James processed from Westminster Hall into Palace Yard. A man more superstitious than Pepys might have wondered what was foretold by the embarrassing collapse of that canopy and the fact that the crown wobbled precariously on the King's head, but such doubts, if they arose at all, were soothed by the gargantuan coronation feast at which he sat listening to the music of Purcell until called to watch the fireworks that exploded in jubilation across the London sky. The succession, it seemed, was assured.

After the celebrations, work. 'The business of the coronation being now over,' Pepys informed the Navy Board, 'and with it the interruptions . . . to His Majesty's bringing other matters of public concernment to determination . . . he is pleased to appoint tomorrow in the afternoon about 4 o'clock for your joint attendance on him at the Treasury Chamber at Whitehall.'[3] Unceasing business and routine alone would secure the future of the navy, and a voluminous correspondence flowed from Derby House concerning such matters as the best way to ensure the preservation of ships' biscuits, the return to France of Charles's extravagant mistress (the detested Duchess of Portsmouth), and such matters of discipline as the rebuke of a captain who had tried to smuggle wine into the country. The gold pen was busy indeed, but to guarantee the success of his wider plans, it was necessary for Pepys to ensure his election to Parliament as Member for Harwich then persuade a sympathetic new House that an adequate revenue would have to be provided for a navy now some £400,000 in debt and wholly deprived of stores.

Others were less than content with the new regime. For all that James had sworn to his Privy Council that he would, despite his reputation for arbitrary power, 'make it my endeavour to preserve this government both in Church and

State as it is now by law established', there were those who doubted his word. A small number were even prepared to flout the law in the most extreme manner. In Scotland the Earl of Argyll raised an army of Covenanters, while undercover information came to Derby House concerning the activities of the Duke of Monmouth, Charles's favourite bastard, now in exile among the republicans in Holland. All of this was deeply disturbing. Pepys wrote to Captain Skelton at Portsmouth, ordering him to keep a lookout for 'a certain ship carrying 32 guns with about 150 men of several nations, and having in his stern the picture or figure of the sun rising out of the clouds'. The ship had been 'lately bought', Pepys declared, 'by the Duke of Monmouth at Amsterdam for the transporting of men and arms to some part of the coast of England in order to the beginning of some commotions here answerable to the rebellion in Scotland by Argyll, which ship if it shall be your fortune to meet . . . it is His Majesty's pleasure that you endeavour by all acts of hostility to reduce, sink or otherwise destroy'.[4] What made the situation particularly alarming was that the impoverished navy had at this time merely two frigates readied in home waters. Urgent letters from Derby House secured a dozen more, along with orders to ready another six.

When news reached London that Monmouth had landed, these vessels were despatched to Lyme Bay and the loathed Herbert was sent with a naval force to assist in the defence of Exeter. The rebellion, pathetic as it appeared, was crushed with such savagery that it was said that the West Country ran ankle-deep in blood. Pepys, for one, was delighted, writing of 'the happy news just now brought to the King of the total defeat and rout given to the Duke of Monmouth's army yesterday upon a moor within two miles of Bridgewater, his foot being all cut off or taken, his horse fled'. He was not yet sure whether the Duke himself was still alive but firm orders were despatched to the fleet to keep an eye open for fugitives.

The infamous Kirke of Tangier was despatched to exact the government's physical revenge in the West, while the odious Judge Jeffreys was sent to administer justice at the Bloody Assizes. Pepys, for his part, gave his support to a captain hoping to profit from transporting those rebels who escaped the gallows, enquiring 'what sort of usage these fellows are to receive' and whether or not they were 'to be sold entirely, as blacks are to slavery for their whole lives'.

With the execution of Monmouth, Whiggery, it seemed, had been destroyed, but Monmouth's rebellion had made all too clear the parlous state of the navy. Pepys now pressed forward with renewed vigour in his plan to raise it into one of the greatest fighting forces in Europe. A royal visit to the dockyards at Portsmouth was planned for the autumn of 1685. Pepys and Evelyn set out in a coach (charged to the Crown at £22. 15s.) and met the King at Winchester. They found James earnestly discussing the supposed miracles of the Spanish *saludadors* with the newly elevated Bishop Ken. Here was a tiny instance of his monarch's superstition but Pepys, who had seen these men in Spain and exposed their pious frauds, 'did not conceive it fit to interrupt His Majesty who so solemnly told what they pretended to do'. It was not a civil servant's place to criticise.

More revelations of royal religious beliefs were to follow when, after their return from a most thorough inspection of the dockyards, Pepys, in deep conversation with James, plucked up courage to ask him if there was any truth in the rumour that his brother had made a deathbed conversion to Catholicism. The King told him delightedly that indeed there was, and produced for Pepys a paper written in Charles's own hand refuting the doctrines of the Anglican Church. An amazed Pepys showed it to Houblon and Evelyn, the latter dismissing it as the usual stuff of Catholic priests seeking to convert men to their faith and expressing the hope that the 'primitive, apostolical and excellent' Church in which he himself had been nurtured would continue to flourish. Men of goodwill still believed that the centre would hold.

An increasing number doubted this but, for the moment, Pepys's principal concern was, as always, with the navy. His visits to Portsmouth and later to Chatham had confirmed his worst fears. The fleet was in a state of ruinous physical decay and those responsible were doing their best to cover up the truth. Action of the most sweeping kind would have to be taken, and Pepys resolved to take it. The fleet would have to be repaired, rebuilt and refashioned after his image of maritime supremacy. Practical advice was his first need and, to this end, Pepys, with an annual Parliamentary grant of £400,000 assured, contacted his old friend Sir Anthony Deane. Deane confirmed that the entire battle fleet was laid up: nine First Rates, fifteen Second Rates and no less than thirty-nine Third Rates. Three-quarters of the Fourth Rates were unfit for sea. This was a disastrous situation, as both men realised, for the nation lay utterly exposed to 'sudden attempts from our neighbours'. Deane insisted, however, that with an immense and highly disciplined effort it should be possible to repair the entire fleet within three years.

To ensure this, the old bugbear of credit would have to be removed by a guarantee of regular funding against the customs returns. All the instructions issued to the navy would have to be followed to the letter, insubordinate officers and idle workmen dismissed, and a system of rewards introduced for those who deserved them. Pepys addressed an attentive Parliament on the matter, reminding them that the Test Act had shown the service resolutely Protestant and recalling the recent dangers posed by Monmouth's rebellion.

The King, however, was already managing to alienate the goodwill with which he had been so conspicuously welcomed to his throne. The large and apparently permanent army he had raised to defeat Monmouth was staffed by an egregious number of recently appointed Roman Catholic officers and, when the Commons voted him a supply but pointedly refused to thank him for his speech, he prorogued the House. This was an augury of worse to come.

Pepys, meanwhile, laughing at the futile efforts made by the Navy Board to set its own house in order, proceeded to gather that information which, on the last day of 1685, he would have finished fashioning into the greatest and most important of his many memoranda: his 'Notes for my Navy Discourse to the King and the Lord Treasurer'. This he delivered on New Year's Day. It was the apogee of his career. To this everything had led: St Paul's School, Cambridge, the vertiginous excitement of the Restoration, Sandwich's help, Pepys's own years of professional experience. Throughout those years James, as Duke of York, had watched over his efforts constantly. Now the former Lord High Admiral was on the throne and Pepys paid suitable tribute to his long-nurtured concern for the navy, declaring, 'I need not open to the King anything of the importance of the Navy of England that he has so often hazarded his life for.'[5] This was nothing less than the truth, but if Pepys was determined to present James as a hero he was careful to offer a portrait of himself as the devoted civil servant, the worthiest advocate of naval reform. 'The length of my experience beyond anybody else's in the Navy entitles me to this liberty,' he asserted. Nor was it only his years of service that gave him authority, for that time had been 'improved by the use made of my leisure during my five years recess in looking through the whole in all its parts, so as I could never have done had I continually remained under an obligation of spending my whole time upon one part'. Even defeat served his present purpose.

Now he could reveal the 'deplorable' state into which this most vital of all national institutions had fallen: the waste, the expense, the incompetence, the shortcomings of the Navy Board above all. To effect a wholesale revival of the navy it was clear to Pepys that a wholesale change in its administration would be necessary. It was impossible to work with an institution such as the Navy Board, sunk as it was in supine apathy and unable to re-create itself for a great challenge. As a result, Pepys proposed a special commission of carefully selected men who were not only thoroughly familiar with practical considerations, administration and accountancy but who had the personal qualities required: they would have to show 'vigour of mind joined with approved industry, zeal and personal aptness for labour'. They would also have to display, as Pepys told James, 'an entire resignation of themselves and their whole time to this your service without liableness to avocation from other business or pleasure'.

Royal approval for a commission was readily granted, and Pepys set about gathering together the supermen of whom he would be the unquestioned head. They included Will Hewer, Sir Phineas Pett, of the great shipbuilding family, the rather unlikely figure of Balty (who had proved his industry when collecting information for Pepys during the menace of the Popish Plot) and, of course, Sir Anthony Deane. But it was with this last figure that Pepys encountered his first serious obstacle: Deane, it appeared, was not willing to help. His advice had made him indispensable and now he was determined to secure the most advantageous terms for his employment. He had a large and thriving private business, he explained. Government service could not equal the profits he drew from it and he had, besides, fifteen children to support and was not 'without expectation of more'. Five hundred pounds a year could not tempt him. It was a grave disappointment.

Pepys read out Deane's letter to the King and the treasurer and they tried to patch up a compromise: if Deane would accept their proffered fee he would be allowed to continue running his own business. Deane still felt that he could not accept. The amount of work involved in saving the navy was enormous. His whole time would have to be given to it and Deane valued his time at £1,000 a year. While the treasurer exploded in fury Pepys resolved on a more subtle ploy. He knew that Deane was indispensable and sat down to prove it, drawing up a list of all the other leading shipwrights in the country and describing each name with a degree of caricature that gave an overwhelming impression of incompetence. Age, gout, inexperience, illiteracy, drunkenness and personalities 'supine to the last degree' disqualified them all. Armed with this powerful paper, Pepys cornered the King and the treasurer, who were forced to submit to Deane's demands. This was a necessary victory. Pepys, Deane and the invaluable Hewer would now form the triumvirate that would restore the nation's defences.

Pepys had assembled his team at last and he treated them to a two-hour lecture on their responsibilities before they were addressed by the King in 'a very earnest, plain and serious discourse', also prepared by Pepys, on what he, too, expected. In the meantime, the old Navy Board was removed from its comfortable office and commanded to sort out old accounts as they saw their other duties taken over by the new men. Pepys had got his way, and now in no part of the navy would he tolerate incompetence, inefficiency or the familiar abuses.

One particular abuse concerned Pepys above all, and this he set out to rectify in the proposals he made in yet another paper. 'His Majesty's Regulation in the Business of Plate Carriage'. Pepys would stamp out 'good voyages' once and for all, and would do so by making it an offence punishable by immediate discharge for any captain in the navy to carry any sort of merchandise without a royal warrant. Captains in foreign ports were required to keep the secretary informed of all their proceedings (a rule that also ensured log books were accurately kept) and to deposit a copy of this report with the English consul. To remove the financial problems that lay at the heart of the abuse, Pepys also instituted a system of rewards and allowances for officers, which would compensate them for 'good voyages' by paying a known and regular sum above their regular salary. The rewards were generous indeed, in some cases nearly doubling an officer's pay. Steps had been taken to remove one abuse and now, to ensure the quality of newly recruited officers, Pepys reintroduced his examination for lieutenants. He instituted rules that governed every aspect of their lives as midshipmen, and made it perfectly clear that none of these teenagers (they were all to be under sixteen) received any pay until they could present Pepys with 'a perfect journal, fairly written, kept and signed by himself, expressing in distinct columns the place where the said ship shall have been each day at noon, the daily change of the wind, and all the extraordinary accidents happening in the voyage'.

Pepys saw himself as the lynchpin of these reforms, the centre from which all flowed and to which all returned. There would not be a serving officer, however young or lowly, who did not recognise him as the seat of authority. This was his way of imposing order. This was his way of serving and protecting the nation. It was, in the short-term, extraordinarily effective, but the psychological and emotional cost were high indeed – and sadly dehumanising. Letters of magisterial rebuke continued to pour from him. Pepys wrote to a captain who had returned home from the West Indies without leave informing him that 'His Majesty has been pleased to tell me that he will have the matter full enquired into' – an eloquent circumlocution for a court-martial. When the clerk of the survey at Portsmouth had the temerity to present the King and the Lord Treasurer with a collection of tabulated information (a presumptuous piece of self-seeking made ridiculous by numerous mistakes) he received a crushing reproof. 'This only in the truth of friendship I must take the liberty of saying to you,' Pepys wrote, 'that, by the time you shall have conversed in the world and business as long as I have done, you'll find it of much more use to you rather to distrust than to presume too easily upon the sufficiency and unanswerableness (as you term it) of your own conceptions.' This was portentous, heavy-handed, and lit only perhaps by the smile of self-satisfied irony that may briefly have flickered across his face.

The self-important have no real humour. Nor do they necessarily have any easy access to their more shameful memories. Years before, a very different Pepys had pursued an honest carpenter's wife around the dockyards, promising advancement for her husband in return for sexual favours. Those favours he had taken, and now Mrs Bagwell – she who had so resisted Pepys that he had sprained his thumb in the tussle – had returned. Could the secretary help them again? He could not. Promotion, argued the King's representative, using all the ghastly logic of the bureaucratically circumscribed, was wholly in the King's gift and he himself was above being influenced. To prove the point, he wrote to Mrs Bagwell's husband telling him 'that I advised Mrs Bagwell, as I do everybody else, not to lose their time in attending, at least upon me, because that occasions them but an increase of expense in staying in town and does them no advantage after once they have informed me in their case and request'.

The Admiralty was to become a place devoid of personal nuance, an institution where no one was indispensable. Pepys made the latter abundantly clear when he wrote to James Pearse, whose mother had been trying to get her ne'er-do-well son a job. Once she had tried to have him made a purser, now she hoped he might replace the recently deceased Mr Walbanke as an Admiralty clerk. The poor woman had been foolish enough to over-praise Mr Walbanke's 'mighty sufficiencies'. Pepys was at pains to set the record straight. Many of those who did not know him had harped on the dead clerk's virtues:

> whereas I never thought fit to rely on his clerkship for the drawing up of one letter or paper of moment in my life, nor have felt any want of him during his long absence, poor man, by sickness at a time wherein matters of more importance to the Crown have been transacted in reference to the Navy than ever passed this office since England had a Navy. Not that he wanted talents very useful in their kind relating to the keeping of the books, marshalling the papers and examining of passes and divers other things wherein time only had made him fully master of the methods of the office, and he his brother by his continually employing him for many years under him. So that the affairs of this office are no more affected by his death than they would, were he still alive or had never been born.[6]

There is a repellent self-aggrandisement under this feigned impersonality, and an all-too-gloating delight in 'the methods of this office'. The letter is an example of bureaucratic sadism. The downtrodden, faceless clerk is glimpsed here, but so, too, is he who grinds the features of a helpless pen-pusher in the mud.

For his own part, Pepys enjoyed the rewards of power. His salary and the perquisites of office were adding to his already considerable wealth. Fees for passes and for new appointments – whether these were to such positions as master shipwright or lowly chaplain – ensured that this was so. Much of his money was spent on display. At the start of 1688 Pepys moved both himself and the Admiralty into 14 Buckingham Street. This was a sumptuous residence looking out on one side over a tree-planted walk to the river, a façade that he was soon to aggrandise at the Crown's expense. The door facing the Thames was ornamented with a vast shield displaying the Lord High Admiral's anchor, while above was an even larger display of the royal arms. The outside of the building thus proclaimed to all the glory of the office while the interior emphasized to a chosen few the status of its master. Vast maps and splendidly illuminated nautical manuscripts vied for attention with great pieces of tapestry, secured at a bargain rate for Pepys by his friend James Houblon. The elusive Mary Skinner had, perhaps, some responsibility for the household, which was plagued from time to time with the fractiousness that was Pepys's familiar lot with domestic servants, but 14 Buckingham Street was above all his palace, his place for personal display, the centre of his life. Here he housed his ever-growing library, his medals and his globes. Here, too, he could indulge his delight in music, persuading the great Cifaccio to sing for a private party – 'a mere wanton, effeminate child, very coy and proudly conceited', Evelyn thought him – while the 'stupendous' Baptist played what some thought was the finest harpsichord in England.[7]

Nor was it only music that tempted the virtuosi to Pepys's house. Scientific experiments were also conducted there, and Evelyn recorded how he was invited to a memorable occasion when, various liquids having been mixed and 'a little shaken together, [they] fixed divers suns and stars of real fire, perfectly globular, on the sides of the glass, and which there stuck like so many constellations, burning most vehemently and resembling stars and heavenly bodies'. The phosphorescence, Evelyn thought, seemed like God's creation of primal light, for all that the ingredients were in part at least 'made out of human blood and urine'. It was, he declared, 'a very noble experiment', and he recognised, too, that it was his friend Pepys who had done so much to see that the Royal Society, which promoted such investigations, had not fallen into decay. Indeed, the fellows had been so grateful for Pepys's efforts that, in December 1684, they had elected him their president. With characteristic energy and commitment Pepys regularly chaired the Society's meetings and it was while he was acting as president that the Society issued the most momentous of its publications: Newton's *Principia*, which appeared with Pepys's imprimatur on its title page.

Honours continued to cluster to him: in July 1685, Pepys was made master of Trinity House for a second time, having already been appointed a deputy lieutenant of Huntingdonshire, but it was his work for the navy that remained his most signal achievement. The first six months of the special commission showed what he could do. The thirty ships it had been his earlier triumph to build were no longer in danger of decay. The yards were full and busy, and there were high hopes that sixty-five vessels would soon be readied for the defence of the realm. It was a staggering achievement, for all Pepys's carping that those outside his inner triumvirate contributed little, 'what with the laziness of one, the private business or love of pleasure in another, [and] want of method in a third'. Despite such alleged shirking, a vast new dry dock was built at Portsmouth, storehouses and magazines were constructed, repairs fully and thoroughly carried out, and a most demanding timetable more than kept to. Eventually the commission could report that no less than eighty-nine ships had been rebuilt or repaired, twenty-nine vessels not included in the original estimate attended to, and three Fourth Rates constructed. No wonder that there were those, like Lord Ailesbury, who were ready to declare that 'Mr Pepys put this ships and docks in the greatest order beyond what can be expressed.'[8]

Yet even as Pepys's triumph became evident his success was undermined by the one man from whom he might have expected unqualified support. King James II's religious beliefs and his conduct of politics were rapidly bringing the monarchy to a point of crisis that that brave, foolish, obstinate man had neither the wit to appreciate nor the ability to contain. The depth and sincerity of James's Roman Catholicism were beyond question. The Church gave him that sense of absolute certainty for which he craved, there being, he thought, 'no other which claims, or can claim, infallibility, for there must necessarily be an infallible church, or otherwise what

Our Saviour said cannot be and the gates of hell would prevail against her'. These convictions underlay all the King's political thinking. He did not wish to force his faith on his disgusted fellow countrymen but he was determined that his co-religionists should not labour under disadvantages. The Test Acts excluded them from Parliament and public office, the Penal Laws forbade them openly to practise their religion or to teach and publish their ideas. These obstacles James was determined to remove, and he nurtured the secret hope that, once they had gone, thousands of English people would see the light and recant their heresy.

James wished to achieve his objectives through the law, and therein lay the rub. A solid phalanx of the Tories in Parliament had welcomed his accession on condition that he protected their Church and offices. They and the rest of the nation (united in this at least) would never consent to reforms that threatened Protestantism, and even the most intelligent people, while prepared to extend 'liberty and ease to tender consciences', were entirely convinced that once Catholics had been admitted to office they would do all in their power to destroy heretics. Evidence for this seemed all too terrifyingly clear: across the Channel, that most Catholic of kings, Louis XIV of France, had recently revoked the Edict of Nantes which for years had provided some measure of protection to his Protestant subjects. Now the people of England saw their fellow believers stripped of their security, their possessions, their livelihoods and, all too often, their lives. This is what Catholicism was: absolutist in its political methods and remorseless in its intentions.

As James determined to pursue his policy, an increasing number of alarmed people came to believe that a similar fate awaited them. Absolutism, it seemed, was seated on the English throne and people watched fearfully as its influence radiated outwards. A packed ecclesiastical commission sought to stifle criticism of the Catholic Church in Anglican pulpits, Catholic peers were admitted to the Privy Council, and a horrified Evelyn 'watched the Jesuits in their rich copes officiating at the altar in Whitehall'. The bench, too, was reshuffled, the more independent judges replaced with those who would comply with James's wish to dispense his co-religionists from the penalties of the Test Acts and so free all Roman Catholics from laws aimed against them. The country was appalled. If the King could suspend these laws, he could suspend any law. Persons and property were no longer safe. The London apprentices, often an accurate barometer of public opinion, rioted in the streets while the shrewder made shift for themselves. Arthur Herbert, the Rear-Admiral of England, swore on his non-existent conscience that he could not comply with the King's suspension of the Test Acts and was dismissed. There was a change in the wind and soon it would be blowing from Holland where Herbert and an increasing number of the disaffected were in exile at the court of the Protestant heirs, William of Orange and his wife Mary.

In the meantime James pursued his policies like a man obsessed. Unable any longer to rely on the alienated Tories, he turned instead to the Nonconformists, who, like the Catholics, laboured under legal disabilities, naively believing that one minority would support another simply because both were disaffected. Parliament was duly packed with men whose social status and religious beliefs failed to represent the majority of English opinion. Here, it seemed, was absolutism yet again. Just as the law had been arbitrarily suspended, so the body that made the law had been summarily refashioned into what James hoped could be used as a rubber stamp for the royal will. The majority of people found the situation gravely disturbing, and when James made a progress through the Midlands Pepys, who accompanied him as far as the ultra-Royalist stronghold of Worcester, saw how few turned out to support him. His own Tory friends stayed at home, and it was with these people that Pepys chose to stay. It was time, he decided, to keep a low profile. 'To tell you the truth,' he wrote to a friend, 'I was got with Mr Dean of Worcester into the library among the manuscripts and pored away my time till (at my going out) I found nobody left in the town but myself.'

The accelerating pace of James's desire for reform was now driving him headlong to disaster and Pepys was inevitably swept up in its wake. He expressed not a word of public criticism of his master's plans for he was, as always, the King's man and utterly devoted to the legitimate rule he believed the Stuarts represented. That cause he would continue to serve with all the professionalism at his disposal. He would continue to wield his golden pen. Duty, hard work and an unflagging concern for the efficient running of the navy would be his stay in a time of mounting confusion. On 4 April 1687, when James issued his first Declaration of Indulgence granting freedom of worship to Dissenters and Roman Catholics alike, the terrors of popery and arbitrary rule seemed to hang ever more threateningly over the country. Nor was it only the English who were concerned: while the King produced no legitimate male heir from what many saw as his barren second marriage, his daughter, Princess Mary, wife of the ultra-Protestant William of Orange, would succeed to the throne. Now, to their horror and amazement, people learned that James's queen was pregnant. If the child was a boy and was raised as a Catholic, then Antichrist himself would be placed as the legitimate power behind the English throne. The Whig magnates became increasingly alarmed and William's agent returned to Holland with letters from a number of influential men implying that they looked to William as the man who could lead their opposition to James and so save Protestantism and English democracy.

There was no stopping the King. As his wife's body

rounded out, so James issued a Second Declaration of Indulgence and demanded that it should be read aloud from every pulpit in the land. No move could have been more foolishly designed to alienate the forces that had once provided his most loyal support. The King's order was widely ignored, at the instigation of seven of the bishops who, meeting in Lambeth Palace, drew up a petition begging him to withdraw his demand since they could not obey it and keep the law. As copies of the petition flooded the coffee-houses of London, six of the bishops who had drawn it up presented their case to James. His fury knew no bounds. Pepys and the lords of the council were rapidly summoned to the council chamber and there, in an ugly scene, the bishops were interrogated by James and Judge Jeffreys. They admitted to signing the document and were informed that they would consequently be tried in the Court of King's Bench for publishing a seditious libel. It was then ordered that they should be committed to the Tower of London. The barge that took them there was watched by a vast, sympathetic crowd, desperate for the security of their faith now that the Queen had given birth to a male heir. They were terrified by the swelling ranks of the standing army the King had encamped on Hounslow Heath and certain that the terrors of popery were about to descend in all their horror.

Thus, it appeared, was Stuart rule. On 29 June 1688, the bishops were brought to Westminster Hall, there to stand trial. Angry citizens in the hall itself and the streets outside howled in contempt at the actions of a king who, in his infatuated support of the abhorrent papists, acted as if he were above the law. As Mr Justice Powell for the defence was led to declare, if the King could indeed dispense with the laws as he chose then 'there will need no Parliament; all the legislature will be in the King, which is a thing worth considering and I leave the issue to God and your consciences'.[9] A verdict of not guilty was inevitably returned but, while relieved Londoners erupted in celebration, burning effigies of the Pope, ringing bells and firing guns, those of a more ruthless persuasion decided that the time had come to act. Admiral Herbert, dressing himself as a poor seaman, left for The Hague and the court of Prince William. Secreted about him was a letter signed by seven Whigs inviting William to invade England at the head of the Dutch army. Here was the one force that could genuinely threaten James's regime.

The invitation confirmed William's plans. He had already resolved to invade England 'if he was invited by some men of the best interest to . . . come and rescue the nation and the religion'.[10] He believed, or chose to believe, that James's new male heir was a 'suppositious' child, smuggled into the palace, as some said, in a warming pan. He had also formed the view that a strong republican current was flowing through English life and that if his father-in-law's actions became too extreme there would be another civil war, which might well result in a republican victory, the frustration of his wife's claim to the throne and, consequently, the ruin of his chances of bringing England into the next war against Louis XIV. Here, in this last consideration, was the mainspring of William's entire foreign policy. He was determined to form a grand European alliance to prevent the French King from establishing his rule over the greater part of western Europe and then annihilating Protestantism. By forcibly asserting his wife's claim to the English throne William would not only acquire the extra wealth and men required to secure his aims, he would also acquire the spectacular English fleet so lovingly created by Pepys. By these means it might be possible to challenge the power of France. William, too, was a man obsessed. As the Marquess of Halifax put it, the Prince of Orange had 'such a mind to invade France that it would incline one to think he took England only in his way'.

The plan of invasion William formulated had the reckless audacity of genius. The launching of a major naval expedition during the winter months involved the Dutch fleet in the hazards posed by contrary prevailing winds. William only had the word of his English allies that, if he were able to make a landing, James's army would not take up arms against him. If he were to fail, catastrophe would ensue since the English and French fleets would combine in a mighty Catholic armada that would surely annihilate the Dutch fleet. William coolly assessed the risk and, believing that all was in the hand of God, started preparations on a massive scale and threw the full force of his administrative ability behind them. He had to mobilise a vast army of federal Dutch troops paid for by the States General, along with two regiments of English refugees, some French Huguenots, Brandenburgers and Scandinavian mercenaries. Some two or three hundred transports had to be requisitioned to carry the troops, their horses, equipment and provisions. Fifty fighting ships also had to be readied and sailors found for them. Such preparations could hardly be made in secret, for all that James thought he was arming against the French, and by the early summer of 1688 the nature of William's intentions was becoming clear. Pepys and Deane worked tirelessly to ready Fourth and Fifth Rates in the Downs and recruit 6,500 men. Frigates were commanded 'to speak with all ships passing . . . and to gain what intelligence they could of the number, force and motion of the ships of any foreign Prince or State'.

It was the news that came in from The Hague that was most alarming. Early on the morning of 16 August Pepys left in a hurry for Windsor to inform James that he had heard for certain how William was preparing some ninety ships at Amsterdam, Helvoetsluis and elsewhere. His intentions could no longer be in any doubt. All leave in the navy was stopped, a partial mobilisation of the fleet was ordered and Pepys saw to the preparation of fireships. To save the detested regime to which he had committed himself Pepys worked in his office through the small hours and had constant meetings with the

King and senior naval men. James, he wrote, was 'greatly awakened' by the emergency, and Pepys believed that thanks to their joint efforts and 'by God Almighty's ordinary blessing with the concurrence of the season we may at last reckon ourselves safe against any extraordinary mischiefs that might be otherwise apprehended from so unusual a proceeding and insult from a neighbour in alliance'. Faith and common sense told him that William's plans were preposterous.

Preparations were essential none the less, but while they were being made, there were the familiar problems of shortages and delays, and equally damaging failures of morale and discipline. Pepys became increasingly harassed, writing to Lord Dartmouth, the commander of the fleet, to tell him that he did not ever 'expect to see it otherwise till commanders will think fit to observe their instructions more'. It was exasperating. Pepys had brought all his strength, efficiency and experience to the task of readying the fleet. Everything that logic, order and labour could do had been done. But what Pepys could not overcome was the remarkable work done by William of Orange's agents and propagandists: the Exclusion crisis of Charles II's reign had shown the importance of such efforts, and printed propaganda now flooded the country to feed the notion that James was out to subvert the people's liberties and beliefs. Pepys was defending a regime that a growing number of people feared and detested. Now the armed forces were being directly targeted, the aristocratic Edward Russell and the ubiquitous Herbert spearheading these efforts in the navy.

The result was widespread ill-discipline among naval officers, who were difficult to control at the best of times. Dartmouth noted the familiar signs of this, as did Pepys, who was horrified when attending a cabinet meeting one evening to find the captain of a Third Rate idling in the palace when he should have been with his ship. It was as if such people did not care that the country was facing the gravest crisis since the civil war. So angry was Pepys – so dismayed that his disciplinary procedures were not being followed – that, not for the first time, he briefly wondered why he bothered at all. He was working night and day to put the country on a war footing – chivvying, rebuking and remonstrating with men in the dockyards, with victuallers, slop-sellers, and the Ordnance Office – and he was repaid with insubordination. He wrote wearily to Dartmouth:

> unless there be another spirit put into some of their commanders (I mean as to diligence and concernment for the Service and not making it as a bye-business, annexed only as an inconvenience to their employments elsewhere), I shall bid goodnight to the expectations of any good to the Service from them, let you and myself make as much on't as we please . . . But for ought I see gentlemen are got above being jealous of any censure, or else they would not appear to the King every day at Court complaining that their ships are not ready, while nothing is wanting towards making them ready but their own attendance on board.[11]

All of this was trying enough, but the maritime defence of the realm faced one more and altogether graver problem. Dartmouth was not a man in the great tradition of English naval commanders, an admiral capable of extreme action in extreme circumstances. He had been put in charge of the greatest fleet the country had ever possessed and he would not hazard it, as he thought, recklessly. A close blockade of the Dutch coast was, he judged, sheer foolishness. It was the received wisdom that the fighting season in the Channel ran from May to July, and that to open a campaign in November was reckless. Daylight was short and storms of such ferocity that ships would be smashed to matchwood were all but inevitable. Prudence kept the admiral bottled up in the Thames and, for all that a favourable wind was blowing, Dartmouth argued that he was inadequately supplied, that he faced tactical problems, that the weather posed risks too great. He would not even attack the enemy's transport ships, fearing that the danger inherent in such an action was more than the threat offered by William's preparations. These last Dartmouth continued to consider so foolhardy that they would surely end in their own destruction. 'Their growing mad,' he wrote of the Dutch, 'shall not provoke me to follow their example.'

Such thinking was judicious, level-headed, professional – and wholly inadequate. Suddenly the wind changed. The English fleet was now delayed in the Thames not by its admiral's prudence but by forces altogether beyond his control – the forces that bore William's navy, with Herbert in command, down towards the south-west coast of England. The invading fleet was a magnificent sight as what many blessed as a 'Protestant wind' filled its sails and bore the ships to a safe landing at Torbay. Meanwhile, the marvellous fleet that the secretary to the Admiralty had laboured so hard to build had failed utterly in its first task of defending the realm. The news reached London as James, at Pepys's request, was having his portrait painted. Suddenly the commission belonged to a bygone era.

For all the evident catastrophe, Pepys did not despair. Still he wielded his golden pen and still the momentum of his duties sustained him. He wrote frequently to Dartmouth to reassure and send him the King's realisation 'of your incapacity for doing more in that exigence for his service than you did, considering the place in which you were then hooked and the wind that then blew to the benefit of the Holland's fleet and disadvantage of yours'. This was the bureacrat's response, the gentleman's response. Manners, self-control and proper form had to be preserved among the leaders at this of all times. The King, meanwhile, prepared to ride out and lead his army in one last defence of his realm, but the Whig magnates, sensing victory, were already making their way to William's camp and there was deep pessimism in the court as news of the desertions came in.

On 17 November, just before he left for the West, James summoned members of his cabinet to witness his last will and testament. The Lord Chancellor, two Catholic peers, two secretaries of state and four senior officials, of whom Pepys was the first, appended their names. Pepys accompanied his master as far as Windsor where, with a sure instinct that his world was fracturing around him, he asked the King to sign a paper witnessing to his 'long and faithful services' and requiring the Treasury lords to pay him the arrears due for his work both as secretary to the Admiralty and treasurer of the Tangier Committee. He never received the very considerable sums outstanding – Pepys calculated them at over £28,000.

The return of the King, broken and despairing, within ten days of setting out on his futile expedition to the West showed Pepys with terrible certainty how the familiar world was now collapsing. Even the King's general had deserted to the enemy and, for all the talk of calling a Parliament and forgiving those who had risen in rebellion, the smell of defeat was everywhere. Desperation gripped the court. At a secret cabinet meeting held on the King's return, Pepys was asked to draft an order to Lord Dartmouth 'containing a matter which will not bear being known to more than was at the debate of it till we may be morally sure that no advice of it hence by land could prevent the execution'. James had resolved to send his infant son into French exile, and Pepys was required to order the yachts that would take him and his entourage down the river.

Even this plan came to nothing when Dartmouth, terrified that the boy would become a hostage to fortune and an excuse for the French to invade, prevaricated. The prince was returned to London and other plans had to be made to spirit him away. Then, when the King knew that his son was safe, he made preparations for his own flight. As his parting gesture he would wilfully, spitefully drag the country he had so ineptly ruled to what extremes of uncertainty he could. He had been the head of government and now he would make that government unworkable. James destroyed the writs he had ordered to be drawn up for a general election. In all probability he also ordered the Great Seal of England to be thrown in the Thames. There would be no Parliamentary authority and no legitimate monarchical power. Finally, he ordered his military officers to disband their men without any provision for disarming them. His wild army, which had so terrified the people, would be let loose in the land. As for his navy, that great creation of the loyal Pepys, it could sail for Catholic Ireland, if its officers could persuade the men to it; if not then 'there is no remedy'. With these things done, James believed he could flee. As he made his way down the darkened Thames one of his pages knocked at the door of Pepys's house and, presenting Pepys with the King's orders to Dartmouth, told him of James's ignominious flight.

Anarchy across London witnessed to ordinary people's detestation of the regime Pepys had so loyally served. The embassies of Roman Catholic countries were sacked, chapels were burned, and that most detested of all James's aides, Judge Jeffreys, was so viciously attacked that he broke down weeping and was smuggled for his own protection into the Tower. In the meantime the great of the land set themselves up as a provisional government under the Archbishop of Canterbury, faced the inevitable and declared for William of Orange, hinting strongly that they expected him to summon Parliament. Among their many other pressing concerns was the navy and they rapidly sent for Pepys. Bewildered and ill as he was, Pepys attended their call. His duty required it. At the lords' behest he wrote to Dartmouth requiring him to refrain from attacking the invading Dutch ships and to sack Catholics from his fleet. He wrote to the ports, insisting that all outward-bound vessels be searched. He issued orders that no one was to go down the Thames without an official pass from the Lord Mayor.

Then news came that the King had been captured and was even now being returned to his erstwhile capital 'to the great but short content', as Pepys wrote, 'of all his subjects'. This was at best a half-truth. William had James arrested and moved his own troops on London as he arranged for the defeated King to flee. He then drove in triumph down a rain-soaked Piccadilly to his first levee at St James's Palace. The following day he required Pepys's presence and, with Russell and Herbert as his principal officers, asked him to remain at his post. Pepys again complied. For the time being at least (and comforted by the warm letters of personal encouragement sent him by Evelyn and Hewer) he would be coldly, properly, scrupulously the 'faithful and most humble servant' of men who represented all he despised and who, in their turn, loathed him.

As always there was work to do and Pepys sustained the massive demands of the routine of the Admiralty. His expertise was invaluable. He set about dealing with the intractable problems of victualling the fleet from inadequate supplies of money and sending frigates to the Channel Islands and to the coast of Ireland, which was now on the verge of rebellion. The discipline he tried to impose was rigorous, even in the face of mutinously angry unpaid seamen. But it was gradually becoming clear that Pepys had had his term as secretary. When writs were issued for an election and he sought to stand for his old seat the voters of Harwich rejected him. Two days later, on 22 February, Pepys was still sending out official letters, but they were his last. He had already made his decision. The world about him had changed utterly. Pepys would resign and his golden pen would toil for the Admiralty no more.

CHAPTER FIFTEEN

Retirement

In his friend Evelyn's phrase, Pepys had, 'laid down his office, and would serve no more'.[1] This did not mean that he was free of difficulties and responsibilities. He was inevitably bitter and angry, his life's work for the navy having fallen into the hands of those whom he not only regarded as his enemies but men whose attitudes – coarse, ill-disciplined and arrogant – sent shivers of revulsion down his spine. As the grandees of the new regime, people such as Russell and Herbert were also potentially dangerous since they could readily secure their positions by attacking Pepys. He was well aware of this, and indignation combined with concerns over his own safety led him to compose a justification of his conduct of Admiralty affairs, his 'Memoirs . . . of the Royal Navy . . . for Ten Years, Determined December 1688'.

Detailed argument was, as always, Pepys's best defence and, as he worked on the 'Memoirs', he was determined that he would always keep to hand his records of his work. It was only with the greatest difficulty that he could be prevailed on to pass any papers over to his successors. In particular, he hung on to his Letter Books tenaciously and had copies made of everything he considered important. The papers were both his armour and his archive. Pepys used them with his customary thoroughness and he read the finished 'Memoirs' to Evelyn on 10 June 1690. His friend wrote in his own *Diary* how Pepys had successfully showed in his work 'with what malice and injustice he was suspected . . . about the timber of which the thirty ships were built by a late Act of Parliament: with the exceeding danger the present Fleet would be shortly in by reason of the ignorance and incompetency of those who now managed the Admiralty and affairs of the Navy'. This is a fair summing up of the contents, but Evelyn was fully aware that Pepys's work was a moral justification as well as a technical one. In a letter he wrote to Pepys a few days later Evelyn declared that the 'Memoirs' would 'stand like a rock, and dash in pieces all the effects and efforts of spiteful and implacable men, who because they cannot bravely emulate, envy your worth, and would thus secretly undermine it'.[2] In spite of their efforts, the 'Memoirs' proved 'that you, and your colleagues, have stood in the breach, when the safety of the nation was in utmost danger'. This was nothing less than the truth and a few days later Evelyn urged Pepys to publish his work since 'you owe it to God, to your country, and to yourself'. Perhaps Evelyn already appreciated how urgent the need for a public defence was. Pepys's enemies were gunning for him.

His record and his principled decision to number himself among those so-called non-jurors who refused to swear the oath of allegiance to William and Mary made him a natural target for attack. In early May 1689 Pepys, along with Hewer and Deane, was arrested on suspicion of 'dangerous and treasonable practices against His Majesty's government' and was not released until the start of July. When questioned, Pepys managed to prove to Parliament by dint of comprehensive citation from his records that the navy had in no way been wilfully weakened during King William's savage efforts to subdue Ireland. When he was arrested again in June the following year the case against him collapsed. He was bailed after five days and soon the charges against him were dropped altogether. Yet another Parliamentary attack on his administration in 1691–2 similarly failed to bring Pepys down, although the efforts he felt compelled to make in his own defence at times verged on the melodramatic. This was a potentially dangerous season: Pepys never knew when his papers might be searched and he could never be certain that he was free from the threat of arrest.

In order to prepare his detailed defence Pepys went to ground. He made sure that everybody knew that he had hired a house in Epping Forest for the summer then hid himself in his office at York Buildings for three months. The result of such enforced self-confinement was painful indeed, for 'my constant poring, and sitting so long still in one posture, without any divertings or exercise . . . brought a humour down on to one of my legs, not only to the swelling of it almost to the size of both, but with the giving me mighty pains, and disabling me since this day to put a shoe on that foot'.[3] Such was the cost of a measure of security and when, with the help of Houblon and a good lawyer, an attempt to indict both Pepys and Sir Josiah Child of the East India Company for piracy was shown to be groundless, Pepys could at last devote himself to the most fruitful uses of retirement: the cultivation of his friends, his family and his intellect.

As so often, Pepys had to look after his brother-in-law's career prospects for him, but efforts to obtain Balty a job were unsuccessful and were soon followed by a row. It seems likely that Mary Skinner, Pepys's housekeeper, was in some way involved in this. Certainly, Balty wrote to Pepys complaining of 'the malicious inventive ill offices of a female beast, which you keep', and Pepys's fury was not at all lessened by crawling allusions to his 'generous usual goodness . . . and former kindnesses'. He broke off all personal contact with

Balty but may have provided him with a small allowance. Nor were relations with his nephew, Pall's son Samuel Jackson, much happier. Pepys had designed that the young man should be his heir but, after Jackson had abandoned a career at sea and married a woman of whom Pepys disapproved, he was disinherited in favour of his younger, more dutiful brother John.

Pepys went to great efforts to set up John as a polished and educated gentleman. In particular, he was determined that he should make the Grand Tour. The somewhat stolid young man was not an ideal candidate for an educational experiment that Pepys himself regarded as being of the highest importance. He himself was envious of his friend Evelyn's early travels on the Continent and was determined that his heir should have this advantage. The Houblons were mobilised to arrange contacts abroad and the means of exchanging money, while a plethora of letters from Pepys himself gave John detailed instructions about acquiring books and prints, essential sightseeing (the celebration of Jubilee Year in Rome during 1700 was an especially important goal), manners, moral pitfalls and such minor courtesies as dusting off his letters with lettuce seed for the benefit of Lord Clarendon 'who you know is a great saladist and curious'. John's letters of reply, although duly dusted with lettuce seed, were hardly inspiring. He was bored when contrary winds kept him in New Shoreham at the start of his journey, disappointed by the wines in Burgundy, irritated by the difficulties of mountain travel, bored by the music in the Sistine Chapel, censorious of Naples and only too willing to let others take the initiative in Spain. Nor did John's epistolary style provide much matter for conversation back in England. 'You should,' Pepys lamented, 'furnish me with something to say to those friends of ours who have endeavoured to oblige us by their recomendatory letters on your behalf; whatever the fruit of them may have really proved to you.'[4] It was all rather disappointing.

Other correspondence was more fruitful. 'What troubles are avoided when one has nothing to do with the rabble? What is sweeter than scholarly leisure?' Cicero's words, which Pepys chose as the epigraph for his 'Memoirs', aptly suggest the tenor of his final years, and an extraordinary stream of letters and jottings witnesses to the range of his intellectual interests and his undimmed curiosity. He discussed liberty of conscience with such friends as Sir William Petty and the erudite Dr Gale, and came to the conclusion that 'when all is done reason must govern all since our very faith must be a reasonable faith'. Here is an intellectual balance very different from the passion and sectarianism that had surrounded his youth then erupted periodically with such destructive fervour in his later years.

It has an eighteenth-century tone but had its origins with the founding fathers of the Royal Society and their concern with a plain, natural way of speaking, the avoidance of cloudy metaphysical confusion. Pepys was comfortable with men like Petty, who could roundly declare 'that much the greatest part of all human understanding is lost by our discoursing and writing of matters nonsensically, that is in words subject to more senses than one'.[5] Practical, material problems mattered: accurate weather forecasting, exchange rates, the advisability of a national lottery and Sir Isaac Newton's views on probability and gambling. And, as always, anything that would bolster maritime supremacy fascinated Pepys. He was the friend of the most eminent and respectable men but also an eager listener to the pirate William Dampier, who knew better than any other Englishman of the time that there were new worlds to be charted oceans away, that the current maps were false, knowledge of the winds was inadequate and that journals such as the ones he kept were essential to expanding knowledge and opportunities for trade.

Pure scholarship mattered to Pepys too. He had a wide and

much valued acquaintance with the great modern scholars, antiquaries and palaeographers at Oxford, and he brought to their company not only his own erudition but – characteristically – his interest in method and system. Pepys was keenly interested in the great project for a national bibliography of manuscripts, sensing at once how much time could be saved and what discoveries could be made by so valuable an undertaking. He was at first chary of contributing the catalogue of his own collection – he foresaw what a potential nuisance a stream of unwanted visitors might be – but altruism got the better of reluctance and he agreed to contribute, since his own magnificent library had become the centre of his life.

As an expression of Pepys's mind the library is also the image of the man. Naturally its contents are as comprehensive as its owner's interests while its rigorous cataloguing shows that love of order so wholly characteristic of Pepys. One particular detail demonstrates this especially: the books, which are catalogued by number rather than by subject, are ranged in the lovely presses by size, little leather-covered blocks raising slightly smaller ones to the height of their neighbours. Those on the highest levels Pepys had to reach down with the help of a stool. Two or three clerks (including Paul Lorrain who wrote up Pepys's papers on the villainous Scott) helped with the delightful labours of the bibliophile. Pepys made it clear in his will that, with the exception of any obvious omissions, the library was not to be expanded after his death. Preserved in the serenity of the Pepys Building in Magdalene College, Cambridge, the library gives the most life-enhancing sense of dignified scholarship, along with a slightly eerie sense of intimacy. The *Diary* is here, of course, and along with this and the beautiful manuscripts there are good collections of theology, poetry and travel books as well as specialised collections of material relating to the *Navalia*, ballads and a large hoard of prints.

Collecting prints was a particular passion and one in

which Evelyn was closely involved. The later correspondence between the two men is rich with this shared enthusiasm. Pepys had collected prints throughout his life and now he pasted into his albums heads of noblemen, ecclesiastics, virtuosi, lawyers and other professionals. Some of these men were acquaintances and a few were friends. 'I want Mr Evelyn's head,' he wrote to his fellow enthusiast, who replied, 'I send you Sir my face, such as it was of yore, but is now not so more . . . and with it (what you may find harder to procure) the Earl of Nottingham, Lord High Admiral, which, though it make a gap in my poor collection (to which it was glued) I most cheerfully bestow on you.'[5] This is the true tone of cultivated friendship and Evelyn paid proper tribute to the range of Pepys's collection. The letters make clear that he was the more discriminating and informed of the two and the collector better acquainted with artists, whose monograms he could usually identify where Pepys often could not.

The prints are one evidence of their friendship but the finest expression of its fertility is one of the great buildings of England: the naval hospital at Greenwich. Pepys had long treasured the idea of erecting such a building, an enthusiasm shared with Evelyn, whose public work had made him painfully familiar with the suffering of seamen. The genius of a third friend was required to turn thoughts into stone, and the letter Pepys wrote to Evelyn about it is a fascinating and important example of the thinking behind late-seventeenth-century public works. There was already a building by John Webb on the site (and Wren would later adapt what he first proposed to honour Inigo Jones's Queen's House as well) but in November 1694 what his magisterial imagination had in mind was

> the raising of another wing of building answerable to that already there, with a gallery between both, and an apparatus

> of every sort, as well as for elegancy as bulk, within doors, as without, that may render it an Invalides with us for the sea, suitable in some degree to that of Paris for the land, and so much more as it is to take in a provision for the widows, orphans, and seamen slain, as well as for the persons of such as age, infirmities, or wounds, shall have rendered incapable of further services.[7]

The combination of intellect, public spirit and concern for grandeur is evident and the result was a masterpiece.

It was men and ideas of this calibre that were typical, too, of the Saturday gatherings Pepys held while he was still living in York Buildings. These were greatly appreciated by some of the most able men in England. ''Tis never any drudgery to wait on Mr Pepys,' wrote the great palaeographer Henry Wanely, 'whose conversation, I think, is more nearly akin to what we are taught to hope for in Heaven, than that of anybody else I know,'[8] and Evelyn for one missed these occasions sorely when they came to an end with the turn of the century. Pepys was getting old and, in the spring of 1700, he paid a long visit to Hewer's house in Clapham. It was a grand establishment, for Hewer had made himself into a wealthy man, rich enough indeed to buy the house once lived in by Denis Gauden the victualler. The establishment had been described by Pepys many years earlier as 'very regular and finely contrived, and the gardens and offices about it as convenient and as full of good variety as ever I saw in my life'. It was an ideal place to retire to and, a year after his first visit, Pepys was invited to live there permanently.

The letters he and Evelyn exchanged (more frequent now since age and declining health made regular visits difficult) dwell with dignity on the familiar concerns of the elderly. As early as 1692 Pepys was declaring that 'the world and I have been strangers a great while', and those from the following decade are much concerned with health. Pepys urged on Evelyn the advantages of barley water 'blanched with a few almonds and sweetened with a little sugar'. Evelyn in turn recommended 'the wonders of a nephritic powder lately brought into England'. Pepys was having trouble with his urinary system. He was not fully aware that the problem was the one that had tormented his childhood – his old complaint of the stone. No less than seven of these were developing in his left kidney 'fast linked together and adhering to his back'.[9] Together they weighed some four and a half ounces.

The end was now not long in coming and the pain was very great, for all Pepys's stamina. He bore it with exemplary fortitude. 'The greatness of his behaviour,' wrote a friend, 'in his long and sharp trial before his death, was in every respect answerable to his great life'. The final agony lasted some forty hours as his ulcerous, stone-filled kidney filled with the pus that was poisoning him. As he struggled so his contempt for the world became ever more marked, his confidence in a life to come ever more resolute. It was a Christian end, as George Hickes, Pepys's friend and attendant cleric, noted. He was profoundly moved, profoundly impressed:

> I never attended any sick or dying person that died with so much Christian greatness of mind, or a more lively sense of immortality, or so much fortitude and patience, in so long and sharp a trial, or greater resignation to the will, which he most devoutly acknowledged to be the wisdom of God.[10]

The end finally came on 26 May 1703 at '47 minutes past 3 . . . by his gold watch,' wrote John Jackson, clearly in obedience to a final request.

The funeral took place nine days later. It was, suitably, an evening occasion, and St Olave's was filled with the great and the good who were Pepys's peers. Only one close friend was unable to attend and bid farewell as the coffin was laid beside Elizabeth's. Evelyn was ill but, in his *Diary* he wrote his tribute to 'Sam. Pepys, a very worthy, industrious and curious person, none in England exceeding him in the knowledge of the Navy'. He was, Evelyn continued, 'universally beloved, hospitable, generous, learned in many things, skilled in music, a very great treasurer of learned men'.[11] This was nothing less than just, a tribute to a mind of extraordinary vitality and, as was the mind, so was the man.

REFERENCES

Chapter One: Educating Samuel

1. For details of the execution, see C. V. Wedgewood, *The Trial of Charles I*, pp. 188–193.
2. *Diary*, 1 November 1660.
3. For the physical life of the capital, see Liza Picard, *Restoration London, passim*.
4. From *A Hue and Cry after P. and H.*, a pamphlet attack on Pepys published in 1679.
5. *Calendar of State Papers Domestic*, 1641–3, p. 214.
6. For Pepys's health, see 'The Present Ill State of my Health, 7. 11. 1677', Rawlinson Mss, A 185, ff. 206–13.
7. H.M.C. *Calendar of the Mss of the Marquis of Ormonde*, N.S. 1 (1902), pp. 114–15.
8. Cited in Stephen Porter (ed.), *London and the Civil War*, p. 12.
9. *Diary*, 30 May, 1663.
10. John Milton, *Of Education*.
11. See 'St Paul's School' in *Companion* volume to the Latham and Mathews edition of the *Diary*.
12. Cited in G.B. H. Pawson, *The Cambridge Platonists*, pp. 13ff.
13. *Diary*, 30 July 1666.
14. *Ibid*, 30 January 1664.
15. Rawlinson Mss, A 185, ff. 206–13.
16. R. G. Howarth (ed.) *Letters and Second Diary of Samuel Pepys*, pp. 9–11.

Chapter Two: Waiting on Events

1. Cited in Peter Padfield, *Maritime Supremacy and the Opening of the Western Mind*, p. 2.
2. See 'Exchequer' in *Companion* volume to the Latham and Mathews edition of the *Diary*.
3. Cited in Arthur Bryant, *Samuel Pepys: The Man in the Making*, p. 57.
4. See 'Rota Club' in *Companion* volume to the Latham and Mathews edition of the *Diary*.
5. R. G. Howarth (ed.) *Letters and Second Diary of Samuel Pepys*, pp. 11–18.
6. *Diary*, 1 January 1660.
7. *Diary*, 11 February 1660.
8. *Ibid.*, 6 March 1660.

Chapter Three: Restoration

1. *Diary*, 22 March 1660.
2. *Ibid.*, 18 June 1660.
3. *Ibid.*, 20 April 1660.
4. For shipboard life see *Ibid.*, 1 April 1660 ff.
5. Pieter de Groot, cited in Peter Padfield, *Maritime Supremacy*, p. 136.
6. *Diary*, 22 May 1660.
7. W. Prynne, cited in David Ogg, *England in the Reign of Charles II*, p. 136.
8. *Diary*, 2 June 1660.
9. *Ibid.*, 12 January 1661.
10. *Ibid.*, 4 September 1660.

Chapter Four: Getting Started

1. *Diary*, 14 October 1660.
2. For Pepys's account of the coronation, see *Diary* 23 April 1660.
3. *Diary*, 9 March 1666.
4. See *Diary*, 13 January 1662 ff.
5. *Diary*, 7 January 1669.
6. *Diary*, 19 March 1666.
7. Quoted in Bernard Pool. *Navy Board Contracts*, p 5.

Chapter Five: The Life of this Office

1. Henry Peacham, *The Complete Gentleman*, cited in David Ogg, *England in the Reign of Charles II*, p. 136.
2. *Diary*, 2 February 1664.
3. *Ibid.*, 30 October 1662.
4. J. R. Tanner (ed.) *Further Correspondence of Samuel Pepys*, pp. 122–3.
5. For Tom's illness and death, see *Diary* 8 March 1664 ff.
6. *Diary*, 13 November 1662.
7. *Diary*, 9 January 1663.
8. *Ibid.*, 24 March 1663.
9. For Elizabeth's relationship with Mr Pembleton, see *Diary*, 4 May 1663 ff.
10. *Diary*, 15 May 1665.
11. *Ibid.*, 29 June 1663.
12. The 'great letter of reproof' is transcribed in *Diary*, 18 November 1663.

Chapter Six: The Right Hand of the Navy

1. See *Diary* 20 July 1664 ff.
2. *Ibid.*, 23 July 1664.
3. *Letterbook* f. 149, 24 January 1665.
4. *Diary*, 1 June 1664.
5. *Ibid.*, 14 July 1664 ff.
6. *Ibid.*, 10 September 1663.
7. *Ibid.*, 2 February 1664.
8. For a discussion of Pepys's business morality, see Bernard Pool, *Navy Board Contracts*. pp. 37–40.
9. *Diary*, 18 January 1665.
10. Clarendon (Edward Hyde), Earl of, *The Life of Edward Clarendon*, vol. II, p. 192.
11. For Downing's scheme see. *Ibid.*, pp. 190–91.
12. *Diary*, 12 April 1665.
13. For the Press Gangs, see Christopher Lloyd, *The British Seaman*, pp. 75–8.
14. *Diary*, 30 April 64.

Chapter Seven: The Years of Agony

1. *Diary*, 8 June 1665.
2. See *Ibid.*, 30 June 1665 ff.
3. R. G. Howarth (ed.), *Letters and Second Diary of Samuel Pepys*, pp. 24–5.
4. See *Diary*, 10 September 1665.
5. For the incident of the prizes, see *Diary*, 10 September 1665 ff.
6. *Naval Minutes*, p. 250.
7. For Pursers, see Christopher Lloyd, *The British Seaman*, p. 90.
8. See Bernard Pool, *Navy Board Contracts*, pp. 1–43. *passim*.
9. For Mrs Knepp, see *Diary*, 5 January 1666 ff.
10. *Ibid.*, 13 June 1666.
11. See J. R. Jones, *The First Whigs: The Politics of the Exclusion Crisis, 1678–1683*, pp. 1–19.

12. Andrew Marvell, *The Last Instructions to a Painter*, ll. 286–94.
13. For Treasury administration, see Howard Tomlinson, 'Financial and Administrative Development in England, 1660–88' in J. R. Jones (ed.), *The Restored Monarchy, 1660–1688*, pp. 94–117.

Chapter Eight: Perpetual Trouble and Vexation

1. *Diary*, 14 July 1667.
2. For Pepys and the defence of the Navy Office, see *Diary*, 21 October 1667 ff.
3. For the ticket system, see Christopher Lloyd, *The English Seaman*, pp. 82–4.
4. *Diary*, 30 October 67.
5. See *Diary*, 4–5 March 1668 ff.

Chapter Nine: Darkness

1. *Diary*, 31 March 1668.
2. Notes on the journey, made between 5 and 17 June, were written on sheets of paper inserted into the *Diary*.
3. *Diary*, 18–19. June 1668.
4. *Ibid.*, 29 June 1668.
5. *Ibid.*, 27 October 1668.
6. *Ibid.*, 20 November 1668.
7. The memorandum is reproduced in J. R. Tanner (ed.) *Further Correspondence*, pp.230–35.
8. *Diary*, 12 January 1669.
9. *Ibid.*, 31 May 1669.

Chapter Ten: An Encirclement of Enemies

1. For Pepys's health, see '*The Present Ill State of my Health, 7. 11. 1677*', Rawlinson Mss, A 185, ff. 206–13.
2. See *Miscellanies*, vol. VI, Pepys Library, 2874.
3. *Ibid.*
4. John Evelyn, *Diary*, 19 February 1671.
5. For Mary Skinner v. Arthur Bryant, *The Years of Peril*, pp. 48–9.
6. Rawlinson Mss, A 182, f.475.
7. Cited in J. R. Jones, *Charles II: Royal Politician*, p. 98.
8. For full details of this aspect of Pepys's job see G. F. James and J. J. Sutherland Shaw, 'Admiralty Administration and Personnel, 1619–1714', *Bulletin of the Institute of Historical Research* XIV (1936–7), p. 168.
9. J. R. Tanner (ed.), *Further Correspondence*, p. 273.
10. A. Grey, *Debates in the House of Commons*, vol. II, p. 408.
11. Lord Peterborough, in *Succinct Genealogies*, cited in J. R. Jones, *The First Whigs*, p. 16, fn. 2.
12. Rawlinson Mss, A 172, f. 135.

Chapter Eleven: At the Admiralty

1. Rawlinson Mss A 181 f.11.
2. Cited in Arthur Bryant, *The Years of Peril*, p. 100.
3. *Admiralty Journal*, Catalogue Pepysian Mss, IV, p. 383.
4. Cited in Bryant, *op. cit.*, p. 124.
5. R. G. Howarth (ed.), *Letters and Second Diary of Samuel Pepys*, pp. 67 ff.
6. For this incident, see Richard Ollard, *Samuel Pepys: A Biography*, pp. 224 ff.
7. J. R. Tanner (ed.), *Samuel Pepys's Naval Minutes*, p. 62.
8. *Ibid.*
9. J. Houblon to Pepys, 23 April 1675, cited in Bryant, *op. cit.*, p. 120.

10. Edward Barlow, *Journal*, cited in Christopher Lloyd, *The British Seaman*, p. 86.
11. For Pepys's speeches to Parliament, see. A. Grey, *Debates in the House of Commons*, vol. III, pp. 34 ff.
12. *Ibid*, vol. IV, pp. 103–15.
13. Cited in Bryant, *op. cit.*, p. 199.

Chapter Twelve: Pepys and the Popish Plot

1. Cited in J. P. Kenyon, *The Popish Plot*, p. 97.
2. For the fullest available account of the enormous quantities of material on Scott gathered by Pepys in his *Two Books of Mornamont* and elsewhere, see Bryant, *The Years of Peril*, chapters 8–13.
3. Cited *Ibid.*, p. 227.
4. Rawlinson Mss A 190, f. 56.
5. Cited in Bryant, *op. cit.*, p. 283.
6. *Ibid.*, p. 276.
7. *Plain Truth of Closet Discourse Betwixt P. and H.*
8. Rawlinson Mss A 194 f. 67.
9. *A Hue and Cry after P. and H.*
10. Pepysian Mss, *Mornamont*, vol. II, 1.192 ff.
11. Cited in Tim Harris, *London Crowds in the Reign of Charles II*, p. 150.
12. *Ibid.* p. 131.

Chapter Thirteen: The Uses of Adversity

1. John Evelyn to Pepys, 25 June 1680, in Guy de la Bedoyere (ed.), *Particular Friends: The Correspondence of Samuel Pepys and John Evelyn*, p. 102.
2. John Evelyn to Pepys, 3 January 1680, *Ibid.*, p. 94.
3. John Evelyn to Pepys, 7 July 1680, *Ibid.*, p. 103.
4. Cited in Arthur Bryant, *The Years of Peril*, p. 375.
5. J. R. Tanner (ed.), *Samuel Pepys's Naval Minutes*, p. 102.

6. Cited in Bryant, *op. cit.*, p. 387.
7. *Ibid.*, p. 378.
8. Pepys to John Evelyn, 7 August 1683, *Particular Friends*, p. 141.
9. Edwin Chappell (ed.), *The Tangier Papers of Samuel Pepys*, p. 295.
10. *Ibid.*, p. 117.
11. *Ibid.*, pp. 21–2.
12. Cited in Arthur Bryant, *The Saviour of the Navy*, p. 59.

Chapter Fourteen: Return to the Admiralty

1. Cited in Bryant, *The Saviour of the Navy*, p. 87.
2. Pepysian Mss, No. 1534.
3. 27 April 85, Pepysian Mss, *Administrative Letters*, vol. X, p. 444.
4. *Ibid.*, 9 June 1685, vol. iv, p. 37.
5. Cited in Bryant, *op. cit.*, p. 144.
6. 16 December 86, Rawlinson Mss A 189, ff. 261–3.
7. John Evelyn, *Diary*, 19 April 1687.
8. Cited in Bryant, *op. cit.*, p. 235.
9. J. P. Kenyon, *The Stuart Constitution*, p. 445.
10. G. Burnet, *History of My Own Time*, cited in J. Miller, *The Glorious Revolution*, p. 12.
11. Cited in Bryant, *op. cit.*, p. 288.

Chapter Fifteen: Retirement

1. John Evelyn, *Diary*, 26 May 1703.
2. John Evelyn to Pepys, 11 June 1690, in de la Bedoyere, *Particular Friends*, p. 315.
3. *Correspondence*, vol. I, p. 59.
4. Cited in Richard Ollard, *Samuel Pepys: A Biography*, p. 388.
5. *Ibid.*, p. 329.
6. John Evelyn to Pepys, 26 September 1690, in *Particular Friends*, p. 225.

7. Pepys to John Evelyn, 7 November 1694, *ibid.*, pp. 253–4.
8. Cited in Ollard, *op. cit.*, p. 333.
9. John Jackson to John Evelyn, 28 May 1703, in *Particular Friends*, p. 315.
10. Cited in Ollard, *op. cit.*, p. 340.
11. John Evelyn, *Diary*, 26 May 1703.

BIBLIOGRAPHY

A Hue and Cry after P. and H., London, 1679.

Aylmer, Gerald E., *The State's Servants, The Civil Service of the English Republic 1649–1660*, Routledge and Kegan Paul, 1973.

Bell, Walter G., *The Great Fire of London* (reprinted), Bracken Books, 1994.

Bennett, Martyn, *The English Civil War, 1640–1649*, Longman, 1995.

Beresford, John, *The Godfather of Downing Street: Sir George Downing*, London, 1925.

Brome, Vincent, *The Other Pepys*, Weidenfeld and Nicholson, 1992.

Bryant, Arthur, *Samuel Pepys: The Man in the Making*, Collins, rev. ed. 1947.

Samuel Pepys: The Years of Peril, Collins, rev. ed. 1948.

Samuel Pepys: The Saviour of the Navy, Collins, rev. ed. 1949.

Calendar of the Manuscripts of the Marquesses of Ormonde, N.S., London, 1902.

Calendar of State Papers, Domestic Series, 1860–1921

Carlton, Charles, *Going to the Wars: The Experience of the British Civil Wars 1638–1651*, Routledge, 1992.

Chappell, E. (ed.), *Shorthand Letters of Samuel Pepys*, Cambridge University Press, 1933.

The Tangier Papers of Samuel Pepys, Navy Records Society, 1935.

Clarendon, (E. Hyde) Earl of, *The Life of Edward Earl of Clarendon*, Oxford, 1760

Commons' Journals

Costello, William T., *The Scholastic Curriculum at Early Seventeenth Century Cambridge*, Cambridge, Mass., Harvard University Press, 1958.

de la Bedoyere, Guy, (ed.), *Particular Friends: The Correspondence of Samuel Pepys and John Evelyn*, Boydell Press, 1997.

Erhman, J., *The Navy in the War of William III*, Cambridge University Press, 1953.

E.S. de Beer (ed.), *The Diary of John Evelyn*, 6 vols., Oxford University Press 1955.

Fox, Frank, *Great Ships: The Battlefleet of King Charles II*, Greenwich, Conway Maritime Press, 1980.

Grey, A., *Debates in the House of Commons*, 1769.

Harris, Tim, *London Crowds in the Reign of Charles II: Propaganda and Politics from the Restoration until the Exclusion Crisis*, Cambridge University Press, 1987.

Howarth, R.G. (ed.), *Letters and the Second Diary of Samuel Pepys*, 1932.

Israel, Jonathan, *The Dutch Republic: Its Rise, Greatness, and Fall, 1477–1806*, Clarendon Press, 1995.

James, G.F., and J.J. Sutherland Shaw, 'Admiralty Administration and Personnel, 1619–1714', *Bulletin of the Institute of Historical Research*, xiv, (1936–7), pp. 166–83.

Jones, J. R., *The Anglo-Dutch Wars of the Seventeenth Century*, Longman, 1996.

Charles II: Royal Politician, Allen and Unwin, 1987.

The First Whigs: The Politics of the Exclusion Crisis, 1678–1683, Oxford University Press, 1961.

(ed.), *The Restored Monarchy*, Macmillan, 1979.

Kenyon, John, *The Civil Wars of England*, Weidenfeld and Nicholson, 1988.

The Popish Plot, Penguin Books, 1974.

The Stuart Constitution, Cambridge University Press, 1966.

Kishlansky, Mark, *A Nation Transformed: Britain 1603–1714*, Penguin Books, 1996.

Lloyd, Christopher, *The British Seaman, 1200–1860: A Social Survey*, Collins, 1968.

Latham, Robert and William Matthews, (eds.), *The Diary of Samuel Pepys*, 11 vols., Bell and Sons, 1970–83.

Miller, John, *The Glorious Revolution*, Longman, 1983.

Milton, John, *Tractate of Education*, London, 1644.

Marvell, Andrew, *The Last Instructions to a Painter*, London, 1689.

Ogg, D., *England in the Reign of Charles II*, Oxford University Press, 1934.

Ollard, Richard, *Cromwell's Earl: A Life of Edward Montagu 1st Earl of Sandwich*, Harper Collins, 1994.

Pepys: A Biography, Hodder and Stoughton, 1974.

Oppenheim, M., *A History of the Administration of the Royal Navy and of Merchant Shipping in Relation to the Navy, from MDIX to MDCLX with an Introduction Treating of the Preceding Period*, 2 vols, London, 1896.

Padfield, Peter, *Maritime Supremacy and the Opening of the Western Mind*, John Murray, 1999.

Pawson, G. P. H., *The Cambridge Platonists*, S.P.C.K., 1930.

Picard, Liza, *Restoration London*, Weidenfield and Nicholson, 1997.

Plain Truth of Closet Discourse Betwixt P. and H., London, 1679.

Pool, Bernard, *Navy Board Contracts 1660–1832: Contract Administration under the Navy Board*, Longmans, 1966.

Porter, Stephen (ed.), *London and the Civil War*, Macmillan Press, 1996.

Ranft, B. M. 'The Political Career of Samuel Pepys', *Journal of Modern History*, xxiv, no. 4, pp. 368–75.

Rawlinson Manuscripts.

Roseveare, Henry, *The Financial Revolution*, Longman, 1991.

Tanner, J. R. (ed.), *A Descriptive Catalogue of the Naval Manuscripts in the Pepysian Library at Magdalene College, Cambridge*, 4 vols, Navy Record Society, 1903–23.

Private Correspondence and Miscellaneous Papers of Samuel Pepys, London, 1926.

Further Correspondence and Miscellaneous Papers of Samuel Pepys, London, 1929.

Samuel Pepys's Naval Minutes, Navy Records Society, 1926.

Tedder, Arthur, W., *The Navy of the Restoration from the death of Cromwell to the Treaty of Breda; its Work, Growth and Influence*, Cambridge, 1916.

Truesdell, Helen (ed.), *The Letters of Samuel Pepys and his Family Circle*, Oxford University Press, 1955.

Wedgewood, C. V., *The Trial of Charles I*, Collins, 1964.

Wheatley, Henry B. (ed.), *The Diary of Samuel Pepys*, Supplementary volume, *Pepysiana*, London, 1899.

Whitear, Walter H. (ed.), *More Pepysiana: Being Notes on the Diary of Samuel Pepys and on the Genealogy of the Family with Corrected Pedigrees*, London, 1927.

Wilson, Charles, H., *Profit and Power: A Study of England and the Dutch Wars*, Longmans, 1957.

INDEX

actresses 80
Admiralty 254, 261, 264, 288
  Special Commission (1686–88) 332–3, 338
Africa, Company of Royal Adventurers into 96
Albemarle, Duke of *see* Monck, George
Allbon, Dr 224
Amsterdam 52–3
Anderson, Charles 15, 50
Anglesey, Arthur Annesley, Earl of 217, 248
Anglo-Dutch Wars
  First (1652–54) 16, 18
  Second (1665–7) 148, 157, 158, 164–5, 168, 175–8, 191–2
    costs 184
    preparations 151–5
  Third (1672–4) 228, 250–1, 253
Argyll, Archibald Campbell, Earl of 328
Arlington, Henry Bennet, Earl of 230
Ashwell, Mary (companion to EP) 116, 117, 118, 123
Atkins, Captain Charles 276
Atkins, Samuel 264, 285–6, 303, 321
Aylmer, Captain 318
Aylmer, Lieutenant George 268

Backwell, Edward 149, 197
Bagwell, Mrs 121–3, 131, 134–5, 160, 164, 188, 335
Bagwell, William 122–3, 135, 335
Banks, Sir John 245–6
Barlow, Thomas 58, 60–1
Batten, Sir William 61, 69–70, 72, 89, 91, 92, 182, 205, 248
  timber contracts 143–4
Beale, Charles 59, 60
Becke, Betty 124
Beggars' Bush (play) (Fletcher) 80, 81
Berkeley, Charles, Earl of Falmouth 158
Berkeley, George, Baron 136
Berry, Sir John 314, 319
Birch, Jane (SP's maid) 25–6, 73, 110, 179, 183
Birchensha, John 79–80
Blake, Robert [General at Sea] 18, 19
Booth, Sir William 314–15
Bowyer, Robert 28, 41
Bowyer, William 28
Boyle, Richard 158
Brereton, William, Baron 240, 241
Brooke House Committee (1668–70) 205, 206, 238–43
Brooke, Sir Robert 204
Brouncker, William, Viscount 136, 165, 166, 204, 208, 220, 238, 323
Buckingham, George Villiers, Duke of 222
Burnet, Dr Alexander 138, 163
Burr, John (SP's clerk) 45
Burrow, Elizabeth 188

Cade, John 34
Cambridge University
  curriculum (1650s) 12, 13
  SP at 12–15
Carteret, Elizabeth, Lady 160, 161
Carteret, Sir George 58, 61, 87, 89, 144, 160, 161, 205
  attitude to Coventry 100, 101
Carteret, Lady Jemimah (*née* Montagu) 160, 161, 162
Carteret, Sir Philip 160–1, 162
Castle Rising, Norfolk 255–6

Castlemaine, Barbara Palmer, Countess of 119–20, 173
Catherine of Braganza, Princess 88
chaplains, naval 266
Charles I (1600–49), King 4–5, 98
  execution 1–2
Charles II (1630–85), King 37–8, 49–50, 210, 211, 284, 286, 303
  Restoration arrangements 47–8, 54–5
  prerogative powers 48, 98, 228, 244, 296
  tells of escape from Worcester 54, 302
  coronation 72–4, 75
  excessive self-indulgence 119
  mistresses 119–20
  Great Fire of London 180, 181
  the Grand Design 228, 244–5
  and Brooke House Committee 239, 240, 242, 243
  French subsidies 244, 249, 303
  becoming alienated from subjects 249–50
  puts Admiralty in commission 254
  replaces Admiralty commissioners with opposition members 288
  dissolves Parliament (1681) 304
  consults SP on naval matters 308
  dissolves Admiralty Commission 323
  death 326
  deathbed conversion to Catholicism 329
Chatham Chest 92, 248, 308, 324
Chatham dockyard 62, 106, 308, 330
Child, Sir Josiah 353
Christ's Hospital Mathematical School 265–6, 309, 310
Clarendon, Edward Hyde, Earl of 50, 74, 149, 150, 190, 228
  relations with SP 141–2
Clarke, Dr Timothy 87–8, 88–9, 115
Clifford, Sir Thomas 148, 220–1
Cocke, Captain George 96, 165, 166–7, 168, 189–90
Committee for Accounts (Brooke House Committee) 205, 206, 238–43
Committee of Miscarriages 202, 203–4, 205
Committee of Navy Accounts 184
Committee of Safety 32, 33
Committee to investigate Miscarriages of the Navy 288, 290
Cooper, Richard 87, 115–16
court, public criticism 173, 193, 206
Coventry, Sir William (1627–86) 58, 144, 159, 171, 195, 206, 210, 217, 218, 230, 238
  Secretary to Lord High Admiral 53
  appointed Navy commissioner 100
  row with Carteret 101
  growing friendship with SP 101
  view of public service 102
  battle of Lowestoft 158
  attends Myngs' funeral 177
  Treasury commissioner 190–1
  resigns as Secretary to Lord High Admiral 205
  advises SP how to handle Parliamentary committees 205
  speaks up for SP in Commons 291
Crew, John 36
Crisp, Diana 65, 66
Crisp, Mrs 65, 67
Cromleholme, Samuel 10
Cromwell, Oliver (1599–1658), Lord Protector 16, 18, 19, 29–30, 71–2
Cromwell, Richard 30, 31
Cumberland, Richard 15

Dampier, William 355
Danby, Thomas Osborne, Earl of 265, 291
Daniel, Mrs 188, 189
Dartmouth, George Legge, Baron 272, 321, 322, 325
  expedition to evacuate Tangier 312, 313, 320
  fleet commander 345, 346–7, 348, 349
Davenant, Sir William 80, 81, 175
Davis, John 63
Deane, Sir Anthony (?1638–1721) 104–5, 141, 289, 291, 330, 352
  Admiralty commissioner 332–3, 344
Declaration of Indulgence (1672) 249–50, 252–3
Declarations of Indulgence (1687, 1688) 341, 342
Deptford dockyard 62, 63
  shipwrights 135–6
Diggers 16

dockyards, naval 63, 105, 107, 151, 325, *see also* Chatham; Deptford; Portsmouth; Woolwich
Donluis, Phelix 298–9
Dover, (Secret) Treaty of (1670) 245, 249
Downing, Sir George 51, 218, 239, 249
  early career 26
  English Resident at The Hague, intimidatory methods 26, 97
  financial reforms 149–50
  secretary to Treasury Commissioners 190–1
Dryden, John 136
The Duke's Company 81
Dutch Republic 51–2
  maritime trade 52, 96
  merchants 52–3

East India Company (Dutch) *see* United East India Company
Evelyn, John (1620–1706) 247, 329, 337, 340, 354
  friendship with SP 165–6, 245, 291, 350, 352, 357, 358–9
  encourages SP to support Royal Society 305
  encourages SP to write *Navalia* 306–7
  tribute to SP 359–60
Exchequer 26, 27, 150
Exclusion Crisis 280, 285, 287, 291, 295–6, 303, 304, 345

financiers 149
fireships 177–8
fishermen, Barking and Greenwich 152
Ford, Sir Richard 91, 92
Four Days' Fight (1666) 176–7
Foxe's *Book of Martyrs* 183–4
Fuller, William 28

Gale, Dr Thomas 307–8, 355
Gauden, Sir Denis 62, 154, 168, 169–70, 190, 358
Gibbons, Grinling 245
Gibraltar 321
Gloucester, Prince Henry, Duke of 53
Godfrey, Sir Edmund Berry 283, 284, 285, 296–7
Godolphin, Sir William 232
Gosnell, ?Winifred 113
Grafton (ship) 312, 313–14, 320, 322
Great Fire of London (1666) 179–83
Great Plague of London (1665) 158, 159–60, 162–4
Greatorex, Ralph 85
Gresham College 85
Gwyn, Nell 81

Hales, John 78
Halifax, George Savile, Marquess of 303, 343
Harbord, Sir Charles, jnr 232
Harbord, William 281, 288, 289, 298, 299, 301
Harris, John 144
Harrison, Major-General Thomas, execution 71
Hart, Charles 81
Hartlib, Samuel 28
Hawley, John 27–8, 36, 131
Hayter, Thomas 182, 208
Hely, Mrs 6
Herbert, Arthur [admiral] 323, 328, 340, 345, 347, 350, 351
  naval abuses 314, 318, 319, 321, 324
  takes letter to William of Orange inviting invasion 343
Hewer, William (1642–1715) 87, 129, 183, 195, 208, 245, 299, 302, 325, 350, 352, 358
  employed by SP 61
  friendship with SP 61, 207
  acts in Deb Willet affair 226, 227
  lends SP rooms in York Buildings 293
  expedition to evacuate Tangier 312, 314, 318
  Admiralty commissioner 332, 333
Hewson, Colonel 32, 33
Hickes, George 359
Hinchinbrooke, Hunts 7
Hollier, Thomas 22, 23, 138
Holmes' Bonfire (1666) 178
Holmes, Sir Robert 115–16, 178
Hooke, Robert 85, 136–7, 247
Houblon family 293, 354
Houblon, Sir James (?1629–1700) 246, 267, 270, 291, 303, 311, 329, 337, 353

Howard, Henry, Earl of Norwich 255, 256
Hughes, William 91, 92
Hyde, Edward *see* Clarendon

Jackson, John (SP's nephew) 354, 359
Jackson, Paulina (Pall) (SP's sister) 4, 110, 114, 189
Jackson, Samuel (SP's nephew) 354
Jaggard, Abraham 197
James, Duke of York (1633–1701) 58, 170, 311–12
 relationship with SP 99, 148, 210, 217, 219, 311
 and Restoration 53
 as Lord High Admiral 61, 62, 93, 95–6, 238
  anti-Dutch policies 96, 97
  raises funds for Second Anglo-Dutch War 148
  battle of Lowestoft 158
  discusses reform of Navy Board with SP 218, 222
  approves SP's paper on Administration of the Navy 230
  battle of Sole Bay 250
  resigns office 253
 and Great Fire of London 180, 181, 182
 marries Mary Beatrice of Modena 256
 and Popish Plot 284, 285
 temporary exile 287
 and Exclusion Crisis 291, 295–6
 Lord High Commissioner in Scotland 296
 and naval reform 322, 323, 325
 succeeds to throne 326
 coronation 327
 as King James II 327–8, 329, 333
  alienates goodwill 330
  pursues Catholic policies 338, 340, 340–1, 342
  and Seven Bishops' Case 342
  futile expedition to repel Dutch invasion 347–8
  flees the country 348–9, 350
James I, King 97–8
James, John 262, 289–90, 290–1, 293, 299–300
Jarvas, Richard 129
Jeffreys, Sir George 329, 342, 349
Jenkins, Eliezer (SP's foot-boy) 45
Joyne, John 295

Ken, Thomas, Bishop of Bath and Wells 312, 329
Killigrew, Thomas 80, 81
The King's Company 80, 81
King's Theatre 82
Kirke, Lady Mary 316, 317
Kirke, Colonel Percy 317, 329
Knepp, Elizabeth (*née* Carpenter) 174–5, 189, 214
Knight, Sir John 281
Kynaston, Edward 81

Lane, Betty *see* Martin, Betty
Lane, Doll *see* Powell, Doll
Langley, John 10
Lawes, Henry 79
Lawrence, Goody 2, 6
Lawson, Sir John 45
Legge, George *see* Dartmouth
Levant Company 152
Levellers 9, 16
lithotomies 22, 23
London 2–3, 4–5, 7, 8–9, 32–3
 growth of sectarianism 9, 63
 Great Plague (1665) 158, 159–60, 162–4
 Great Fire (1666) 179–83
 rebuilding 197–8
Londoners, health 3
Lorrain, Paul 302, 356
Louis XIV, King of France 98, 99, 175, 228, 244, 245, 250, 251, 253, 303, 339
Lowestoft, battle (1665) 157, 158, 175
Luellin, Peter 28

Martin, Betty (née Lane) 28, 65, 121, 129–31, 131–2, 188, 189, 198
Martin, John 84
Mary Beatrice of Modena, Duchess of York 256
Mary Stuart, Princess of Orange (later Mary II, Queen of England) 340, 341
Mason, John 206
Medway, Dutch raid (1667) 191–2, 193
Micrographia (Hooke) 85

A Midsummer Night's Dream (Shakespeare) 82
Milton, John 246
Mitchell, Ann 28
Mitchell, Betty (née Howlett) 28, 189
Mitchell, Miles 28
monarchy 97–8, 99
Monck, George, Duke of Albemarle 154, 158, 168, 176, 187, 192
  marches on London 36–7, 38, 39
  Restoration arrangements 47
Monmouth, James Scott, Duke of 257, 296, 328, 329
Monmouth's Rebellion (1685) 328–9
Montagu, Edward, 1st Earl of Sandwich (1625–72) 26, 29, 44, 141, 160, 232
  relationship with SP 46, 47, 56–7, 63–4, 126
  early career 8, 18
  Joint General at Sea 18, 19–20
  Baltic mission 31–2
  stripped of appointments 32
  invites SP to become his secretary 39–40
  Restoration arrangements 45, 46, 47, 48, 53
  created Earl of Sandwich 56
  attends on Charles II 57
  obtains promise of Clerk of the Acts for SP 57–8
  at Charles II's coronation 73, 74
  serious illness 124
  liaison with Betty Becke 124–5
  SP's letter of reproof 125–6
  battle of Lowestoft 157, 158
  commands fleet 164–5, 166
  prize goods affair 166, 167, 168
  ambassador to Spain 169
  death and funeral 250, 251
Montagu, Edward, 2nd Earl of Manchester 8
Montagu, Edward, Viscount Hinchinbrooke (Sandwich's son) 49–50, 232
Montagu, Jemima, Countess of Sandwich (My Lady) 112
Montagu, Paulina, Lady (née Pepys) (SP's great-aunt) 8
Montagu, Sidney 232
Montagu, Sir Sydney (Sandwich's father) 7–8
Moore, Henry 28
Morelli, Cesare 263, 290, 291, 293
Morland, Sir Samuel 13–14
Muddiman, Henry 36
Muskerry, Lord 158
Myngs, Sir Christopher 176, 177

Narborough, Sir John 276
Naseby (ship) 46, 47, 48, 51
  rechristened *Royal Charles* 54
national debt 150
national revenue, administration 127–8
naval abuses 171, 266–8, 272, 317–18, 324
  'good voyages' 266, 308, 318, 319, 321, 333–4
Naval Hospital, Greenwich 165, 357–8
Navy Board 57, 164, 264, 308, 327, 331–2, 333
  principal officers 61
  responsibilities and duties 61–2, 91
  victualling the fleet 62, 154
  want of money 62
  Lord High Admiral's Instructions 91, 92, 218
  timber requirements 103, 104
  considers Holmes' case against Cooper 116
  timber contracts 143–4
  financial difficulties 127, 128, 151, 172, 186, 187, 190, 252
  asks King and Privy Council for funds 186–7
  answers to Committee of Miscarriages 203
  Committee of Accounts examines expenditure 205
  defence before Commons 209
  failings 217, 218–19
  members aggrieved at SP's indictment 220, 222
  budget fixed 227
  responsibilities defined 229
  SP defends before Brooke House Committee 238–43
  required to report to SP on state of navy 324
Navy Board commissioners 69
Navy List 321–2
navy, Parliamentarian 61–2, 127

navy, Royal, *see also* Four Days' Fight; Lowestoft (battle); Medway (Dutch raid); Sole Bay (battle)
victualling 62, 154, 169–70, 178, 272–3
ships 107, 151
impressed crews 152–3
gentlemen *v.* tarpaulins 153–4, 176, 269, 314
pursers 171–2
ships laid up in Medway 190
winter and summer fleets 227
officer training and examination 271–2
need for expansion of fleet 273–4
deterioration and decay 308, 314, 320–1, 325–6, 330
New York 96
Nieuw Amsterdam 52, 96

Oates, Titus 283–4, 286
Ormonde, James Butler, Duke of 88, 268
Ossory, Lord 272

Paget, Edward 310
Parliament 4, 11, 31, *see also* Committees
Rump Parliament 16, 31, 32, 33, 37
Nominated Parliament 16
and Restoration 47
grants of supply 128, 140, 148, 172, 184, 252
Members' groupings 184–6
takes on more powerful role 187–8
scrutiny of royal plans and spending 205
votes supply for building ships 278
Pembleton (EP's dancing master) 117, 118, 123, 189
Penn, Sir William 70, 72, 87, 89, 92–3, 152, 164
career 69
Pennington, Mrs 173–4
Pepys, Elizabeth (1640–69) (SP's wife, *née* St Michel) 66, 70, 159, 189, 195
background 17
domestic shortcomings 21, 64
health 21, 64
and servants 25
marries SP 17
early married life 17, 21–2, 27, 34
arrangements for while SP at sea 41, 42
moves to Seething Lane 60
visits Brampton 87, 109
desire for lady companion 113–14
quarrels with SP 114–15, 117
Mary Ashwell as companion 116, 117, 123
and dancing master 117, 118
sent to Brampton 118
and Great Fire of London 179, 181, 182, 183
takes SP's gold to Brampton 194, 199
quarrels with SP 199–200
Deb Willet as companion 200
holiday in Brampton 213, 214
holiday tour with SP and Deb to West Country 214–15
expresses resentment 215
craves tenderness 216
angry with SP over Deb 221, 222, 223, 225–6, 227, 231
determined to humiliate SP 223, 226
marriage saved 233
drives out with SP in new coach 232–3
continental holiday with SP and Balty 235–6
death and burial 236, 237
Pepys family 6–7
Pepys, John (of Ashtead) 6
Pepys, John (SP's brother) 4, 42, 110, 247–8
Pepys, John (SP's father) 2, 3–4, 6, 7, 11, 41, 67, 189, 194, 302
disputes over brother Robert's will 111–12
Pepys, Margaret (SP's mother) 2, 4, 7, 159, 189
Pepys, Paulina (Pall) (SP's sister) *see* Jackson, Paulina
Pepys, Robert (SP's uncle) 7, 25, 40, 73, 111
Pepys, Samuel (1633–1703)
appearance 78
attitudes
monarchism 38, 74, 100, 282
philosophy of pleasure 76
to work 90–1, 100, 128–9, 135–6, 139, 237, 265

character and personality 17, 20, 64, 76, 90–1, 100, 169
clothes 66, 78, 146, 157
drink, hangovers 41, 70–1, 75–6
family matters 189
  death of brother Tom 110–11
  disputes over uncle Robert's will 111–12
  assists John (brother) to become Clerk of Trinity House 247–8
finances 21, 25, 34, 35, 36, 56, 64, 66, 68, 73, 146, 150, 157, 168, 245, 262
food 76–7, 109
friendships 15, 27–8, 29, 245–6, 306
  Sir William Coventry 101, 171, 291
  Sir Anthony Deane 104
  John Evelyn 165–6, 245, 291, 305, 306–7, 350, 352, 357, 358–9
  William Hewer 61, 207, 293, 350, 358
  Sir James Houblon 246, 291, 303
health 33, 263, 353, 358–9
  eye trouble 88, 137, 154, 219–20, 233–4, 235, 237–8, 253, 263
  kidney stone 5–6, 15, 22
  lithotomy (1658) 22–3, 46
  renal colic (?) 137–8
interests
  books and reading 82–5, 263
    library 83, 178, 263, 356
  collections 263, 356–7
  music 14, 129, 337
    Beauty Retire 78, 174–5
    lessons 79–80
    love of 79
  science 85–6, 87, 88, 337
  theatre 80–2, 116, 195
perquisites of office 40, 43–4, 104, 144–5, 147–8, 168, 245, 262, 279, 336
relationship with Elizabeth 64, 66, 68, 112–13, 189
  early married life 17, 21–2, 27, 34, 41, 42
  meanness towards 112
  disregards requests for companion 113, 114
  destroys her letters 114–15
  makes up quarrel 115
  suspects relationship with dancing master 117–18
  squabbles alternate with content 123
  relationship deteriorates 199–200, 215–17
  quarrels 221, 222, 223, 225–6, 231
  promises to see no more of other women 222
  realises Elizabeth will have upper hand 224
  asks Will Hewer to mediate 226
  fearful of Elizabeth 230–1
  marriage saved 233
  drives out with Elizabeth in new coach 232–3
relationship with Edward Montagu (Sandwich) 46, 47, 56–7
relationship with Balthasar St Michel (Balty) (brother-in-law) 44, 189, 247, 353–4
relationship with Mary Skinner (companion) 246–7
relationship with Duke of York 217, 219, 287, 311
religion 17, 29, 65, 90
residences
  Salisbury Court 2, 182
  Whitehall apartment 18, 21
  Axe Yard 25, 33, 65, 66
  Seething Lane 60, 67–8, 109, 245, 252
    dinner parties 67, 68–9, 232
  Derby House 261–2, 263, 324
  York Buildings 293, 325, 353, 358
  14 Buckingham Street 336–7
  Clapham 358
Royal Society, association with 86, 136–7, 305–6, 337
sexual curiosity and appetite 15, 28, 109–10, 119, 129
  prurient interest in royal mistresses 120–1, 164
sexual attractions and encounters 64–5, 157, 160, 164, 173–4, 188–9, 198–9, 221
  Betty Martin (Lane) 65, 121, 129–30, 131–2, 188, 189, 198

Mary Ashwell (EP's companion) 116
Mrs Bagwell 121–3, 131, 134–5, 160, 164, 188
Jane Welsh 129, 131, 133, 134
Elizabeth Knepp 174, 189, 214
Doll Powell (Lane) 188, 189, 198
Deb Willet (EP's companion) 200, 201, 213–14, 221, 222, 223–5
fear of disease 133
visits Fleet Alley brothels 132–3
writings
Books of Mornament 302
Diary 34–5, 46, 194, 234, 252, 356
Memoirs 351–2
Navalia 263, 306–7, 356
Tangier Journal 313
birth and infancy 2
boyhood 3, 4
witnesses Charles I's execution 1–2
Puritan upbringing 4, 7
great discomfort from kidney stone 5–6
boards at Kingsland 6
visits Ashtead 6
calf-love 6
lives with Cambridgeshire relatives 7
returns to London 8
schooling
attends Huntingdon Grammar School (*c.*1644) 8
attends St Paul's School (*c.*1646–50) 9–10
influence of teachers 10–11
wins Mercers' Company scholarship to Cambridge 11
university education
enters Trinity Hall, Cambridge (1650) 11
transfers to Magdalene College 12
university studies 12–14
acquires shorthand facility 13
unofficial curriculum 14–15
sexual interests 15
composes romance 15
graduates (1654) 15
returns to London 15–16
marries Elizabeth St Michel (1655) 17
Montagu's man-of-business and informant 18–20, 22
clerk in the Exchequer 25, 26, 27, 28–9
member of the Rota Club 30
takes letters to Montagu in Baltic 32
Montagu's London correspondent 32–3
reviews his life 33–4
commences *Diary* 34–6
notes preparations for Restoration 37, 38–9
secretary to Montagu 39–42, 43–4, 44–5, 45–6, 57
at sea 46–7
Restoration arrangements 48, 53
in Holland 48–51
makes will 42
hears Charles II's account of escape from Worcester 54
commitment to Stuart cause 55
secures appointment as Clerk of the Acts (Navy Board) (1660) 57–60
moves to Seething Lane 60
agreement with Barlow 60–1
employs William Hewer 61
first brushes with MPs 62
visits Deptford dockyard 63
clerkship, Privy Seal Office (1660) 63–4
throws first dinner party at Seething Lane 67, 68–9
opinions of Batten and Penn 69–70
attends Harrison execution 71
attends Charles II's coronation 72–4, 75
takes music lessons 79–80
learns multiplication tables 86–7
visits Portsmouth 87–9
disagreements with Batten and Penn 89–90, 92–3
unmasks numerous abuses 91–2, 100
fears Coventry as rival 100–1
growing friendship with Coventry 101
determined to have Coventry as ally 101
appreciation of merchants' abilities 102
learns about timber industry 103

mutually beneficial agreement with Warren 104
learns about timber measuring from Deane 104
visits naval dockyards 105–6
learns about ship construction 107
Younger Brother of Trinity House (1662) 108
relinquishes Privy Seal Office post (1662) 108
appointed to Tangier Committee (1662) 108
investigates complaints about Cooper 115
confrontation with Holmes over Cooper 116
concerned at gossip over Sandwich's liaison 124
sends letter of reproof 125–6
acquires job on Fishery Commission (1664) 126
detailed study of Navy Office contracts 128–9
becomes Fellow of Royal Society (1665) 136
Warwick instructs on public finances 138–41
offends Clarendon 141–2
successfully defends timber contract with Warren 143–4
dealings with Warren 143, 144, 145–6
Treasurer, Tangier Committee (1665) 147–8, 157–8
preparation of navy for war 151–5
celebrates naval victory at Lowestoft 158–9
and the Great Plague 159, 162, 163
arrangements for Carteret/Montagu marriage 160–2
celebrates Sandwich's capture of Dutch ships 165
prize goods affair 166–8
tackles navy victualling problem 169–71
Surveyor-General of the Victualling (1665) 171, 172–3
recommends budgets for pursers 171–2
attends Myngs' funeral 177
refurbishes study 178–9
and Great Fire of London 179–83
answers Parliament's questions on cost of war 184
presents case for funds to Privy Council 186–7
privateering ventures 190, 201, 207
breaks with Warren 190
safeguards gold and private papers after Medway raid 194
attends meeting of Privy Council 195
expedition to Epsom 195–7
surrenders post of Surveyor-General of the Victualling (1667) 201
lends money to Charles II 201
answers to Committee of Miscarriages on Medway defence and seamen's tickets 202, 203–5
Coventry advises how to handle Parliamentary committees 205
concerned at possible examination of private dealings 206–7
comes to understanding with Warren 207
prepares to defend Navy Board 207–8
acclaimed defence before Commons 209–10
valued in royal circles 210, 211
holiday tour to West Country 214–15
private conferences with York about Navy Board reform 217–18, 222
prepares and submits reorganisation proposals 218–19
Navy Board members aggrieved at indictment 220, 222
advises Charles II on navy readiness 228–9
defines Navy Board responsibilities 229–30
paper on Administration of the Navy approved by York 230
concludes *Diary* entries 234
unsuccessful attempts to enter Parliament 235, 253
continental holiday with Elizabeth and Balty 235–6
Elizabeth's death and burial 236, 237
defends Navy Board before Brooke House Committee 238–43

prepares navy for war 245, 248–9, 250
attends Sandwich's funeral 251
Seething Lane house wrecked in fire 252
appointed Secretary to Admiralty Commission (1673) 254, 255, 262
elected MP for Castle Rising (1673) 255–6
Commons attacks on 257–9, 260
accused of popery 258, 259
confrontation with Shaftesbury 259–60
moves to Derby House 261
honours following Admiralty appointment 262
conduct of Admiralty affairs 264–5
instigates founding of Christ's Hospital Mathematical School 265–6
attempts to root out naval abuses 266–8
institutes system of officer training and examination 268–72
tries to improve conditions for seamen 272–3
proposes to Parliament expansion of fleet 273–6, 276–8
corruption allegations by opposition MPs 278–9
thwarted by organised opposition 280–2
readies fleet in record time 282
attends Charles II at Newmarket 282, 284
opposition attempts to destroy 285–6, 287, 288–90
secures acquittal of Samuel Atkins 286
elected MP for Harwich (1679) 287
resigns as Secretary to Admiralty and Treasuer for Tangier (1679) 288
defends himself in Commons 290–1
committed to the Tower 291
accumulates evidence against Captain Scott 291–3
moved to the Marshalsea 293
granted bail, resides with Hewer 293
efforts to clear his name 294–5, 298–300, 301
satirised 297–8
bail fully discharged 300
proceedings abandoned 301
takes down Charles II's account of escape after Worcester 302, 311
consulted by Charles II on navy matters 308
reports on Christ's Hospital Mathematical School 309–10
courts favour of royal circles 310–11
accompanies York to Edinburgh 311–12
accompanies Dartmouth on expedition to evacuate Tangier (1683) 312–18
visits Spain 318–19
voyage home 320, 322
convinced of necessity for trained commanders and rigorous discipline 320
formulates plans to reform the fleet 321
appointed Secretary for Affairs of the Admiralty (1684) 323–4
elected MP for Harwich (1685) 327
royal inspection of Portsmouth dockyards 329
resolves to repair, rebuild and refashion fleet 330
addresses Parliament 330
'Notes for my Navy Discourse to the King . . .' 331
obtains Royal approval for Special Commission (1686) 332
commences to rectify naval abuses 333–4
reintroduces examination for lieutenants 334
achieves objective in rebuilding fleet 338
readies fleet against Dutch invasion 344–5, 346
acts for provisional government following King James's flight 349–50
asked by William of Orange to remain at post 350
resigns Admiralty Secretaryship (1689) 350
refuses to swear oath of allegiance to William and Mary 352
arrested and imprisoned 352–3

retirement 353
arranges Grand Tour for heir John Jackson (nephew) 354
final years of scholarly leisure 355–8
lives with Hewer at Clapham 358
final illness and death 359
funeral and burial 359
Pepys, Talbot (SP's great-uncle) 7
Pepys, Thomas (SP's uncle) 111–12
Pepys, Thomas (Tom) (SP's brother) 4, 6, 110–11
Peterborough, Henry Mordaunt, Earl of 232
Pett family 107–8
Pett, Peter 107–8, 115, 136, 195
Pett, Sir Phineas 332
Petty, Sir William 306, 355
Pickering, Edward (Ned) 124
Pierce, Mr 50
Pierce (Pearse), Elizabeth 88
Pierce (Pearse), James 115
plague 3, 158, 159–60, 162–4
Poole, Captain 267
pope-burning demonstrations 256, 296–7, 343
popery 256
fear of 173, 183–4, 193, 206
Popish Plot (1678) 283–5
Portsmouth dockyards 62, 329, 330, 338
Portsmouth, Louise de Kéroualle, Duchess of 327
Povey, Thomas 108–9, 147, 233, 299
Powell, Doll (née Lane) 28, 188, 189, 198
press-gangs 152–3, 177, 257, 272
Priestman, Captain Henry 267
Privy Council 284, 288, 340
Puritans 5

Rainbowe, Dr Edward 11
regicides 71–2
Restoration drama 80, 81
Roman Catholicism 173, 249, 253, 339
Romeo and Juliet (Shakespeare) 82
Rota Club 30
royal absolutism 98
Royal Charles (ship) (formerly *Naseby*) 54, 107–8, 192
Royal Society 85, 86, 136, 305, 337
Roydon, Captain Charles 268
Rupert, Prince 158, 176, 187, 253–4, 272
Russell, Edward, Earl of Orford 345, 350, 351
Ruyter, Michiel A de [Dutch admiral] 175, 191

Sabbath observance 5
Sadler, John 11–12
St Michel, Balthasar (Balty) (SP's brother-in-law) 44, 189, 247, 332, 353–4
finds companion for sister 113
continental holiday with sister and SP 235
helps SP's efforts to clear name 292, 295
St Olave's Church, Hart Street 66, 237, 359
St Paul's Cathedral 182, 197
St Paul's School 9–10
Salisbury Court 2, 182
saluting flags at sea 93, 303
Sandwich, Earl of *see* Montagu, Edward
Sawyer, Robert 15
scientific instruments 87
Scott, Captain John 285, 288–9, 291, 292–3, 295
Scroggs, Sir William 293, 300
seamen's pay 62
abuses 272
in arrears 63, 188, 202–3
tickets 202, 204, 241–2
Seven Bishops' Case (1688) 342–3
Shaftesbury, Anthony Ashley Cooper, Earl of 252, 254, 301
works against SP 255, 257, 258–60, 278, 285, 286
leads Parliamentary opposition 257, 276
and Popish Plot 284, 285
and Exclusion Crisis 295–6, 303
sacked from Council 296
Shakespeare plays 82
Shelton, Thomas 13
Shere, Henry 312, 314
ship construction 106–7
shorthand 13
Shovell, Captain 318
The Siege of Rhodes (music-drama) (Davenant) 175

Simpson, Thomas 178
Sir Martin Marr-all (play) (Dryden) 81, 195
Skinner, Mary (SP's companion) 246–7, 337, 353
Slingsby, Sir Robert 61, 63
Sole Bay, battle (1672) 250–1
Southampton, Thomas Wriothesley, Earl of 151, 190
Southwell, Sir Robert 288
Spong, John 59
Stop of the Exchequer (1672) 249
Stuart, Frances, Duchess of Richmond 120–1, 173
Sweepstakes (ship) 267–8
Swiftsure (ship) 45, 176
Symons, Will 28

Tachygraphy (Shelton) 13
tally sticks 27
Tangier 108, 146–7, 315, 316, 320
  expedition to evacuate (1683–84) 312–20
  haven for corruption 317–18
Tangier Committee 108, 146, 147, 157, 312
Test Act (1673) 253
Theatre Royal, Bridges Street 81
theatres 80, 81, 82, 116–17
Thomas, Sir Robert 259
Thomson, Colonel George 240, 242
timber industry 103
Tonge, Israel 283–4
Tooker, Miss 173
Tories 339
  propaganda 301
Treasury Commissioners 190–1
Trumbull, Sir William 312
Turberville, Dr Daubigny 219, 220
Turner, Jane (née Pepys) 6, 22
Turner, Miss 195, 221
Turner, Thomas 58

United East India Company 52

Venner's Rising (1661) 63
Vere Street Theatre 80, 81, 82
Vincent, Dr Nathaniel 307
Viner, Sir Thomas 149
Vines brothers 28

Waneley, Henry 358
Warren, Sir William 103–4, 143, 144, 145–6, 190, 207, 242–3
Warwick, Sir Philip 138–41
Welsh, Jane 129, 131, 133, 134
West India Company (Dutch) 52
Whigs 298, 299, 300, 301, 304, 341, 343
  propaganda 298
Whore, Dr William 29
Wilkins, John 136
Willet, Deborah
  companion to Elizabeth Pepys 200–1, 213, 214
  SP's advances 214, 221
  trip with Elizabeth and SP to West Country 214–15
  dismissal 222, 223
William, Prince of Orange (later King William III) 49, 251–2, 254, 340, 341, 349
  preparations for invasion of England 343–4, 347
  lands at Torbay 347
Williams, Dr John 64
Williamson, Captain Robert 43
Witt, Jan de, Grand Pensionary 175
Wood, Dr 309–10
Wood, William 103, 143, 144
Woolwich dockyard 62, 91, 135
Wootton, William 28
Wren, Sir Christopher 245, 306, 357

York, Duke of *see* James, Duke of York